An Introduction to

CLIENT MANAGEMENT
for Solicitors

Cavendish
Publishing
Limited

An Introduction to

CLIENT MANAGEMENT
for Solicitors

*A practitioner's guide to help solicitors
satisfy their clients and improve their
own profitability*

by John H Freeman
Solicitor

Cavendish
Publishing
Limited

First published in Great Britain 1997 by Cavendish Publishing
Limited, The Glass House, Wharton Street, London WC1X 9PX
Telephone: 0171-278 8000   Facsimile: 0171-278 8080

Freeman, John
Client Management for Solicitors
I. Title
344.10068

ISBN 1 85941 039 1

Printed and bound in Great Britain

Foreword

John Freeman has produced a highly individualistic but interesting account of issues which solicitors can only ignore at their peril. He brings to the subject enthusiasm, common sense, and above all a commendable lack of jargon. His views seem relevant to small practices in a way that many books have failed to achieve. He is neither dazzled by fashion nor instinctively opposed to change.

I am sure all those who delve into his text will find more than a few pearls of wisdom.

John Hayes CBE
Chairman
OPRA

Preface

I would like to acknowledge the help and support of the following people and organisations (not in order of priority) without whom this book would not have been written. To all my clients during my career to date who have prompted me to consider their opinions and perceptions and with whom I have tried some client management techniques, with varying success! To my own firm which has allowed me the opportunity to develop some of my ideas on client management. To my wife, Nanette, who has given me the support and encouragement to stick at it and complete the book despite many other pressures on my time and energy. To Duncan Finlayson of LawNet who has read through some of the text and who has made some invaluable comments and suggestions. To my sister, Madeline, and her husband who have made available their cottage nestling in the hills of North Worcestershire where I was able to retreat occasionally with notes and computer for a few days' uninterrupted sessions of writing, thinking, reading and word processing.

My thanks to the many people both inside and outside of the legal profession with whom I have discussed the ideas in this book and who have responded with interest and promises of advance sales! To my publishers who were patient and encouraging; and last, but not least, to my children, Kate and Edward, who have for the last 18 months seen more of the back of my head as I gazed into the VDU than they ought, and in whose homework I would like to express renewed interest, would that I could now even understand the questions!

John H Freeman

Introduction

The legal profession in the mid-1990s is very different from what is was only a few short years ago. Deregulation, increasing competition both from within and outside the profession and a long and bitter recession have forced solicitors not only to reorganise and manage their practises as businesses but also to rethink the fundamentals of what being in legal practise is all about.

Being a hard-working and competent lawyer is in itself no longer enough to guarantee success in this competitive legal world where client satisfaction has assumed a new and paramount importance. The way we present and deliver our legal work to our clients is often more apparent and more real to the client than the legal work itself. The modern solicitor in private practise, therefore, needs to possess not only skills in law, finance, business, marketing and staff management but also he needs the ability to satisfy his clients by understanding and responding to their perceptions, needs and expectations.

Client Management for Solicitors examines the client issues which are now becoming an integral part of the work of all practising solicitors. It focuses on the proactive management and development of the solicitor/client relationship in a systematic and practical way that will enable the practising solicitor, as well as the new entrant to the profession, to learn and apply techniques and work practices that will help to ensure that the needs and perceptions of his clients are satisfied regularly and systematically.

In an irrevocably changed profession, where the battle for clients is being lost or won on the issue of service, it would be an unwise and dangerous strategy to leave the issue of service any longer to chance. The prize for success in satisfying clients is increased client retention, market growth and improved profit margins whereas the sanction for failure could result in reduced performance and decline.

Solicitors and law firms can adopt a new and exciting strategy which focuses everyone in the firm, from senior partner to office junior, on meeting and exceeding client expectations – set out in simple, practical and realistic stages in this book.

As a practising solicitor for over 20 years, my three guiding principles have always been to try to do good quality legal work, to keep my clients happy and to make a profit. I have also tried to get on with the people I work with in order to achieve these things more effectively and in order to get some enjoyment from working in my chosen profession.

Increasingly over the last few years, during the rigours of the recession and now in this post-recession world where legal work is more demanding, where clients are harder to find and keep, where competition is fiercer and where it is harder to make a profit than ever before, I have thought and talked with others long and hard about what exactly it is that makes a good and successful solicitor. Qualifications, legal knowledge, social skills, communications skills, hard work, energy, ability and motivation were all mentioned, but overall it kept coming back to one overriding criterion – the extent to which he satisfies his clients.

No matter how highly we lawyers rate our own legal skills, no matter how sophisticated are our financial reports and computers, and no matter how nice the people are with whom we work, those features alone did not appear to guarantee success with fee-paying clients. Speaking to clients on the matter of solicitors, they all seem to talk about availability, understanding and communication, or the lack thereof. It became ever more apparent that what we, as lawyers, think we are good at, is not necessarily what clients think about us.

What do clients think? When I tried to find out, I was amazed at the dearth of published information and hard data about client views and opinions. Although everyone has their own views about clients, very little written information seems to be available for the student of client management.

Then I tried to think about what it is that clients like and don't like and what it is that really satisfies them. Putting together the things that clients had said to me over the years and things I had seen and heard during my years of practice, it again appeared to me that it was not necessarily expert legal skills that were in issue. It appeared that legal competence is assumed by most clients but that it is the service they get from their solicitors as perceived by them that really either got their blood boiling or gave them cause for satisfaction or delight.

If, as it seems, the issue of service is so important to clients in the legal profession, I wondered where I could look to find out more about service, what was written about it, how could I learn to do it better and what training was available. I was surprised to find that apart from some books on marketing, customer service and client care, there was very little in depth and practical advice or training available. It also seemed to me that in these highly competitive days, for a solicitor and a law firm who could excel in service as well as in legal competence, there are virtually unbounded possibilities for growth, profitability and perceived pre-eminence.

So, in the summer of 1994, I slipped away from the office for a few days with my PC and a few files of notes and cuttings from assorted magazines and journals I had been accumulating and, in a small cottage overlooking the Malvern Hills, I started to write down a few principles and practices of client management which I thought would provide a short booklet on the subject. What I wrote there in three days now forms the basis of 'the client manager's toolkit' in Chapter 10. I was amazed to find that the subject and content of client management kept on growing to what has turned out to be a new system of doing legal work and a book on its own account.

The case studies and people referred to this book are all based on incidents and on people, firms and clients I know or have known but the circumstances and details have been altered in order to preserve client confidentiality and to prevent individual identification. Some are amalgamations of events and characters. No similarity to any person, firm, or client, whether living or dead, is made or intended. The essence, however, has been retained for illustrative purposes. In referring to the solicitor, partner, client manager or other legal professional, I have used the masculine gender throughout for the sake of brevity. It is, of course, recognised that women form a very substantial part of the profession with new entrants to the profession being almost evenly split between men and women. Masculine and feminine genders throughout the book are interchangeable.

Client Management for Solicitors is my own personal view of legal practice with clients and does not necessarily represent the views or policies of my firm. This book does not purport to tell solicitors how to manage their relationships with their clients and I certainly do not hold myself out as a paragon amongst client managers. What the book does try to do is to highlight the strategic importance of client management and to examine some ways of going about it. Client management is not just a set of theories and aspirations – it is a practical method of doing the things that we do so as to increase client satisfaction and profitability. In these challenging times of change, client management does present us with lots of ideas, innovations and perhaps even radical practices. For some, client management may be found to be no more than what they are already doing, it may be found to be idealistic or controversial but, for those who are prepared to take a fresh approach to client satisfaction and profitability, I hope that client management may offer them a helpful and positive way forward.

Table of contents

1 Looking after your clients

The three Cs

One day, whilst serving my articles of clerkship in London in the early 1970s, I was taken quietly aside by my principal and introduced into the secret art of legal practice. 'Of course,' he whispered, slightly apologetically and with an air of conspiracy, 'you only need to do three things to be a good solicitor.' After pausing for the drama of the wisdom he was about to bestow and leaning slightly forward and piercing me with his gimlet, bespectacled eyes, he reverently spoke the following three words; 'Case, Costs, Client,' and stepped back to observe my reaction. The whispered words hung in the air and time stood still. I stared back, perplexed. After a short pause, he said again, and this time with more emphasis, 'Case, Costs and Client – you know, the Three Cs!' After three years at university and fresh (or rather stale) from the College of Law at Lancaster Gate, my head stuffed full of cases, statutes, rules and exceptions to rules, I was confused and a little shocked to hear a real-life practising solicitor summarising the science and art of legal practice in three simple words beginning with a 'C'!

Undeterred by my lack of response, 'First,' he explained, 'the case must be carried out in a proper and effective manner, complying with the law, established legal precedents, forms and procedures. Your legal studies and training are important here. For example,' he continued, 'your legal advice must be sound, the writ needs to be issued in the correct form, within the limitation period, properly and correctly drafted and issued in the proper court of jurisdiction. The property contract needs to comply with the rules of contract and conveyancing, the Land Registry Rules, the Law of Property Act and so on.' He solemnly cautioned, 'We must not expose ourselves or our clients to error or risks, taking particular care with undertakings! The case', he summed up, 'is doing what we as lawyers are trained to do – the mechanics, the process, the systems, the rules, the forms and the law. Finally,' he stipulated, 'to do the case properly, you have to be a good lawyer!' This all seemed pretty obvious to me, I was with him so far and happily nodded my agreement. I had already observed that he was a very able lawyer. Surely, I thought, advising on the law and doing the legal work in the case, that's all there was to it? What else could there be?

'Second,' he continued with growing excitement, (and on reflection he may in fact have put this first), 'you have to get costs!' He intoned, mantra-like, 'You have to make sure that you get costs for doing the case.' He stated it like an eternal truth about which there could be no possible argument or exception. 'It's no good doing all the legal work in the case if you don't get paid the costs' he exclaimed indignantly. He was always up-front, direct and unyielding with his clients over costs, in every case. Even as an articled clerk, I could appreciate that lawyers did have to be paid. I had also observed that he appeared to run a successful and profitable practice.

Moving reluctantly from costs and on to the third and last 'C', clients, he concluded by admonishing me with a wag of his finger, 'And don't forget, you must look after your clients!' The lesson was over and he retreated to his room. In those seeming far-off days of scale fees, and the conveyancing monopoly, this third 'C', clients, the looking-after of, sounded a bit lame to me. It hadn't been taught at Lancaster Gate, there was no set textbook on it and there had been no interesting options in my last year at university about 'clients', or even 'costs', come to that. It had all been about cases and the word 'client' had hardly featured in my training at all. What could he mean? Was he mad? What had 'looking after your clients' got to do with being a lawyer? I had to admit, though, that he did appear to have a large, loyal and growing client base.

Over the following weeks and months as my articles slowly expired by effluxion of time, whilst busy writing letters, seeing clients, delivering briefs to the Temple, sitting behind counsel in court and taking my first faltering steps in conveyancing, debt recovery, legal aid, personal injury, company annual returns and in delivering bills to clients, my principal's whispered words kept coming back to me, occasionally, at first, but then louder and more frequently until the words kept repeating themselves over and over in my head like the tolling of a bell – 'Case, Costs, Client!' I found myself thinking at odd times during the working day, 'Am I doing this case properly, are we going to get paid the costs for what I am doing and is what I am doing actually looking after the client?' His three C's had really got me thinking!

The first 'C', the case, being about the law and the legal work, must be the most important of the three C's by far, I reasoned. It is about the study and application of legal principles and is surely what we as lawyers are here to do. As for the second (or first) 'C', costs, I could appreciate that it is important for solicitors to get paid for the work they do. Yes, the second 'C', 'costs', was definitely admitted. But as for the third 'C', looking after our clients, I thought this must, at most, be an afterthought, a nice idea, a vague aspiration and relatively unimportant compared to the other two.

How things have changed since then! Due to the gradual deregulation of the profession, we are now actually allowed to 'market ourselves', although still in a restricted way. We all 'specialise' in ever narrowing bands of legal expertise and the sole practitioner is being blamed, perhaps unfairly, for some of the ills of the profession. We are all currently confronted by ISO 9002 and the standards of quality and performance demanded by the Legal Aid franchise, the Law Society and other quality assurance systems. So we all are still very much concerned with the 'case' and many, if not most, solicitors would argue that this is still the paramount task of a lawyer, that of practising the law and doing the legal work. Our law libraries, textbooks, reports, databases, precedents and the new 'quality' systems that are being built into our practices are evidence of this.

The second 'C', costs, has been developed into a science and management practice in its own right, spurred on by the recession, deregulation and increasing competition from both within and outside of the profession. Billing targets, computerised time recording, work in progress, credit bill performance, write off statistics, utilisation percentages, recovery ratios and so on have all been devised for us by our in-house or accountancy colleagues to plan and monitor our financial performance. No sane or solvent law firm would now deny the importance of 'costs' as well as the 'case', but what about the third 'C' for 'clients'?

Putting the client first

Now in the late 1990s, it seems that everyone is talking about the third 'C', 'clients'. Everybody seems to be saying, 'It's all about satisfying the client' or 'We must think more about what the client wants' or 'We must put the client first' and even 'We are committed to the highest standards of client care.' But, if asked what this might actually mean in practical terms, things tend to become rather vague and unstructured. There seems to be agreement that the main issue is now about satisfying the client but in specific and practical terms of what can actually be done in our day-to-day dealing with clients, there seems to be something of a vacuum. It is this space that client management seeks to fill.

Few solicitors would now deny that the client is the most important part of our practices, that the client must come first, that the client is our future and that it is we who depend on the client for our incomes and not the other way around. We all acknowledge the client care ideals, the idea of listening to the client and trying to satisfy the client. Many of us agree that there must be some changes in what we do and how we do our work for our clients but many of us still return to our desks from the annual partners' conference and carry on just as before, though perhaps less profitably and perhaps woth some foreboding about the future.

The client management mincer

If it is considered in the simplest of terms, it could be said that we as solicitors carry out the case that will earn us the opportunity to charge costs to our clients. What, if anything, can be done to improve this position? What can be done to get more work? What can be done to improve our profit margins? What more can be done to satisfy our existing and potential clients? Rather than looking at the bottom end of the mincer and the mediocre financial results that some firms are suffering, we should instead turn our attention to the top and action end of the mincer, and try to alter what goes into the mincer in the first place – quality work and client service. The case, or the quality of the legal work, and the quality of service, or the way we present ourselves and deliver the case to our clients are the two principle ingredients. To further the analogy, if the two ingredients of case and client are put in at the top of the mincer and a client manager turns the handle, costs and client satisfaction will be produced at the other end.

Our current obsession with costs, profit margins, recoverability percentages and chargeable time needs to be matched or exceeded with an obsession for service and client satisfaction in a managed and systematic way. The better the ingredients of quality legal work and the way the case is presented and delivered to the client, the better the financial results will be. This is the essential message of client management – to carry out quality legal casework with a presentation and delivery service that will satisfy the client, who will in turn perceive that they have had value, which will in turn produce an acceptable level of profit.

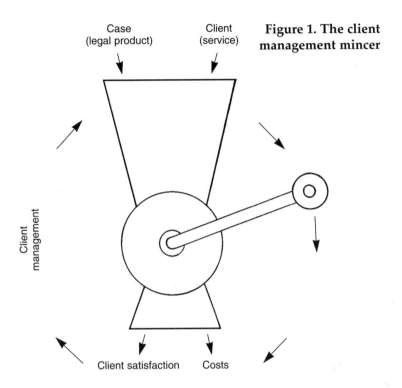

Figure 1. The client management mincer

Case (legal product)

Client (service)

Client management

Client satisfaction   Costs

The turnover days

Prior to the recent recession, the measurement of our legal work was primarily concerned with quantity rather than quality. Whenever one solicitor met another the usual question was, 'Keeping busy?' We felt happy only when the desk was groaning with the weight of papers and files, the phones constantly ringing, everyone rushing around to meet deadlines, going to meetings, doing completions and then moving on to the next case as quickly as possible, with scarcely a backwards glance to the exiting client. We measured our performance in terms of 'busy-ness' and with the old profit margins intact, this was enough to ensure a successful practice and a comfortable income to a hard-working solicitor.

By the mid- to late-1980s, measures of performance relating to bills delivered, individual fee-earner billing targets and time recordings were introduced. However, these again dealt in volume and did not give a clear picture of profitability. Very few of us could have said what the level of profit was on a case-by-case or client-by-client basis. It was sufficient to keep busy and 'keep the bills going out' and profitability looked after itself. As long as the work kept pouring in, we were all happy and life was simple, busy and profitable.

In these post-recession, deregulated and competitive times, the critical issue for the profession is now not only how to keep 'busy' and how to increase turnover, but also about how to increase profitability and productivity on a case-by-case, group-by-group, department-by-department, branch-by-branch and firm-wide basis. These all add up to the overall profitability of the firm. If you are still doing volume work at £X per case but it's costing you £X+Y per case to do it, how much longer can you keep this up? Can you afford to wait for the next boom? Can you afford to do work like that if and when the next boom comes? Can we afford to be 'busy' like that again? Who is predicting or wants a boom anyway?

Turnover, as a measure of performance, must be supplemented with measures of profitability, productivity, product quality, service and client satisfaction which provides value to the client and better management for the firm.

Reforms to make lawyers howl

It has to be admitted that the changes implied in putting clients first with client management systems consistently applied across the firm, are changes which may not present themselves easily to some of us. Whilst most will agree with the principles and ideas of client management, when it comes to actually doing something different about it some lawyers may find it difficult and unsettling. Not only doing things differently and doing different things, but thinking differently is required, and some will find this challenge difficult or even unacceptable. Client management is, in the ultimate analysis, an attitude of mind rather than a system of techniques and procedures. Client management converts client-oriented attitudes and aspirations into systems which will be of practical use and benefit to both the firm and its clients.

The legal profession has traditionally taken pride and strength in the virtues of solidity, reliability, caution, prudence, precedent and established rules, practises and procedures. The unprecedented changes, threats and opportunities to the profession brought about by the combined effects of deregulation, competition and the recession, have shown that these accepted virtues need to be accompanied by a whole new set of words which will need to be imported into our working vocabulary. Words such as new, creative, innovation, experimentation, testing, market research, redesign, client satisfaction ratings, initiative, feedback and relationship will need to be incorporated into our vocabulary if we are to take client management seriously.

Speaking and listening more often with clients, even when not strictly necessary for the case in hand (and without charge!), may be a new idea to many lawyers and the thought of actually asking clients about their perceptions, values and opinions may be seen as revolutionary to some. But, when it is done properly, it is nearly always received well by clients and often to their surprise and pleasure. Although it is now being done more often, until recently, very few law firms deliberately went out to seek client opinion. This is now one of the main points of differentiation for our law firms. By getting and staying close to your clients, by asking what they think and then by doing something about it, your firm will be seen as different from other firms in the eyes of your clients. Being different, or differentiation, is something that is now more important than ever before in this competitive legal profession.

Clients don't pay for our files, for our precedents, for our forms, for the legal processes, for our law books or even for the law – they pay for a service that provides the benefits and solutions that they perceive as being worth the price charged. In order to ensure that what we do actually does achieve the benefits and solutions that clients need and expect, we need to ask clients about their perceptions and take action accordingly. To do all this we will need to act and think differently if we are to have any hope of success.

The other end of the telescope

Clients don't always see us as we see ourselves or each other. It's easy to lose sight of the main function of the firm – that is, to provide clients with what they want and thereby to make a profit! We may think we provide what clients want but, if we don't have in place any systems for checking and confirming this, how can we be sure that we are doing this fully and effectively? Herein lies the big difference between the successful and less successful firms: those who do provide what clients want and are responsive to clients' needs; and those who just go on providing their clients with what the firm thinks the clients want and what it has always done, but without checking for value and satisfaction.

Here can be found a new way of looking at ourselves and what we do. We should look at our work as that which ensures that every client's needs and expectations are identified and agreed, that the case plan and charges are agreed and that the legal product is delivered to the client with a service which the client perceives adds value to the generic legal product. Instead of looking at the client as someone 'out there', we should start to look at the client as an integral part of what we do and to understand more fully how the client sees us and what he expects from us. Client management focuses on the client's 'buying' experience. To do this requires looking at things from the client's viewpoint down the other end of the telescope.

The solicitor/client relationship

The special relationship that exists between a solicitor and his client should be re-examined and strengthened as a matter of strategic policy. Whereas in the 1980s many lawyers specialised in work types rather than client types, many became specialists in legal knowledge rather than in client relations and many of us got caught up in expertise and turnover issues, we should now remind ourselves of what was, is and should be special about the solicitor/client relationship. This includes:

1 client confidence that the solicitor will be able to do the job;
2 trust in the solicitor held by the client;
3 the independence of the advice given;
4 the fact that our advice and service is confidential;
5 the fact that the solicitor/client relationship is privileged; and
6 the fact that the solicitor is accessible, has a good knowledge and understanding of the client's interests and needs.

The client management programme set out in this book illustrates one way of how client management can be developed across the firm and its people and its practices to combat client indifference, dissatisfaction or falling profitability.

We employ accountants to help us manage our finances, some firms employ personnel managers to help manage their staff, we employ qualified solicitors, legal executives and paralegals to help us to do the legal work, but who manages our clients? Only the solicitors and staff who do the work for the client and who can really influence the client relationship can do this. This is as it should be because, as will be seen later, the solicitor as a service provider is himself an integral part of the service. We can employ market research and marketing people to help us gather and analyse information about clients but, in this world of change, it is still the lawyer on the job who is the most important person as far as the client is concerned. The lawyer on the job who is involved in and part of the client relationship is the client manager.

The management of service

Doing the case, applying the law and following the procedures is very important – it is what we were trained to do and it is what we have always done. It is why we became solicitors. Now, in addition, we need to do all this with quality procedures and systems, with more standardisation, consistency, compliance, specification and measurement. The successful implementation of and compliance with case management standards could in itself improve a law firm's profitability by as much as 15–20%, with fewer mistakes and less costly corrective and time-consuming re-working measures.

It is necessary and important to discuss and agree costs with your clients at the outset and make sure that any variations or additions are agreed throughout the course of the case and that regular interim bills are delivered and paid as the case progresses. Financial management at both macro and micro levels in the firm is essential. With both the management of the case and the costs under control, you will have an efficient legal practice.

If you then take this efficient legal practice and then add to it the attitudes, culture, systems, techniques and procedures for client management, you will be creating the combined three-part formula of case, costs and client which will lead to the firm's perceived pre-eminence in the marketplace as a firm which cares for and looks after its clients with a reputation for providing quality legal work service and value for money.

The change of emphasis and practice from file management only to include client management as well cannot be resisted much longer because economic pressures and competition are forcing solicitors to review what they do and the way they do it at a fundamental level. If clients like what you do and how you do it and perceive it as representing value for money, they will stay with you, bring you repeat work and recommend your services to others. If clients don't like what you do or how you do it or think that what you provide for them is not worth the money charged, they will move to someone better able to meet their needs and expectations.

9

The message of client management is that a managed service is vital for the regeneration or development of our post-recession practices, that service must be improved, that it must be perceived to be done by our clients and that we must be perceived as being different by the service we manage to provide.

Exclusion clause

Every lawyer has his or her own particular way of dealing with clients. If lawyers sat down and talked about what they do that clients like and about what clients do not like, there would be a wide consensus of opinion. Client management tries to draw together some of these basic issues as well as suggesting ideas for possible development.

It is necessary to understand from the outset that unlike most other law books, which are based on precedent, case studies and established, well-tried rules, practices and procedures, this book, in attempting to deal with the often intangible and personal aspects of client management, has little published or hard data, facts and information to rely on. There is not a vast amount of published material or case studies on client management. As a profession we are seriously under-researched in the subject of client perception and opinion other than the published reports of the Office for the Supervision of Solicitors and the National Consumer Council. These are worthy of study but tend to concentrate primarily on complaints – a good a place to start as any, however.

In client management, there is some theory, there is a need to experiment and there is no binding precedent. Client management is pragmatic. Some of the things set out in this book may not work in some firms, some may be risky, most will be capable of improvement through practice and some may be very successful. It is a fundamental principle of client management that *everything* in and about law firm management is up for review and possible change and improvement in the cause of improving client satisfaction. We must put the client at the centre of things and then design our products and services around the client, as shown in the diagram below.

It is necessary with client management to test, try, review and redesign based on experience. Think about it, ask the clients about their perceptions, do it, redesign it and do it again. There are not many sacred cows in client management where everything depends on whether or not clients like or value or are satisfied with what we do for them. This is why client management has been described as 'manag-

**Figure 2. The
client care wheel**

ing the intangibles' and this is why client management may be found
to be challenging to many of us technically trained lawyers who like
things to be precise and predictable. Client management is not precise
where there is only the common lore of clients.

A word of caution is required. I do not advocate any lawyer or firm
to wholeheartedly import a new client management system lock, stock
and barrel, because each lawyer and firm is different. Each firm is
unique and needs to develop from where it now is. The ideas and practices of client management will need to be introduced carefully and
incrementally on a trial basis for a limited period of time on a small
controlled sample basis. For example, if you decide to introduce the
client agreement, you should design the form of agreement to suit
your firm, your people and your clients. You should try it out in one
group, department or branch for a limited period to enable your staff
and clients to comment and get used to it. Expect to find comments,
feedback and improvements. Only when you and your staff are satisfied that it is working and that it is beneficial and that your clients do
actually like it, should you consider introducing the client agreement
to the wider areas of the firm.

We should also recognise that the introduction and development
of a client management system falls into the category of what is
sometimes called 'transformational management', where the design,
introduction and implementation of new practices and procedures is

11

the main driving force in management. Ideas and innovation in matters of the client are now more important than ever before in a profession which so far may not have been noted principally for its innovation. The ideas and practices in this book may be found by some to be challenging and controversial and by others exciting and beneficial because they touch and concern the very essence of our professionalism, that of our relationship with our clients.

Client management for solicitors

This book suggests that we should try to see ourselves as client managers, as well as fee earners and case managers, by looking at what we do from the client's point of view. Having ascertained what clients want, client managers do what is reasonably necessary to satisfy clients and improve profitability. Client management proposes some ways of doing just that.

Action checklist

1 Commission a sample questionnaire with a small section of your clients – are they satisfied with your service, what do they perceive and what do they value? Why do they come to you rather than go to your main competitor? Why did they go to your competitors? What would induce them to use your firm again and to recommend others to do so?
2 Plan that your next partners' conference will feature 'client management' as the main topic. Ask a few clients to attend. Invite a guest speaker.
3 Consider adopting as your mission statement: 'To be known to our clients and in the marketplace as a firm which listens to its clients and provides quality legal work, good service and value for money.'
4 Consider that if you are already in control of your finances, if you are reasonably competent lawyers and if you manage your staff well and productively, what else is there to do but to do whatever is necessary and effective to ensure that your clients are satisfied with your service?

2 The management revolution

The challenge of change

Having lost their traditional monopolies, law firms are finding themselves in a deregulated and competitive profession. When viewed in the context of a post-industrial economy, a clear process of change can be seen. The industrial revolution of 200 years ago came about when home-based craft skills were harnessed into the factories and the product-deliverer dictated the terms of sale, the product and the price. The factory owner decided what to make and what to charge. Another industrial revolution happened 80 years ago when mass production techniques were introduced into an economy where demand outstripped supply. The factory owner was the king. The techniques of mass production which were operated kept staff and the customer apart. 'You can have any colour you like, as long as it's black', said Henry Ford. This was the hallmark of a market geared to mass production, where demand exceeded supply and where the supplier could dictate the terms. It was not customer responsive because it did not need to be.

Now a new service revolution is happening where the client has become the king because the customer has choice as never before. In the business of service, everyone now needs to focus on supplying the customer with quality products, in reducing costs and waste and in improving the product-delivery service. The new strategies for survival and growth in a competitive market place are:

1 Client responsiveness – how quickly and how precisely can you identify and interpret client needs and expectations?
2 Anticipation – how well can you anticipate and supply to new client demands?
3 Legal products – how quickly can you develop new legal products and reduce or discontinue entirely the old, unprofitable or unwanted legal products?

4 Quality standards – how well can you eliminate wasteful work practices, reduce costs and improve product quality?
5 Technology – how well and how soon can you apply your computers, software, databases and information technology skills to reduce costs and improve productivity?
6 Quality of people – how effectively can you recruit, train and manage your staff into being a highly productive, adaptable and flexible workforce? Have you introduced short-term contracts, salaries linked to performance and consultancy contracts? Do you have fewer long-term full-timers, more retraining and people prepared to change careers more than once in a working lifetime? Do you believe that there are no more jobs for life?
7 Change – how well can the people in the firm read what's happening and adapt to the new business realities?

Partners, management and staff must together become company workers and colleagues because all the people in the firm *are* the firm, from the clients' point of view. The 'feel-good' factor can only be achieved when everyone in the firm is working together in satisfying the clients, reducing costs and improving the quality of products and service. We have been forced to change by the economics of competition and deregulation. The new key issues are that firms must produce client-driven, value-added, differentiated, quality products, using innovation and people trained in client service as well as in technical legal skills.

We need to acknowledge that just being good lawyers is no longer enough in itself to achieve the growth or even the survival of a law firm. Financial management, commercial awareness, business planning, client management, staff management and marketing skills are needed in addition. You cannot compete on legal knowledge alone and you cannot compete only on financial management but you can compete on client management to become known as a firm that cares about and looks after its clients.

The new management

The old management style had partners in charge and staff did what they were told. Clients were 'out there'. Administration rather than management was the norm. Marketing was not permitted and staff training and development was random in other than strictly legal subjects. The firm was organised according to the function of the people in it. There were 'conveyancing departments' and 'litigation departments' and lawyers classified themselves as 'conveyancers' or 'litigators'. Client work was split by function and sequence and people worked in separate and largely uncoordinated ways. Typists typed, the accounts were done by cashiers, fee earners did the legal work and partners spent time with the clients. The system worked well in a stable and undifferentiated profession where the supply to the demand for legal services was regulated and where work was abundant.

By the 1980s, it was recognised that some policy was needed to maintain office efficiency, control and consistency. The reactive, partner-nudged and retrospective control systems could no longer cope with the increasingly complex demands of running a multi-million-pound-turnover firm. A new degree of control and centralisation was needed. This created a layer between the lawyer's work with his clients and the control of his business, and it was called bureaucracy.

This classification into function and its consequential centralisation of management introduced a functional layer between the lawyer and his client which in turn produced a systems rather than a service approach to our work. Our firms were run principally on financial lines. The real lifelines of the firm in terms of quality products, client service and staff development were perhaps not given enough prominence in this departmental and financial management structure. Although the drive towards departmentalisation improved technical skills, it tended to lack client focus and inhibited interaction with the other departments of the firm, with little transfer of skills or expertise and little or no sharing of client information.

The new management will see groupings of lawyers form around the type of clients they serve. Two broad classifications only might apply – the business client department and the private client department. Within each will be situated people whose technical legal skills will include both contentious and non-contentious skills. The litigator, the conveyancer and the company-commercial lawyer will work side-by-side in the same team in servicing a homogenous client base. The self classification according to function will give way to a classification according to client type.

Another grouping could be that people may work in groups for a key client who has a range of requirements, both non-contentious and contentious. This multi-skilled team will be formed to meet all the legal needs of a particular client or a particular type of clients. There will be a client partner leading each team, whose main role will be to stay close to the particular client or type of clients, understanding, anticipating and supplying their needs. He will also manage the team and the production of the legal work to meet that client's requirements. In this way the group will be putting the client first by forming itself around the client's needs, rather than around its own skills, functions and traditional working structures.

The new management is about the control and organisation of the firm's available resources in such a way as to maximise the opportunities of achieving the agreed twin objectives of increasing client satisfaction and profitability.

The need for vision

The busy lawyer's world is about clients, files, telephones, meetings and deadlines: it is very much about the present moment and the immediate future. Long-term vision has no place amongst day-to-day legal work. It is difficult for many of us whilst doing our legal work to look beyond the ends of our desks, or into next week, let alone three years ahead. But without vision, we risk being caught unprepared by the tremendous changes now surging through the profession, the market and the economy. We must take time out to think and plan, for it is the quality of the thinking and the effectiveness of the planning and execution which will determine where and what we will be in three years' time.

In this competitive age there can be only one approach from which all else flows – that of consistently achieving extraordinary levels of client satisfaction. The transformation of our firms must have client satisfaction as the central theme. Start by listening to clients, analysing the results and re-appraising the whole firm from top to bottom with these principles as the guidelines. Treat every person, product, process and service for its value-added contribution to the client satisfaction process. This particular vision is the one from which all else will flow.

In the old days of 10 years ago, words like 'management' were hardly ever used. Even in the late 1980s, if you used words like 'proactive', 'change', 'new', 'different', 'initiative', 'innovation', 'test', 'try', 'questionnaires', 'marketing' or 'empowerment', you were sure to evince frowns and enquiries about the state of your health and perhaps a note on your personnel file marked 'unsound'. But now, in this new challenging time of change, it is the quality of our vision, ideas, market information, decisions, culture and actions which will precisely and unerringly determine the quality of our financial and professional future.

The management of change

The task of management is to match the internal resources of the firm with the external requirements of the market. By first looking outwards, observing the market, measuring and evaluating it, management should then look inwards and make such provision and changes as are necessary to ensure that what the firm does is what the market wants. As the markets change, so must the firm. Viability and success depend on the firm's ability to convert market information into productive value. A failure to do this will result in the firm not having the capacity or expertise inside the firm to respond to change and the new demands of the market from outside the firm. The competitive advantage of the firm depends upon the ability of the business to do just this, to respond quickly and effectively to the market.

The ability to look at the markets, the ability to plan the necessary internal changes and the ability to carry them out and measure its relative success is the role of management. It will not happen just by everybody working harder – we have to work smarter. Vision, information, discussion, decision, communications, implementation and review is the matrix of the new management activity. Market information generates a new understanding of the business by enabling us to see ourselves as our clients see us. This new understanding produces a new way of working.

The management of change is perhaps the most difficult of all management issues to be dealt with. If we take the view that basically everything is OK and only a few touches to the rudder here and there are needed, then we must be either perfect already (but may not be one year from now) or be doomed to decline. Such an attitude is a vestige of the old days of practice when very little did change externally and so little needed to change internally. This attitude can no longer be maintained in an economy and a profession where the only constant is change. Managing change successfully requires determination, training, sensitivity and a thick skin. It can only happen in a learning and innovative culture.

The need for action

All firms are now exhorted to produce mission statements, practice purpose statements, objectives, budgets, business plans and the like. Lawyers are good with words and many firms have produced some impressive mission statements. But if you look at them you will see that most are very similar, but many of us have yet to achieve substantial progress towards our stated mission. This is because some mission statements fail to recognise and respond to the changes in the market, because they are based on what we think we should do rather than upon market research and client data.

Lawyers like precedent, evidence and facts. We feel uncomfortable about setting sail in the choppy waters of ideas, vision, change, innovation and pro-active planning. Shall we do this or shall we do that or shall we just stay as we are? Many law firms have produced a business plan and so really it is all down to implementation. Most firms have taken management very seriously indeed. But mission statements *per se* do not make change happen, they do not add one degree to the level of client satisfaction and they do not increase profitability. Strategic plans with beautifully-crafted phrases, produced after long and heated conference debates, are worthless without action.

In order to achieve real advances in management, direction and profitability, we need to supplement our training and working in black letter law with equal helpings of training and practice development in service, client management, staff management and product quality. We need to learn the new group partner and client partner roles, we need to learn leadership skills and we need to learn team-working skills which break down the barriers we erect and maintain between partners and staff, between 'us and them'.

Take training as an example of management in action. The old firms with the old ways said, 'Spending more money on training will improve our legal skills and so enable us to attract more clients and do more work. The need for leadership and service skills in partners and staff is useful but subservient to all this.'

More recently, some people are saying, 'We don't allow unstructured or reactive training. All our training is linked around the planned requirements of our people in line with the approved business plan of the firm which includes client and service training.'

The most action-oriented law firms simply say, 'Human relations skills training courses are of fundamental and paramount importance to the success of the business and are on-going and mandatory for everyone in the firm, including partners.'

The attitude of, 'Yes, that's all very well, if you've got nothing better to do but I've got to dash – I've got work to do' is an attitude which can retard progress and undermine the efforts of other people in the firm. Fee-earning is critically important but so is improving our systems and culture to make fee-earning more effective. Without managed improvements being made and sustained, the effort in fee-earning will yield poorer results and poorer prospects than could be achieved with better direction and strategic planning.

The four main things in law firm management

In the management revolution the essentials of law firm management may be seen as falling into four main activities.

Case management

Doing the legal work well was always the first concern of the practising lawyer and it still is one of his four main concerns. Being a good lawyer in today's climate, however, needs to be demonstrated by compliance with a quality system. 'Quality', the buzz-word of law firm management over the last five years is not new; it is just a new name for doing things consistently. Quality is perhaps most easily seen to be relevant to our case work and file management. Opening files, dealing with correspondence, giving legal advice, preparing case plans, doing the case work itself – all now demand that they are done consistently in accordance with pre-defined standards of practice and work methods.

Financial management

Up until the 1980s, financial amnagement was regarded ad the main concern of practice management. Financial management became an issue as firms grew bigger and more profitable in the 1980s and it became a crucial issue as firms, along with the rest of the country, went into the recession of the early 1990s. The financial performance of a law firm is one of the results of how well it performs in the three other main areas – client management, staff management and quality management. Depending on how well we satisfy our clients, depending on how well we manage our staff and depending on how well we manage the quality of our legal work, the financial results will follow. Turnover, chargeable time, utilisation percentages, cash-flow forecasts, profitability ratios, work in progress percentages, and aged debtors are all part of financial management, but financial management is the measure of our success or failure, it is not the only cause or reason for our success or failure.

Staff management

The biggest single item of expenditure in a law firm's budget is the cost of employing staff, typically as much as 40% of a firm's total annual expenditure. The aspect which most distinguishes a successful business from its less successful competitors is the quality of its people. The task facing law firm managers is how to ensure that staff are managed in such a way that our greatest item of expenditure or 'overhead' is converted into our greatest asset. We are a people business and, in order to develop our relations with our clients, we must also ensure that our relations with our staff are equally developed. You cannot decree a new client management culture to be implemented by alienated, 'sufficing' and unempowered members of the firm. Client management is an attitude and system of working that can only grow and develop in a culture which is people oriented, both within and without the office walls.

In order to satisfy our clients, we need the full and effective support of our staff and to adopt practices to use this resource more effectively – in short, we need to manage our staff relations better in order to manage our client relations better. We need to recognise that partners, solicitors and all our staff *are* the firm as far as our clients are concerned. By understanding this, law firm managers will place staff management as an important strategic objective.

Client management

We are trained in the law but not specifically in dealing with clients. In terms of systems, policies and management practices, perhaps the most unmanaged and unsystematic aspect of a law firm's business is that of doing the business itself, the solicitor's relationship with his client! This surely must be an aspect of legal practice that can benefit from a managed service system. Low client satisfaction levels produce low profitability levels. A client consults a solicitor for advice and services in order to achieve a solution to a problem or to achieve a benefit or some state of welfare. The law is the tool that we use but it is not law that the client 'buys'. It is more often the way the legal advice and service is delivered to the client that the client judges our performance than the legal advice or our knowledge of the law itself. It is of course important that we advise on the law correctly and carry out the correct legal procedures but this legal ability is assumed by clients. It is this other vitally important though intangible aspect of the solicitor/client relationship, the product delivery mechanism, that can give great scope to the development of a solicitor's practice. It is something that can be learned and which can be proactively managed.

The role of the client partner

One of the first principles of client management is that the relationship with the client needs to be proactively managed by the person supplying the legal product and service and who has formed a relationship with the client. That link should not be broken or interrupted. This also means that a particular partner is required to take overall responsibility for that particular client's experience of the legal products and services delivered to him by the firm overall and all those in it.

Not only must the client partner manage the production of the legal work for the client from his own group, A, but he must also manage the client's relationship with the firm and the overall service which the client receives from the firm and, in particular, he will be responsible for the client satisfaction rating by that client of the firm overall. So whilst his own group, which may handle most of the client's corporate legal work, has a CSR (client satisfaction rating) of say 75%, if he refers some of that client's other legal work to another department or group, it is he as the client partner who must make sure that group B delivers the service to the client to a similar standard. If he just sends the work through to group, B, and then leaves it, he is in delegation terms 'dumping' the key client on someone else. This is a high risk strategy in these competitive and client discriminating days.

To that key client, the client partner and his group *are* the firm. If the client partner suddenly drops out of the picture, that to the client is like having a different firm and he may as well go elsewhere. Where the client is king and where the client is put first by the client partner, this can no longer be allowed to happen.

The role of the group partner

Client management re-defines the role of each partner within the firm. Instead of seeing himself as a fee earner, or as a super fee earner, or even as a 'fee earner, manager and owner', the group partner sees himself as a lawyer who generates profits for the firm by satisfying his clients and adding value to the basic legal product by the efficient and effective management of the production and delivery of legal services by the group of people with whom he works.

The days of a partner seeing his role as only doing legal work for his clients, having one or more assistants and dictating instructions to a secretary may be considered by some to be expensive, inefficient and obsolete. Each partner, whether or not he 'does management' in any formal sense, must realise that he does have an important management role in his own group, as follows:

- management of the group's financial performance;
- management of the group's staff and productivity;
- management of the group's quality of legal work; and
- management of the group's clients.

This is where the group partner's new role is essential for successful client management in all its aspects.

Characteristics of a group partner

Good characteristics	Bad characteristics
Approachable	Remote or 'too busy' to talk with
Easy to get along with	Arrogant or stuffy
Open-minded	Fixed views
Reliable and predictable	Breaks the rules, inconsistent
Accepts criticism	Defensive/over-sensitive
Works with foresight	Work is reactive and unplanned
Has vision	Lacks imagination
Decisive	Lets things happen
Willing to innovate	Reluctant to change
Listens, talks and consults	Autocratic management style
Supports his staff	Blames and bullies
Good delegator	Hogs work and dumps files
Good with clients	'File manager' mentality
Sets objectives	No goals, no planning and no objectives

Gives praise when due	Takes all the credit
Sets standards	Poor control of group legal work
Strong financial control	Vague about figures
Holds regular group meetings	Only meets when he has something to tell the staff
Works hard and gets the job done	'Nine-to-five' mentality
Commercially aware	Thinks legal practice is not a 'business'
Enthuses for the firm overall	Only cares about his own group or department
Will do whatever is reasonably necessary for the firm	Suspicious of others and wishes to preserve the status quo
Manages the production of legal work	'Top gun/fee earner' mentality
Good leader, director and empowerer of people	'You must do what I say because I'm the boss!' mentality
Fun to work with	Humourless/unexciting/boring

The business plan

Firms that do not plan are planning to go nowhere fast. Firms that do plan but then fail to do what they planned to do are firms that are planning to go nowhere slowly. Firms that do plan, execute, measure, review, adjust, plan and re-execute are firms that will survive and thrive. One of the most prevalent reasons for business failure and under-performance is where a business lacks a clear or agreed plan or neglects to implement the plan that it has made. It is the well-planned and well-managed firms that will thrive.

We must start the process of business planning with the premise that *everything* we do is up for review annually. There can be no sacred cows, no 'no-go' areas and no certainty except the certainty of change. The only two certainties about the future are that the future will happen and that it will be different from the past and the present. A service business must start with its clients – who are they, what do they want and what will they pay for? We must not make the same old mistake and debate what *we* think they want. We must ask our clients what they want and what they perceive as value and then do something about it. The basic operational method for the client management firm is:

1 ask the client what he wants, perceives and values;
2 check the markets for new legal products and services;
3 do a SWOT analysis to identify the opportunities and strengths of the firm as well as its weaknesses and threats;
4 (re)design the legal products and service delivery system accordingly;
5 provide the new products and services;
6 measure and review it for success and ask the client again;
7 update the business plan.

The business-planning wheel of the client-oriented firm can be illustrated by the diagram:

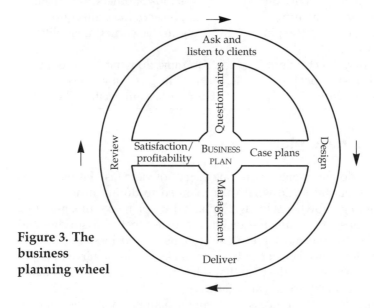

Figure 3. The business planning wheel

Many firms have produced business plans as aspirational rather than operational models. We would all like to be client-oriented and maximise profitability, but working out and doing what is necessary to achieve this fully and effectively can elude many law firm managers. Client management can provide the structure of a new and effective business plan which can be implemented in planned and practical ways.

The mission statement

Many law firms will have spent many hours of discussion and debate in producing the carefully-crafted mission statement. Most are then consigned to the shelf whilst everybody goes back to 'real work'. But mission statements can be useful if kept simple and if communicated to everyone in the firm. Even better, the mission statement should ideally be evolved after discussion with staff and clients, so they identify with it and take 'ownership' of it, rather than having it imposed from the high altar of the partners' annual conference. Keep it simple, for example:

THE MISSION STATEMENT
of
JARNDYCE & JARNDYCE
Solicitors
'TO KEEP OUR CLIENTS HAPPY'

This Mission Statement of Jarndyce & Jarndyce has been agreed after discussion with a number of clients and after consultation with all members of the firm. In order to achieve our Mission we have agreed that:

We shall:

1 do quality legal work that conforms to written specifications and which are adapted to and agreed with each individual client to meet his needs;
2 deliver our legal products to our clients with standards of service that are designed to meet and exceed the client's identified expectations;
3 agree charges with clients so as to produce value for money as perceived by the client whilst also producing acceptable levels of profitability.

In order to do this, we will:

1 listen to our clients regularly and systematically;
2 do something about what our clients say;
3 be innovative and creative in service;
4 involve all members of the firm;
5 achieve and maintain and try to constantly improve a measurable standard of client satisfaction.

The typical old and unstated mission statement that, 'We do legal work and the client must pay us for what we do' has given way to the statement, 'We are trying to run a law firm but it's really difficult to get the client to pay' which in turn is now giving way to the statement, 'We do what the client wants and has agreed to pay for'.

Law firm mission statements may indicate three broad approaches:

1 Firms that retain the old functional structures and culture with a turnover and hierarchical management style.
2 Firms that implement quality systems and look outwards in implementing marketing and client management systems.
3 Firms that are listening to clients, have a passion for asking without fear of criticism, that empower the members of the firm to do their jobs better and that design and implement legal products, services and systems to match client requirements and to exceed client expectations.

Any mission statement from a service-based business must of necessity involve the clients, the service providers and the service 'product' itself. Any mission statement which has not involved consultations with clients and staff first will not be fully effective. The overall objective of a client management firm may be encapsulated in this mission statement:

To be perceived in the marketplace as a firm that is pre-eminent in providing its clients with quality legal work ('It works and it's what we want'), good service ('They really understand our needs and always seem keen to satisfy our requirements') and value for money ('A pound spent with Jarndyce & Jarndyce goes a long way!').

The response to change

When faced with change and financially challenged, the initial reaction is to cut costs, to right-size (reduce) partners and staff and to 'do marketing' (spend large and often wasteful sums on advertising and brochures). These measures, however, are often only capable of slowing down the decline in profits rather than turning it around because they attempt to:

● change the culture whilst improving performance at the same time – the ultimate, but very difficult, challenge;
● gradually change the culture while gradually improving performance – effective but slow; or

- improve performance through management hierarchies, budget control and targets – effective in the short-term but no overall change in firm's direction and culture.

Where markets, the economy and our professional rules have changed, it may be seen as self-evident that our work practices and management styles must also change. This requires client managers and new approaches to management.

It has been said that there are two types of manager: the transactional manager and the transformational manager. The transactional manager is able to carry out standard and established tasks and responsibilities in an efficient and reliable way. He manages the affairs of the business, he produces regular monthly reports, he acts within laid-down guidelines, he implements the approved business objectives and he doesn't cause any shocks or surprises. He is solid and reliable in financial matters and 'knows about computers'. He may not be so good at marketing and staff management but at least he holds things steady and does not challenge people with too much change and innovation. This style of management is suited to law firms in a stable economy and a stable profession and with a stable market. It is now out of date and out of synchronisation with our market- and quality-driven economy.

In these unprecedented times of change a transformational management style is needed that promotes and encourages a change culture throughout the firm. Lawyers have debated long and hard about what needs to be done and the acid test is the ability of a firm to plan and implement the necessary changes. To do this successfully management needs first to ascertain the views of one of its principal group of stakeholders, its clients, and then debate these views. In order to stimulate debate, the transformational manager will produce a detailed client survey and questionnaire including feedback and statistics. He will provide information about competitor law firms. He might even introduce a few clients and referrers into the discussion. He has his ear close to the ground and is constantly looking outwards to the markets and the clients. He will be close to clients and get regular feedback from them about their perception of the firm.

These changing times do require a different kind of management response in addition to the transactional style of management. This new sort of transformational style of management needs lots of walking about and spending time with all the people in the firm as well as with its clients and external contacts and referrers of work. Just doing the same old things in the same old ways is a head-in-the-sand management style that cannot succeed in the mid- to long-term.

Management by client managers

Given that clients are the most essential part of our businesses, how is it that we appear to have little system or structure to deal with the management of the client relationship? We have detailed reports on disbursements, profit and loss, depreciation, turnover and productivity, but what have we done about clients other than give them advice and send them bills? To be a good client manager needs not only proven ability to do legal work efficiently, technical legal skills and the ability to satisfy and retain the existing clients of the firm, but also the ability to develop relationships and work with existing clients, the ability to introduce new clients and the ability not only to cover one's own group or departmental costs but also to contribute to the overall net profits of the firm.

A client manager is expected to bring in new clients, retain the existing clients and produce legal services to attract and retain them accordingly. Some new ideas and innovation are needed to assist the hard-pressed partner in all these apparently conflicting tasks and this is where client management may be of help in combining them all.

The task of a client manager is to maximise profits by achieving two things: (i) a reduction of production costs; and (ii) an increase in income. The trick is knowing what resources to cut without impairing service and in knowing what type of clients and work will actually produce an increase in income as opposed to just an increase in activity. What is at stake between the two is profit or loss. In order to improve income, it is necessary to improve the quality of the product as well as the quality of the service which presents and delivers the product to the client.

Management attitudes

What we think determines what we do. Management action is, therefore, predetermined by the quality of the thinking that goes into law firm management. As form follows function in architecture, action follows attitude in management. There are broadly three main differences of attitude which are found in law firms towards the problems that we all face in trying to run successful practices. There are those firms who just keep on doggedly doing the same old thing in the same old way, regardless of profitability and effectiveness, but with lower profit levels and lower staff and partner morale than before and with an increasing foreboding about the future. Then there are those firms who are adapting to the new and more effective and profitable ways of doing quality work. Lastly, there are those firms who have a clear understanding of their clients and of market forces and who are actively doing something about it.

Try the following management attitude test by ticking the box against one only of the three statements in each section which most closely corresponds to your own attitude as follows:

Attitudes to clients

1 'We know what our clients need.' ☐

2 'We carry out surveys and produce questionnaires to find out what our clients need.' ☐

3 'We send out service questionnaires to every client and we visit our key clients regularly to discuss their current and future requirements. We try to design our legal products and services to match our clients' requirements. We then deliver, review and keep checking with clients.' ☐

Attitudes to staff

1 'Staff are our biggest overhead.' ☐

2 'We train our staff to make them more efficient.' ☐

3 'Our staff are not only our best asset – they are members of the firm and part of it.' ☐

Attitudes to management

1 'The managing partner implements the partners' decisions.' ☐

2 'Each partner tells his fee earners about their targets and performance'. ☐

3 'Each group partner with his group members set their own group budgets and targets.' ☐

Attitudes to performance

1 'We strive to meet our monthly billing targets.' ☐

2 'We are committed to the highest standards of client care.' ☐

3 'We are all involved in developing a firm which is responsive to client needs and expectations.' ☐

Attitudes to business plans

1 'The business plan is produced by management and is marked "Confidential-partners only".' ☐

2 'We send out an abridged version of our business plan to our senior staff.' ☐

3 'We ask each group and department to produce their own business plans. We link these with client feedback to produce the firm's annual business plan, produced by and for the whole firm and its clients.' ☐

Attitudes to communications

1 'I tell my staff if there's anything important to say.' ☐

2 'I discuss targets and performance with my work group.' ☐

3 'I listen to and consult the members of the firm in regular group meetings about quality and service improvements.' ☐

Attitudes to the recession

1 'We've had to reduce staff and freeze salaries.' ☐

2 'Some of our partners and staff are being encouraged to consider early retirement.' ☐

3 'We have encouraged our people to develop new products and services; we have increased our training and retraining programme and we have reduced some unprofitable services and introduced some new services.' ☐

Attitudes to the performance culture of the firm

1 'We can't afford to pay bonuses linked to performance.' □

2 'People work in teams and some are paid bonuses.' □

3 'Groups are encouraged to set their own performance targets. They regularly achieve group bonuses for exceeding their own approved targets.' □

Attitudes towards quality

1 'We're qualified solicitors – of course we do quality work!' □

2 'Of course quality is a good idea, but many of our clients just won't pay for it.' □

3 'By first finding out what the client wants to achieve and by agreeing the work with him as well as the charges, we are seeing that quality is driving our expenditure down and profitability up.' □

Attitudes towards finance

1 'The more we bill the better!' □

2 'We all have targets for time recording, billing and aged debtors and generally we perform to our targets.' □

3 'The more we satisfy our clients by identifying what they want, by agreeing a case plan and the charges and by providing them with a service they value, we are able to bill more profitably.' □

Adding the numbers of each question you have ticked, a total score of 0–10 may indicate that management attitudes are still bound by a backward-looking, functional, controlled and hierarchical management structure.

A total score of 11–20 may indicate that the management attitudes have addressed the new management but is still not fully effective in terms of significantly increased client satisfaction and profitability.

A total score of 21–30 indicates management attitudes that are highly market aware and linked to effective implementation.

The management revolution

Many law firms are now familiar with the following:

1 PCs and keyboards on case managers' desks;
2 targets and performance measures;
3 work specifications and case plans;
4 job descriptions;
5 annual appraisals;
6 client agreements;
7 teams for performance, profit and cost centres;
8 the separation of ownership, management and fee earning;
9 staff empowerment; and
10 flexible, client-oriented structures.

Many of us may have felt a little alienated by all of this and some may have taken refuge from it by determining to be good lawyers and leaving management to those who want to do it. But for those of us who have stayed at the coalface of client work and have left others to devise more efficient management machines and to find new seams before the current ones run out, cannot escape the need to provide a valued service to clients. Client management must be the concern not only of the managing partner who will see service as a means of improving turnover, profitability and reducing costs, but also of those 'real' lawyers in the firm at the coalface of client work who are working harder and often with smaller returns and less job satisfaction than ever before.

The issues for law firms in the mid- to late-1990s are the management and quality issues that stem from two overriding objectives – the need to satisfy clients and the need to make a profit. The well-managed law firms with quality products and services will grow and prosper. Financial management coupled with client management will make the critical difference between the successful and the less successful firms because the distinction between the two will be made by the only person competent to do so – the client.

Action checklist

1 Start with a blank sheet of paper and write down what you think are the 10 main attributes of a successful law firm. Then write down the 10 main attributes of your own firm. Compare the two. Produce

a detailed plan of how to make them match over a given period, stating who will be involved and what costs and resources are required. Ensure that someone is empowered to put the agreed plan into action with an approved budget and timescale.

2 Design a management structure which focuses on achieving higher levels of client satisfaction and profitability than at present. Everything else in the management structure will be determined by these two principles.

3 Implement a management action plan which focuses on client satisfaction, staff productivity and empowerment, quality legal work and financial accountability.

3 The client revolution

The client revolution started when scale fees for conveyancing were abolished in 1973 and now the battle for clients is being fought and won with the weapons of quality, staff management, value for money and service to clients. The victors in the client revolution are those firms who find out about what their clients want and then make sure that they get it.

It is we who are dependent on our clients for our incomes – clients do not depend on us for theirs. The tables have turned subtly around on us since the old days when clients had little real choice in the selection of their lawyers and no easy way of differentiating between the good, the bad and the unsatisfactory. Clients may not understand the law and the legal process but they do understand value and they do understand service. Therefore, in order to win the battle for clients, lawyers need to start with a fresh sheet and start asking their clients some straight questions:

1 what do you value?
2 what are you willing to pay for?
3 what kind of service do you require from us?
4 what do you like about our service? and
5 what don't you like about our service?

Firms who proclaim in their brochures and mission statements that, 'We pride ourselves in our commitment to provide the highest standards of service to our clients' may in fact be firms who have not actually asked their clients the above questions but are convinced that they know best. They may be genuinely trying to provide best service but, unless they start by asking their clients, only time and the clients will tell whether or not they will get it right.

Clients are revolting!

Clients will no longer put up with high levels of fees and low levels of service. If they do not get what they feel they deserve, they will go looking elsewhere. High fees, poor service, delays, patronising attitudes, remoteness, indifference and self-satisfaction are some of the perceived attributes of the profession that clients are refusing to tolerate any longer. Whether such perceptions are justified is another question, but the fact that clients have those perceptions means that we must take them seriously.

Automatic client loyalty and high incomes for lawyers can no longer be assumed. Clients want to see an agreed basis of fees with the understanding that any variation from what is agreed must be first approved by themselves. The billing criteria that were enshrined in the Solicitors' Remuneration Order 1972 have been superceded by the 1994 Order, which recognises that, in addition to the eight criteria for assessing whether fees charged are 'fair and reasonable', there is an ninth factor to be considered – namely whether or not the fee or the basis of charge has been agreed with the client. This factor, agreement with the client, is an important principle of client management.

Even where technical legal competence is high, the level of service may be found to be inadequate, from the client's point of view. Solicitors have been criticised, perhaps unfairly, for appearing to take their clients for granted. This image, aided and abetted by the few, has tinged the general public perception of the profession as a whole. It is the attitudes within the firm and the method of presenting and delivering the technical legal services to the clients that clients will no longer tolerate unless they are satisfactory to the client. Technical legal competence is assumed. It is in the service element that accompanies the legal product that clients will no longer be taken for granted.

A director of GEC, a leading UK electronics manufacturer, who regularly instructs outside lawyers, has said that the most important attribute in a corporate lawyer is good judgment. 'Basically, I am looking for an individual partner whom I feel I can trust and whose judgment I will value. All larger firms have competent legal expertise, but it is these individual qualities which really count.'

To be able to give such advice and to exercise such judgment, the lawyer needs to develop his knowledge of his client's business or of his private affairs. This is where client management comes into play, by enabling the lawyer to get the information he needs, to analyse it into what is useful and relevant to the client and to give himself the tools that he has not had before which will enable him to develop and maintain that relationship.

The business of a law firm starts and ends with the client. As with any business, it's not what we do that clients pay for but the benefit, welfare or solution that is achieved as perceived by the client that generates in them a level of satisfaction, in turn producing a willingness to pay our fees. Pointing to the Solicitors' Remuneration Order is no longer sufficient justification in itself for the level of fees. You may be legally correct to make the charge and you may even be vindicated on taxation or in an application for a remuneration certificate but, unless the client perceives value, he will not be satisfied. You will be right, but you will have lost a client. Being right is no longer sufficient – we have to be right *and* have a satisfied client.

'A business exists to create a customer' is the pertinent statement made by Peter Drucker, in his seminal book *Management by Objectives*, to highlight the truth that for all businesses, whether manufacturing or service, it is not what they do that counts but what they are doing for the paying customer. The creation of a client, the delivery of a legal product and service that produces a benefit to the client, the making of a charge that represents value to the client and a profit for the firm and the retention of the client's goodwill for repeat work and recommendation, is what contemporary legal practice is about.

The effects of the recession, deregulation and the increase in competition have combined to turn our traditional market from a regulated and controlled sellers' market where solicitors dictated the rules, the processes and the price, into a buyers' market where clients are free to choose their legal advisers, to stipulate the service they need and to agree the price they wish to pay. It is to help us to adapt to and cope with this new buyers' or client market that client management is needed. Now that the tide of market conditions has turned 180 degrees in favour of client choice, we need to respond by a similar 180 degree turn that puts the choosing and paying client at the front of all things. Client satisfaction in a dynamic, choice-oriented and competitive market is too important to be left to chance.

The client pyramid

Which of your clients account for the biggest fees per annum? Which clients use you for all their legal work? Why don't they use you for all of their legal work? What more could you do for them? Have you asked? How much of your work comes from existing clients? If you keep all your clients and develop them to use a wider range of your firm's services, do you need vast numbers of new clients? If you count your new clients but not your lost clients, are you achieving any real growth? Are new clients replacing lost clients quickly enough? Is too much time, attention and money being given to chasing new clients whilst existing clients may remain unsatisfied and are drifting into the hands of our competitors?

A client pyramid should be drawn for each firm where lots of small client/customers form the flat base of the pyramid in terms of numbers but produce only A% of turnover and B% of profit. The fewer larger and regular clients higher up the pyramid produce C% of turnover and D% of profit. What does this indicate? Should we develop the profitable ones and reduce the unprofitable ones? Why are some clients profitable and others unprofitable? Building up this picture can give a useful overview of the composition and relative value of the client base of the firm.

Figure 4. The client pyramid

The client, lawyer and service paradigm

If we look at things in the same old 'functional way' and from the same old perspective, things will not change; but our clients will. If we get up and walk around the problem it may appear different from another angle. Our clients see us from a different angle from that which we see ourselves. The wider the angle, the wider the difference and greater the lack of conformance in that view and the less will be the degree of understanding between the supplier and the receiver of the service. The narrower the angle, the less the difference and greater the understanding. This difference in perception depends on positioning and perpetuates the gap in client alignment. Rather than seeing yourself as a fee earner, or as a partner, or as a lawyer, try thinking of yourself as a person who gets paid by clients for providing them with benefits and solutions through the delivery and management of your firm's people skills and resources. Look at it in a way which shows that you are paid for your service to your clients which involves the law but is not comprised solely of the law. Service, not law, is your principal business. Achieving benefits for clients as a result of doing legal work is the client manager's theme. If you start to look at it differently, it may offer pointers to new ways in which to deal more effectively with clients and this is the start of client management.

Perception is a filter whereby both lawyers and clients assess things according to their own experiences, values and expectations. It's not what actually happens that is important or real, but how we interpret what happens that is real and important. So if, as we have established, clients do perceive the service element of our work in different ways from us, then, if we start seeing it more from their viewpoint, it will appear to us in a similar light. This match, or client alignment, and the consequential action, is the key to client management. The point was more succinctly stated by Robert Burns:

> O wad some power the giftie gie us to see oursels as ithers see us.
>
> Robert Burns, *To a Louse*

The client is always right

Good client care is what clients think it is and not what the lawyer says it is. If your client is dissatisfied, then you should accept that he is dissatisfied and not argue whether or not he is right to be dissatisfied. His dissatisfaction is a fact. Having acknowledged that your client feels that way, you don't necessarily have to agree with him but you should try to ascertain why he feels dissatisfied. For example, he may say that he has been overcharged. You may feel indignant about this because of all the work you have done for him. 'What work have you done? I haven't seen it!' exclaims the client. You begin to explain the things that have been done that the client was unaware of. You produce a hefty file, perhaps in several volumes, a documents file, a deeds packet, streams of computer printouts of recorded time and point to the bill narrative in self justification. 'No, I didn't tell you about all of this because I did not think it was necessary – I just got on with the job!'

you meekly explain. The client somehow remains unimpressed. The fact that you did all that work is no longer a guarantee in itself of client satisfaction.

So while you may think your client is wrong to criticise your bill and you feel you are right and he is wrong, he equally feels that you are wrong and he is right. He feels you are not justified in making that charge based on his perception of the work and you feel that you are justified because of the work you know that you have done and which was necessary. You're both 'wrong' at the same time. It's a 'lose-lose' situation. Your client has been left feeling unsatisfied and you have been left with a loss. This situation need not occur had the principles of client management been applied.

Accepting this, it is all a question of communication, perception and (mis)understanding. The solution is to ensure that your client's perception of the work matches the work actually done for him. For example, client satisfaction will be improved at the outset by the client agreement, the case plan, and during the progress of the case by regular client reports and frequent use of the telephone. Fee resistance will reduce when there is a client agreement, when you have discussed and agreed a case plan, and when you have performed accordingly. He's happy because he knows where he stands and you're happy because you know what work has been agreed, how much you will be paid and when you will be paid. You're right and your client is right. Client agreements, case plans and agreed charges help to promote a 'win-win' relationship between the solicitor and his client. Here both the client and the solicitor are always right.

The best solicitor in town

I often recount a commercial property case where I was instructed to represent the land owner and a certain well-known local solicitor was representing the developer. I duly sent out a draft development agreement and waited. The developer's solicitor never replied to my letters, he never returned my telephone calls, he never even amended the draft development agreement – no sign of a red pen anywhere! He just wasn't playing the game! 'Where is he and what is he doing?' I used to wonder. I tried to comfort myself with the thought, 'He can't be that good a lawyer after all!' It was not until I met him with his clients at the completion meeting in my office that I discovered the answer. Clearly, his clients idolised him! They were full of praise for him and hung on his every word. When he spoke, it was as if the assembled Law Lords were sitting ghostly on either side of him, nodding in silent agreement. To his clients, he was the law. My clever legal points went unheeded. His clients just gazed at him and waited for his authoritative and binding dicta.

Why was this? What had he done that I hadn't? What was so special about him? It clearly wasn't the depth of his legal skills, which I judged to be adequate though not profound. I later discovered that he spent lots of time out of the office with his clients, in their offices, at their shops and factories, with them in the pub and restaurant, in their homes and at the weddings of their daughters. In their eyes, he was the best because they saw a lot of him and because he showed them by his actions that he was interested in them. He used to tell them he was the best and they as paying clients were happy to accept this.

This particular case later hit a boundary problem which could have been avoided by more thorough preliminary legal work. But, instead of being blamed by his clients for the delay, cost and aggravation this caused in being sorted out, he emerged as a champion of their rights against an oppressive and inflexible property owner. He was not a lawyer's lawyer, but he was very successful with his clients. I have come across his reputation on many occasions before and since then and with the usual refrain, 'Mr X? Of course we know him, he does all our legal work – he's the best solicitor in town!'

There is an important lesson here in client management. Whilst we should not neglect our legal work and the files, we should try to spend more time with our clients, demonstrating our interest in the client and his business. Time spent with clients makes a stronger impression than 'unseen' time spent slaving over the file in the office. This work is invisible to the client and no matter how good it is, it will not of itself necessarily increase his level of satisfaction. Client satisfaction lies mainly in the realm of the service intangibles.

Our clients aren't really interested in our files, our precedents, our forms, our law books, our computers, our software or our offices – they are interested in us because of the benefits, solutions and welfare that we can provide to them. They want to know and be involved in what's going on, they want added value, they want something different and they want service. They want the best solicitor in town!

Thinking about clients

In order to be able to deliver a service that clients want and value, it is important to know how we really think about clients. How client-oriented are you? Tick 'Yes' or 'No' to say whether or not you agree with the following statements:

Statements about clients	No	Yes
1 Clients are the most important people in our business.		
2 We depend on our clients for our living.		
3 Service is our business.		
4 The level of client satisfaction is more important than the numbers of new inceptions.		
5 We send out regular client questionnaires and systematically analyse the feedback we receive and act upon it.		
6 We do a client satisfaction survey at least once a year.		
7 We treat complaints as an important and 'free' form of client feedback.		
8 The client is always right.		
9 The client is the best judge of our service – not us.		
10 We see effective client management as an important strategy for the success of the firm.		

You may score 0 for a 'No' and 1 for a 'Yes' to work out your client-orientation rating as follows:

0–2   it may be that your clients are not as important to you as you thought.

3–5   you have client awareness but are you doing much about it?

6–8   you are saying and doing the right things but could you do more?

9–10 you are interested in and understand your clients and you are doing something about it. You can rightfully claim to be client-oriented.

Client focus

If clients are the most important part of our businesses and client satisfaction is one of the principal objectives of doing work for them, what do we need to do to ensure that these principles become embedded into our work practices? There is far more to client management than 'smile technology' or splashing out on a new tea tray and cups and saucers for clients in reception. These are often mistaken for being what client care is about, but there is far more to it than that.

When clients become the focus, it will touch and concern everyone in the firm. It is not just for partners, or fee earners, it is for everyone. It has been proven over and again that it is easier, quicker and cheaper to do business with steady, loyal and satisfied clients than to pursue new and unknown target clients at great cost in terms of time and money.

Marketing activity chases new clients and marketing reports enumerate 'new' clients. But, who in the firm is responsible for chasing old and lost clients, who counsels existing clients, who does the 'exit' interviews – in short, who focuses on clients? Logic as well as business sense tells us that new clients pouring in at one end will be of little benefit if an unknown number of lost clients are allowed to seep out at the other end. An increase in new clients of 10 % per annum is less encouraging when it is reported that the number of lost clients has increased to 15% per annum.

It is important to know what's going on at both ends and to be in control of both new and existing client relations and it is even more important to manage what goes on in between, with existing clients. This is client management. If the first half of the 1990s has been about quality, the second half is about client management. This was succinctly put by Donald E Petersen, the Chairman of Ford Motors, who said, 'If we are not customer driven, our cars won't be either.'

Some useful work showing valuable insight into the profession's view of itself and its clients was done by Yallop Marketing Consultants. They suggest that you ask yourself to tick which of the following statements you most strongly agree with:

Statement	Agree	Disagree
1 The quality of our professional expertise sells itself and clients will always need our products.		
2 The only way to keep our clients is to reduce our price and be more price competitive.		
3 We need to get in more clients and do more bills!		
4 You just can't plan ahead in this profession – noone knows what's going to happen from one day to the next.		
5 We make our profits by creating opportunities to effectively satisfy our clients' needs within the constraints of our resources.		

Comments on the above statements are as follows:

1 This statement indicates a product-oriented attitude and is often heard from solicitors who like the law for its own sake and who regard clients as a necessary appendage.
2 This is a cost-oriented attitude and is often heard from solicitors who work in a fiercely competitive marketplace where price appears to be more important than service or quality.
3 This displays a volume or turnover mentality and appeals to the solicitor who works a 10–12 hour day, who likes being 'busy', who appears to thrive under pressure.
4 This is erratic and dis-oriented and is the constant cry of the 'busy' solicitor who may not be as effective as he could be.
5 This is a marketing and client-oriented mentality.

To change or increase your focus on new, existing and lost clients, it's not enough to just talk about it or delegate the function to a marketing partner or, even worse, to a marketing committee. You need to develop common values that are based on client feedback derived from questionnaires and surveys and by taking small, practical steps to remedy perceived client problems and opportunities. Only by sharing, listening and doing with measurable results, communicated to all will you make any real progress in your efforts to sharpen the focus on clients.

Attitudes and perception

Client management is not only about the process of law; it is also about an attitude that permeates an organisation where the people in it set themselves the task of providing extraordinary client service to each and every client. It is the attitude that holds that the purpose of your work is to provide your clients with something that will delight them and make them want to pay your salary or profits by buying the benefits of the legal products and services that you deliver to them. Whether or not and to what extent you achieve this will be decided by the perception of your clients. You may have all the necessary legal expertise and experience, but if you haven't satisfied your clients fully then more needs to be done.

Client management won't work fully unless everyone in the firm is committed, involved, enthusiastic and determined. Not only can a chilly (or over-busy) receptionist make a poor impression on a client, but also the case manager's approach to dealing with the client's affairs. We should try to bridge the gap and see it the way the client sees it. For example, a divorce client may be laden with thoughts and feelings of personal failure, whereas an inexperienced client manager may see the situation only as a file with a green form. A house-moving client may be ending an old chapter in his life and starting a new one, in which moving house is just a part. He may have got a new job or a new partner and be moving to a new area, whereas the lawyer may see it only as a linked sale and purchase with the discharge and grant of a mortgage with registered titles. If you try to see it as the client does, it will improve the understanding and communication. Try to see the benefits that the client needs and then match your service to help him achieve this. Try to provide benefits or solutions through your legal processes, rather than just the processes themselves.

The top of the mincer

Financial reports and analysis will not in themselves substantially improve the performance of the firm. Financial performance is one measure of how well we do what we do, but it does not measure what we do for our clients in order to achieve that financial result. The production, delivery and presentation to the client of the legal product is what we do to produce a result or benefit or solution to the client. This is what needs to be proactively improved and managed by the practice of client management. Looking back at Chapter 1, and the section on 'the client management mincer', we can see that, if we put in a quality legal product and a quality delivery service at the top of the mincer and if we are assisted by our staff in turning the handle of the mincer, then the financial results at the other end inevitably will improve.

File management versus client management

One of the first work habits that needs to be re-examined is the underlying culture that what lawyers do is to work on files. In our offices we keep drawers full of files, we dictate on files, we write on files, we open new files, we close old files – much of our time and attention goes on to the file. The files are important and do need to be well kept in accordance with quality standards and file management principles. But it is a fundamental misunderstanding to think or conduct our offices in a way which makes file management the main thing that we do for our clients. Files are the tool, the process and the method for producing the benefit, the solution and the result, but the file is not the result or benefit or solution. The file is the lawyer's equivalent of the painter's brush, the mason's chisel or the baker's oven. The file is only one of the tools we use to help produce the benefit, solution or welfare for the client. Client management ensures that what we do in our files and on our desks and in our offices produces the result, the solution and the benefit that the client wants and is prepared to pay for.

Client management puts the client first and relegates the file to be a subsidiary though important tool. The file is a means to an end, but it is not the end itself. If we take as our starting point the statement that we are in business to satisfy our clients, then the first question must be, 'What must we do to satisfy this client?' rather than the implied statement that says, 'This is what we do – who will buy?'

File versus client management is the underlying cultural issue that a firm needs to decide before it can set sail on the rising tide of client management. The case for client management is one that is being put ever increasingly by our own clients whilst the case for file management is a quality issue. It's a matter of emphasis – both file management and client management are important but, in the matter of the client versus the file, the clients are both judge and jury and the case for client management will be won, with costs, by clients every time.

Client policy

All well-managed firms have a documented financial policy containing details of how to draw cheques, pay in monies, order telephonic transfers and so on. Most well-managed firms will have written policies on how to do case work, how to manage files and how to comply with quality systems. Some well-managed firms will have policies on how to manage staff, how to do appraisals, how to increase productivity and improve communications, and how, in short, to maximise the results from the people in the firm. But how many firms have a documented policy on how to manage their relations with their clients?

The statutes and rules which govern and regulate the framework of our relations with clients are not designed specifically to improve that relationship. They deal with compliance. The fuss that the introduction or imposition of Rule 15 caused in the profession indicates the intensity of the profession's reaction to being told what to do as far as our clients are concerned. If we are intent on being or becoming client-oriented, then we should ensure that we have a system in our firms to ensure that client relations are managed proactively and positively, so that client satisfaction is consistently provided to comply with quality standards and so that all clients are retained as long-term clients of the firm.

There are four principle themes to a client policy:

1 that client satisfaction is acknowledged to be the critical success factor in the management and development of a law firm;
2 that putting the client first in devising systems to ensure client service and client satisfaction is the first task of the firm;
3 that it is important to try, test, review and adjust or reject. This is where the profession must now be willing to welcome and encourage innovation, ideas, creativity and enthusiasm for developing new and better client satisfaction systems; and
4 that if it works for clients as well as for us, we must build it into our product and service systems.

We are all good with our own clients, what about the hundreds or even thousands of other clients of the firm? Are they being fully and effectively satisfied? Are opportunities for the use of wider services and of your particular services being properly diagnosed and developed?

What about those clients who never see a partner? What about your clients when you are not there? Client management provides policies for dealing with these issues

Clients – who, what, where, when, why and how?

Who are our clients and what do we know about them? What do they want and expect? Where do they come from? When do they require our legal services? Why do they come to us and not go to another firm? How much are they prepared to pay for our services?

How many 'old' clients keep coming back? Which clients produce the most profit, the most turnover, the lowest margins, the most problems and the most complaints in the firm? What do clients like? What don't they like? If they don't complain, is it safe to assume that they are happy? What more can we do for them? Are we doing enough for them? Are we over-reliant on a few big clients? What repeat work do we get? What percentage of our turnover comes from new services? Have we introduced any new services in the last year? What new services do clients want? How many clients did we lose last month? Why did we lose them? Should we have lost them? How can we get them back? What is it that satisfies a client?

A traditionally reactive profession is being forced by the market to become more responsive towards its clients and to ask itself important and fundamental questions about its clients. Not only does this mean new work practices but also a fundamental shift of emphasis which puts the client and the satisfaction of the client first.

Who are our clients?

Do we do credit checks or do we blithely incur substantial work in progress costs before submitting a bill? Is Mr Jones, who is buying a house through your conveyancing department, also the chairman of ICI? Is the 'new' client an 'old' client of the firm? Were there problems? Knowledge about clients can both protect and develop the client relationship and needs to be systematically gathered and analysed.

What do they want and expect?

What do clients want? Do they want your file, your precedents, your forms, your brochures, your departments and your smart offices? Or do they want:

1 a responsive service;
2 to be understood by the person they deal with;
3 reasonable charges that they can understand and agree with;
4 reliability of the person and the product;
5 accessibility of the person; and
6 a person who is interested in them?

Where do they come from?

Do clients just appear from nowhere? Are they refugees from a competitor firm? Are they firm-hopping? Are they shopping but not buying? What's their background? Do they come from the competitor in the High Street or from a rival city firm? Why did they leave that firm? Are they just doing a cost comparison? Are they splitting their legal requirements between several firms? Are they dumping an unwanted or difficult case on us? Are they shopping around for other services?

When do they need our services?

I recall telephoning for a quotation from a commercial supplier on a Saturday morning to be told, 'You're lucky we're open on a Saturday!' to which I replied, 'No, it's you who are lucky that I phoned you at all!' The reply I received suggested that the supplier had not yet adopted the philosophy that 'the customer is always right'.

I saw a client recently who said, 'I want you to be proactive with us – tell us what you can do for us and where you think you can help us. Don't wait to be asked – come and see us!' Doing a property purchase here, a share transfer there, a change of name and so on are just pieces of a jigsaw that help us build up a picture of the client. It's patchy and slow. This invitation from a client is very valuable for the client manager. Clients will appreciate proactive suggestions even if they don't immediately instruct us to do the work for them. They will register that we are interested in them and remember to come to us when they are ready. Client managers don't just sit and wait for instructions; they get to know the client, they go to see them, they keep in touch and they are there just when the client needs them.

Why do they come to us?

A client-oriented firm will know why it is distinctively better than or different to its competitors and it will be interested to know why its clients come to them in particular. What is our unique selling point? What is our differentiation? Why us and not another firm? Only the clients can tell us.

How much will they pay for our services?

Low levels of productivity, client satisfaction and quality will not justify high fee levels. In a competitive market, the Solicitors' Remuneration Order may protect you in a taxation but it will not win you work. Time costing, value costing, percentage work and fixed costs are in regular use and contingency fees have arrived, albeit in limited types of cases. I believe we will see a lot more of charges which are agreed with clients in advance and which are linked to a written work specification and timescale. 'No deal, no fee' agreements are increasingly being done in non-contentious and property work.

Client managers seek answers to all these questions but there is no single universal answer for all clients, because every client is different. What is important is that we should try to systematically get to know and understand our clients better in order to provide a better service by planning and managing our relationships with our clients.

The client is our business

We should question our basic assumptions from time to time in order to avoid forming false illusions. Watch your competitors, find out what they do well, plan and do it better and then check with client feedback to measure its effect. Everything we do is driven by our clients. When the client's preferences change, so must we also change to mirror this. Is the client satisfied, will he come back and will he tell his business associates, family and friends about us? The question for law firm managers is, 'What do we need to do to deliver quality legal products with quality service and value, reliably, consistently and comprehensively across the whole firm so as to ensure consistent high levels of client satisfaction and profitability?'

There are some basic issues here with which many will now agree:

1 client and competitor research and product testing will enable us to get closer to our clients;
2 the value chain must be looked at from the client's point of view at all times; and
3 client satisfaction is our business – the client is our business.

This is the fundamental principle of client management and its meaning, implications and application is the concern of the client manager.

The five most important people in the firm

The five most important people may be thought to be the senior partner, the managing partner, the finance director, the marketing partner and the staff partner. To think this would be wrong. In any professional firm, the five most important people are the client, the client, the client, the client and the client. It's not the new accounts manager, it's not the brilliant rising legal eagle, it's not your secretary and it's not even you. It is the people who pay your bills and on whom you depend for your living – your clients. At any one point in time, the clients telephoning your office, speaking to your secretary, sitting in reception, travelling to your offices, going to your office toilet, having a coffee, sitting in your room listening to your advice, travelling back from your office or going home, thinking about impressions afterwards, trying to remember what was said, reading your often long and technical letters, struggling to fathom the meaning of your Rule 15 client care letter, waiting to hear from you, waiting, wondering – all these clients are experiencing the overall service of your firm in ways unique to them and these are the most important people at any one particular point in time.

We see what we do from our own perspective, it's only human, our advice, our desks, our office, our letters, our contracts and our clients sitting politely opposite at the other side of our desk. But what happens when you're not there, when you're not available, when your client doesn't hear from you, when he needs to speak to you but you're not around? Your client in your absence may be a seething mass of confusion, doubt and frustration. It's hardly ever the legal advice or the legal work that clients complain about. They are far more likely to complain about delays, not knowing what's going out and not feeling cared about because this is what they perceive more than anything else. We might think these things are minor problems and not really important but the client patently does not. The most important people in our offices are our clients and we must take active steps to manage the client's experience of us and our service.

Plus ça change

There is nothing really new in client management, other than that it is more important now than ever before. What is new about client management is that it should be a managed and consistent process and that it can be learned and that it should involve everyone in the firm. The old style general practitioner who looked after all the legal affairs of a client and his business is not very different in some respects to the modern client manager. It has been recognised that a solicitor can no longer be an expert in all branches of the law and it was this relentless drive to specialisms which caused so much harm to the traditional solicitor/client relationship. Client management does recognise that clients should have one main point of contact, that specialist work is done by the specialist but that the overall product and service supply to the client is co-ordinated by the client partner. The difference and the opportunity is that with client management we are able to more actively manage and develop our relationship with our clients.

Action checklist

1 Check your complaints system for invaluable feedback from clients.
2 Start a regular client questionnaire system.
3 Do the client attitude tests on pages 42 and 44.

4 Quality and client management

Understanding quality

One of the buzz-words for law firms in the 1990s is 'quality'. Previously, if quality was mentioned, it was assumed that professional legal work was self-evidently quality work on account of the training that solicitors had to undertake in order to qualify. It was thought that professional training and practice were enough to denote quality. It was said that something was either good or bad quality or high or low quality. None of these, however, were linked to a precise definition or to a satisfactory understanding of what 'quality' actually means.

The Law Society produced a definition of the word in its booklet, *Quality – 1991* which comprised three parts – professional competence, client care and business skills. It is interesting to note that this definition did not see quality only as a matter involving what we as lawyers do but that it also recognised that quality also involved the client. It acknowledged that quality is not only about the standard of legal advice. Quality is not only about being a good lawyer. It defines quality as something which involves both the lawyer and his client.

In the context of legal work and the various quality standards that abound, quality has more recently become to be understood to mean two things:

1 the degree to which the legal work conforms to an agreed and written specification of work; and
2 the degree to which the legal work satisfies identified client needs and expectations.

These two parts of the definition of quality are also fundamental to the definition and understanding of client management which is founded on the twin principles of providing at the outset a written specification of the work and the service and agreeing the specification of work with the client, and of checking with the client, during or at the end of the case, the level of his satisfaction with the work and the service.

Quality in the context of client management takes quality beyond the mere listing of a procedure, process or specification to that of seeking agreement with the paying client and also checking for satisfaction. Client management provides the techniques, tools and practices which will enable solicitors to put quality in both its parts into everyday practice.

First, a detailed examination of the two 'limbs' of quality are required in order to understand why client management is quality in action and how it may be put to work in our everyday work practices.

Quality – conformance to specification

The first limb of quality, the degree to which the work conforms to a written work specification, involves three things:

1 the standard of work in a case must be legally correct. Legal knowledge, procedures, forms, precedents, time-limits, expertise and the written work must be correct and conform to established practice. Standard case plans for routine case work should be established for all groups and departments and should be reviewed and updated at periodic intervals;
2 increasingly clients are asking to know more precisely what work will be done, to have some input into discussing and agreeing the work stages and to be assured that the work will meet their requirements;
3 having discussed the work and agreed what is to be done, many clients also then appreciate having a written specification setting out the agreed work and timescale, broken down into stages. This is where the use of the case plan is becoming more prevalent in quality managed case work.

This is the first part of quality. It means that the work will conform to pre-set standards and agreed specifications. Conformance to written standards and specifications will act as a useful and important checklist, will reduce error and streamline the work. This will lead to savings in time, and, therefore, in the overall measured cost of doing the job. Your recoverability rate will improve on a case-by-case basis and your ability to handle more cases will improve, giving rise to consequent improvements in turnover and profitability.

Quality – meeting client requirements

The second limb of quality, that of identifying, working to and then checking on client requirements and satisfaction, brings into play another aspect of professional work, an aspect which involves a subjective assessment being made by the client of the legal work and the systematic and applied client management techniques of the lawyer. The importance of this client management aspect of quality has come more into prominence since the abolition of scale fees, the progressive deregulation of the profession and the unprecedented rise in competition. The identification and satisfaction of client needs and expectations as a part of a quality standard is the task of the client manager. This is where quality and client management coincide.

Those who have been involved in setting up quality systems may complain about the paperwork and the fact that quality systems do not in themselves improve the service to the client or increase client satisfaction. This is true if only the first limb of the quality definition is developed but the second limb, the meeting of client expectations, is overlooked or just assumed. The first part of the quality definition, conformance to agreed standards, will reduce costs, delays, errors and reworking. It may also improve client satisfaction by reducing misunderstandings and cost overruns but it will not necessarily improve the service to the client.

The meeting and exceeding of client expectations is not given adequate practical attention in some quality systems and it is this particular part of quality that client management is largely concerned with; the identification, agreement, measurement and improvement of client satisfaction through the design, implementation and review of proactive client service measures and product design to meet ascertained client requirements.

It can be seen that this second part of a quality service is concerned with the delivery mechanism and the service element on which the client assesses the quality of the overall product. The first part of quality is measured by us lawyers as the degree to which the work we do varies from agreed standards, and second part is measured by the client as the degree to which the service we provide to the client meets or exceeds his identified needs and expectations. Quality measures the degree of variance from or conformance to agreed written standards of product and service. The greater the conformance and the lesser the variation, the higher the quality. In short, it can be seen that a good quality legal service means that:

1 the work which has been done achieves a high degree of conformity to written standards, which we can measure and assess ourselves; and
2 identified client needs and expectations are achieved as closely as possible, and this can be assessed only by the client.

Quality, therefore, is something which is assessed by both the lawyer and the client in its two constituent parts respectively. There is both an objective standard in assessing to what extent the legal product conforms with the agreed case plan and a subjective standard whereby the client assesses the level to which the legal product and service has met or exceeded his identified expectations. The lawyer assesses the former and the client assesses the latter. Case plans and client agreements (see Chapter 11 and Appendices 1 and 2) are, therefore, essential tools for use in quality and client management in achieving and increasing the quality of legal work and service.

It can be seen that client management is a quality system affecting the whole spectrum of the solicitor/client relationship. It does this first by the systematic use of case plans and client agreements to deal with the first limb of quality. Secondly, it does this by the systematic identification and satisfaction of client needs and expectations at the outset and throughout the course of a case by the use of client management techniques and work practices which are designed to increase the likelihood and level of client satisfaction.

The second limb of quality, that the service should meet or exceed the expectations of the client, is one that is less tangible and, therefore, more difficult but not impossible to define and manage. Whilst putting in place systems for case management, costs plans and the client agreement, it is yet another matter to find out what the client expects and then to check at a later stage whether or not his expectations have been met or exceeded.

Quality: BSI-style

The British Standards Institution describes the quality of a service as:

the totality of features and characteristics that bear on its ability to satisfy stated or implied needs.

One of the problems that we as lawyers have encountered in providing a quality service is that perhaps we have predominately concerned ourselves with the legal advice and the legal work and perhaps have not paid enough attention to the identification, satisfaction and measurement of client needs and expectations. Perhaps not enough attention has been given to getting clients to state or articulate their needs at the beginning, during or at the end of a case. In saying this, it is in no way being suggested that we should give less importance to our standards of legal advice or expertise. On the contrary, the first limb of quality accents the importance of this but now with the rider that there should be an agreement with the client about the work to be done. Quality requires not only correct legal work and advice, but also that client needs and expectations are identified and satisfied as well. In these days of intense competition for client attraction and retention, we can no longer afford to rely on what we think the client needs or expects, we have to find out by asking and then ensuring that we deliver what the client wants.

Our concept of quality is an evolving thing. It is clear that quality does not necessarily mean expensive, long-winded, over the top or a Rolls Royce service, or even doing lots of unnecessary work that the client doesn't want and won't pay for! By definition, and by linking the work to a case plan and a client agreement, quality work is doing *exactly* what the client needs and expects and *exactly* what the client has agreed to pay for. Quality focuses on the work and the client's perception of it. The quality of a product or service is not good or bad in itself, but is only good or bad to the extent to which the product or service conforms to or varies from agreed standards and the extent to which it satisfies client expectations. Quality is no longer to be assumed, but is something that needs to be actively built into every case and every client relationship by the use of client management techniques.

Quality and client managers

The first aspect of quality, conformity to specification, is one which we as lawyers are particularly well equipped to deal with. The law, legal procedures, checklists, work specifications, case plans, precedents and the established processes are the nuts and bolts of what lawyers deal with every day. Case managers will find this aspect of quality particularly appealing because it deals with the law, legal procedures and the 'due diligence' approach to doing legal work. Now, with the increased emphasis on doing the job right (see Chapter 1) and with the penal amount of the uninsured excess in professional negligence insurance policies, it is ever more important and cost effective to ensure that our work and case management systems conform to standard written procedures.

The second aspect of the quality definition is that the work must be agreed with the client. No longer is it sufficient for us to take instructions in the office and show the client to the door with a hearty pat on the shoulder saying, 'Well, Fred, don't worry about it, just leave it all to us and we'll sort it all out for you!' Clients want to know what 'it' is, what the steps are, who will do it, how long it will take, how much it will cost and when bills will be payable. This second aspect of quality is one that appeals to the client manager in us because it requires reaching an agreement with the client on the work to be done, his needs, expectations and objectives, and then it requires communication and feedback throughout the case about client perception and client satisfaction. Quality makes legal work a truly two-way process between the solicitor and his client.

The first limb of quality is about case management, and the second limb of quality requires client management.

Fitness for purpose

'Quality' as a working practice as opposed to a theoretical concept may still be fairly new to some lawyers and so it may be helpful to think of it in terms with which we are familiar, namely fitness for purpose. At common law, this means that the goods or service must be reasonably capable of being used for the purpose which the customer reasonably expects and be of merchantable quality. There are two elements of fitness for purpose:

1 the product or service must work reasonably well; and
2 it must do what the customer reasonably expects it to do.

Both these elements are virtually identical to the definition of quality we have looked at above. The first element is dealt with in case management by the use of the case plan. This is a standard list of features and actions which ensure that the legal product is effective and free from error. The second element of quality is dealt with by the client agreement, the care plan (see Chapter 11) and the client questionnaire. In doing these, you sit down with the client at the outset and identify his needs and objectives and then plan what work is to be done, by whom and by when in order to achieve this objective and later check for results.

Quality and the client

The quality of the legal product is defined partly by the lawyer, who specifies what needs to be done in order that the legal work is done correctly and efficiently, and partly by the client, who should be asked to specify his requirements at the outset of the case and to assess the level of his satisfaction during and at the end of the case. This is the key aspect of the new understanding of quality – that the client is integrally involved in determining what is to be done, thereby determining the quality of the matter. The writ needs to be issued in a certain form and in a certain way and over this aspect of quality you – the lawyer and the law – have control. Whether or not you will actually serve the writ once it has been issued is a client matter. The progress and features of the case are to a large extent determined by the client. The quality of the product is determined by the client in discussion and agreement with the solicitor. Satisfaction is determined by the client alone.

Chapter 6 looks at the service aspect of the total legal service between a lawyer and his client. The quality of service is largely what the client perceives it to be and not what we perceive it to be. It is the task of the client manager to ensure that the quality of service matches or exceeds the client's expectations.

The case for quality

Quality is not new. Jean Baptiste Colbert, the Finance Minister of France in 1664, wrote a letter to King Louis XIV in which he said:

> If our factories through careful work assure the quality of our products, it will be to the foreigners' interest to get supplies from us and their money will flow into the Kingdom.

The rise in consumerism, competition and the pressure on clients themselves to comply with ever increasing standards of quality control and assurance are combining to compel law firms to introduce and operate quality systems, from the basic standards (every piece of paper on the file must bear a number and case reference) to sophisticated levels (zero defects in all work). It is no longer sufficient for us to assume that what we do must be quality work, because what we do relates only to a part of the first limb of quality. Work cannot be quality work without input from the client. In tendering for work and even in retaining work for existing clients, the pressure is on us to be able to demonstrate to our clients and our potential clients that our quality procedures will give them assurance of quality work. Quality procedures and systems do not mean the best, better than, or even good or bad. Poor quality denotes non-conformance to measured pre-set standards and low client satisfaction, high quality means conformance to measured pre-set standards and high levels of client satisfaction.

The case for quality can be summarised as follows:

1 Benchmarking – so that you can accurately measure the performance of your own business with that of a competitor. Instead of just saying to a prospective client, 'Of course, we're better than Kenge & Carboys!', you would be able to say with greater authority, conviction and credibility, 'Our quality standards are recognised and accredited and are subject to regular external audit. Our quality standard is unrivalled in this town, not even Kenge & Carboys conforms to this standard! We also conduct regular client satisfaction ratings; and this is currently 78% and rising!'

2 Productivity – in the case of Rover cars, who in 1988 were sold to British Aerospace for £80 million, having introduced a company-wide quality policy in 1986 that resulted just four years later in an increase in productivity of 50%, and achieved a sale value to BMW in 1994 of £800 million. That turnaround and tenfold increase in value, according to John Towers, former Rover Chief Executive, was due entirely to their quality programme which was introduced by force of circumstances. In his own words, 'One of the things that was clear then was that we couldn't remain as we were.'

3 Client satisfaction – working to a quality system improves the satisfaction for clients because both supplier and receiver know exactly what is agreed and both are satisfied when it is achieved.

4 Staff satisfaction – if a quality programme is introduced for all the people in the firm, it will affect and benefit everyone, not only by reducing waste and error and so increasing productivity, but also by increasing people's pride in the workplace with the knowledge that what they are doing meets acknowledged standards of quality and client requirements.

5 Continuous improvement – quality means that nothing stands still as it requires people to work continuously towards improving whatever they do.

6 Less error and costly reworking – case plans agreed with the client in advance, written work specifications and file audits will together reduce the opportunity and incidence of error and the cost of unbillable time or even compensation, in putting things right.

7 Cost – doing what the client wants right first time can produce substantial savings in production costs.

Why quality and why now?

Conformance to standards and specifications is so much easier to measure and correct in the manufacturing and industrial sector because the physical aspects of a concrete product are more capable of precise definition than an intangible service. For example, a television may be specified as a colour portable with a 14-inch screen, 20 channels, remote control with teletext. Between the various products that are available in that range, it is easy to compare specifications and identify extras and compare value. This is why the manufacturing industry has managed to make so much progress over the last 20 years in improving the quality of their products. Quality is now built into products throughout the entire manufacturing process.

The Japanese, in particular, have brought quality in manufacturing to a new level of 'zero defects'. There is the story of the Japanese computer-chip company who received an order from an American company for 1,000 computer chips in which it was specified, 'There shall be a failure rate of no more than 0.6%.' This greatly puzzled the Japanese who could not understand why the Americans wanted six faulty chips! It surprised the American company even more when on opening the shipment of computer chips they found taped to the box of 1,000 chips, all of which worked perfectly, a little packet containing an extra six faulty chips 'as per your order'. Not only did the Japanese company agree a specification with the customer up-front, but they also ascertained and complied with the customer's expectations.

Now in the last few years of the 20th century, the quality spotlight has moved onto the professions and other service providers, but the task will not be so easy or straightforward. How do you set standards for legal work and service? How do you measure conformance with those standards? How do you set standards for client expectations and how do you measure conformance with expectations? The methodology of quality is that you write down measurable standards or criteria of performance, get agreement with the client and then carry out the work in conformity with them and then measure the degree of conformity actually achieved. Being a 'good lawyer' or a 'good firm' is no longer a sufficient assurance for the purpose of demonstrating quality. A good reputation may help but unless it can be measured and quantified, it will not be in itself any assurance of quality work. You're only as good as your current caseload. Even the firms with the best reputations stand to maintain or lose that reputation on the quality of the work turned out by their latest batch of recruited fee earners.

It is, therefore, impossible for a firm to hold itself out as providing a quality legal service unless it has systematic and consistent ways of taking instructions and agreeing a case plan and work specification with a client and unless it also has systematic ways of obtaining client feedback and of measuring the levels of client satisfaction actually achieved.

The new quality way is to find out exactly what each individual client wants and then to design and supply the service in a cost effective way that produces profit for the firm and satisfaction for the client. This is the client-driven approach to quality and is appropriate in a client-dominated market where clients have abundant choice and competition is fierce. This is why quality and why now, and this is the reason we need to change 180 degrees from the old ways when we simply assumed what the clients wanted and thereby addressed only one part of the quality formula.

'You get what you pay for'

It is a mistake to groan about quality, 'Our clients don't want quality, they just won't pay for it!' The whole point about quality is that it is about just that – identifying and then supplying *exactly* what the client has agreed and at a charge he has agreed to pay. Quality depends in part on the client and is not just an objective standard that exists in the vacuum of the office manual.

The client on the receiving end of a quality service gets exactly what he has agreed to be done and at the price he has agreed to pay. This will vary from one client to another but both will receive quality work. The same product at the same price to two different clients may be perceived in entirely different ways because each client may have different expectations of the product or service. The debt recovery client who puts hundreds of matters through the firm's computerised debt system can get the same quality of service as the management buy-out client who receives intense input from the lawyer on one matter. One needs minimum personal input whilst the other demands maximum solicitor/client time. Both are quality services because in both the work plan and charges are agreed and both meet the client's expectations. Quality does not only mean legal skills, reliability or cost. It means what the client perceives and expects. Both a Metro and a Rolls Royce are quality cars for the clients who buy them. Each is designed to meet the customer expectations for that particular vehicle at that particular price.

Quality – who needs it?

If you have already adopted a quality system and have gone through the pain barrier of implementing it, all you are likely to see at first is a mountain of extra paperwork, aeons of recorded non-chargeable time and no perceived improvements in the bottom line. You are still in business, though, and that is no mean achievement. You might acknowledge that it is easier now to find a client's title deeds and quicker to retrieve a file but have you also put quality principles to work in your working practices? Do you use case plans to set out the standard work to be done? Do you go through this with the client to reach agreement on the work and the timescale? Do you then follow through the agreed case plan in the management of the case? Do you identify with the client the objectives of the work and the level of service he requires by completing a care plan at the outset? Do you then measure whether the agreed work is done to plan and whether and to what extent it achieves client satisfaction?

Quality can be seen to affect not only central management, but also every case manager and every client as well as every file. By gathering the data at the start of the case about the client, the case plan and the client's expectations, you can then monitor the progress and achievement of this throughout the course of the case. This can help you to eliminate from your work practices things that are not agreed and are not necessary and incorporate things that the client wants. This process raises the whole client focus and makes it consistently more achievable to attain higher levels of client satisfaction. It can be seen that, in the new competitive and cost-conscious 1990s, quality is needed to provide cost savings and client satisfaction when quality practices are combined with client management.

Quality in practice means that we can adhere to accepted written standards, reduce the room for error and improve efficiency. Quality in practice means that we can involve the client more, agree the work stages and charges and meet his identified requirements. Both lawyers and their clients need quality to reduce error and to improve understanding, client satisfaction and profitability.

The cost of quality

The cost of quality is easier, perhaps, to define as being the cost of the lack of quality, or the cost of 'unquality'. The items which increase the costs of doing the work include:

1 the lack of a case plan can produce costly errors;
2 a badly written or incorrect case plan can cause costly errors;
3 a failure to agree a case plan with the client at the outset can cause misunderstandings;
4 the failure to follow a case plan once agreed can cause costly errors,
5 correcting mistakes made due to the foregoing absorbs otherwise chargeable time;
6 the costs of reworking work that has not been properly done; and
7 doing work which was not planned or anticipated can reduce or even wipe out any profit margin.

The cost of 'unquality' has been estimated to be between 20% and 50% of the overall production costs of an organisation or business. The conversion of such hidden 'costs' to quality is straight profit. In other words, up to 50% of your total firm-wide expenditure, which includes production costs, non-chargeable, written-off and unrecovered time, could be converted to profit by the implementation of an effective quality programme. If your total 'costs' are £1 million, and your cost of 'unquality' is, say, 25%, then a fully effective quality programme when implemented could earn or save as much as £250,000. If only 20% was achievable within the first year of the quality programme, then £50,000 is the cost of quality, or the lack of it – a quite staggering figure and one that cannot be ignored in any law firm wishing to achieve or increase its profitability.

Poor quality costs money, good quality saves money. We have all seen posters at the supermarket which say, 'Good food costs less at Foodco!' How is it that the supermarkets can compete with slogans like that? Is it just a slogan or is it actually true? It can be true because quality processes reduce costs and the benefits of cost savings can be passed on to the customer.

The drive in a law firm to reduce overheads should not be confined to cutting the cost of letterheads, premises, staff costs, computers and paperclips. The drive to reduce expenditure also is in the hands of each fee earner or case manager to a degree which, as has been seen, can produce far greater costs savings than the odd £1,000 or so shaved off the annual expenditure budget.

The managing partner will manage expenditure with financial budgets but he does not as a rule produce financial management reports about the costs of quality. If all the time taken in the above 'cost of quality' list was recorded by each fee earner and partner and measured, the cost would be very substantial indeed. The cost of poor quality is the aggregate of:

1 time and expense of remedial case work;
2 time of other work involved in the problem or in putting it right;
3 the lost productivity time of those people;
4 the time taken to find out if the rework is acceptable; and
5 cost incurred in failing to meet client expectations.

Attention to these quality issues will convert itself into bottom line performance figures where management understands that the cost of quality is directly translatable into margins, profitability and turnover. Case managers need to become more aware of the cost of reworking and thus reduce it. Where quality is absent or deficient because a job is not specified, planned and agreed with the client from the outset, an overrun of time and costs will not only incur further unrecoverable costs, but also client dissatisfaction will increase. This may lead to less repeat work, fewer recommendations, and a lowering of the firm's reputation in the marketplace. It will also reduce the time available for other clients, thereby compounding the problem all the way down the line.

By identifying and then measuring the cost of quality failures, both in the legal product and the service delivery mechanism, the cost savings of a quality system will be understood. By comparing the profitability of a firm and the costs of 'unquality', both before and after the implementation of a quality system, the cost saving achievements will be clearly seen.

Having identified the instances of 'unquality', in process deficiencies, overlap of work effort, the cost of reworking and the removal of non-value-adding work practices, the potential of delivering higher than before client satisfaction by reducing cost, waste and time, will be considerably enhanced. 'Unquality' incurs the cost of non-chargeable reworking time and non-billable chargeable time as well as the cost of incurring and then writing-off large amounts of work in progress. By reducing these areas of unquality, the firm will be better able to produce an agreed legal product with a service level that satisfies and at a cost which represents value for the client and consistent profit for the firm. Quality costs nothing and will save you something in terms of reduced process and product delivery costs.

Where profit is defined as the difference between income and expenditure (total costs of production), then it can easily be seen that, in a law firm, the introduction of a strategic quality policy where turnover is constant can yield an equal or greater increase in profitability than an expensive marketing campaign aimed at increasing turnover.

Quality and the competitive edge

According to a joint DTI/CBI Report entitled *Competitiveness – How the Best UK Companies are Winning*, no matter whether a business is a manufacturing or a service industry, the study of 100 of the best United Kingdom companies identified some key characteristics that all the successful companies had in common. These include:

1 a management and leadership style which recognises the need for change and which provides the drive to carry it all through over an extended period. Management understands change as being a continuous process and a way of work-life rather than a fixed term project with an end date. You can't do quality and then stop and relax – once you've started, there is no finish;
2 winning companies realise that the challenge of change can only be met by realising the full potential of the people already working in the business but who are not currently working to their full ability or capacity. New, flatter work and management structures are required and an emphasis on training and communication will put decision making closer to the customer;
3 winning firms focus on the needs of customers and welcome their demands and comments;
4 winning companies understand that the most important task of the firm is to develop new and differentiated services or products based on information about markets, customers and competitors; and
5 winning firms continually try to produce services that meet and exceed client expectations. They see service and support as the key to competitiveness.

The report states that the most successful companies have in common three main things at their core – managing change, managing staff and managing customers. It concludes by saying that the challenge to us all is to ask ourselves, 'How do we measure up to the best and how are we going to change?'

Why did the Japanese motorbike finish off the British motorbike industry in the 1960s and 1970s? It was not because they made a better motorbike but because they made one which was better in meeting identified customer demand. They had more specified features that the customer wanted compared with the British motorbikes. Instead of adopting the 'take it or leave it' attitude of the British motorbike industry, they asked customers what they wanted and then delivered it. They did not make the mistake of assuming they knew best. They addressed the second limb of quality – the meeting of client requirements.

What is at the heart of the quality revolution as much as the client revolution are three things:

1 the power of client choice;
2 the need to be able to respond to client choice effectively; and
3 the desire for continuous improvement.

BS 5750 and ISO 9002

These are quality systems aimed primarily at management of the production process. The system ensures that the client gets what has been contractually agreed with him and that any deviations are to be agreed with the client first. It requires that the procedures of how a firm works are written down and then it requires the management of the firm to ensure compliance with those principles. The standard does not necessarily ensure that the system is good or the best. The system deals with management responsibility, clarity of system and method, consistency, internal quality audits, management reviews, corrective action, training and document control.

A quality system has the advantage that it requires the business to think about and map out what it does and how it deals with its internal affairs. It helps a firm to predict and avoid problems. It helps to avoid recurrent problems. It should increase morale and efficiency because it should involve everyone in the firm. It requires that the firm produces systems and then keeps them under review. This promotes a consistent level of performance to agreed standards. The main features of the system are:

1 a commitment to quality by partners and staff;
2 a documented quality system;

3 clear procedures for taking instructions. In client management terms, this focuses on the first phase of the client relationship where the client manager uses the client agreement, agreed charges and case plans;

4 a clear procedure for monitoring the progress of a case. In client management terms, this is where case plans are important because it would be otherwise difficult to monitor progress unless you have something against which to measure progress. The principles of client management and quality make it essential that the client be kept informed of progress at regular intervals throughout the case, whether or not anything is actually happening. The client's perception of service is not suspended while you wait for the next letter to arrive, it's continuous;

5 a clear procedure for document control;

6 a policy and procedure for the selection of subcontractors including the selection of counsel, expert witnesses and so on;

7 a procedure for handling client documentation that includes checking, listing, storing and protecting the client's documents in your possession;

8 case reference systems;

9 case monitoring systems;

10 procedures for inspection of work and suppliers;

11 service review. This is where the client manager sends out a client questionnaire during and at the end of every case to ascertain client opinion on service, product quality and value, as well as to get a measured client satisfaction rating;

12 monitoring of inspection procedures;

13 recording identified problems (complaints handling systems);

14 taking necessary remedial action;

15 safeguarding materials in storage or in transit;

16 recording verification findings;

17 audit of the quality system (did the case plan work; did the client have his expectations met or exceeded?);

18 training of staff to deliver services to required levels of quality;

19 after care, follow up; and

20 statistical techniques.

The application of these principles to client management is of fundamental importance and the benefits may be summarised as follows:

1 the taking of instructions is improved;

2 case progress reports are produced;

3 document control is improved;
4 systematic selection of outside services;
5 improved retention of client documents and materials;
6 case references used throughout;
7 case monitoring improved;
8 work verification against case plans improves quality control;
9 maintenance of precedents is improved;
10 complaint handling is systemised; and
11 audit of the above for compliance or variance.

It should be understood that BS 5750 is not enough in itself to promote client satisfaction and that it needs client management in order to fully develop the client satisfaction and value potential of the product, the service and the firm. Client management encompasses both client care and quality systems. Client skills without quality systems will not achieve their full potential and quality systems without client skills will be limited in effect.

The BS 5750 kitemark has been achieved by a number of law firms and has been widely regarded as the badge of quality. Since its arrival in the legal profession, however, it has become increasingly acknowledged that BS 5750 and ISO 9002 which has replaced it, does not, in itself, necessarily improve the service to clients from the client's viewpoint. It is seen by many as a paper exercise in only requiring a firm to write down what it does and then to stick to it. It does not contain quality assurance. Rather it is concerned with documented procedures for the internal workings of a business. It will reduce inefficiency but of itself it will not improve the vital product and service element. A firm that gives poor legal advice and poor client service would not necessarily fail the accreditation.

BS 5750 was not designed for lawyers but for the manufacturing process. It is an achievement for any firm to obtain it but many people will agree that it is but a first step only on the road to total quality management and total client satisfaction. A firm may already have embarked on the design and development of client management systems that address these additional aspects of client perception and client satisfaction. This book contains an outline of a quality client management system that a firm may wish to adopt, in whole or in part.

The benefits of having a system such as BS 5750 or ISO 9002 include:

1 it is a marketing differentiator, but only if you have not got it;
2 it assists in meeting some client requirements;

3 it may assist in meeting tendering conditions;

4 it may produce staff management improvements; and

5 it will produce cost savings in terms of reducing the amount of wasted time in reworking, document retrieval and taking instructions. Quality will promote doing it right first time, identifying and avoiding problems, having up-to-date precedents and introducing an effective complaint handling system to reduce the wasteful and often avoidable involvement of the Office for the Supervision of Solicitors.

The LawNet Quality Standard

One of the main reasons for the foundation of LawNet was that members recognised that the consistent management, measurement and improvement of the quality of their legal work and services are essential to the survival and growth of their practises. Not only is quality necessary in order to maintain good work, to increase efficiency and to avoid errors, but it is also necessary to give the member firms a competitive edge.

LawNet recognised that something more than internal quality systems were needed to achieve client assurance in a consistent and measured way. Doing the work in accordance with quality systems is one thing, but delivering it to the client in a way which the client liked and wanted was another and second aspect of quality.

LawNet decided to create a standard which contained a fuller application of quality rather than one which was primarily concerned only with internal rules and procedures. The LawNet Quality Standard was designed to be compatible with and to contain all of BS 5750 whilst also containing standards relating to client service and satisfaction. The resulting LawNet standard is one which goes beyond BS 5750 and approaches a total quality management system.

The LawNet Quality Standard concentrates on four key aspects of law firm business, including the quality of management, the quality of people and the quality of image. The fourth aspect is concerned with the quality of client services.

The LawNet Quality Standard recognises that quality is assessed to a large degree by the client. The first limb of quality deals with objective standards and agreed work specifications, but the second limb, which is relevant here, deals with the subjective input the client has, first in stating his expectations, and then in assessing the degree to which he perceives that his expectations have been satisfied. In order to meet this second limb of quality, the LawNet Quality Standard requires a member firm to:

- put in place a system to research, review, record and monitor the opinions of clients with regard to service levels and expectations;
- to take such steps as are necessary to ensure that their standard of service is that reasonably expected by clients;
- to establish clear procedures for taking instructions from clients;
- to establish clear procedures for planning the progress of a case, including in complex cases the preparation of a case plan setting out what work is to be done, when it will be done, and stages of communication with a client;
- define and adhere to a level of contact with the client during a case;
- ensure that information about progress of a case is given to the client at regular intervals;
- keep the legally-aided client informed of their potential cost liability;
- ensure that the firm has procedures at the end of a matter for reporting to the client, accounting for any outstanding monies, returning documents to clients, advising the client as to future reviews of the matter, checking that the client is aware of important dates and where agreed with the client, maintaining a central diary to record such dates;
- put in place a complaint handling procedure; and
- comply with Rule 15.

The LawNet Quality Standard went 'live' in October 1994 and since that time all member firms have been undergoing the first round of external quality audits carried out by LawNet's own quality compliance and assessment team. Most member firms have put in great effort and commitment to installing and complying with the system. It has not all been fun and easy but, for the vast majority of firms who have gone through the audit with a high degree of compliance, most say that it has been and will increasingly be seen to be worth the effort. Quality is here to stay.

Total quality management

Total quality management ('TQM') has been brought into prominence because of the astounding success the application of its principles has brought to the Japanese economy over the last 30 years. In a country that lay in ruins after the Second World War, new ways and ideas to regenerate business prosperity were sought from the West. A solution was found in Doctor Deming and the 14 principles of business management he had developed and which became known as TQM.

The resulting success story of the Japanese businesses that adopted it are powerful proof of its efficacy. Having been rejected by Ford in the early 1960s, TQM was developed and implemented in Japan during the 1960s and 1970s, to be eventually adopted by Ford in the 1980s.

TQM is about producing the best products and the best service, using all the people in the firm, through constant innovation and striving for continuous improvement and holding the perception of the customer as the means of assessing success. It applies equally to products and service. This is where client management is particularly relevant because it concentrates on the delivery process of the legal product. For example, you may do a very good piece of legal work for a client with which he is pleased, but if the firm's invoicing system contains errors, if the client is chased for payment after he has paid the bill, if the computer wrongly locks onto him and goes on to threaten the client with legal proceedings, then the client's degree of satisfaction will decrease considerably. It can be seen that the accounts and administrative staff of the firm do have a direct effect on the client and his level of satisfaction. This is why all members of the firm are recognised in TQM as having an important role to play in total quality.

It will be seen that customer prominence is at the forefront of these principles. Particular attention in TQM is paid to the following.

Why things go wrong

Being aware of and identifying the causes of failure is the first step towards putting them right and more importantly, of redesigning your systems to ensure that the same errors do not recur. Fixing a problem without planning to reduce or avoid its recurrence in the future is like running up and down the dry side of a leaking dyke, putting your finger first in one hole and then into another without plugging the first hole before you dash to the next one. In client management, it is essential that where mistakes do occur, these recorded and the product or service is redesigned so that they never happen again. This is the task of the quality partner as well as of each group partner. Without systems to check why things went wrong, the firm will not allow itself to learn from its own mistakes.

The internal client

The assistant solicitor dictates an urgent letter to the client, but forgets to press the record button for the third paragraph, the secretary takes a telephone call for someone else after typing two paragraphs and restarts at the fourth paragraph, the letterheads she ordered from stores have not arrived and she is out of stock, the new office junior has forgotten to reload the toner cartridge in the printer and she is due for training on it tomorrow, and the receptionist is off sick but has not yet telephoned in. All these everyday happenings can combine to result in a dissatisfied client and also in unhappy internal relations. Everyone relies on someone else to do their own job properly. If not, the whole house of cards can tumble down and reduce the best of lawyers and law firms to ineffectiveness. If the participants get together at regular intervals to discuss problems that have occurred and to devise ways of remedying and avoiding them, then such a firm is well on the road towards total quality management.

Communication

The Charge of the Light Brigade is perhaps the most famous illustration of the damage that can be done by poor communication. Was the order to charge, or not to charge? Similarly, costly damage, though thankfully less mortal (at least in the short-term), is perpetrated daily due to lack of information, wrong information or merely poor channels of communication within a firm. Does your receptionist need to know what's contained in the marketing plan in case of a telephone inquiry? Does your secretary need to know the contents of the client information pack, just in case a client should comment on it? Would it help staff to know that the average levels of client satisfaction across the firm is improving? Should non-partners be told only what they need to know for their immediate job description?

TQM is a strategic planning and development issue which should be at the forefront of every law firm's business development plan and should be communicated throughout the firm in order to have maximum effect.

Total quality service

According to most clients, it is the level of service which is more apparent to them than product quality. Clients are more likely to be pleased by a draft sale contract of a property being sent out on the date agreed than one being sent three days late but with up-to-date Land Registry office copy entries. This does not mean that clients will accept poor quality work or that doing good quality legal work is not important. Clients assume that a qualified solicitor knows how to do his job. In addition, the client wants the legal work to be agreed by him, to meet his requirements and expectations and to achieve some benefit or solution. It is the recognition and management of these intangibles, in addition to doing quality legal work, that marks a legal service as being a quality service. In the context of a law firm, this requires client management as well as quality management.

Measuring quality

The financial performance of a law firm may be measured in the monthly management and annual reports and it is measured externally by the annual audit. Finance is the area of performance where measurement and reporting is easiest to do. It is one tangible measure of what is largely an intangible service. But finance is not the only measure of performance.

If we accept that the financial performance of a firm is the direct result of the quality of its products, its staff and its client satisfaction, then we should also design, measure and produce reports on the quality of our products, our staff and our client satisfaction performance to show more accurately exactly how and why the financial results were achieved.

As quality is now being made the subject of external audit, in terms of the legal aid franchise, BS 5750 and ISO 9002, it may not be long until we have external audits of our staff management and client management performances. There might even be a time when results and league tables of measured client satisfaction ratings are published! The top 10 law firms, instead of being rated only in numbers of partners, fee earners, turnover and incomes per partner might also, and more interestingly, be ranked in order of client satisfaction. Imagine what such a published annual account might look like:

Annual Report of Jarndyce & Jarndyce – 1996	
1 Client satisfaction	The firm showed an improvement over 1995 in increasing its performance to 63% from a low start of 52%. Complaints were up by 23%, largely due to the firm asking clients rather than waiting to receive complaints. 95% of complaints were resolved within seven days and to the client's satisfaction. There were no referrals to the Office for the Supervision of Solicitors.
2 Quality of work	The loss of productive time due to reworking reduced from 22% to 17%, producing a net increase in chargeable time of 5%.
3 Quality of staff	Staff turnover dropped from 4.5% to 3.7% and staff morale increased from 43% to 62% due largely to improved communications. Bad timekeeping and absenteeism reduced by 5%.
4 Finance	Turnover was up slightly by 5% but profits increased by 9% to 23% of turnover.

Quality management

Quality standards set the minimum level of acceptable performance and it is the task of the group partner to achieve the substantial savings that are possible by managing and motivating his group staff in accordance with quality standards.

Quality means the degree to which the product is effective (does it work?) and the degree to which it meets the client's expectations (does the client want it?) and so it is both standards and client-driven. This involves both the lawyer and his client. On the other hand, productivity means efficiency and is process-driven. Are the two mutually incompatible or exclusive? Client management states that its systematic application will improve both product quality and client satisfaction. It is a fundamental misapprehension of both quality and client management to think that the two are inconsistent.

Product and service design is also the responsibility of the group partner. It is up to him in discussion with his group clients to ensure that the legal work and the service with which it is delivered to the client is what the client wants and is prepared to pay for. He must ensure the value added process is sustainable at the price being charged. If it is not, then he must redesign and redirect his resources.

The implementation of a quality system goes hand in hand with the implementation of a client management system. You can't have one without the other. A firm that wishes to implement a quality policy will need to take the following steps:

1 obtain full commitment from all partners;
2 appoint a quality partner;
3 inform and involve all staff in the quality drive;
4 set out a quality implementation programme linked to a client management system with clearly identified goals, time-scales and allocation of responsibilities;
5 implement the system by stages;
6 train all staff in quality procedures;
7 review and monitor progress; and
8 aim for external audit at an agreed stage and timescale.

Case management

The carrying out of the legal work is what we have traditionally regarded as being the work of the lawyer, pure and simple. Seeing clients, writing letters, drafting documents, attending meetings, handling negotiations, giving legal advice, making court appearances and so on are what we lawyers do. It is important to actively manage our cases as part of our service to our clients. Whereas, traditionally, much of the work of a law firm has been reactive to client instructions, case management with agreed case plans, client agreements and progress reports help our work to become a planned process of direction and control.

Case management is also about the systematic management of the legal service from the client's point of view. It starts with the first interview with the client, the agreement of the case plan with the client, its implementation over the agreed time period and lastly the review of the case for conformance and variation and checking on the degree of client satisfaction achieved.

Case management is not, therefore, confined to the file and to the legal work *per se* but also includes the management of the client's perception of service. Client management encompasses both case and file management as well as the management of the service to the client.

File management

There is more to file management than paper clips and sellotape. The file is the tangible record of the legal work that is being done for the client. The file will contain a file management clip for checking the progress of the legal work as a well as a client management clip for checking that the work has been presented and delivered to the client in accordance with the firm's client management system.

The file management clip will typically contain a checklist to ensure that the basic client quality standards have been complied with including:

- client inception form completed, filed and copy sent to client database;
- conflict search done;
- Rule 15 letter sent to client;
- client agreement agreed and signed by the client and the case manager;
- terms and conditions of business sent to the client;
- case plan agreed with the client;
- care plan agreed with the client;
- client information pack sent to client;
- agreed charges agreed with client and copy sent to accounts;
- interim and final bills delivered as agreed;
- progress reports to client done as agreed;
- bills delivered and paid;
- pre-exchange report sent to client;
- client questionnaire sent and received;
- client satisfaction level ascertained;
- deeds returned or put in deeds storage;
- complaints and comments acknowledged and dealt with;
- case report sent to client and acknowledged;
- contact dates diarised;
- introductions to other services;
- diarise next client review date;
- client database details updated; and
- audit form completed.

The standards of file management are determined by what the client wants and expects as well as by what the firm itself considers should be done. The point of having a quality file management system is that it ensures the consistent application throughout the firm of practices and procedures that are known to work and that are known to increase client satisfaction and to reduce client dissatisfaction. Without a written system and regular and systematic checking of conformance, there can be no quality.

Case plans

How does one design the legal product? There are three stages involved. First, check the clients and the markets to ascertain what the demand is or likely to be for the particular legal product. This will produce a range of standard services; for example, property sale, property purchase, divorce (petitioner), debt recovery, personal injury (plaintiff) and so on. Second, write down the things you need to do in carrying out the particular job from start to finish. You start by 'taking instructions', completing a standard case plan, doing this and then doing that until a certain stage is reached. This might be the issue of the writ or petition, an exchange of contracts or the submission of a planning application. The following stages may vary. Here you need to leave room for some variables. Then, following the completion or the obtaining of judgement or of the decree, there are certain 'post-completion' stages to deal with including, at the end, the client review and file archiving.

The third stage occurs when a particular client has requested the service and then the standard case plan needs to be adapted to suit that particular client. This is where the client has a positive input to make in designing the legal product. Instead of just telling the client what work will be done in the case plan (and even that may be a considerable advance in itself), client managers suggest the work in the case plan as standard and check with the client whether it is acceptable or whether more or less is required. There must be a discussion at this point with the client.

Putting quality to work

It is only by the pursuit of quality that a firm will be able to develop itself into a truly client-focused and effective organisation. Any firm in any location can do this by forming and acting upon this single resolve. Instead of casting about with the difficult strategic questions about where the firm wants to be in three years' time, quality itself can form the central focus to strategic planning. The production of quality legal work in response to client needs and expectations and which produces high levels of client satisfaction, value for money and profitability is a pretty good strategic plan for any firm, large or small.

When the motivating force and *raison d'être* of every person in the firm is to achieve extraordinary levels of client satisfaction, then the die is cast for the firm to become and remain truly competitive. It is this vision and commitment that puts the pursuit and attainment of extraordinary levels of client satisfaction as the guiding light and benchmark of everything the firm does and stands for that is an absolutely fundamental and essential prerequisite for the firm to successfully implement a quality and client management policy.

Once that vision and understanding has been formed and full commitment to it has been obtained (and this is often the hardest and longest step to take), the next stage is to gather client feedback and opinion on a regular and consistent basis.

This information will enable the firm to commence a top-to-bottom and bottom-to-top reappraisal of every person, every thing and every procedure in the firm in order to assess its contribution to added value for the client and the extent to which each contributes towards the attainment of extraordinary levels of client satisfaction. Only a determined reappraisal of the firm and its innards with no holds barred will work here. Any protectionism, vested interest, defensiveness or resistance to this all encompassing reappraisal will reduce the benefits to be achieved by the process. Vested interests and inertia are the enemies of quality.

It will quickly become apparent that the pursuit of extraordinary levels of client satisfaction cannot happen without also the advancement of extraordinary levels of staff satisfaction and morale. Quality and client management systems depend entirely on the contribution, effort and motivation of the people that are involved in their implementation. A change in the very heart of the firm is a prerequisite for any meaningful or effective advance in excellence. Quality needs people.

A firm needs to identify, develop and celebrate its own unique style. People are different and so law firms are different. This difference needs to be made into a distinctive advantage. So, instead of Jarndyce & Jarndyce just doing quality, 'JARNDYCE & JARNDYCE MEANS QUALITY!' may be a more inspiring description. The turnaround of client perception and satisfaction needs all the forces of the firm to unite in the common cause of quality and excellence in doing what the client wants and what works.

The next stage is to identify who the firm's competitors are, what they do, who their main clients are and what they do that their clients appear to like. A firm needs to aim its marketing efforts at specific clients and specific types of client. The firm needs to adopt best practice by a process called 'benchmarking' where the approach quite simply is to identify the key things in your business and then learn and emulate the best ways of doing it from your competitors.

Talking about quality and planning for it are not doing it. Initially, a firm may become dispirited because it will become even more aware of the amount of work to be done and the number of problems unearthed in the review and reappraisal process. Unless full implementation is pursued with vigour by the whole firm, quality will be misunderstood and undervalued, and the full benefits of quality will not be experienced.

Quality and client satisfaction

The overall objective of implementing a quality system is to achieve consistency in case management and extraordinary levels of client satisfaction, with consequent improvements in profitability. The client's perception of the quality law firm will change from one which may have been seen to have been re-active and introverted into one which has become a client-oriented, quality-driven firm which seeks and achieves continuous improvement in its levels of product quality and client satisfaction because of its constant dialogue with its clients.

Part of this process will involve making the coming to law and dealing with a solicitor a more professional and comfortable experience for the client. Instead of calling ourselves 'fee earners', we should perhaps more appropriately call ourselves 'client managers', moving away from a sales and turnover mentality to one which recognises that each member of staff plays an important part in satisfying client requirements. Far from exhorting lawyers to become 'salesmen', the drive to quality and client management through achieving extraordinary levels of client satisfaction is a drive away from the sales mentality of the 'fee earner' and is instead a drive towards the professional, client-oriented approach of the client manager.

The demystification of the profession as a by-product of the quality drive is an attribute from which we all stand to gain, both lawyers and our clients. Let the client see your computer time print-outs, let him see a tariff of charges for specified standard legal products and services, let him see the range of services and products and be fully informed about them and let him play a more involved part in agreeing case plans and service expectations. All this is designed to make the legal process for clients a more open relationship where value is added to the product, the service, the solicitor and the client. There is nothing that will be impossible for a firm which attains a true and comprehensive quality and client focus.

Quality and client management

The quality aspect of client management involves hard work, discipline and motivation to put into effect. The role model of leadership has to come from the partners. A law firm should not give up at the thought of trying or when quality is only partially implemented. It is better to aim at quality and fall slightly short than not to aim at all. Within only a year or two from now the possession of accredited quality systems will no longer give a firm a competitive edge but it will be the ticket for entry into the race for clients. If a firm does not have an accredited quality system or similar in place by then, the firm may not even make it to the starting line.

The four main aspects of law firm management of clients, quality, staff and finance need to be evolved into effective management systems to provide a level and consistency of performance which linked together will provide the firm with a successful and profitable management structure. Client management cannot be developed fully in isolation from quality management. Quality standards apply to the legal work we do, from client satisfaction to case planning, precedents and checklists. It does not specifically quantify the quality of legal advice, which is beyond the scope of these management systems, but it does quantify and measure the legal processes for delivery of the legal product. The product and its delivery to the client go hand-in-hand in a linked quality and client management system.

If quality is understood to be about conformance to specifications and stated client requirements, then it will be understood also that the process whereby we ascertain or agree what are the client's requirements will be seen to be fundamental to quality. The quality aspect of client management falls into five phases:

1 ascertaining and agreeing client expectations;
2 designing the product or service to meet those expectations;
3 delivering the product or service to meet or exceed those expectations;

4   measuring variables in conformance; and

5   measuring client satisfaction.

The quality movement signposts the way for solicitors to re-engineer their working practices along quality lines. For example, the 'old' way was for law firms to 'do conveyancing' and to organise themselves internally into departments for the delivery of conveyancing work in the most efficient way. All the firm needed was a queue of conveyancing customers at the door and the profit costs flowed. This is the traditional supplier-led approach which worked satisfactorily when the suppliers dominated the market and demand was high. Supply rather than demand was then the only issue. Quality now balances the relationship between the supplier and the receiver.

Action checklist

1   Recognise that quality is determined in part by the client – it does not exist *in vacuo*. Build client input into your product and service design with the application of the principles of both case management and client management.

2   Accept quality as not being optional and implement a quality system.

3   See the improvement and maintenance of quality through client management as the number one strategic development plan for the firm.

4   Set standards of performance in response to best practice and client expectations.

5   Audit quality performance regularly for consistency and conformance.

6   Check with clients for effect and respond as appropriate.

7   Watch your market share, turnover and profitability grow.

5 Understanding your clients

Client perception

One of the principles of client management is that, in order to provide a service which clients want and value, it is necessary to understand more precisely what it is that your clients and potential clients actually need and expect. Before we start carrying out the case and before we start our marketing activities, it is necessary to understand more about the clients we hope to attract and retain based on market research, questionnaires, surveys and client feedback.

Client management is about the delivery of the legal product to the client. Instead of leaping straight into brochure design, advertising and public relations we should first find out what it actually is that clients want and what is important to them. The first and most fundamental step to be taken before any meaningful or effective marketing strategy can be undertaken is to find out information about client perception. This information, once obtained, will form the platform from which your purposeful and effective marketing plans will be launched.

Client: 'They gave appalling service – no feedback, no chasing for action, no telephone calls, no pro-activity! I have withdrawn instructions.'

Client: 'Don't live on past glories. If you don't change, you'll go out of business.'

Here be the dragons of client perception. What do clients perceive? Is it really important what clients perceive? Does not a job well done speak for itself? Does anyone still seriously think that we can go on doing what we do regardless of client perception? Only a regular series of client questionnaires and periodic client perception surveys will be able to provide answers for this. Based on a customer survey reported by Tom Peters (*The New Masters of Excellence*), a business

83

discovered that one of the main reasons for customers leaving their usual supplier and going elsewhere was 'perceived indifference' on the part of the business itself. Customers felt that the business was not interested in them or even the future trade that could result from them. We as lawyers need to know how many and why clients leave us and go elsewhere and the only way of finding out is to conduct regular 'exit' surveys of such former clients.

The above survey was carried out in the United States to find out the reasons why customers leave one supplier of products or services for another and the following results were obtained:

1% had died;
3% had moved away;
5% had disliked the product, or the service;
24% had disputed the fees; and
67% had left because they felt that the firm did not care about them.

The vast majority, over two-thirds, left not because of mistakes, fee levels or legal error, but simply because of perceived indifference. If this statistic is true also of clients of law firms, it is a strong argument in favour of law firms becoming more managed in their understanding of and interest in their clients. It need not take much, perhaps only the occasional telephone call, but it needs to be done. Even if you do care but fail to show it, as far as the client is concerned, all he perceives is indifference. Clients perceive understanding and interest far more readily than technical legal skills and are often more concerned about it than fee levels. There are important lessons to be learned here from customers about client management. After all, who else can tell us better – they're the experts!

A better understanding of client perception, based on the facts and data produced by market research, will turn our approach to marketing away from a selling attitude where we say, 'This is what we do – who wants to buy?' to a client management attitude where we instead say, 'We are interested in you and understand your needs and expectations – we think we can help you achieve your objectives! We can provide the benefits you seek!'

Client management is not based on 'selling', which is unpalatable to many professionals, but instead client management appeals to the adviser and the consultant in us. Client management does not require us to turn salesman but to develop our traditional professional skills in this new competitive environment. Client management focuses on the buyer as well as the seller.

The survey of solicitors' clients

A survey report mentioned by the American management consultant David H Maister was carried out in which several hundred regular users of legal services were asked to say what things were important to them in choosing a lawyer. The replies given fell into 10 main criteria:

- reputation for obtaining results;
- competitive fee levels;
- experience in the client's sector;
- having a real understanding of needs;
- being a specialist in the relevant field (technical ability);
- quality of professional staff;
- previous experience with your firm;
- size of the firm;
- ability to come up with imaginative or innovative ideas;
- speed of initial response to an enquiry.

Those replying were also asked to rank the criteria in order of importance to them. Two of the above selection factors were ranked so highly and almost unanimously that the other eight paled into relative insignificance. How would you rank them? A copy of the client survey results is contained in Appendix 15. The two most important and universally agreed selection factors were:

1 having a real understanding of needs; and
2 quality of professional staff.

Understanding the client and the quality of the people in the firm are the two key selection factors. People and the relationship between them are the two paramount criteria and not, perhaps surprisingly, legal knowledge or fees. Competitive fee levels are down at 8, size of firm was last at 10 and previous experience with your firm was last but one at 9. So much for client loyalty!

At first reading, these results may be found to be quite surprising. On further reflection and after discussion with one's own clients, the results can in fact be seen to be very encouraging. If these results are true, it underlines, confirms and highlights the importance of service *from the client's point of view*. This message is of fundamental importance to the attitudes, practices and culture which underlie client management. It's not the extent of your legal knowledge, it's not your firm's reputation, it's not your fee levels – it's you and the service you provide as perceived by the client that really counts where clients are concerned!

If you ask the people in your firm to state what they think are the most important selection factors, it would be interesting to see first, which selection criteria they think clients actually use and second, what order of priority they would put them in. After a discussion of the results, it would be interesting to show them the survey table (without the priority figures) to compare their selection factors with those of the survey and then to ask them to say how they think clients in the survey prioritised the selection factors. The results would give some initial, though rough, indication of how closely aligned the thinking of the people in the firm is to that of your clients.

It would be interesting to see what the results would be if you tried the survey on a few of your own clients. Most clients don't mind being asked, as long as its quick, they will perceive that you care about what they think and you may hear some new and important client perceptions. The ramifications and implications of client perceptions regarding the way we work and the way we present our services to our clients are the theme of client management.

Client alignment

The keys to effective client management include the ability to understand the client, to see what you do from his point of view, to identify his expectations and to manage the delivery of your services so as to meet or exceed his expectations. By understanding the client we will learn to think like a client. By getting and staying close to the client we will be able to understand what we do from the client's point of view. Client management is about the client's experience of what we do, seen from the client's point of view.

If marketing is about selling, then client management is about buying. If you were a buyer, why would you buy from A rather than from B? What do you like about buying and what do you dislike about buying? You can start by remembering the times that you as a client or a customer of someone else had a good or bad experience or perception. Why do you keep going back to the same pub or restaurant? Is it really the quality of the beer or the food on the menu, or is it because of the people that run the place that make you feel welcome and comfortable? Why do you treat yourself occasionally with a shopping trip to the large department store – it's not the cheapest, but maybe it's because of the personal service you get there.

If client service is primarilyy about understanding the client – what does this mean? Does a client choose to instruct you because you are a qualified solicitor or because of your technical skills? Except very rarely, when you possess niche expertise that cannot be obtained elsewhere, it will generally be sufficient that you are a qualified solicitor. Clients expect you to be legally competent – you can't compete on legal competence, but a firm can compete on service.

The client is more concerned about you and whether or not he can work with you, than on the level and degree of your qualifications. In over 20 years of legal practice I can't ever recall being asked by a client or even a prospective client in a beauty parade about my legal qualifications. Lawyers seem to be far more concerned about firsts and upper seconds than clients who, in my experience, are not bothered what degree you have.

In making a decision about his solicitor, a client may feel the following:

1 insecure because he has to reveal his personal or business details to another person, or because he has not used a solicitor before and does not know what to expect;
2 sceptical about whether you can really help him;
3 worried about whether or not he can trust you;
4 doubtful about whether you will really understand his needs; and
5 worried about costs.

Client alignment means getting and staying close to your client so that you understand him better and start to see yourself and what you do for him from his point of view. By taking the selection factors in Appendix 15 and carrying out the same survey on the partners and staff in the firm and then comparing the results, you could work out a client alignment chart for your own firm as follows:

● client selection factors in priority; and
● firm selection factors in priority.

By comparing the two together, paying particular attention to the areas of difference, the degree of client alignment will be illustrated. Then, by carrying out an annual client alignment survey with both clients and the people in the firm, a visual plot of the development and improvement of the client alignment of your firm over a period of time on an individual or personal basis could be obtained.

Tom Peters' onions

I sometimes take a mischievous delight in asking trainee solicitors what a legal service looks like. As I stand by the flipchart in the training room I ask them, 'When you go to the shop to buy a television, what does it look like?' One of them will get up, take the squeaky marker pen and draw a TV on the flipchart. I pause to comment on the artistry and lead them on by asking, 'When you go to the supermarket to buy a bottle of wine, what does it look like?' Another springs up and draws a claret bottle with a flourish. Legal training can be so much fun! Now that they're getting into the swing of it, I close in with, 'OK. Good. Now, when your client comes to you for legal advice, what does it look like?' Snap! Confusion and uncertainty ensue. 'Is it a trick question?' the ones fresh from law school enquire. 'That's not a fair question!' argue the budding litigators. 'We've never been asked that before!' complain those in the conveyancing department.

Well, what does our legal service look like to the client? When you do ask a number of clients what they see, perceive and think about your firm's services, they will mention a number of attributes or characteristics about you and your firm. Reliability, reputation, the degree of interest you show in him, availability, expertise and so on along the lines of the client survey discussed earlier. 'What would it look like if you could draw it?' I ask the trainees, picking up the marker and advancing towards the flipchart. I draw two large circles and then write in the first the ten constituent parts taken from the client survey. In the second circle, I write in the things that we as lawyers tend to think are the important attributes of our legal service.

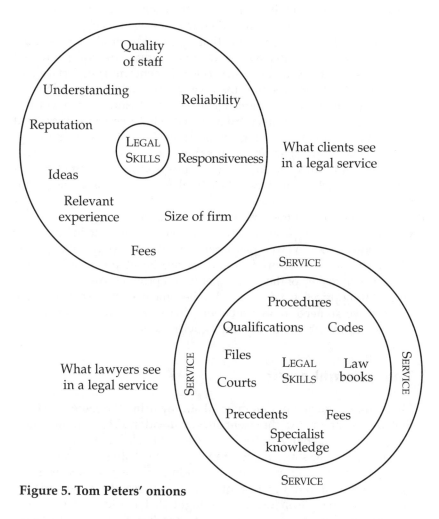

Figure 5. Tom Peters' onions

The legal work that we as lawyers think would comprise about 80% of the circle, according to the client comprises only about 20%. The legal work, though central and important, is only a small part of the overall service as perceived by the client. The other things that he perceives which fill up the remaining 80% of the perceived service circle include those survey selection criteria mentioned earlier.

The ramifications of this view of legal work from the client's point of view are fundamental to the client management system. If it is true that the legal work is only a small part of the overall legal service as perceived by the client, if it is true that the client values all those other service 'intangibles' in the circle, then the message to law firms is clear and intense. If we can also ensure that we provide the client with those service 'intangibles', effectively and consistently, if we can ensure that we build some, if not all, of those service elements into our service production and delivery systems, then we will not only be doing more to provide a fuller service from the client's point of view, but we will also encounter less fee resistance from clients. This 80% of the perceived legal service must be the biggest and ripest area of practice development available to us, an area that some law firms may not yet have actively and fully tackled in a purposeful, systematic and proactive way. It is an area which will yield quick and significant results.

Herein lies one of the central themes of client management. When you ask yourselves, 'What more or what else can we do to improve our profitability?' the answer lies largely in these service 'intangibles' which offer an area of product and service development which may comprise up to 80% of the overall perceived product. We don't need to keep cutting prices, we don't need to become even more expert in the law, but we do need to offer a better service, as defined by the client. We need to work more in the 80% 'service' zone.

The internal audit

My own firm carried out an internal survey using the same questions that were contained in the client survey mentioned earlier. The questionnaire contained in Appendix 15 was sent to all fee earners, support and management staff and the replies were collated. Several people thought that 'having a real understanding of client needs' was the most important but the rest of the survey results were variable. Overall, the people in the firm thought that fee levels were more important to clients than the clients themselves thought them to be. There was a tendency of fee earners to dismiss the importance of having imaginative ideas, ranked by clients in the survey at 5, but by the firm as 9 or 10!

Staff members were also asked to write down what three things they thought would be most useful in improving the service to clients and these replies included the following:

1 'be friendly and helpful' – residential conveyancer;
2 'do more cross-selling to clients' – litigator;

3 'be more aggressive to get results for clients' – litigator;
4 'keep to the basics and do not nit-pick' – commercial lawyer;
5 'better team structure needed' – office temp;
6 'talk to every client at least once a week' – commercial lawyer;
7 'make the client feel important' – legal assistant;
8 'agree realistic deadlines' – commercial lawyer;
9 'improve reception areas' – cashier;
10 'do mailshots to clients for changes in the law' – WP operator;
11 'don't keep clients waiting too long for an appointment' – administrator;
12 'set up joint workshops with clients to identify service improvements' – WP operator;
13 'discuss different ways for clients to pay their accounts by way of payment on account, standing orders, interim bills, etc' – litigator;
14 'reduce delays' – probate legal executive;
15 'communicate more with clients' – commercial lawyer;
16 'avoid using legal jargon' – debt recovery department;
17 'keep in touch with your client because if you don't let them know what you're doing they usually think you aren't doing anything' – legal assistant.

The following replies were received from people generally:

18 'agree costs upfront';
19 'treat each client as the only client of the firm';
20 'get the message to the right fee earner as quickly as possible';
21 'return telephone calls as soon as possible';
22 'hold open days for clients with private interviews available';
23 'agree work specifications with clients';
24 'agree and try to achieve realistic deadlines';
25 'do a weekly progress report to clients';
24 'agree the bill with the client before delivering it';
25 'give the client more information about the firm and its services';
26 'keep in touch with clients after the end of the case';
27 'keep to the basics';
28 'have commercial awareness';
29 'have clearly defined responsibilities between staff and have a team structure'; and
30 'have a back-up contact for when you're not available'.

These ideas came, as can be seen, from a complete cross-section of the firm because all members of the firm were involved. Perhaps surprisingly, the support and administrative staff seemed to be just as well tuned in to client perception as the fee earners and partners.

The purpose of doing an internal audit, ideally annually, is to assess the general level of client consciousness within the firm, to learn about internal staff perceptions and to learn new ideas and understand current concerns from the client managers in the firm, namely all the members of the firm.

The external audit

At the same time as doing the internal audit with members of the firm, it is necessary to carry out an external audit with a cross-section of clients. This approach to clients can be done yourself but there is here a risk that you may not ask all the correct questions and a risk that your clients may be embarrassed or reluctant to be totally frank in giving their replies to you personally. In order to avoid influencing the questions or the replies, you may decide to use an outside research consultant to handle the communication with your clients and to help you to analyse the results in the cold light of day. If you have your own client services and marketing manager, you will be able to do the audit in-house on a regular basis.

The basic methods of gathering client feedback are postal surveys, personal interviews, telephone surveys, questionnaires and the use of consultants. Postal surveys tend to have a low response rate and do not always extract the really important information and feedback that is necessary. Face-to-face interviews can be time consuming to both you and your clients. Telephone research can be useful particularly for researching a particular product, service or department. A cross-section of clients to be audited from each group partner might be categorised into key clients, business clients, private clients, new clients, dormant clients with whom you have not done business for 12 months or more, and former clients who you would not necessarily expect to automatically come back to you. Perhaps a cut-off date of two years may be appropriate here.

The value of client feedback can be very significant. A bridge will have been built between you and your client, you will start to build up a picture of how your own clients and those of the firm see you and the firm, what they like, what they don't like, how they react to new services and procedures and what they think is important. If you collect, collate and then build this knowledge into the design of your services and products, the sky will be the only limit to your practice development.

For example, the survey may reveal that clients have difficulties getting through the switchboard, with lines engaged and delays in having calls transferred. You may probably not have been aware of this but for the research. You can now look into the problem and put in hand the appropriate solution – additional lines, direct dialling, etc.

You may find complaints about increases in fee levels, increases which perhaps have not been communicated to the client until the bill was delivered. You may find that with a referrers survey, some bank managers may not be aware that your firm carries out debt recovery work. You might get a comment from a referrer saying why they don't send work to partner A any more. 'Yes, he's a very good lawyer, but he always seemed to be too busy and clients just can't wait around that long to see him. We'd definitely send more work to him again if he was able to respond more quickly.'

Research and development

In order to carry out client research effectively, you must have the full support of the client managers because they will be required to provide lists of their clients' names for you to interview. They will need to first contact these clients to let them know about the proposed research and they must make it sound positive to the client. It's a complete waste of time and an undermining of effort if they just telephone their regular clients and say, 'Oh, by the way, I'm supposed to tell you that some market research chap will be contacting you shortly with some sort of questionnaire. It's the latest fad from our marketing people – a complete waste of time and money if you ask me!' This attitude will not convince the client that your firm is really approaching client management in a positive and constructive way.

How many of our business clients have research and development departments? How many Japanese companies invest in research and development and how much of their time and effort do they put into it? In a profession where the law is constantly changing and where client perception and client markets are changing as never before, what client-focused law firm can afford not to provide for this function in it's day-to-day management activities? It's amazing how we decide what the clients want without ever consulting their own views and wishes. The assumptions we make about our clients are quite often wrong. What we think is often the very reverse of what clients think.

We may think that what is important is the file, the correctness of the legal advice and how well our documents or procedures work. But clients don't think that at all. They assume legal competence and are more concerned about whether we really understand them, whether we are really interested in them, whether we can really help them achieve the welfare or benefit which they believe they need.

When we have completed the annual internal audit and external client perception survey, the acid test and the real challenge is to compare the results, to find where there is a good or close match and where there is a mismatch. It is then necessary to draw up proposals that will maintain and increase the matched perceptions and which will rectify and improve the mismatches.

This is the central task of the client manager, to ensure that what the firm does is what the client wants, values and will be prepared to pay for. The replies to client surveys will give us that compelling reason to readjust and realign what we are doing so as to match client expectations.

For example, if your survey results indicate that some clients feel that you don't understand them or are not interested in them, we must consider what can be done to understand and be interested in clients more than we do. Visiting the client at his office or factory, building up a client profile, doing a regular or annual client review with regular clients, sending out regular client satisfaction questionnaires or inviting a few clients to enjoy some hospitality may be ways that would be appropriate.

These research projects can also generate new types of work as well as more repeat work. For many clients, such research is often the first time they may have been given the opportunity of expressing an opinion about the firm and its services, having before only ever been consulted about the issues of the case in hand. Client surveys, research, feedback and questionnaires are very important tools in marketing and practice development.

Needs, expectations and aspirations

The client agreement (see Appendix 1) and the care plan (see Appendix 14) deal with the identification of client needs and expectations. You discuss and adapt your client agreement, the care plan and the case plan to do what you agree the client wants you to do. By carrying out the work for the client in accordance with these will enable you to successfully satisfy the clients' needs and expectations effectively and consistently.

Without the client agreement, you may have carried out the case plan well, but you may still have an unsatisfied client because his expectations may not have been defined or met. The client's needs are what the case plan is about, but the client's expectations of service is what the client agreement and care plans are about. The quality of the legal work specified in the case plan will go towards satisfying the client's needs and the quality of service in the client agreement or the care plan will go towards satisfying his expectations.

For example, if you agree instructions to form a new company for a client, you will take details of the proposed new business, its main purpose and the objects clause, its shareholders and directors, company secretary and registered office. You go ahead and acquire the company books and amend the memorandum and articles of association and then send the completed books to the client. You have met his needs, he's got his company. So why is the client dissatisfied? Maybe he expected the whole thing to take two weeks rather than four, maybe he expected you to keep him informed of progress (or the lack of it), maybe he expected your office to be open at 6 pm when he telephoned, maybe he expected you to advise him on a share sale pre-emption clause. Maybe you don't know why he is dissatisfied, but you should. Even better, you should manage to avoid any dissatisfaction at all by dealing with client needs and expectations in accordance with the principles and practice of client management.

There is another 'desire' in addition to needs and expectations. For example, clients may not expect or need you to visit them at their office or workplace, but they may be impressed when you do. Some types of client or case don't usually expect or need copies of letters being sent to the client but they do seem to like it if they get them. They don't normally need or expect monthly progress reports but they are impressed when they do get them. It is this third level of 'desire' or 'aspirations' that the leading client management firms are already aiming their sights at in order to exceed client expectations.

Client questionnaires

There are various forms of client questionnaire to be used on a regular basis to obtain feedback from clients. The science of asking clients is still young in a profession which has only recently emerged from the dark ages of monopoly into the glaring daylight of client perception, discrimination, competition and choice. Regular client feedback is the first system a firm should put in place in order to start on the road to achieving an all embracing client management culture.

There are many types of client questionnaire. Questions may include, 'How often do you consult a solicitor? How many different solicitors do you use? Why do you use our services?' and so on.

Regular feedback from clients is the lifeblood of an effective client management programme. Client management will not work or be effective unless we know what the clients think about it all. We have all seen in the case of Rule 15 how well-intentioned measures can go badly wrong by requiring law firms to use often wooden and technical letters which many clients have found to be too long or too formal.

It is not advisable to introduce new legal products or services that will impact on clients without first consulting with a sample of your clients or at least without having identified a need or perception that clients actually have. If clients suddenly find that something is different, they can become unsettled. Any change in the approach to the client relationship should be gradually introduced and explained to the client in order to avoid damaging the client relationship.

You may start with using a simple short form questionnaire with a limited number of clients. Avoid bombarding clients with long and time-consuming lists of difficult questions. Appendices 6 and 10 contain samples of client questionnaires that can be used in different ways and with different clients and at different times.

The client satisfaction questionnaire in Appendix 6 is designed to be given or sent to clients at the end of their particular case, to find out their views about the way the case was handled, about the service they received and about their overall perception and rating of value for money. There is also included an open 'comments' space for the client to say whatever he likes.

The client questionnaire in Appendix 10 is designed to obtain information from clients about their opinions and perceptions. The questionnaire can be displayed in reception areas for clients to complete in a couple of minutes and post in the client comments box which would be kept in the reception areas.

Another form of client questionnaire may be in a more substantial and detailed form which represents an in-depth probe into the very heart of client perception and client comment. The use of this questionnaire needs to be handled very carefully. It is not designed for casual or first-time clients or for clients who rarely use the services of a solicitor. It is designed for use with a key client who you know to be receptive and supportive of your wish to understand clients better and to improve the quality of your service to clients. It could also be sent to a regular referrer of work or to other professionals such as estate agents, surveyors, bank managers and accountants. The form could be used with non-clients or prospective clients as well. It is important that the form is not just sent by post. The person to whom the questionnaire is to be sent should first be contacted by you by telephone or in person and he should be asked if he would like to participate. You should explain why you are asking the questions and what you intend to do with the results. You should stress the confidentiality of the question-naire. You should ascertain whether the client would prefer just to complete and return the form or whether he would be willing to see you for a short meeting. Alternatively, and only if appropriate, the questionnaire could be completed with the use of your marketing manager or even with the use of an outside consultant.

If you look over the client's shoulder while he completes it or, even worse, if you sit down and ask the questions face-to-face and fill it in as you go along like a legal aid form, you may not get the best, most honest and useful responses from the client.

The regular use of questionnaires is a sign of a responsive and car-ing firm which is interested in its clients, which is trying to better understand what the clients perceive and want and which is actually doing something about it.

Client surveys

In addition to using the regular client questionnaires mentioned above, you may consider carrying out an annual or more frequent client survey to give a general overview of client opinions and percep-tions about the firm. This can be particularly useful in measuring the development of client perception and opinion on a regular basis to ascertain the effectiveness of the firm's client management programme.

The annual survey could be done by an independent outside con-sultant to ensure its effectiveness and objectivity. The consultant could then assist your client partner and marketing manager in drawing up an analysis and set of recommendations for action based on the survey results. The survey and recommendations could be done after your year end and form the basis of the spring partners' conference for approval and inclusion in the firm's client management plan for the year. At this point of development, your client management techniques and culture are becoming sophisticated and capable of accurate measurement.

Typical survey questions may include:

1 How long have you been a client?
2 How did you hear of the firm?
3 Why did you choose us?
4 Have you dealt with other firms of solicitors?

A firm should conduct a client survey at least annually and then produce an action plan for implementation. The firm's client partner needs to take overall responsibility and control of this. The survey results need to be carefully considered in a positive and constructive way. There is no such thing as a negative comment, it represents a client's perception and challenges you to do something about it. If you can deal with such comments in this way, you are already over half way to understanding your clients.

Client satisfaction surveys

A short form of a client survey could deal simply with the one main issue of client satisfaction. This questionnaire seeks the client's perception about the client partner, the case manager, the support staff, the case itself and the overall assessment of satisfaction. The advantage of this form is that it is short and capable of easy measurement and report.

Every case should have this form of feedback from the client as to his overall level of satisfaction on each particular job, with that particular case manager and client partner. The results are recorded and will form part of the monthly group client report (see Appendix 11). Not only should the group partner report to management and his other partners on his bills delivered, inceptions and current number of matters, but he should also be able to report, for example, ' My group has achieved an average client satisfaction rating last month of 73%, compared to 65% and 62% in the preceding two months respectively. We're really pleased to see that the efforts we have been making to be more responsive to the needs of our group clients by completing a client agreement and doing a case review in every case really seems to be working. Staff morale in my group has improved tremendously and, by the way, you will also see that we have exceeded our monthly billing and credit control targets for three months running!'

What clients like

A law firm like any other business will only continue to survive for as long as it continues to supply its customers with the benefits they want, need and value. A quality product or service which conforms to standard specifications and works, and which meets or exceeds the expectations of the customer and at a competitive price are the basic ingredients for this. Zero legal defects, delivery on time, at the agreed charge and with a level of service which satisfies the client and which is viewed by the client as being 'worth it' is what is in issue.

This does not mean the cheapest price – clients will pay for service and value-added, differentiated legal products and services. This is a key message of client management. You can either go on charging less and less for a poor and undifferentiated service which may or may not meet or exceed your clients' expectations, or you can ask your clients what they want and then do something about it and charge for so doing. It's up to you and your clients.

Practising solicitors have a wide knowledge of what clients like and don't like. Do you agree that the list of things your client likes would include the following and what other things would you add?

My client likes it when ...	Agree	Disagree
... I treat him as my only client ... I visit him at his workplace ... I do promptly what I said I would do ... I keep him informed of progress ... we agree upfront what work is to be done ... we agree upfront an estimate of likely charges ... he knows exactly who will be doing his work ... I return his telephone calls promptly ... I send him copies of letters sent or received ... he gets value for money ... his complaint is dealt with quickly and fairly ... as one client has just told me when I asked him, he said he likes ...		

The list of what clients like is almost infinite and it is for the client manager to be an expert in this field and the best way to find out is to ask your clients – they like to be asked.

What clients don't like

We tend to know more about what clients don't like about us and other firms from an examination of our own complaint reports or by reading the reports of the Office for the Supervision of Solicitors. Of course, our clients never or hardly ever complain to us, they must like what we do because we never hear otherwise! If a practising solicitor was to draw up a list of things that his clients don't like, it may read something like. What would you add to the list?

My client doesn't like it when ...	*Agree*	*Disagree*
... he's told that I'm busy on another important case and that I can't see him		
... I fail to do what I promised or when I promised it		
... I see him only by appointment		
... he feels taken for granted		
... he's kept waiting without explanation		
... I write long, technical letters		
... I do not tell him anything about what's going on, even if nothing is going on		
... he's chopped and changed about amongst fee earners		
... I send him written work which is badly spelt and poorly presented		
... as one client has just told me when I asked him, he said he does not like ...		

Promises, promises

One of your best qualified assistant solicitors has a very high productivity rate. He works long and hard and always turns out work quickly and free from error. He is a good, hard-working member of your group. However, you are aware of a problem because one or two of your clients have commented to you that he has been slow on their case. You are surprised but on investigation you identify the problem. He takes on everything that is given to him (such people tend to be given too much work which then makes them less effective), he tells his clients that the work will be done by a certain date. He usually achieves this, but in a few cases he doesn't. It is those clients who complain that he is 'slow'. To himself and to you, he works hard and long and covers a lot of ground, but to the few clients he is unable to satisfy, he is 'slow'.

Your other assistant is of average standard who will never set the world alight, he never gets into a sweat and achieves only a satisfactory rate of production. His clients never complain about him being 'slow' because when he gives time estimates to clients (and he rarely does), he is conservative and always adds a few days extra. As he is able to meet those dates, and on occasion he does it before the due date, his clients think he is 'quick' because he does what he says he will do on time. The former 'fast' and productive assistant is setting traps for himself by unnecessarily promising unrealistic deadlines, and so he makes himself 'slow' to his clients.

Clients don't like to be disappointed. It's not so much that they always want things done quickly, rather they do want to know when things will be done. Certainty and understanding are often more important than speed. So in giving time estimates, don't be vague with if's and buts, but give a date which allows reasonable time to realistically do what is said. Don't assume that third parties will respond as quickly as you. Don't assume that speed is the most important thing. If speed is actually important, it could be dealt with in a different way.

Case study

A long-standing and important client who gives his solicitor and his firm lots of commercial work telephones him on a Thursday afternoon to ask if he can give him some urgent advice on an unusual tax point.

Client: 'I know you don't usually do this sort of work but I must get some advice by tomorrow!'

The solicitor is faced with a quandary – he knows that he doesn't have the expertise in-house, but he doesn't want to refer his client to another firm and he doesn't want to appear inadequate. He quickly sifts through the possible responses as follows:

Solicitor: 1 'Yes, of course we can handle it!' (gulping and checking the PI policy); or

2 'I'm sorry but we don't do that sort of work in the firm' (gulping and checking his billing figures); or

101

3 'Well, the sort of advice you need in this particular instance is not something we specialise in but we do have a very close association with a firm that does have a specialist in this field. I'll telephone them right away and get straight back to you.'

In response 1, he risks everything if he ends up disappointing the client. He doesn't have the expertise and will not deliver a level of legal product to which his client has become accustomed. He may give inadequate or even incorrect advice. This is a high risk strategy and possibly professionally wrong.

In response 2, he will not really disappoint his client because the client is not really expecting his solicitor to be able to help. He feels uncomfortable about not being 'all things' to his client. He is also worried about his client going to the firm down the street which does have a tax specialist and who used to do some of that client's other work as well.

Response 3 is frank and tries to accommodate the client. You have in mind a firm which specialises in tax work and which you have dealt with before. They are some distance away, but you feel sure your client won't mind travelling to see them on this one occasion. Although your client may use the firm you recommend, it is unlikely that he will think any worse of you for being honest and as the other firm is some distance away and doesn't specialise in the sort of commercial work that the client usually has, there is no real risk of losing the client. The client is happy with that advice. He does not expect his solicitor to be 'all things', so his solicitor doesn't need to pretend to be so. You have given him good advice without actually dealing with the technical tax point in question.

Perhaps an even better policy would be to put in place a referral protocol with one or two specialist firms to which you could refer quickly and safely in situations like the above case study.

Added value

Clients, the same as everyone else, like to feel that they are getting something extra, special or different for what they pay, or even something for nothing. These may include:

- fixed fee interview;
- standard form will without charge as an extra for some other work;
- telephone helpline advice;
- discounts for early settlement of bills or for volume billing;

- special offers ('Will week');
- free parking at your office;
- no charge for receiving telephone calls from them;
- easy payment terms, key client discounts, etc;
- 'no deal, no fee' billing agreements;
- all case work supervised by the group or client partner;
- regular progress reports, etc.

Referrers

Much of our work still comes to us as a result of referral and recommendation, often from regular referrers such as bank managers, accountants and surveyors. It is important also to find out the referrer's perception of you and your firm and to know why exactly it is that they refer clients to you and not to someone else and if they do refer clients elsewhere, why is that and what can you do to rectify the situation? Talking to your referrer over lunch or at the golf club can be useful but you could also consider using a form of referrers questionnaire.

The client database could also include a list of referrers containing details of name, company, contact name and main contact name in your firm. This could be used for mailshots as well as referrer questionnaires.

Don't ask the experts

Solicitors have traditionally taken the view that they know best about the service they provide to their clients. The view is embedded in our professional culture that only lawyers know about the law and that, therefore, only we are able to decide what a good legal service is. To think like this is to make a big mistake. If service really is that which is perceived by the client, in his terms and not ours, then this means that only the client is able to decide whether or not he has received a good service. In matters of service, the client who receives the service is the expert and not us who only deliver it.

A firm might proclaim in its brochure that it is '... committed to the highest standards of client care ...' and many firms have indeed done a lot of work to do just that, but perhaps without asking the clients first! We could go to the time, trouble and expense of smartening up the reception area, redesigning the letterhead, increasing our training budget, employing expensive staff, installing a new client database and so on, but does all this necessarily improve our understanding of the client and the quality of the service we deliver, from the client's viewpoint? If the survey results in Appendix 15 are taken seriously, then we could spend the time better in meeting with a few clients and asking them what we can do to understand them better. We should listen to what they say and then do something about it.

The big, new, expensive and sophisticated solutions are always not what the client wants. The real experts here are the clients. Again, it is interesting and instructive to compare the results of the internal and the external surveys discussed earlier about what clients think are important and about what lawyers think are important. These can be contrasted as follows:

Clients say, 'what is important to me about my solicitor is that ...
... he should understand me and my business
... he should be interested in me and my business
... he should be easy to contact
... he should be easy to do business with
... he and his staff should be competent at their job
... he should drive his cases and keep me informed about progress without me having to chase

Lawyers say, 'we think that it is important that ...
... we charge competitive fees
... we have specialist legal skills
... we respond quickly to clients
... we are experts in commercial law/property law/matrimonial law, etc
... we employ only people with top academic qualifications

What we think is important is not always what our clients think and it is this mismatch of perception that reduces our ability to attract and retain clients and to increase our profitability. The prime task of client management is to match what the clients think and want with what we provide for them, increasing in the same process both client satisfaction and profitability.

Where will it all end?

Why do we seem to be so reluctant to ask our clients what they think of the service we deliver? Do we fear increased fee resistance? Do we fear criticism? If there is a problem, it can only get worse by not being identified and dealt with. Putting our heads in the sand and adopting the management technique of the ostrich is no answer. It is often the case that clients actually *like* being asked about what they think and want! Wouldn't you?

A firm that does ask its clients will end up by being known as a firm that cares. Firms which then do something about it, about being more responsive (as opposed to reactive) to client needs and opinions will soon be seen as market leaders.

Client information systems

Doing a client questionnaire should not be a one-off or even an annual exercise. Not only the data but also the exercise itself and awareness of the client in the firm and the firm in the client needs to be regularly and constantly affirmed and updated. The data is so important that it needs to be done as part of a regular system of work, regarding client opinion and client satisfaction as an integral part of your work.

The first part of a firm's client information system is a good and usable client database operated daily by someone who knows about marketing and who knows about clients, not a part-time WP operator, unless that member of the firm has a particular interest, enthusiasm and skill in this field, and adequate time to do the job justice.

The second part is to commission or carry out an annual client survey of a cross-section of your clients with a comprehensive questionnaire. Some of these can be done by post, others with a selected number of interviews and others perhaps by an outside third party. The results must be carefully analysed and these results can then be used to form the basis of the firm's business plan for the following year.

The third element of a basic client information system is to have a short questionnaire sent to all clients at the end of every matter. This needs to be short, simple and perhaps linked to some client offer, discount or 'freebie'. Again, it is important that the results are analysed by a marketing manager who will prepare a monthly client perception report to partners. The report will make fascinating reading and will be as useful in many ways as the usual financial reports.

What you (think that you) look like to your clients

If you think of the total legal service in pictorial form as looking like a perfect circle, how would your own practice look to your clients? Would it be a perfect circle, an oblate spheroid like Saturn, or a small, deformed, twisted and dried up old prune? Based on the Innovation Toolkit issued by the DTI in 1990, it is possible, entertaining and useful to complete the following exercise by plotting the results onto a client perception picture. The test results will be based on the simple questionnaire below sent to a cross-section of your firm's clients on an annual basis. It is over-simplistic, perhaps, but it is a start and it can be fun.

By carrying out this questionnaire with clients, and with members of the firm on a periodic basis, a law firm will be able to obtain a pictorial illustration of how it sees itself and how its clients see the firm. The comparison of the two audit results will reveal interesting and important data on differences of perception and a periodic comparison will show how the firm is progressing to match its own self image with the view of it as seen by its clients.

Under the 10 headings below, the respondent is asked to evaluate his perception of the firm in relation to each statement. The score of '5' means that the respondent strongly agrees with the statement and '1' means that the respondent strongly disagrees with the statement and '3' means that the respondent neither agrees or disagrees and so on. For example, 'X' shows what the firm thinks, but 'Y' shows what its clients think.

Client service perception survey	1	2	3	4	5
1 The firm finds out what the clients wants and values.			Y	X	
2 The lawyer always agrees with the client first what work is to be done.		Y		X	
3 The lawyer and the client discuss and agree the legal charges clearly at the outset.		Y			X
4 The lawyer and the client agree what level of service the client wants and expects.		Y		X	
5 The lawyer and the client discuss and agree who will be involved in doing the work.	Y			X	
6 The lawyer keeps the client informed of progress throughout the matter.	Y			X	
7 The lawyer always delivers what he agreed to do.		Y			X
8 The firm always deals with complaints quickly, fairly and satisfactorily.			Y		X
9 The firm always achieves a high level of client satisfaction.			Y		X
10 Overall the clients get good value for money.			Y		X

Take the result of each score, plot it for each statement number against the radius number shown on the circle below for each statement. When all scores are plotted on the circular chart, it will provide an easy way of showing how the firm perceives itself and how the clients perceive the firm. One audit will be done for the firm internally and one for a random cross-section of clients.

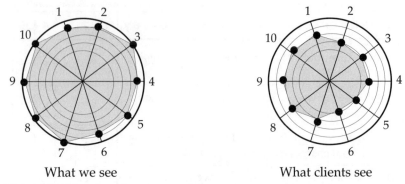

What we see   What clients see

Figure 6. Client service perception survey

The perception survey is based on the principle that, with the perfect law firm, service will be seen to be a perfect circle. The larger the shaded area the better because it indicates a higher level of perception than a smaller area. The more 'rounded' the better because it shows a better balance of overall perceived ability. Large 'spikes' and tiny 'stumps' are illustrative of inconsistent and imbalanced client performance. A small shaded area may indicate a lack of development of client management attitudes and practices in the firm.

Action checklist

1 Do an annual survey of client opinion.
2 Do a survey of opinion within the firm.
3 Compare the responses and then evolve a strategic development plan for the firm based on the findings.
4 Carry out regular client surveys and questionnaires to plot the strategic development of the firm into one which more effectively understands and achieves what clients want.
5 Watch the levels of client satisfaction grow as the firm aligns itself, its products and services with the identified needs and expectations of its client.

6 Service is our business

Service defined

The dictionary definition of 'service' is, 'a contribution to the welfare of others; useful labour that does not provide a tangible commodity'. The legal service we provide, therefore, lies not in what we do, not in what we know, not in our files, not in our law books and not in our computers, but in the extent to which what we do or achieve increases the welfare of the client as perceived by the client. It is not what you do, but what you do for them that clients pay for. Service is an intangible commodity that can be judged only by the client. Service is measured by result rather than by input.

Getting to grips with service may be hard for the technically trained lawyer who may be more comfortable with facts, legal rules, precedents and his own office routine than the intangibles of service. We cannot afford to ignore or undervalue service just because it is intangible. This is the purpose of being a solicitor in private practice, to produce and maintain a feeling of welfare or benefit in the minds of your clients by the application of legal advice and services. Service is result-driven in that it is by definition no good in its functional aspects, no matter how well the process is done, unless it achieves the result for the client. If you don't achieve this then no matter what you do or how good a lawyer you are, the client will perceive that you have given an unsatisfactory service to him and he will be right.

Service thus defined is not unique to service industries. All manufacturing businesses, even those making widgets, are really all in the service industry to the extent that their customers all want a benefit from the use of the product.

Volvo cars are a prime example. The researchers and designers at Volvo understand that they are not primarily in the business of car manufacturing. As a result of extensive customer surveys, Volvo learned that the reason people buy Volvo cars is to achieve peace of mind and confidence by buying into some form of middle-class life-time family transportation system. Reliability, safety, versatility and longevity (lifetime care!) are the benefits that Volvo buyers want and pay for. It's not the engine, or the design or the performance, even though these too have recently been improved to match the best on the market in response to customer surveys. It's not the car, therefore, but what the customer perceives that the car represents that is important.

The same is true for Parker pens. For many years rated as the best fountain pen in the world, but viewed as too expensive for own personal use, sales rocketed when Parker realised that the people who bought their pens had no intention of using them themselves but that they were bought primarily as gifts! This being the case, Parker designed their advertising and marketing to address the giftware industry rather than the scribe, whilst continuing to make a world-class pen. Being world-class alone is not enough, there has to be a perceived benefit to the customer, in this case, enabling a person to make a special gift of an acknowledged quality pen.

This is the service challenge to a law firm – can it ensure that what it does will achieve and maintain a feeling of welfare and benefit in the minds of its clients? If it can't, other firms will do just that. We need to know and understand the business we are in, which is service. We are not in the legal business in the same way as the judges and court officials. The legal work is the means but not the end. This requires a new angle being brought to bear on the traditional understanding that we are working as lawyers and, in addition, we need to be seen by our clients as providing benefits. Client managers need to recognise and come to terms with this new self-image being imposed on us by our clients in a deregulated and competing market.

The legal service triangle

A service is an intangible thing – the client knows it when he gets it but without client feedback it is difficult to be precise about it. There are some principles about service that need to be stated:

1 Service is defined by the client and not by the firm.
2 Only the client can judge whether or not and to what degree he is happy or unhappy with the service.
3 Different clients will have different service expectations. Two identical legal products might leave two different perceptions in the minds of two different clients. One might think that he has been looked after well, whilst the other may feel patronised, ignored or taken for granted. Both these differing perceptions are right because

the client who receives the service is also part of the service and, therefore, makes it unique to him.

4 There is no such thing as 'good' or 'bad' service in the abstract. The legal product can be standardised but the delivery service must be adapted to the individual client in every case. How well it conforms to the agreed standard will determine whether it is good or bad.

5 Service is shaped by the service receiver as well as by the service provider. Clients are not just passive receivers of an abstract service. So many complaints made about solicitors are on analysis found to be not about the legal work itself but about the legal service – poor communications, avoidable misunderstandings, delays, etc. On investigating a complaint, the legal files are in most cases found to be in order but, nevertheless, the client is dissatisfied for some reason or another. It can be seen that he who provides the service has a unique influence on it. It is a personal service and this presents huge opportunities to the client manager.

6 The product is part of the service. The essential legal work is carried out by the lawyer – the draft contract, the letters, the writ, the court appearance and so on. The client expects and is entitled to assume that this will be done competently. The service, therefore, comprises three parts – the legal product, the service provider and the client. This understanding of the overall legal service provides a host of new opportunities to the client manager.

We have seen that the client takes part in the service ('the receiver'), the lawyer who delivers the legal product also forms part of the personal service ('the supplier') and there is the legal work itself ('the product'). These three constituent parts define the service triangle.

Figure 7. The legal service triangle

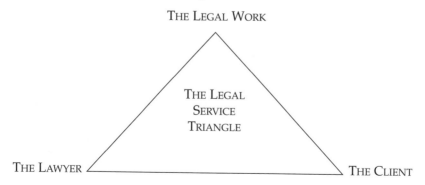

THE LEGAL WORK

THE LEGAL
SERVICE
TRIANGLE

THE LAWYER   THE CLIENT

This is the solicitor/client relationship analysed in a new and practical way. It identifies the three constituent parts that show that two-thirds of the service are people issues; the lawyer and the client. Both take part in and form part of the overall service in a direct relationship, where both the served and the server participate in the production of the service. The production and the consumption of the service take place simultaneously and this again opens up many new opportunities for client satisfaction through service delivery and product improvements.

What are the attributes of good service? What does it mean to say, 'Their firm always gives good service!' These are some of the attributes of a firm with a good service image, from the clients' point of view:

1 the firm is easy to do business with;
2 the firm is easy to approach;
3 the firm gives you the feeling that they understand what you want;
4 the firm is able to deliver what you want;
5 the firm is interested in you;
6 you get the feeling that they really know what they're doing;
7 you get the feeling that the firm really knows what you're doing;
8 the whole business is directed towards and is energised and motivated by clients' comments and perceptions;
9 the firm is well known as one which consistently responds to clients quickly and positively with a 'can do' attitude and which takes a positive approach to dealing with client problems and complaints;
10 the firm drives its casework and gets results.

All these attributes require client feedback in order to be measured and this feedback is the key to good service – knowing what the client wants and then doing something about it.

Service in perspective

The legal profession has traditionally had the image of being a learned profession. Learning and knowledge are its main attributes. This is fine in a profession which is undifferentiated and has a monopoly on legal work. But, in a profession which now competes for clients with fewer and fewer restrictions, each firm must develop its own profile to include a client service profile. It is important to be a good lawyer but it is more important to be a good lawyer who is good with clients.

Ideally, we would all like to be good lawyers with lots of clients. The traditional measures of productivity and effectiveness in terms of bills delivered are now being supplemented by measures of client satisfaction, client retention and client attraction. Whilst knowledge and legal ability must be maintained and improved, we must learn to see these as methods and means, rather than as ends in themselves.

Measures of internal financial performance must of course be maintained but in themselves these do not measure service. Financial measures must be supplemented by client measures which include detailed reports about inceptions and client satisfaction. The old attributes of legal knowledge, 'doing the case' and 'being busy' must be accompanied with service abilities in 'satisfying the client'. Clients see lawyers and law firms as just another service provider.

'Innovate or liquidate'

These words were used by the former President of the Board of Trade, Michael Heseltine, at the launch of the DTI/CBI Report *Innovation – the Best Practice* in January 1993. This report, based on surveys of manufacturing and service industries, showed that those businesses which scored highly in innovation were also those companies which were continuing to grow, despite the recession. Mr Heseltine said:

Innovation is clearly a vital component in improving the competitiveness of business ... innovation begins with people. The report shows that in many cases a change in corporate culture has proved necessary to the promotion of innovation. Communication and team working – involving staff at all levels of the business – emerge as the key ingredients.

Howard Davies, the Director-General of the CBI said at the same launch:

Innovation is a way of life in the most successful companies which are continually asking themselves: "Are we doing things the right way?" and "Can we do it better?" Innovation does not necessarily mean new ideas and inventions, but can be just the development and implementation of new services and processes. Doing something that has not been done before or doing it in a way which has not been done before, with the motivation of trying, testing, measuring success and re-designing – that's innovation.

There is an important message here for the legal profession, a profession that is, perhaps, more traditional and less innovative than the businesses of our industrial and commercial colleagues – and clients! The ways of thinking in doing legal work are detailed, logical and lineal. 'If this, then that' is the lawyer's thought process. In client management and innovation, these thought processes are sometimes found to be inadequate and inappropriate. You can't just look up from the legal work on your desk for a couple of minutes and plan a client management programme. The subject-matter requires lateral thinking and the timescale is quite different. One is factual and knowledge-based, one is pragmatic, perceptional and experimental. We need occasionally to be able to put on one side our lineal thought processes and start to do new things and in new ways, with the client and the service intangibles as the focal point. Instead of seeing what we do only or primarily from our point of view, try seeing it from the client's viewpoint. Try and test everything in the firm and what you do against one criterion, 'Does it satisfy my client as much as it could within given cost constraints? If not, I'll improve it. But first, I'll ask the client.'

Price versus value

If you want to charge more for your legal work, you will have to provide a better service. The leading edge strategy now is to deliver a higher quality product but at a lower cost and with better service, so providing better value for money and satisfaction for the client. This is the client management objective.

Profitability on a case-by-case basis, has been secondary when for many years 'costs' charged to clients were, by definition, based on a pricing policy which was based on the cost of production plus a reasonable level of mark-up.

In these competitive and deregulated times, your profit will be a direct function of the added value you build into your service. You may demonstrate on a remuneration certificate that the costs were justified, but you will have lost a client. The value added service principle, therefore, is:

to identify, meet and exceed client expectations with performance targets and measurement. To listen to clients and what they want, to design the required features into our service as far as possible within cost constraints and to implement and then review for effectiveness. The measure of our success is not only the bill but also the levels of client satisfaction achieved.

It is not the problem of doing low margin work – but of doing the work from an entirely different perspective and approach. Those firms which have evolved from the 'price' culture to the 'value' culture, will recognise that there are now four main objectives in doing legal work:

1 do the case well   – quality;
2 satisfy the client – service and value;
3 make a profit   – costs; and
4 job satisfaction   – people.

Law firms are becoming more 'client-driven ' in moving towards a total quality service and measurement system. The role of partners is not only to earn fees but also to create a culture where innovation, client satisfaction, staff empowerment, experimentation, reward and results are encouraged, and thereby earn more fees and operate more profitably. Law firms must be managed so as to provide value to clients rather than just requiring clients to pay the price of the legal process.

The legal process

As lawyers we are constantly involved in the detail, the process, the procedures, the systems, the law and the minutiae of case work but, if we stand back and look objectively at what we do, we can see that it can be seen as a five-part process as follows.

Ascertain the facts

When we first see a client, we listen to what he says and read the paperwork. We may need to ask further questions and we may need to get further statements or evidence. We gather the relevant and important facts first so that we can properly and fully advise the client.

Legal advice

Having obtained the facts, we then apply our legal knowledge, experience and expertise in advising the client of his position. We advise him whether or not he has a case, whether it's strong or weak and what the law says. We describe the various courses of action that are possible, with the consequences of each one in turn being explained to the client.

Case plan

Having advised the client on the legal position, it is then necessary to discuss with the client the alternatives of what can be done, how long it will take and how much each alternative will cost. Input from the client is needed here because he will need to know and agree in advance what will be done if we are to ask him to pay for it. Preparation of the case plan is a vitally important part of the legal process.

Do the case

This is the stage where we carry out the agreed legal work in accordance with the case plan and as varied where necessary by subsequent agreement with the client. This is the case management stage which takes most of the time. We must ensure that we keep to the case plan and keep the client regularly informed of progress.

Review the case for satisfaction

When the legal work is done and the file is finished, what has been the result of our work? Is the client satisfied with what we did for him? After all, is not that the overall objective? Did anything go wrong? What can we improve for the next time? The case is not completed until we have ascertained the level of client satisfaction.

So the legal process, seen in this way, is really a service process that involves both the solicitor and his client at all five stages. Service comprises the service provider, the legal work and that which is perceived by the client to be the benefit or result of the legal service. The client, the solicitor and the perceived benefit *are* the service. Unless the benefit is identified at the outset and measured at the end, we really will have no idea about the true quality of our work.

Process versus benefits

Our clients do not pay us to open files, to use precedents, to record their finances on our computers or to do many of the things that we spend so much of our time actually doing. In the legal process described above, it is the results and benefits that most absorb the client's interest. The getting of the evidence, the negotiations and amendments, the court procedures and forms, are all just part of a process that converts legal advice into a client benefit. We should consider the various ways that our new and redesigned services to our clients can promote and improve the results and benefits, where the client places so much emphasis.

If we are to be successful with our clients, we must be able to tell them not only what we do, because clients aren't really interested in our departments or how we organise our functions internally, but what we can do for them, what benefits they can get from our services and what difference and added value they will receive from us but from no other solicitor or law firm. The old assumption that all lawyers and law firms are the same must be superseded by the responsive attitude that we can do what the client wants. In short, we must define ourselves not in our terms of what we do, but in the client's terms of what we can do for the client. Not only a 'can do' attitude but a 'can do something extra of benefit for you' attitude is needed.

The benefits we (can) offer

In marketing and delivering our services to our existing and prospective clients, it is the benefits to the client of what we do that we should seek to emphasise over and again. For example, in presenting our debt recovery services to a prospective client, first ask the client what he is seeking to achieve. A quicker recovery rate? A better recovery rate? A cheaper service? Regular progress reports? A reliable service? Or just the money as quickly and as cheaply as possible? It is then up to you to emphasise in your presentation how you can achieve these objectives and then ensure in doing the work that these objectives are built into the service you actually deliver.

Products and service

It may be helpful in the context of client management to think of the legal work as 'the product' and to think of the delivery mechanism as 'the service'. Marketing is the presentation to the client of the product and service. The three component parts of what clients buy are the product, the service and the benefit of the product and service, which together may be called 'the total legal service'. So although we see ourselves as a service industry that doesn't 'make things', let us not confuse what we do with the way we present and deliver it to our client. In those firms which have separate client interview rooms near the reception area, this is where you see the client and he sees you. You take instructions and give advice and report on progress and results there. That is what the client sees and that is what he pays for. This is what may be thought of as the 'service area'. When you go back to your room, where you actually keep all the files, do all the drafting, write all the letters and make all the telephone calls, that is the 'production area'. The trend towards the use of interview rooms or 'service rooms' reflects what is happening in the profession, of a distinction being made between the product and the service.

Staying close to the client

This means that you should go over to where your client stands, sits, works or plays and look at things from his point of view. In order to do this, you need to get away from your desk, away from the office and to see clients in their natural habitat outside your office.

You could also use the DDR (Daily Dose of Reality) Form mentioned in Chapter 10 . If you are the senior partner, make it a daily routine that you will telephone one client of the firm that you have not met before. Over the course of a month you will have spoken with 20 clients of the firm who you knew little or nothing about, and who knew little or nothing about you. Both you and your clients are sure to learn something of value in this front line, client-oriented communication. Don't forget to check with the appropriate client partner first before telephoning his client!

Make it a weekly habit to go out and see at least one client in his own office, factory or workplace. You will begin to see and understand your client in a new way, and he will perceive you as a solicitor who is interested in him and who is trying to understand him and his business better.

Once a week go to see at least one main referrer of work, perhaps over lunch, to see how things are going in his marketplace. Once a month you should invite a selected small group of clients and referrers to a light buffet lunch. You might make a short speech after lunch but, otherwise, let the event take its own course. You are mixing, matching and staying close to your clients. Of course, it is not only partners and admitted staff who need to get out and about to stay close with their clients. If you keep your staff away from clients, you are building up internal walls that divest your staff of any responsibility towards your clients and so they become introverted and file-management orientated. If they never see the person who receives their output, why should they give that little extra effort when required?

Ways of staying close to your clients might include:

1 your team assistant receiving all incoming calls for you and so building up a relationship with the clients;
2 include a question on staff assessment on your client satisfaction questionnaire;
3 job rotation between groups so that ideas from one may cross fertilise the other and vice versa;
4 junior team workers being present at some client receptions;
5 junior and support team staff on client action teams to discuss client behaviour, requirements, complaints and ways of improving performance and service;
6 development of a client relationship/contact plan. What is your plan? Just seeing clients and talking to them about the case is not enough any more. How often should you see a client, how often should you telephone and how often should you drop in to see them? etc;
7 how do you measure your performance to your client contact plan? The ultimate measure is that you should never receive a surprise telephone call or a complaint from a client.

Developing a client care plan

In the developing relationship between you and your client, you can put a simple client care plan in place as follows:

1 a copy of all letters to be sent to the client;
2 daily/weekly/monthly progress reports;
3 meetings at his office or yours;
4 definition of client objective;
5 redefinition of client objectives which may change over a period of time;
6 discussing and identifying the client's future needs;
7 following up on his previous suggestions and requests;
8 carrying out exit interviews and telephone calls for ex-clients;
9 knowing all key clients by first name and their home telephone numbers. Do they know yours?

Client-driven product design

Do you say to a client, expressly or by implication, 'We will decide how to do the job because we are the legal experts and you will pay for the work we do.' Or do you actually say, 'The usual way of doing this is set out in this standard case plan. Here, you can see what is usually involved and how long it usually takes. Do you have a budget sum for legal charges in mind? If you prefer, I can take out this and this from the case plan but you may need some extra work doing there. This will result in a reduction in the standard charge of £XXX to £YYY. How does that sound? OK? Well, if anything changes or if you decide you'd like us to do those omitted items, we'll look at it again.'

If you analyse what you do in terms of time for a client, the legal procedures and points do not take up the largest part of the time in a matter. Most time is spent dealing with the client and the variables that most cases seem to throw up. These variables needs to be clarified with the client in advance.

Case/client study

I advised a tenant company on taking a new short-term standard lease on a new industrial estate. We did lease amendments, searches and inquiries and had a meeting followed by a written report. All went OK and the bill of £XXX was paid without comment a week or so after completion. Three months later, the same client telephoned to ask if I could do another lease for him on the same estate at the same rent. I said, 'Of course' and he said, 'How much?' I said the legal charge would be the same as the last time but the client hesitated. 'Can't you do it for less?' he asked. 'Of course I can', I replied, 'I'll just do less work!' We agreed that the same lease amendments would be done, but that no meeting was necessary. He was happy with that. He stipulated that the lease must be completed within two weeks. We agreed a charge of £XXX/60%. I got the client to sign a letter of confirmation of these instructions and did a short report on the lease to the client for the sake of the file as much as for the client. All went well, the lease was completed on time and the bill was paid on completion. The client was delighted. On checking my recorded time, I found that we made more profit on the second case than on the first! Our finance director was delighted.

It was then that I realised that case planning with clients can increase both profit and client satisfaction. The client took an active part in the design of the legal product and service. If we accept that clients are the judges of the quality of our service quality and partly the judges of our product quality, then we should accept that clients should be involved in the quality of every case. The variables of quality and service are infinite. What suits one client may not suit another. Some clients insist on full written reports before exchange, others just want you to get on with it and tell them when its all been done.

There used to be a lot of talk in the 1980s about the Rolls Royce service and the Metro service. There was a tendency to assume that all clients had to have the Rolls Royce service whether they wanted it or not. I've even heard solicitors exclaim, 'But you can't do that – that's cutting corners. The client has no choice in the matter!' Client management is about client choice but that does not mean that clients tell us how to do our job. We explain and make recommendations. In some extreme cases, we would be right not to do the work but, in the vast majority of cases, a sensible agreement can usually be reached.

Client-driven service design

If you are going to be proactive in dealing with the service element of the overall legal service, you should agree it with the client from the outset. See the care plan in Chapter11 and Appendix 14. The point is that the service element of the case, from the client's point of view, is often the largest part of what he perceives, experiences and pays for. It should not be left to chance. As we have seen, there is no such thing as 'the service' in the form of a fixed commodity just waiting for a client to come along because each service to a client will vary according to the service provider and the client. Even the legal product is capable of variation of design from client input. Likewise service. Does the client want more than one meeting? How many? Does he want copies of all letters sent? Does he want copies of all letters received? Does the service provider supply an emergency telephone number? Does he go to visit the client or does the client come to him? In some cases and with some clients this level of service care planning may be useful and necessary.

Listen, design, deliver and review

What we do for our clients is not just a fixed product and a fixed service. The twin elements of product and service need to be kept in a dynamic flux between you and your client. The process has a number of distinct stages:

1 start by listening to the client and how he wants or expects the product and service to satisfy his needs and wishes;

2 sit down with your group and work up a case plan based on the standard case plan for that sort of case and adapt it to meet that particular client's requirements;

3 work out a care plan to ensure that the delivery and presentation of the work agreed in the case plan will satisfy or exceed the client's expectations;

4 work out a charge for the agreed case plan and care plan based on the standard tariff but adapted to fit that particular client. Discuss the proposed charge with the client and record the agreed charges in the client agreement;

5 you and your group then carry out the case plan and the care plan marking any shortfall or problems in performance;

6 during and after the production and delivery process, you will obtain feedback from the client and then you will ask the client to evaluate your performance in terms of the client satisfaction rating;

7 you then review the product and service as delivered to see what went wrong, what went well and what was unnecessary and what could be improved. You then design the improvements back into the 'standard' case plan and care plan.

By now you may be groaning, 'How does anyone find the time for all this client care and client contact – I'll never find time to get my work done!' But if you pause to consider what actually is the work of the lawyer, then you may think again. It's true that you will not be able to do all this yourself. You should involve all your staff and particularly your group staff in the management of clients. You can't do it all yourself and you should not try.

The levels of service

Tom Peters talks about the different levels of service that he has heard described and which may be transposed by the client manager to the legal service as follows.

The generic service

This is the most basic aspect of the work. For example, in conveyancing, there has to be a transfer signed by the parties. There may be a contract. Title is usually investigated. There are the usual searches. You have to do at least these items of work to provide a basic conveyancing service which works. The standard case plan will design the basic service with options for additional work, such as a written report, additional inquiries and so on.

The expected service

Your client will have some expectations about the service you will be providing. He will expect you to have an office, he will expect you to write some letters, he will expect to make an appointment to see you at your office, he will expect to pay a bill and so on. Nothing exciting so far, unless he expects something else. It is important to use the case plan, the care plan and the client agreement to find out just what it is that the client expects.

The actual service

This is the service that your client actually gets from you. For example, you may have several meetings with the client. You might send him a progress report. The actual service is how well you deliver your legal product, as perceived by the client.

The potential service

This brings us into the 80% slice of Tom Peter's onions illustrated in Chapter 5, where almost anything intangible which satisfies or delights the client is included. For example, giving your client your home telephone number for emergency contact where necessary, working late or at weekends to meet the client's deadlines, offering a free legal audit, client discounts and introductory or special offers are additional items that clients don't always expect or get, but would be happy to have them if actually delivered. The things that clients don't expect but are pleased or even delighted to be offered are all part of the potential service. What governs the potential is your ability to think of them, your client's perceiving them as beneficial and the cost constraints in actually delivering them.

These descriptions of the various levels of service may be rather generalised, but they do serve to illustrate the point that service is variable and has potential for development. A firm which seeks to differentiate itself on service is a client management firm.

Service: the good, the bad and the unsatisfactory

We all pride ourselves in providing the highest levels of client service and many of our brochures proclaim it, but how many of us ask the clients whether or not we actually achieve what we say? Is the highest standard of service required in both the £3m management buy-out and the £150 debt recovery case? What if they are both for the same client? Handling thousands of debt recovery cases would not demand a high level of personal attention or expertise in each case, but the overall account would require a high level of service for a major client with several thousand cases under your care and control.

Good service is what your client says it is, not what we think it is. We might think we have done excellent work but, if our client does not agree, then our work is not excellent – it is bad service.

Example

In a property case I did for some new Far Eastern clients, the project team flew into the United Kingdom in October and instructed me through an interpreter to complete a lease of a new factory so that they could start production 'on Monday, 12 March at 9.30 am' Apparently, they had an important order which had to be met without fail. As I began to explain, through the interpreter, the *habendum* and *reddendum* provisions of the 60-page draft lease and just as I was getting into my stride, the company chairman nodded politely for me to stop, drew two lines and scribbled some words on a piece of A4 paper and slid it across the table towards me with a bow. Intrigued by this interruption, and bowing back, I saw the following.

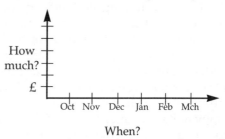

It was a graph to plot cost and time. He had obviously decided to do the deal and only wanted to know two things. I told him what he wanted to know, meekly putting aside the red, amended draft lease. That evening they drove back to Heathrow for their flight back home, having paused to take photographs from their hired car of the mud-patch that was to be in production in only five months time. I did long fax reports to tell them what I was doing and what my advice on the draft lease was, I made many telephone calls at 8 am or 8 pm to their head office seeking instructions. We did complete on time and they did start production exactly on time at 9.30 am on Monday, 12 March. My bill was paid on time. That was the service they wanted and that's what they got. Everybody was happy.

Whether service perceived is good, bad or unsatisfactory – it all depends on the needs, expectations and perceptions of the client.

Service included, value added

When you have dined at a well-known restaurant that was so busy you were kept waiting for a table, even though you had made a reservation, do you become outraged when the bill, already high, is marked, 'Service Not Included'? Do you wonder, 'What service?' Do you resent paying such amounts? Do you grumble to your wife/partner/friends on the way out, 'I wouldn't have minded so much being kept waiting for a table for 35 minutes but we had booked in the first place! Do you think that waiter was new? He didn't seem to know what was on the menu. They're not usually that bad, though.' Do you then compare it wistfully with the same restaurant you visited for the first time only a month before, 'It's a far cry from last month when we were really well looked after. Yes, darling, I know it was expensive, but I thought it was worth it then. I'm not so sure now though!'

The dissatisfaction of the diners was not about the meal itself (the product) but about the service that accompanied the meal, which together with the price made up in total the overall dining experience. The meal and the dining-room were not at fault. The problem lay with the service and the people.

It is more often the service element that colours one's judgment of the whole buying experience. Service itself costs very little, it is the thousand and one little things done better that produce added value and delight the client. What value could be added to a legal product or service and do your bills have service included? Some principles here might include the following:

1 service is what your client expects it to be;
2 good service is meeting those expectations;
3 excellent service is exceeding those expectations;
4 service costs little or nothing;
5 value can be added to the legal product by service improvements; and
6 immediate improvements in client satisfaction and billing are obtained by service improvements.

Client retention and service to sales

It is generally acknowledged that as much as 80% of our work comes from existing clients. This may be even higher in respect of commercial work where repeat work from a relatively small number of high activity niche work clients can keep a partner and his group fully occupied without the need for the constant injection of new high turnover clients. With certain kinds of litigation and conveyancing work, there is a higher turnover of clients, although many are 'former' clients from previous years. Like lawyers, clients like to stick to what they have done before unless there is a strong reason to leave. The acid test of service quality is the degree to which you can retain clients for future work. The 'seepage' factor of non-returning clients needs to be closely monitored.

It is a principle of client management that good service more so than product quality is what leads to client satisfaction and client retention. More work is generated from an existing client where that client feels understood and looked after with the service he has received and expects to receive again. Communications, accessibility, responsiveness and value are some of the main service intangibles that lead to more work. Service to sales should be a key strategic marketing policy.

Service culture levels

When you receive a complaint, is your immediate reaction to feel hurt, misunderstood, undervalued and defensive? Do you close ranks and blame the client? Or do you think, 'The client has a complaint – we'll deal with it and sort it out to his satisfaction.' Or do you rise to the occasion and exclaim, 'Here's a client who really cares about our service and is helping us to improve in areas we did not know about. This is an opportunity to show him what we can do – I'll get straight on to him!'

Exaggerated, perhaps, but it illustrates that what is important is our attitude to clients. This depends on the level of client service culture that exists in the firm. Take the following statements – which of them most closely corresponds to your own views?

Statement	
1 'Yes, of course we have a complaints procedure and use it when necessary to deal with one-off problems. Our main drive is in cutting costs and in increasing turnover.'	
2 'We respond to our clients' problems as quickly and as openly as we can.'	
3 'We treat each client as an individual with his own needs for product, service and value. We stay close to our clients and design and deliver a product and service to match their agreed needs as well as trying to anticipate their future needs.'	

From low service culture in 1, through medium service culture levels in 2, to a high service culture level 3, we can progress our own implementation and evolution of a service culture in the firm. The process can't be rushed and has to have one or more 'drivers' in the firm to get it to embed itself in the practice culture.

Service is our business

Clients are far more aware of the service features in how we deliver the legal service to them rather than features of the legal product itself. Lawyers may think that being a good lawyer is what is important in our business, but our clients are really the only ones entitled to say what is important. Clients may not understand or appreciate the legal content of what we do, but they can judge whether or not they are satisfied, rightly or wrongly, with what we do for them.

In a service business, we all must constantly seek ways to exceed the client's expectations. To do this, we must recognise that service is not peripheral to the real work of lawyers, but that it is the real work of lawyers in business to satisfy their clients by providing legal advice and services which in turn produce a benefit for the client. In order to satisfy clients, we need to know what it is that clients want, what it is that satisfies them, what it is that exceeds their expectations, what it is they expect and then design or alter our systems to ensure that is what we and our staff actually deliver to our clients.

Example A

The typical car service involves you checking your car service manual and your car's mileometer to check when the service is due. You then telephone the service manager to book the service. You may have to wait seven to 10 days and you are asked to bring the car in at 8 am. So far so good. On the day of the service, you arrive at the garage at 8 am and there are two customers already at the service desk. You wait only a few minutes and your car is booked in. Yes, they can arrange a service car and off you drive to work in a used but acceptable older vehicle. You get on with your day and receive a telephone call from the garage to say that everything has been done and your car will be ready to collect at 5 pm. You drive back to the garage, park the service car in the car park next to your waiting car, pay the bill, which has only a few minor 'extra' charges, and collect the keys. There is another customer already waiting but you are not kept more than five minutes, your car gets the 'all clear' and you are given the keys and away you go.

How do you rate this level of service on a scale of 1 to 10? Perhaps 7 or 8? It's about what you expected, the normal service.

The high service level businesses would rate this service as low as 1 or 2. The service experience was as expected, predictable, not unusual, average, unremarkable and one which any other garage could have done just as well. It lacked differentiation and it lacked added value. The customer could just as well use another garage next time. There's no compelling reason to go back.

If you wish to excel in the service industry, you have to find ways of doing more than the average and more than the expected. So let's look at a re-run by the same garage six months later which has implemented a customer management programme as a result of customer service questionnaires.

Example B

The customer receives a telephone call from Steve Jones, who introduces himself as the service manager of the garage where you had your car serviced six months ago. According to his records, he says, and your average mileage computed from the time of the previous service, your car should be due for its next service within the next few weeks. Is the mileage around 50,000? 'Well, yes, actually it is about that', you agree, making a mental note to check the mileometer in the car on the way home. Steve says that he could book your car service provisionally for next Monday at 8 am. After you have checked the car mileage, you can confirm or cancel. He says that the garage has arranged a service vehicle for you. In fact, it's their new four-wheel drive Turbo Estate launched only last week that was featured on TV and in the national press. Did you see it? Well, you might like to drive it for the day. You promptly confirm the service appointment and you can hardly wait for that 'free' test drive. You arrive at 7.45 am to collect. You leave your car keys on the service desk as Steve hands to you the keys of the new service car. You sweep off to the office and notice a few heads turning en route. The client you take out to lunch admires the 'new' car. As you reluctantly leave the service car on the garage forecourt that evening, you notice that there is a car parked alongside that looks a bit like yours, only in much better condition. You take another look at the car next to you as you shut the service car door with a satisfying 'clunk'. You rub your eyes and realise – it is your car! The garage must have given it a clean. Just look at that shiny roof and polished chrome!

As you collect the keys and the bill, which is the amount Steve said it would be, Steve explains what work has been done, shows you the ticked-off check-list and advises you that the two front tyres will need a change within the next thousand miles. As you drive off the forecourt homeward-bound, you re-adjust to the 'new' car, which does seem smoother and more responsive than before, and you notice a new licence holder on the windscreen showing the date and mileage for your next service. You smile as you think that will not be necessary as you will be ordering one of those new Turbo Estate cars for your vehicle replacement due next month. You wonder idly if Steve knew you were approaching the next car change as you park your car on the driveway at home, noticing the roses reflected for the first time on the wheel plates of the new clean car.

Now that's a service with added value and which exceeded expectation. There is of course a small cost to this extra service and I'm not suggesting that we should go over the top and decrease our profit margins by giving away free service 'extras'. Many of these service extras do not cost or do not need to cost much at all. In short, if you want a better business, you'll have to provide a better service and to provide a better service you'll have to start by providing your clients with what they want, with something extra and with something different.

What's this got to do with solicitors? Everything.

Example C

The same day, whilst his car was being serviced, another customer from the garage drove his service vehicle to keep an appointment with his solicitor which he had made two weeks earlier. After parking 'his' new car in the multi-storey car park some 10 minutes from your office, he arrived on time at the reception and was kept waiting for 20 minutes. After he had thumbed twice through a dog-eared edition of *What Car* kept in the reception area, unable to find a test report on the new Turbo Estate, he was eventually seen by an assistant because the partner, who the client had hoped to see, was 'delayed in court'. The advice from the assistant seemed over-complicated and 'bookish' and the client thought the fees quoted were excessive. As he drove away from an unsatisfactory experience with the firm, he reflected, as he eased himself into the soft but firm support of the car's sports seats and felt the exciting surge of the turbo kick in as the car urged its way through the city traffic, that 'lawyers get money for old rope! When are they going to wake up and earn it by giving a good service. They could learn a thing or two from Steve Jones!' he thought. 'Come to think of it, that chap coming out of the garage this morning – I remember him, he's a solicitor I used to play squash with five years ago. He used to do the legal work for my former company. He was very good. I'll give him a ring on the car-phone!' As he was put straight through to Mr J Jarndyce Jnr, who said he could see him right away, his foot kissed the accelerator and the car leapt willingly into the fast lane towards his next appointment.

We are compared not just to our competitors but to other businesses. Our successful business clients will expect us to be equally competitive and successful. If we want to stay in business, even businesses who are not our direct competitors can put us to shame in terms of service. We must realign our work practices so that we continue to do and improve the legal work (the product) but also to improve the way we relate to the clients and present and deliver our services to them, just like some garages have done.

At the 1995 Conference of the British Chambers of Commerce in Aberdeen, John Welsby, Chairman of British Rail, said that total quality means continuous improvement. It focuses on the customer. We must ask ourselves, he said, 'What contribution can we make to the well-being and welfare of the customer now and in the medium-term? What we did yesterday is less important than what we could do today and tomorrow. We are all engaged in the provision of affordable benefits to the customer. Customers want and expect to be told what's happening, even when nothing is happening – that's what's happening.'

At the same Conference, Professor Donald Mackay, Chairman of Scottish Enterprise, said that success requires you to be market-driven. Derek Marnoch, Chief Executive of the Aberdeen Chamber, said that most businessmen are too close to the action to be able to take time out to plan, to devise strategies and to implement change. In a market-place where change is prevalent, those who do not keep up or ahead of the game will not survive. The acid test is in finding out the answer to the question, 'Is our service worth paying for more than that of our competitors?'

Action checklist

1 Write down three recent instances when you have received bad service. Then write down three instances when you have received good service. Do you think that good service is more costly to deliver than bad service?
2 Examine the details of the last 10 reported complaints in your firm. Were they in general avoidable? Did it cost more in time to sort them out than it would have to have avoided them in the first place?
3 Do some sample client service questionnaires to find out what your clients really think and then do something about it.
4 Ask the members of your firm how they think service can be improved.

7 You and your clients

The solicitor/client relationship

Most law firms have by now accepted that running a law firm is the same as running any other business and that the same principles of business apply. As for the client, this does not mean that going to law is the same as going shopping to the town centre where the product and price are the only determinant factors in influencing the customers' perception of value for money. Going to see a solicitor is done because a client wants to achieve a benefit or solution and much of that will depend on the personal input and skills of the lawyer he consults. The client may be in a distressed or anxious state or is vulnerable to potential loss or has suffered some form of loss or injury. The relationship, therefore, is important to him and its success will depend on a number of attributes being present.

The client looks to his solicitor first for some understanding of him and his problem. He also expects some interest to be shown in him and his situation. He expects legal expertise or experience of the solicitor to help him achieve the benefit or solution that he requires. The client speaks to his lawyer in confidence, safe in the knowledge that his personal, private and confidential details will remain so. He also knows that his lawyer is independent and that the advice he receives will be the free from personal interest or unfair gain or advantage from the lawyer's side.

The relationship between the client and his solicitor and its many constituent parts is what the legal service is all about. What the client feels and thinks about his lawyer and the service he receives often depends as much on these intangible relationship features as on the actual legal work itself. The client wants to feel that the relationship is beneficial to him and that it promotes his interest.

It is axiomatic, therefore, that if you wish to influence what the client thinks and feels about you and your legal service and is satisfied with what you are doing, you must pay serious and systematic attention to the feelings and perceptions of the client and the relationship that develops between you. This can and must be actively managed in a way that is an integral part of the overall legal service in accordance with the principles and practices of client management. There are a number of distinct stages through which the typical relationship develops and it is useful to examine some of them to understand them and to identify client management techniques that are appropriate to each distinct phase.

The client partner

The role of the client partner has been introduced on page 21. This denotes a major shift of emphasis in doing our legal work, from file or case management to managing the client's overall services which he receives from the firm. The client partner will have typically some 10 key clients for whom he is responsible for ensuring that:

1 the client is satisfied with the services of the firm overall, whoever provides the legal product and service;
2 the client is fully supplied with all the work that the firm can do for him. At a law conference I was told by a solicitor, 'We do all the litigation work for a large plc but we don't have their property work.' It was understood and accepted that the client's property work was done elsewhere. On further questioning, it transpired that that client had never been asked if that firm could do their property work, because, '... we are only their litigation solicitors'! If we just accept the mindset that we have allowed both ourselves and the client to assume, it can forgo many possible opportunities;
3 the basis of charges is agreed with the client and reviewed annually with the client to ensure that the client receives value for money;
4 the client will receive services from people within the firm who can actually provide the legal services the client needs and expects. A problem can arise where a client whose client partner does all his company work refers an urgent commercial litigation case to the litigation department. The company client is treated to the same, no doubt adequate but different, type of service than that to which he has become accustomed in the company department. This can lead to inconsistent client service and satisfaction levels, internal conflict and possible endangerment to the client relationship;
5 he takes a monthly report from all case managers in the firm for each of his key clients. It is not for the client partner to chase these reports but for the case managers to provide them on the first of the month, without fail.

6   he co-ordinates all activities of the firm for that key client;

7   he carries out the annual client service review; and

8   he deals with all client transfers (see Chapter12) for that client.

That's all very well to say, you may respond, but how can an already too busy partner find the time for all this non-chargeable work? The answer is that if it is accepted that the main task of a partner is to increase profitability by producing, maintaining and increasing client satisfaction, then such activities ought to become part of his regular work practices. He should be busy doing that whilst delegating and transferring much of the routine legal work that can quite adequately be dealt with by others in his own or other groups.

This role is called the client partner role, though some firms call it the lead partner. The client partner is generally the partner who introduced the client into the firm or who does most of his work. He is the one to whom the client addresses key cases or problems and to whom the client talks first about any major new case or service problem.

The client partner is identified as taking this lead role. It must be in agreement with the client. You can't just tell a major client that from now on partner B will take the lead role rather than partner A to whom the client has become accustomed. Partner A may well be overwhelmed with clients, and you may wish to give partner B a key client. This cannot be done, at least not without the client's agreement. It may take some time for partner B to build up that relationship with the client. You cannot delegate personal service; but you can delegate function.

Client classification

An increased understanding of clients will result from increased focus and attention to clients and this in turn will lead to some useful client classifications. Depending on the stage of the relationship with the client, clients may be broadly classified as follows.

Potential client

Every person, firm and company is a potential client. Usually the term describes someone for whom the firm has not acted before at all. It can also mean someone for whom the firm would like to act, being a specific target or being included in a list of potential clients to whom the firm believes it can be of service and with which the firm or specific partners in it are taking steps to become acquainted.

New client

A new client is one who has instructed the firm for the first time in at least one new matter. The new client may be achieved as a result of a tender, a beauty parade, a quotation, a concerted campaign, an advertisement, an acquaintance or just plain chance. Special treatment is required here to ensure the new client has the best service the firm can provide for that particular client and that the firm's services as a whole should be offered to him where appropriate.

Current client

A current client is one whose matter is being dealt with and who has received and paid at least one bill. The first bill payment marks an important milestone in the solicitor/client relationship and it may be useful to do a client satisfaction rating with the first bill. This may identify any problem or potential problem areas with the service and client expectations. Normally, a high satisfaction rating during the first 'honeymoon' period would be expected.

Existing client

An existing client is one for whom more than one matter has been carried out by the firm. There are signs that the client is pleased with the service, product quality and value for money so far and is prepared to continue using the firm for repeat work of the same type. He may also use another firm or firms of solicitors for work of a different nature or calibre.

Established client

When a client has used one department for one particular type of repeat work and then has also used another department and another partner or group for other types of work, and for whom a client partner has been allocated, that client can be described as an established client. He has been embedded into the firm's advice and services and appears content to continue using the firm for all of his legal requirements.

Key client

Where a client has been allocated a client partner who oversees all of that client's various matters with several parts of the firm, and where the aggregate fee income from that client forms a substantial and quantifiable part (circa 10%) of the client partner's annual group income budget, then that client is a key client. Special attention needs to be given here as the dissatisfaction or loss of a key client can have a severely adverse affect on the income of the group or department.

Major client

A firm may have a number of clients who have contributed to the establishment or growth of the firm and who may individually account for as much as 10–15% of a firm's total annual income. This can be a fortunate and precarious position for the firm to find itself in. Some major clients may be able to negotiate fee discounts which keep margins low on a case-by-case basis but keep the firm's personnel and resources tied up in the volume operation needed to maintain an acceptable degree of profitability from that client. A firm has to think long and hard about doing such work and weigh up the consequences of keeping or losing that client.

Dormant client

A client whose last case has been finished for six months or more without repeat instructions being received or contact being made may be regarded as a dormant client. A dormant client may usually be capable of resuscitation where contact is maintained and interest is shown. Where this is not done, a dormant client may lapse into a former client.

Client/customer

A new client who had just one case handled by the firm and who has not given any more instructions within six months of the end of the last one and only case may be regarded as a one-off customer rather than as a client. He may have been shopping around, have bought once and then continued shopping elsewhere. Often these new client/customers are able to negotiate substantial introductory discounts and added-value services with a succession of firms, which nevertheless fail to establish that client. Whilst an essential aspect of client growth, sometimes these serial client/customers can distract the firm from looking after its existing clients.

Former client

Where a client has just drifted away or has not reinstructed the firm for more than a year, then that client cannot be counted on the firm's client database as anything but a former client. To think that such clients remain on the 'active' list is to court self-delusion. Clients need to receive regular contact from the client manager to maintain the service link.

Ex-client

When a client has parted company with the firm over a dispute, complaint, or an unpaid bill, that client can be regarded as an ex-client. Nevertheless, if the firm sees value in regaining that client, the client manager needs to dig deep into his client manager's toolkit (see below and Chapter 10) to find an appropriate way to regain contact with that client in order to rebuild the relationship. Of course, there may be reasons why the firm may not wish to represent that client again under any circumstances, though these are generally very few.

The first interview

The first meeting between a solicitor and his client is one of the 'high' service points of the overall relationship and it is absolutely vital for the client manager to make the right first impressions at this meeting, as well as to cover the basic ground that the case manager needs to cover. The solicitor needs to establish a relationship with his client that will develop from that moment on the 'client for life' principle. He also needs to establish the terms of the contractual relationship in the client agreement and also to get charges agreed from the outset. First impressions last.

How you conduct the first meeting with the client is critical. Does the new client feel comfortable with you? Does he feel you are being precise about the legal issues and about costs? Does he see how well you have prepared for the meeting by briefing yourself with information about his business as well as mastering the facts and legal issues of the case?

Is the client really interested in your departments and internal structure and functions or would he prefer to hear you talk about him and his business? He wants to hear you talk to him about how you can help him. Going to see the new client at his office for the first meeting can be a strong demonstration of your interest in him and your wish to help him by saving his time.

Can you tell the client something he doesn't know or give him an idea he had not thought about before? For example, with a new property client who is expanding his business and taking a new lease, you might suggest that an option to renew might be useful, or an option for the freehold or a break clause, whichever may suit his business needs now and in the future. It shows you are thinking about him and his business.

If you know something about the type of business he is in, try to resist telling him about the business he's in or what's important or that he's doing the right thing. Rather, make your statement a question such as, 'Do you think that getting a legal commitment to this deal before you expand your new operation in Europe is important?' The client will be able to outline his business objectives, whilst noting that you have asked a pertinent and informed question. You need to build on your understanding of the client.

Who is your client? Try to find out the position of the person sitting there in front of you, who he reports to, the extent of his authority, who reports to him, what his budget constraints are and who are his main customers and main competitors. Try to avoid making it sound like an inquisition or as though you're conducting a cross examination or just mechanically completing the details on the client profile form.

What you are really trying to do is to identify common values, mutual understanding and empathy. Try to find out what the client's main concerns are and then try to adapt your service and advice in such a way that the client's concerns are being, or will be, met by the work that you will be doing for him. For example, if he is concerned about who will do the case, because 'you lawyers keep chopping and changing, we never see the same chap twice!' then you will comfort him with the statement that you personally will retain the day to day control and management of his case(s). You may mention that you will be the client partner, what that role means to him, that you will be assisted by Mark Smith and Jill Brown who are assistant solicitors, and preferably you will introduce them to the client before he leaves. You will explain that they will help to speed things up and also save some costs, and that you will have daily supervision of their work. You may give the client your personal direct number, home and mobile telephone number.

Try to give your new client some options that he can consider and make a choice about. It is important that the client makes an input at this stage. You should outline one or two alternative ways of proceeding, commenting on their relative merits in relation to his stated concerns and ask the client to comment.

Having heard the client outline the problem and having gathered some of the facts, you may give some preliminary advice on the legal position. You may also produce a standard case plan, if appropriate, and discuss the work stages with the client. You may need to amend and adapt it to suit the client's and the cases's particular requirements. You can offer to follow it up with a written case plan with agreed charges in the costs plan or, even better, you can complete the case plan and agree the charges there and then. Bear in mind that if you don't cover these points there and then, the client will probably have made a decision about whether or not to use you before he reaches the door. Always ensure that at the end of the first interview you summarise what has been agreed, the next steps to be taken and by whom and that you have both agreed and identified when and where the next meeting or telephone call or contact will take place. Contract for it by getting the client to sign the client agreement and/or a copy of the notes of meeting you have taken.

Above all, try to resist becoming fascinated with just the facts and legal aspects of the case in hand. Instead, try to turn that fascination also on to reaching an agreement with the client about the relationship and the service, his objectives and concerns, and the benefits or welfare he hopes you will achieve for him. Your legal and technical skills are a condition of the instruction and not the reason for it. Demonstrating that you understand the client and the world he lives and works in and that you are willing and able to help him succeed in that world by working with him – that is one of the tasks of the client manager.

Establishing the relationship

When acting for a new client, usually at the first interview everything is fine. The client has told you his problems, you have listened politely and you have asked a few questions, you have given him some advice on the legal position and you have agreed a case plan of some sort. You may even have agreed about charges and in what manner and at what time the client will pay for your services.

At the end of the first interview, the client goes away feeling that he has been able to talk about himself and his aspirations or problems with someone who understands and who has agreed to help him in ways that have been clearly explained and agreed to suit him in particular. He understands what the next steps will be and when he will hear from you again. He has also agreed with you how much the charges will be and who will be doing the case work. You go back to your room or turn to the next file pleased that you have added a new client to your client list, that you have agreed the charges and when to do the bill and when you will be paid and you have even planned the case, in whole or in part up to an agreed point. Now you are able to get on with the legal work. Everybody is happy, the new relationship has got off to a good start.

There are a number of things that need to be checked off at the outset to ensure that all has been done which needs to be done:

The client agreement

The client agreement is dealt with more fully in Chapter 12. You need to ensure that the client agreement is completed at the first interview. Not only is it good practice and complies with Rule 15, but it also shows to the client that you are managing the case and the relationship and that in signing the client agreement there is a contract and a defined basis of the relationship. The signature and shaking of hands can add a nice 'contractual' touch to the proceedings.

Case plan

The vast majority of the work we do is routine and standard. Whilst the client and the facts differ in every case, the stages and procedures tend to be well-established. In commercial conveyancing and property work, for example, it is possible to list the main types of transactions and then to produce and use standard case plans or specifications for the work usually or likely to be involved. The case plan will be useful to you and your client as follows:

1 to discuss the work plan with the client, adding in extras or taking out stages that are not required;
2 to enable you to give a quotation or even better to agree a fixed charge with the client for a fixed amount of work;
3 once agreed with your client, to annex a copy of the case plan to the client agreement (see Chapter 12 and Appendix 1);
4 to act as a checklist in the case management (see Chapter 4);
5 to be a useful guide to the client so he can understand the progress of the case.

In the case of a specialised area of expertise, then the work may be capable of being broken down into stages.

General advisory work is less easy to plan precisely, but you can agree time or cost limits with the client to impose some kind of parameters of what you will do for the client. By keeping a full file diary on your time recording system you could, for example, agree to supply monthly print-outs to your client so that he can see what's been done and how much work in progress is being clocked up. It's a good way of reporting progress, or the lack of it, as well as agreeing costs, variations and doing a case plan review. It's also a good opportunity to send an interim bill, provided you have agreed monthly interim billing in the client agreement.

It is very important to note that the case plan is designed for the client – it is not a detailed legal checklist for the case manager. A case plan can be supplemented on the file with a detailed 'how to do the case' checklist. These can be found in standard texts and precedent books.

Care plan

As we have seen, the overall legal service as perceived by clients comprises three parts: the legal work itself ('the product'); the way the product is presented and delivered to the client ('the service'); and the charges made for the product and the service ('value for money'). You need to establish the product, the service and the value parameters at the beginning of the client relationship. The case plan deals with the product, and the agreed charges deals with the financial obligations of the client as well as the value to be achieved. But often we overlook or undervalue the service element in our work. What kind of service should you deliver and what kind of service does your client expect or would find to be satisfactory? It may be possible to work out with your client at the outset what kind and level of service would be appropriate and satisfactory in the form of a care plan (see Chapter 12 and Appendix 14).

It is obvious that the service level to a large client trading company with several thousand debt recovery cases with your firm would be different from the service expectations of a client making a standard will. But with both clients, it is are important to agree and deliver to plan. Some care plan service features might include:

1 copies of all letters you write on the file to be sent to the client;
2 copies of all letters received to be sent to the client;

3 copies of all letters sent and received to be sent to the client;

4 copies as above to be faxed on the same day to the client;

5 monthly written progress reports to the client (see Chapter 10) ;

6 monthly progress meeting with client at your office/his office;

7 copies of all draft documents to the client with all amendments made and proposed being shown;

8 extra sets of copies of same to be sent to client (one for the managing director, one for finance director, etc);

9 full written report to client pre-exchange;

10 copies of all searches, inquiries, reports, etc to the client;

11 'bible' of all copy documents to client post-completion; and

12 retention and storage of deeds for client with/out charge for agreed period.

The list and range of services will vary depending on the type of work and client. The client management principle is to agree with your client at the outset what type and level of service he expects or would find satisfactory and then to ensure that the agreed care plan or service level is recorded on your file and is taken into account in the agreed charges. It is then the task of the client manager to ensure that the service is actually delivered to the client during the conduct of the case.

The process of doing the care plan not only helps you to understand your client better, but it will also ensure that you do satisfy his actual rather than his supposed requirements. Every client is different, what one wants may be irrelevant to another. Moreover, it will impress your client as to your professionalism and client focus – he probably will not have received this degree of attention before!

Diagnosis and introductions

Your new client consults you about doing his will. In the process of taking instructions you realise that your new client is a man of business, who employs staff, who has funds available for investment and who is looking for new business premises. Although you may be the firm's expert on wills, and do this and nothing else, you will ensure that you tell the client that Mr Jarndyce in your firm will be able to advise him on employment contracts and staff problems and that Miss Emmerson will be able to help him in the property acquisition he is considering. If your new client is receptive and interested, you will introduce him to the named people before he leaves your office. You will also record his potential requirements in the client plan (see Appendix 9) which is recorded on the client database.

Referrers

Your new client has not appeared in your office by magic. He may have received a recommendation from one of your clients or referrers. You should enquire and make sure that you contact the referrer to thank him and let him know, for example, if the referrer is the local bank manager, that you are looking after your new client who is also his customer.

Agreed charges

It is important to agree charges with your client from the outset. He is certainly thinking about it and so are you. There is no real medium or long-term benefit in ducking the issue. Clients don't always ask about charges and if you don't deal with it, the client will go away after the first interview feeling uncertain about costs and may even think you have been evasive. As long as you take the approach, that the charge is a matter for agreement rather than one of prescription or deferral, then the matter of money should be able to be dealt with quite satisfactorily.

Maintaining the relationship

The 'honeymoon period' with the new client has commenced and for the first few weeks things tend to go along alright. You write your letters, draft your contracts or issue the proceedings and all seems to go well. You are developing a nice neat file, your correspondence and documents are all in order, you are following the case plan and everything seems fine. You have not contacted the client since the first interview because you are doing what was agreed and there is no need to contact the client. You have heard nothing from your client and you assume he is happy. You have heard nothing from the other side and you see no need to hurry at this stage. The client hears nothing from you and assumes – what?

During the honeymoon period your client may assume that you are doing what you said, and being a well-behaved client and thinking that telephoning you will increase the costs, he keeps quiet. Eventually it may get too much for him and he telephones to enquire politely about progress. Such calls seem innocuous enough and some may be no more or less than that. But others are the result of a growing worry, then anxiety and then fury at not knowing what's going on. When a client telephones to ask about progress, the first black mark has been scored against the client manager because the client should not have to ask. There are a number of things that can be done to keep the relationship in good shape, though it is difficult if not impossible to maintain the honeymoon period level of service forever. These include the following.

Progress reports

You don't have to do the full and comprehensive report at this stage. It may be sufficient just to telephone to say what's happening or simply that nothing is happening. Both are statements of progress. You could do the written progress reports to give the client a view of what stage has been reached (see Appendices 3 and 4).

Call forward diary

It is a good case management practice never to put a file away without first diarising the next call forward date. This can be in a call forward diary or even in your own diary. Don't just wait for things to happen before you react – make things happen by taking a planned, measured and proactive approach to both client and case management.

Weekly client contact list

Make a list of all your new and current clients, divide into four and telephone the clients in each group once a month, taking one list per week. You will telephone such a client in the group unless you have spoken with that client during the last 14 days.

Monthly client matter review or round-up

Once a month on billing day (see Chapter 13), you will review the progress of each and every case in your group with the case manager concerned to ensure that progress and bills are being made on each one and according to the case plan and the client agreement.

Monthly bills

Agreed regular monthly billing is a good way to remember to contact your client and to make a progress report if you haven't otherwise done so. Combining client contact, progress reports, bill delivery and collection is a feature of client management which benefits both the solicitor and his client.

Doing what you said you would do

Honeymoons tend to go into decline when there is a failure to deliver what was promised or expected. It's the same in law. If you agree to do something, then not do so ranks as a capital offence in client management terms. One thing promised but not done can undo so much goodwill that has been developed in the relationship.

Doing what you said only quicker/better

It is good client management to deliver the legal product or service in accordance with the agreed case plan and care plan, but even better client management to exceed those expectations. For example, if you promise to send out draft contracts 'by Friday' but in fact send them out the Wednesday before, the client will be pleased to see you doing something more than he expected.

Renewing the relationship

Clients are for life and there is no such thing as 'the end of the case' where client contact ceases. Having served the client well, as ascertained from the client satisfaction case questionnaire completed by the client at the end of the matter, you have established a basis for moving on to other services now and in the future. Once you can agree some further work with the customer, then you are on the way to developing that customer (one matter only) into a client with repeat instructions. This is where the after-sales service, contact diary, client plan and assistance from the client database and marketing manager will assist.

Reviving the relationship

If you have had no contact with the client for six months or more, you can regard that client hopefully as 'dormant'. If you make contact again with that client between six and 12 months after the end of the last matter you did for him, and providing the client is receptive to the contact, then he can be marked on the client database as 'dormant' as opposed to 'lost' or 'former' client.

When you make such a contact call, you may ask how things are going, perhaps mention the work you did for him where appropriate and by his responses you can gauge whether he might be in need of further services and whether or not he is likely to come back to you. Perhaps you could leave the call with an invitation to one of the firm's social events or perhaps agree to call around to see him.

You should not expect to receive immediate new instructions from the dormant client contact call, though this does often happen. The client might say, 'I'm glad you've called because I've been meaning to ask you about something ...' The contact call helps to make an impression that you are aware of the client and his needs even after six months and that you have organised yourself to make regular contact with clients, both current and dormant. He will form an impression about you – that you and your firm are people that care about clients and keep in touch even when you're not being paid to do so. Not long after making the contact call, do not be surprised to get a call from that 'dormant' client with some new instructions. Even if he does not, you will be the first solicitor he thinks of when he next has need of legal advice. In my experience, five out of 10 contact calls to 'dormant' clients produce immediate instructions of some sort, and, of the other five, a further three to four call within two to three months with requests for advice.

Rescuing the relationship

With regular progress reports during the course of a matter, it should be possible to avoid or ward off potential problems or misunderstandings. If problems do arise that threaten the continuation of the relationship, it is essential that the problem is dealt with quickly and positively. There generally is little point in delaying matters. The make-up of the rescue package during the course of a matter will depend on the particular problem and it may include:

1 a change of client partner by agreement with the client;
2 a change of group partner or case manager;
3 a review and redesign of the case plan with the client's agreement;
4 a review and redesign by agreement of the care plan;
5 a review and redesign by agreement of the agreed charges.

If there has been some mistake or omission or even possible negligence, special consideration will need to be given to ensure that the client's overall objectives are not defeated or imperilled. It's not just a question of saying 'sorry!' and reducing costs. First, you will need to find out exactly what it is that the client is concerned about. Complaints about cost are often found to be concerns about value, and concerns about delay are often found to be due to poor communication. The rescue package varies according to the client and the circumstances, and it needs prompt, sensitive and expert attention which seeks to rectify and additionally to out-perform expected service levels. This kind of rescue package response, when linked to an effective follow-through operation, will impress all but the most worsted of clients. If it does not save the day or the client, you will have achieved partial redemption of your reputation by showing care and attention, albeit too late.

The end of the relationship

The provisions that apply here should be covered by your standard terms and conditions of business agreed with the client at the beginning of the matter. Usually, the client may terminate on giving written notice provided that all outstanding and accrued charges and expenses are paid, with interest where appropriate. The client manager will be concerned to know and understand the reasons for termination by the client. It may be obvious of course. The personality issue, the mistake, the alleged negligence, the neglected or aggrieved client, the client going out of business, the moved away and, unfortunately, the deceased client. Whatever the reason, you need to find out what it is and record it. With so much effort going on at front-end marketing and operational client management, a firm cannot allow client seepage just to happen, it has to become part of the firm's client management culture. It may not always be possible or opportune to carry out an 'exit interview' but it should be attempted wherever possible. The exit interview can be a valuable tool of market research which may also serve to restart the relationship in some cases and with some clients.

A firm may not have a lost client policy or, at least, not one that is recorded and consistently applied. Like life and death, clients do come and go. When clients leave, there is often a sense of personal or professional failure and the sad episode is often just swept under the carpet. This is not only not best practice but it also may lose opportunities for valuable client information and client recovery. Client management requires that every aspect and stage of the solicitor/client relationship should be examined, evaluated and planned systematically for client attraction, satisfaction, retention and client salvage opportunities.

The telltale signs of breakdown

As with marriage, where the husband is often said to be the last person to know that all is not well, the same can be said for the solicitor/client relationship where the solicitor may be blissfully unaware that problems are brewing with a client. He may only find out when it's too late. He is so busy with his legal work, with his eye focused down on the details and minutiae of day-to-day legal work that he may never lift his gaze up above the desk to see what's going on or to sniff the wind or to get out and look around. Nevertheless, there are well-known signs indicating a problem in the relationship that the client manager should be on the alert to spot and intercept as follows:

- the client doesn't call you back or is slow to do so;
- your client's secretary deals with you;
- the client does not accept two successive offers of hospitality;
- the client questions you more closely than usual over the terms of some work that you have done or are doing;
- you hear from others about deals your client has done that formerly the client would have consulted you about;
- you are not invited to the dinners and hospitalities that you have formerly been invited to attend;
- you sense that things with your client are different but can't quite put your finger on what it is;
- the client stops telephoning you for the many little pieces of free advice that you are used to discussing with him;
- your client's staff sound distant and evasive;
- your bills are more closely scrutinised than previously;
- payment of bills grows later than previously;
- your offers to pop in for a chat are not warmly received;
- your client is 'out' when you do call by;
- you are seen, if at all, in reception or public areas rather than in the director's inner sanctum to which you once enjoyed easy access;
- while you are waiting in your client's reception, you think you recognise a partner from a rival law firm going into the MD's office;

149

- the client's body language shows little or no eye contact;
- there is a reduction in the value and frequency of instructions from the client;
- relations seem to be more formal and with less humour than before;
- you feel that you are losing touch with the client;
- you feel you are being avoided by the client's middle and technical managers who once had easy and frequent access to you;
- when you sign in at the client's reception, you notice the name of a rival law firm in the visitor's book;
- such meetings as you are able to get with the client are short and often interrupted for longer than seems usual; and
- you notice that you are starting to feel paranoid about your clients.

As you read through this list you may feel an uneasy feeling setting in and find your hand reaching automatically for the telephone to make a few calls to one or two clients you have not spoken to for a week or more. This shows that your client antennae are working but that you may be over-reacting. A managed approach to clients on a systematic basis will be better than panic or reactive measures.

Salvaging the relationship

You may be confronted with a situation with a client and a matter in which it's too late to do anything about it. It's all gone wrong, the client is definitely 'ex' and considering legal action, heads may have rolled, ranks have closed and the file has been consigned to the insurer's solicitors. Nothing can be done now except litigate and at best settle, or can it? If there is no litigation issue as yet, it's always possible to say sorry. A letter to the client expressing regret at what's happened and saying that the firm understands and respects the client's wishes, may not get the client back or even right the perceived wrong, but it may achieve an acceptable 'sign-off' for the firm. It may at least leave the client with the impression that you did express regret and apologise, even though you may have stopped short of actually admitting that you made a mistake. Admission of error is, of course, constrained by the professional indemnity insurance policy, the partnership agreement and employment contract. We all make mistakes. My nightly prayer is, 'Please let me not make mistakes, but those that I do make, Lord, please let them be capable of remedy.' In so many cases with so many clients, a simple apology is often all that is required. The client feels strongly about being worsted by the firm, that to be confronted with closed ranks only makes it worse and the only way it can go is to court. The apology and offer to rectify are powerful tools in the toolkit of client management. It may not always salvage the relationship, but making the attempt is always of some benefit.

Lost client policy

When you lose a valued client either on a tender, or because of a complaint or mistake or other cause, what do you do about it? Do you sweep it under the carpet, do you just keep quiet, do you feel hurt, undervalued, bitter and misunderstood? Or do you go out after that client and keep in touch until you win him back again? Are you persistent and not over-sensitive?

An 'exit interview' may be useful in some cases. Contact the client and with a standard questionnaire try to obtain some feedback as to why the client went elsewhere. It may be difficult to obtain a response but not always impossible and you must judge as to the right timing and method of approach. But you should never just leave it as a defeat, which is bad for morale and often found to be avoidable. With many clients, the exit interview has been seen to be a way of keeping channels open, of finding out what the client wants and perceives (it's never too late!) and in many cases of keeping the door open for future work. I have known cases where potential clients, who have been lost on a tender, give instructions after a few months where contact has been maintained. You should never admit or accept defeat in the battle for clients.

Changing the relationship

Things may have got off to a wrong start or, having got off well, things may have changed. For example, you may have taken on a client for some court work only to find that a later joined third party is a client of the firm. You may be doing a property sale for new client A only to find out that the purchaser is your existing client B. Conflicts may arise that must be dealt with in accordance with professional rules. The case may have changed from an undefended divorce into a full blown fight. What to do? Provided you have in place a client agreement that deals with variations and alterations and possible termination by the firm, then the situation needs to be brought to the attention of the client at the earliest possible moment.

One reason why some lawyers may be reluctant to use the client agreement or case plan may be that they think it will limit what they can do and what they can charge for, particularly when the case itself changes after it has started, as many cases do. The client agreement and the case plan both recognise that the plan is provisional and that a review may need to be made. This does not indicate a lack of control or poor case planning, but it realistically recognises that things might change and, therefore, so must the plan, the timescale and perhaps the charges. The client agreement and the case plan in fact plan for alterations and changes in a neat and clear way. I have not yet come across a client who finds any difficulty with this planned and flexible approach which keeps the client informed and in control.

How well do you know your clients?

As a solicitor in private practice, you know your clients' cases pretty well and you may know your clients pretty well. Without referring to your print-outs and database information, you could probably write down the names of all your clients from memory. You could probably even list them in order of importance based on bills delivered over the last 12 months. You could probably write down an estimate of bills delivered for each client over the last 12 months. You could even write down their occupations and businesses. You may have visited a number of these clients at their own workplaces. You are on first name terms with most of your clients.

If you are in a firm that has several hundred or several thousand current matters, and several hundreds or even thousands of clients, you are probably pretty well aware of the main clients of the firm. You may not deal with them personally yourself or maybe only occasionally when their legal affairs stray into your own particular field of expertise. When someone in the firm passes on work to you to do for that client, does he also pass on information about the client which, though not vital for the file or case work, may be useful and interesting from the client management and client service point of view? As a test of how well you know and understand your clients as a client manager, how would you answer the following questions:

1 Who are the 10 most important clients (key clients) of the firm in terms of bills delivered over the last 12 months?
2 What was the approximate amount of fee income from each of the firm's 10 key clients over the last 12 months? If you cannot estimate the figures, arrange the names in order of importance.
3 What is the estimated fee income from each of those 10 key clients over the next 12 months?
4 Write down the number of cases currently being handled for each key client.
5 Who is the client partner primarily associated with each of the top 10 key clients of the firm?

If you did the test on your own, check your answers with the information available in accounts or on the client database. If you did the test in a group, without conferring, compare the variations in answers given. You may be surprised at the wide degree of variance in the internal perception of the key clients of the firm. As a result of the test, the firm may decide to do a regular key client report to all partners showing who the key clients are, how much has been billed year to date and the target for the year, actual figures for last year, the name of the client partner and a section for comment by the client partner. This is a step towards client management on a firm-wide basis.

You may agree that as a client-oriented law firm, the partners should know about the clients of the firm. Each partner is responsible for *all* the business of the firm and he should take an interest in the parts of it he does not actually get involved in from a functional point of view. A partner may not have anything usually to do with client Y, but as a proprietor of the firm, being responsible financially for any mistakes or profits earned from that client, he should at least be kept informed about the state of each main key client account. The client focused firm will have as one of its hallmarks a firm-wide and less parochial group partner view of the firm's clients.

The client manager's test

If you found the above test of interest or value, then you may wish to probe further into the knowledge which you and the people in the firm have of your clients and their attitudes towards them. Partners, associates and case managers could take the client manager's test set out below. The test answers are to be given to your best belief and knowledge, without preparation or conferring. The answers you give should be what you actually think, not what you would like to think. Don't give the best answer, give the answer you think is correct for you.

The client manager's test			
	Yes	No	Don't know/ other
1 The firm is more interested in bills delivered than in the levels of client satisfaction.			
2 Everyone in the firm knows who our best clients are.			
3 We know what's different and special about our firm.			
4 We find out why clients chose to instruct us.			
5 We do not let our most demanding clients dictate the quality of our work.			
6 Complaints are dealt with quickly and fairly.			
7 We go out to visit clients regularly.			
8 We find out what clients want and then do something about it.			
9 We regularly monitor levels of client satisfaction.			

The staff and members of the firm are the firm's main actual or potential assets. In matters of client management, they *are* the firm. As a client-focused firm, you may, therefore, see the advantage of involving your staff by asking them to complete the team test above.

Not only will the test results reveal what your firm's client management looks like to you from inside the firm but, by doing the test at, say, annual intervals and comparing the results you will see the development of your firm's client awareness progress over a period of time.

If you or your firm has never done anything like this before, you will find that the process of doing the tests and the discussion of the results with all concerned will in itself be a considerable step towards the firm becoming more client-focused. The fact that it's new, different, interesting and outward looking will open up new perspectives and opportunities. In order to be successful and effective, the test process must have the full confidence and support of the firm, with a determination to continue the process at regular intervals, to look at the results with a new resolve to involve and direct everyone in the firm along the path of client management, a path which starts with awareness and then develops into action.

Personal communications with clients

Nick Butcher, the Managing Director of DHL International, said at the BCC Conference in Aberdeen in May 1995 that retained customers offer a ninefold opportunity of increasing profits. Customer loyalty can only be earned by good service given by one individual person to another within the context of a client-oriented business environment. This requires good channels of communications, personal contact and personal service.

Database marketing helps us to find out who uses our products or services and why. But relationship marketing helps to spread the word about your firm in a way that is personal to the individual client's needs. Clients respond to relationships rather than to products. This is why personalised and targeted marketing is more effective than the 'blunderbuss' approach. Customers want to be in control of what they receive, they want it personalised and they want it to meet their own particular needs.

The telephone, the letter and meetings are the contact and communications media. You need to stress your service levels that can't be matched elsewhere. Direct mailshots go hand-in-hand with database marketing and it's becoming more personal and more specific. It is targeted and pertinent, it is no longer junk mail. Clients are generally happy to receive direct mail so long as it is relevant to their needs. Clients say that they perceive a benefit from receiving regular *relevant* contacts and information that is aimed specifically at them. Clients want the personal touch – to be treated as an individual – don't you?

Communications with clients during the case

In client management it is emphasised that you must take steps to keep in regular contact with your clients, even when it is not strictly necessary from the point of view of the file or the legal process. The small amount of non-chargeable client contact time is time well invested with clients. Try to avoid thinking, 'Nothing has happened yet so there's no point contacting the client!' because things will have been happening to the client and contact may alter things. Even saying to the client, 'Nothing's happened yet' is a progress report. There follows a brief list of ways of contacting clients during the case.

The telephone

Without the telephone, communications with clients would not have advanced much since Dickensian times. This instrument is still sometimes, however, used in Dickensian ways. Case managers can easily lapse into dictating a letter rather than picking up the telephone to speak to the client. It can be frustrating when the client is not there when you telephone. In such an event, leave a message and determine to master all the facilities on your office telephone for redial, automatic call-back, repeat calls and memory functions. Telephoning the client is usually quicker, cheaper and more personable than writing a letter. The service content of a telephone call is greater than that of a letter because it is 'live'.

The letter

Letters can provide a barrier at times when you need to say something difficult or to send an unagreed bill. They are expensive to produce, slow and can be challenging to clients. Moreover, they cannot be withdrawn once sent. Use enclosures and reports to deal with technical matters. Letters are sometimes necessary to record what has been agreed, or simply to put advice given 'on the record'.

Progress reports

There are various forms of progress reports to clients and each can be adapted to suit the needs of a particular client or firm. The simplest and best report is the telephone call to the client, even when not strictly necessary from the point of view of the case. Remember that clients are often more sensitive to service features than to product features. Sometimes your written progress report is used by the client in reporting to his own board, and makes his life that much easier.

Checklists

The file checklists should also include a reminder to contact the client, either event or time triggered. It's so easy for the busy solicitor with a busy client to find that two or three weeks go by without contact either way. In the client's perception, this may imply that nothing has been done for him.

Quality control system

As we have seen in Chapter 4, quality involves agreeing and meeting client expectations as well as product specifications. The firm's written quality control systems will become quality assured systems when its written procedures provide for regular progress contacts with clients. These contacts can range from simply a telephone call to a full-blown progress report meeting covering a multitude of cases for that particular client.

Diagnostic interviews

The initial interview with the client or subsequent contacts or feedback data may indicate that the client has need of other legal products of the firm. At the appropriate time, the client manager will suggest a discussion on the client's wider needs and this may perhaps produce further instructions and a more satisfied and better served client.

The partner in charge

He should contact the client during the case to check on satisfaction with the case manager, etc and trouble-shoot any problems. He usually is the group partner who supervises the group where the legal work is being done for that particular client. He may or may not be the client partner.

The client partner

As seen above, the client partner must keep an overview of *all* of the cases in the firm of his key and major clients. He must not assume that having referred the work to another group, department or branch that all will be satisfactory to the client. Even where the work is being done properly, the client partner knows that his key or major client is receiving service from someone else and, therefore, by definition, the service is different. He must be sensitive to client reaction or rejection and by keeping in touch can ascertain how things are going. He is checking here on service rather than product quality.

Interim bills

The delivery of a bill always produces a reaction from the client and it is good practice to agree the amount of the bill with the client before sending it out. This creates an opportunity for a progress report and case review on which the client may well assess value. Linking billing to progress reports is generally acceptable to clients.

Visits to the client

A visit to your key and major clients from time to time is often well-received and appreciated by clients. It shows a client that you are interested in him and may give you a chance to learn more about your client and perhaps ways to provide a better or wider range of services to him.

Meetings

A progress report meeting either at your client's premises or in your own offices can be useful where there are a number of current matters on which to report. Whilst each case manager will report on each individual case direct to the client, these case meeting overviews can be useful to pick up any cases that are slipping or that the client may have forgotten about. It also gives the managing director in the client company an overview of the cases being instructed by his sub-managers.

The group secretary

The group secretary is the principal secretary working for the group partner and other case managers in the group. She can provide an important support service here to the group client managers by ensuring that contact dates and progress report intervals are diarised, reviewed and actioned.

Communications with clients after the case

After the case has been legally completed, the client manager knows that the relationship with the client must be maintained until the next instruction is received, be it within one week, one month or one year. There are a number of things that can be done to keep in touch in this interlude with a client as follows:

Case report

The client manager knows that a case is not completed until a case report has been made to the client and a check has been made to assess client satisfaction. Quality demands that such a check is made because without it, how will we know whether and to what degree the client has been satisfied? Relying on instinct or assumptions is not good enough any longer. A brief case report and a client satisfaction slip (see Appendix 6) for the client to complete and return will usually be adequate for most cases.

Client questionnaire

Sometimes a more detailed questionnaire will be used for certain clients to get more useful information about client satisfaction. Perhaps one a month per group or one for every 20 clients may be deemed to be appropriate. Clients must not be bombarded with questionnaires and their discrete use is essential.

Appointment card

This can be used during the case as well as after the case. I am always impressed when emerging from my dentist's chair that his receptionist not only has the bill ready for payment but also insists on making the next check-up appointment before I can escape into the open air. Depending on the type of client, such future check-up or review appointments may be useful. They also maintain a tangible service link between the client and the firm.

The group client diary

This is maintained by the group secretary for follow-up and contact dates with clients. Like the key dates diary which is essential to preserve product quality, the group client diary is essential in maintaining service quality.

Reminders for future dates

When the case is completed, there is generally no contractual requirement to remind the client in the future about key dates. The case report should of course flag these up (eg 'Note that the option to purchase must be exercised if at all not less than six or more than 12 months before 31 December 1999 – see clause 10 of the Agreement'). If these sort of dates are also put into the five year diary and called forward, then it can be a useful reminder to the client at the time (eg on 1 January 1999 you may write to the client as follows, 'We would remind you that if you intend to purchase Blackacre under the Option Agreement, you must do so by giving written notice not later than the middle of June to be not less than six months in advance. We enclose a draft form of the Option Notice for your consideration and approval'). You will have telephoned the client as well at such time. You must take care in your firm's terms and conditions of business to avoid any contractual or other liability from giving such reminders because the penalty for omission could be high. Of course, where the client asks you to make such reminders, an appropriate fee or retainer should be agreed.

Staged contacts/reminders

Depending on the type of client and expected future business, reminders at three, six and 12 months after the end of the case can be made. These will enquire whether any other benefits and services can be offered. Client managers will use their accumulated knowledge of the client as well as the client profile and database to suggest what they think would be appropriate. Where clients go for more than six months since giving any instructions, and become 'dormant clients' then other client management techniques should be considered, such as a visit or offer of hospitality.

Other client matters

Once a client manager completes a case he will be aware that this may not complete all of the firm's cases with that particular client. The client partner should keep an overview here to see how the client's relationship with the firm develops.

Client newsletter

The case report or questionnaire will have asked the client whether he wishes to receive the firm's client newsletter or other information services. Quarterly or bi-monthly newsletters can be useful in maintaining the client's awareness of the firm as well as of developments in the law, provided they are relevant to his needs.

Seminars

Inviting clients to a seminar which is relevant to their business is a good way of keeping in touch as well as of creating more enquiries.

Legal audits

The completed case may have dealt with a new client's property needs, but he may have need of other business or personal advice. Diagnosis of his needs might have been picked up during the case but, if not, it can be offered as an 'extra' after completion of the case. It can often be useful to do a diagnostic audit within three to six months after the case completion because the client will have had time to assess your service as well as his own continuing and future needs.

Client entertainment

One of the best ways of maintaining and developing the client relationship is to spend time with clients. Entertainment of potential, new and established clients and referrers is an important part of the client manager's activities, because two out of three elements of the overall legal service (the service provider and the service receiver) are not only present but are put into sharper focus in those out of office activities.

Meetings with clients

The face-to-face meeting with a client is undoubtedly the best medium for communication. Meetings are not easy to arrange and can absorb valuable time and so a meeting must be used by the client manager like a craftsman uses his tools. The meeting must be carefully planned and controlled to ensure that the maximum benefits are regularly and consistently obtained. Preparation and forethought are essential in order to maximise the use and benefits of the valuable commodity of client time. You need to consider:

1 What are the objectives of the meeting?
2 At what time will the meeting start and finish?
3 What do you hope to achieve by the end of the meeting?
4 Who will need to attend the meeting?
5 What is on the agenda?
6 Where will the meeting take place?
7 Who will take notes?
8 Who will chair the meeting?
9 Will attendees have authority to make decisions?
10 At the end of the meeting, what action has been agreed and by whom?
11 When and where will the next meeting or contact take place?
12 Have/will all members of the meeting get a copy of the meeting notes?

Meetings should not be allowed to meander on. The meeting should start on time and afterwards the solicitor and client should go through the notes to agree the main points covered and to agree the action plan and timescale. The general rule is not to call a meeting unless the advantages of so doing are clear and agreed.

In the meeting with your client, there is an excellent opportunity to get to know your client better, to look each other in the eye, to read and interpret the body language and to form a closer relationship. The client manager should make the art and craft of meetings one of his principal client management tools because the service he gives to the client is happening there and then, he is 'on live' and because it offers one of the high points for the development of the relationship. If, as has been seen, the legal service is what the client perceives it to be, then the service itself is being assessed, reassessed and evaluated at every meeting between the solicitor and his client. Understanding this, the client manager will be solicitous to ensure that the opportunities and benefits of the meeting are maximised.

Problem meetings

The most common problems with client interviews include:

1 the meeting starts late;
2 the meeting runs late;
3 the meeting does not have a planned start and end time;
4 the meeting lacks an agenda and a structure;
5 the environment is poor or inappropriate. Do you actually bring your client into your own work-room or do you have dedicated client interview rooms?;
6 do you make the client comfortable?;
7 use of inappropriate body language;
8 rushed or ill-considered conclusions by the case manager, such as, 'This is a probate case' when it may also be about tax planning, partnership advice, property transfer and financial services;
9 telephones not switched to divert when the client comes in. It is bad service, as well as bad manners, to allow yourself and your client to be interrupted by telephone calls during a meeting;
10 use of too much jargon;
11 the client does not understand you; and
12 failure to agree a case plan for the client to take away with him or to be sent to him by the next day. After all, you do write it down in the file and in your diary so why not make it easy for the client and send him a copy?

Telephones and the client

Second only to a meeting with a client, the telephone is the next best way of communicating with a client. It is instant, personal, interactional and 'live'. We need to communicate with clients on a day-to-day basis by telephone. It is an important instrument and its use can be made more effective by following a few guidelines.

Preparation

Stack your outgoing calls to be made together. Plan what you want to say and what you want to find out. Make sure you have all the relevant information to hand.

Listen

Listen carefully to your client – things may have changed at his end. Be prepared to hear something different from what you expect. Don't assume that because you've done this kind of case many times before that it will be exactly the same. Every client and case is different.

Speak

Say what you have to say and make sure it is received and understood. Keep the points short and simple. Don't try to cover too much ground; if there is too much to say, call a meeting or go and see the client instead.

Attendance notes

As you speak, make a written attendance note of the call and keep it on the file. It acts as a contemporaneous record of what was said and by whom and the action agreed upon. It can help to avoid misunderstandings. In some circumstances, it could be good practice to sign the attendance note and send a copy to the client 'for the record' or to obtain his signature to confirm instructions. In urgent cases, it could be faxed to the client.

Agreed action

On completing each telephone call, complete the written telephone attendance note, put a copy on the file and, where appropriate, send one to the client for signature. Record the time, carry out the agreed action and diarise for the next action, review and client contact.

The technology of the modern telephone that has facilities for redials, conferences, time recording and instant and direct dialling, needs to be mastered by the client manager.

Letters to clients

The letter is the traditional communication tool of the solicitor to his client. However, its use may be overdone in many situations. With meetings and the telephone being the prime communication tools, the letter should be regarded as a supplement to these and not a replacement. Letters are expensive to produce, slow and not particularly user friendly. Some ground rules for the client manager on writing to a client might include the following:

1 try to write no more than one side of an A4 letter – avoid continuation sheets wherever possible;
2 never write a letter where the telephone will do;
3 use a letter to record advice given, instructions received or action agreed in a telephone call;
4 don't use a letter to give technical legal advice. Prefer to speak to the client by telephone or in a meeting so that you can explain it better and deal with his reactions and questions;
5 when you do report to a client on technical legal advice, prefer to use a 'report to client' by way of enclosure. A report can be structured better and can admit some legal jargon where a personal letter to a client should not. The report, based on a shell report for that type of transaction, can also act as useful checklist to the solicitor to ensure that all the main and relevant points have been covered. The report can be sent in duplicate, with a copy for the client to sign and return by way of record for acknowledgement of the advice and as an instruction to proceed;
6 avoid the use of legal jargon in a letter;
7 consider using a different or italic font style in letters to soften and personalise the communication:

Dear Mr Smith,

Purchase of Unit 123, Newtown Industrial Estate, Anytown

I am pleased to say that I have now completed my preliminary work on your proposed purchase of the above unit, and enclose my report for your attention.

Please let me know if you have any comments or questions and if you are satisfied with the report, please sign and return the copy of the report in the envelope enclosed.

Yours sincerely,
J Jarndyce.
Partner

Encs: report, copy and stamped and addressed envelope.

8 ensure that the letter is set out attractively and that it is easy to read, with all spellings checked by use of the spell-check routine resident in most WP software systems;
9 as a part of the agreed care plan with your client, you may have agreed to send extra copies of your letters to others in the same company or organisation. Ensure that this plan is adhered to;

10 run a daily letter check routine from time to time, either through the computer network or else by obtaining a copy of all letters written by a firm or branch or department or group to assess whether the letters sent out comply with the above guidelines or any other guidelines the firm may agree and stipulate from time to time.

Using the fax

These may be regarded as a benefit or as a bane to legal work. They make communications with clients immediate and can be more user friendly than letters. They do increase the pace of work and should be used instead of letters where appropriate and not in substitution for a letter. The fax itself should be sufficient without the need to send a copy in the post or DX as well. Clients seem to be more willing to send a fax than a letter to their lawyers.

E-mail and the Internet

Computer links between law firms are now quite common but the extent of their use between law firms and clients is not known. It is certainly possible, for example, to link a client's own computer to the law firm's computer where compatible for transfer of data in connection with large and repetitive transactions. For example, where a firm's debt recovery department handles several thousand debt recovery matters for a client, a computer link between computers will save time and money as well as reducing the bulk of paperwork and data input time.

Where a firm has the appropriate accounts or case management software, it may offer selected clients the ability to 'view only' directly into the system to obtain direct and up-to-date progress reports.

Tele-conferencing is an emerging piece of communication technology and some firms and sets of chambers are putting it into regular use, which is likely to continue to become more prevalent.

Body language

Relatively recently, it has been recognised as a serious science that the way we move, use and place our bodies is itself a form of communication that can be read and interpreted as a universal language. The client manager who understands the use of body language can both transmit and receive signals, sometimes simple and basic and at other times subtle and sophisticated. Here are a few examples.

The smile

This is perhaps the most potent signal you can send or receive and its meaning is obvious to all. The person that smiles says that he is happy to see you, that he likes you and is glad to be with you. The person being smiled at will be made to feel good and a neutral or hostile client will find it hard not to react positively to a genuine smile. As the Eastern proverb says, 'The smile that you send out always returns to you'.

Eye contact

Have you ever walked in to a shop and been totally ignored by the assistant and made to feel as though you are invisible or, even worse, that you don't exist? Even when you are eventually served, do you feel that you are being given individual treatment or that you are being treated just as another 'punter'? Have you gone into your favourite restaurant and felt that you have really been well looked after? If you reflect on the two experiences, you may find that one of the main differences is that in the shop the assistant did not look at you eye to eye whereas in the restaurant the waiter probably made you feel special by making eye contact and responding to you personally. All sales people are taught to use eye-to-eye contact to communicate more effectively and personally.

In the office, therefore, you should try to look at your client in the eye from time to time, without staring or challenging him. It is a powerful tool and must be used sensitively – used wrongly it can unnerve or even antagonise a person. Look him in the eye to underline or stress an important point you are making or an important piece of advice.

Likewise you can read your client if he does not give you any eye contact. It may indicate that he is unsure, nervous, upset, annoyed, lacking in confidence or a downright crook! In the former cases, you may find that as the meeting progresses and you put your client at ease, the frequency and duration of eye contact may increase. The client manager may wait until this time before moving on to discuss more important or delicate issues.

If you keep looking around the room or staring out of the window as you talk to or listen to your client, he may feel that you are not really interested in him at all.

Seating arrangements

A solicitor sitting behind his desk with the client across at the other side creates a formal and imposing communication situation. The message it gives to a client is, 'I'm the solicitor, I'm in charge, this is my office and it runs under my rules. You sit in that chair and do as you're told. Don't invade my space. I may not trust you. I am safe over here. We are different.' This implied message may be useful in certain situations, particularly with a new or hostile client or when formal business is being transacted. For instance, when a cheque or some deeds and documents or a formal receipt are being handed over, the desk 'barrier' is usually appropriate. Clients, after all, still expect a certain amount of formality from their solicitor. When you get to know your client better, however, or when you move on to less formal business, for example, working together to go through a draft document or statement, then coming around from behind your desk and sitting with the client at a small round table, can be a way of putting a client at ease. It can be used to do just that, to signal that the meeting is moving on to less formal matters or to indicate to the client that you trust him and feel safe with him, that you like him and want to get closer to him.

A desk imposes a barrier and implies a difference, a round table promotes equality, a long narrow board room table connotes distance and unilateral authority and no table or barrier suggests friendliness and informality. Some client interview rooms are furnished with settees and armchairs, which relax and may aid discussion, particularly a strategic or discursive type of interview. They are not appropriate to writing things down or taking formal instructions.

A word about chairs. If your chair is set high and your client is sitting on a chair which is lower than yours so that his eyes are lower than yours, then you have put yourself into a commanding and dominant situation where the client has to look up at you and you look down on him. If your chair is a high-backed, studded, leather swing-chair and your client is given the office stool, the message is obvious. Understanding these things, the client manager will consider what seating arrangements are appropriate before a client arrives.

A nice little touch the client manager uses is to have the right number of chairs in the room for the number of clients or visitors expected. It saves time of rummaging around or raiding neighbouring offices for spare chairs – it also shows the clients that each one of them is expected and important and that you have prepared yourself to meet with them.

The handshake

This is the usual and traditional form of greeting and departure. It is an acceptable form of physical contact that is non-threatening and non-sexist. In the formal setting of a lawyer's office it can also add a nice 'contractual' touch to shake hands as a seal to an agreement or undertaking to do something of importance. It can also be a thank you message. A few tips on handshakes:

1 Don't crush the other person's hand – apart from being painful, it may be seen as a threatening, aggressive, domineering or just plain insensitive gesture.
2 A limp handshake may indicate nonchalance, indifference or lack of strength. If you've just reassured a worried client that you will hound his debtors all the way through the courts, a limp handshake may be at odds with the assurance he needs.
3 One to three shakes appear to be the norm – any longer may embarrass.
4 A clean and well-manicured hand goes without saying.

Posture

Slumped in your chair, arms crossed, feet up on the desk – the message is strong and unimpressive. When you sit upright with a straight back it indicates (and also aids) attention, control and respect. When you lean forward, you indicate particular interest and attention. It also stresses what you are saying as being of particular importance. Crossing your arms may indicate hostility, defensiveness or perhaps boredom and complacency. Leaning on one elbow on the desk may indicate lack of energy and indifference.

Crossing the legs indicates self composure and perhaps some protectionism, double crossing the legs indicates discomfort and perhaps nervous tension. Leaning back in the chair with arms wide open and legs apart indicates either relaxation or trust, or perhaps a complete surrender.

The occasional nod and saying 'Yes' or 'I see' or 'Hmm' encourages the speaker to continue and indicates that you are still listening.

Complete silence on your part may indicate hostility, disagreement or lack of attention. Constant movement, scratching or bending paper clips may indicate nervous energy, discomfort or distraction.

Perhaps the easiest and most effective form of communication by body language is emulation. If you see the person you are talking to adopting the same body posture as yourself, it generally means that the other person is like you, agrees with you or wishes to be like you or to agree with you. By adopting the same posture or movements as the person you are talking to may signal similarities and a common viewpoint.

Body language can be a very precise form of communication but it needs some practice in observation and interpretation. It enables the client manager to send signals as well as read signals that are important in dealing with the client relationship.

Small talk

This is usually done at the beginning and sometimes at the end of a meeting. Its main purpose is to put people at ease but also it is a kind of 'tuning in' to the other person's wavelength. With both new clients and established ones, when you meet you will both have had various experiences that day that will have influenced how you are thinking and seeing the world. Talking about the weather, the traffic, last night's television or football or cricket, apart from being mildly interesting, is done so that you can perceive whether the other person is feeling confident, positive, tired, worried and so on as well as sending signals to him of how you are feeling. Small talk is not a waste of time but an important prelude to communication. The importance of small talk should not be underestimated.

Clients and client management

Client management focuses on the case and on the service from the client's point of view and as such is distinct from and additional to file management and case management. This does not mean that these latter two things are unimportant. The quality of the legal product is more important than ever in an over populated legal profession where excellence has become a vital differentiator. This aspect of quality is what is most apparent to us as lawyers who daily work with the production and delivery of the legal work.

More importantly, what client management recognises and attempts to deal with is that, in addition to producing and delivering a legal product, it is important that the client's perception and input into the service we provide is managed in an effective way. Clients are not just passive receivers of the legal service, they are part of it. The relationship you have with a client, therefore, needs to be understood and managed and two-way communication is the tool.

Action checklist

1 Consider and implement a client partner system in the firm where named partners take overall responsibility for named key clients.
2 Review with partners and case managers and a few clients the format and content of the first interview in order to work out the basic ground work to be covered. Then design and implement a system, perhaps based around the client agreement and the case plan.
3 Ask your clients about how they would like to see improvements in communications.
4 Study body language as an aid to communication.

8 Staff and client management

A people business

A law firm does not produce goods but it does provide services that produce benefits, solutions or welfare for its clients. The nature of this service is that it is delivered by one person or a group of people inside the firm to one or more clients outside the firm. Solicitors are assisted by their staff in delivering a service to their clients. The solicitor gives legal advice and carries out the legal work and he is assisted in doing this by his assistants and trainee solicitor to whom he delegates the routine aspects of the case management; by the secretary or group paralegals who produce letters, documentation and the routine paperwork; by the receptionist who receives visitors when they arrive; by the telephonist who talks, albeit briefly, to all the clients of the firm and often on more than one occasion; by the cashier who records and analyses the financial transactions in the case and who may deliver the bill and chase and collect the bill payment; and by the archivist who stores the file after the case management has been completed and who is responsible for retrieving it quickly when the client requires it, to name but a few.

Clients perceive our work as providing benefits for them rather than as the functional and procedural aspect of the work that we inside the firm see. Clients rate what we achieve for them, not what we do. The complete legal service is about one person or group of people providing services and benefits to other people. It's not only about lots of legally trained and competent people beavering away on internal systems, processes or legal work. It's about what the client perceives to be the benefits and satisfaction that the people in the firm, who are the firm, produce to him. In short, it's a people business. Recognising this, it is a principle of client management to prepare and train all the people in the firm to be aware of client perception and satisfaction, to be trained in the ways of achieving and promoting client satisfaction and to be able to innovate and be flexible in the ways of dealing with the clients with all this in mind. It may sound idealistic but it's only a matter of getting the people in the firm to see themselves from the client's point of view: from this all else will flow.

In a people business, therefore, it is just not possible to create and develop a client-focused and client management culture without also creating and developing a staff-focused and staff management culture. A firm can't realistically talk about the importance of client perception without also being aware of the importance of staff perception. If it espouses the principles of client management, it will not be supported by its staff unless it applies similar treatment to them in ways which demonstrate that it understands, values and respects them and wishes to make or keep them involved, committed and satisfied in the work they do with its clients.

Staff management

A leading law firm management consultant said on his visit to my own firm in 1991 that the management of staff in a law firm is more important than the management of its finance (John Loosemore of LPS Lawyers Planning Services). Client-oriented firms understand that all impressions formed by their clients about the people in the firm are potentially important and they take care to ensure that these impressions are managed as far as possible so as to project and reinforce the objectives and profile that the firm wants to convey to its clients. They treat every contact with the client as a moment of truth. They understand that these moments of truth occur not only when the solicitor sits face-to-face with his client giving legal advice, but that they also occur on the 101 other occasions where the client has contact with other members of the firm. As the client sits in reception, the receptionist *is* the firm. The office junior idly chatting in the lift as he arrives *is* the firm. *You* are the firm. The cashier who chases the bill for payment *is* the firm. Whatever impression is made will last in the client's mind until it is changed by a more positive or negative impression. This is why every member of the firm is important in the client's perception of the firm. Every member of the firm, or the group or the team has a part to play in creating and reinforcing the overall impression you wish to make on the client.

The need to retain, develop and attract quality staff cannot be overestimated. The huge cost, both direct and indirect, incurred in staff turnover, in the loss of productivity in losing and retraining people, and in having under-productive and under-developed staff is substantial in proportion to bills delivered and the turnover of the firm.

A principal objective of every client-focused law firm should, therefore, be to encourage and develop a highly motivated, technically competent, efficient, effective, enthusiastic and client-oriented workforce of people in order to increase productivity, the return on the investment in salaries and training and to increase client satisfaction. Figures on staff morale should feature in the monthly staff report. Firms will need to have reports on human resource management dealing with the cost effectiveness and management of the people in the firm.

Client management is not itself principally about staff motivation and management which is too big a subject to be covered within the scope of this book. What it is sufficient to say is that good staff and people management which produces highly motivated people will have a very substantial and beneficial effect on client management and, therefore, on both turnover and profitability.

Client management, like staff management, deals with people and their perceptions. Both the client relationship and the staff relationship each involve two parties who interact to create benefits for the other. It is axiomatic, therefore, that an understanding of the other person's requirements is necessary to produce a successful relationship. Client managers and the members of the firm must also enjoy a managed relationship with the firm in order that they can be more effective in their management of the firm's relationship with its clients.

The firm is its people

One of your most important clients is waiting in reception, having arrived a few minutes early for his appointment. As he glances through the daily newspaper, he can't help overhearing the receptionist complaining to one of the secretaries loitering by the photocopying machine about the lack of a pay rise from the firm this year. What they say about management and the firm is not flattering. Their complaints are interrupted by a telephone call from what sounds to be an irate client. The receptionist is clearly unable to deal with it adequately. Your important client is all ears behind your newspaper. Neither of these incidents will make a positive impression on your client. He almost certainly will not mention it to you but may have formed the impression that your firm is one which may be in financial difficulties, which does not deal adequately with complaints, which makes mistakes and which does not pay enough attention to the client or its staff. It may affect his decision in referring further work to you. You may be blissfully unaware of this and if your client seems to become dissatisfied, you may worry, incorrectly, that it is due to the quality of your legal work.

At his next appointment at your office, another legal secretary passes through reception and, noticing your client, she goes over to him and says, 'Hello, Mr Carstone, how are you?' He remembers that she was part of the team working with the commercial partner that dealt with Mr Carstone's successful management buy-out of his company six months earlier. The team had worked long and hard together in order to achieve the deal which has put him and his fellow senior managers in control of the company which is now being turned around from a loss making situation to one which will at least break-even this year and looks set fair to be in the black next year. Many positive memories and impressions come back as he is taken through to see you on time. You are unaware of his encounter with your secretary, but you notice that he seems to be in a very warm and constructive frame of mind.

These two different incidents may give out mixed messages to a client about the people in the firm. Some may undermine the positive impressions that you have worked on for so long to create and maintain and the others may build them up again. You may never be aware of all the impressions and perceptions that form in your client's mind but you should be aware that they do occur and that they do affect the client's view of your firm. To the client, the people in your firm *are* your firm. He takes your legal competence for granted. He takes for granted that you have computers to get his bills right. He takes for granted that you have reasonably pleasant offices. What is variable and what he perceives most and what he does not take for granted is the way he is treated as a client by you and by your staff when you are not around.

Client management achieves the breakthrough when the sum of the perceived parts exceeds the whole. This is the synergy that an effective client management programme can deliver when everyone is involved with the client.

Management styles

What kind of staff manager are you? What style of staff management does the firm adopt? There is a correlation between the client and staff management cultures of the firm.

Hierarchical

This is the traditional 'boss and secretary' style where the solicitor sees the clients, writes the letters, dictates the notes, does the legal work, goes to court, etc. The secretary and other support staff are there to type letters, keep the diary, make tea, do the filing and answer the telephone. They are not expected to have any impact on the client – their relationship with the client, if any, is at best seen by the hierarchical firm managers as neutral. However, many of our secretarial and support staff are both able and willing to do more and to get more involved with the clients with the right encouragement and training. The hierarchical work style in these situations can be expensive, inefficient and under-productive.

Democratic

There is also the solicitor who reluctantly finds that he has a staff management role thrust upon him. He has no feeling at all for the old fashioned boss/secretary role and is always upfront about everything with his staff. He frequently, though irregularly, calls for meetings 'of everyone' to discuss issues ranging from the thickness of photocopying paper to the holiday chart in the staff room. He encourages people to talk and takes notes or minutes. He means well but somehow it doesn't seem to keep people happy. His meetings generally start with suspicion from staff who wonder about 'the hidden agenda'. When at last someone does speak, it tends to be a request for more pay or better facilities. Decisions are difficult because there are so many different views and opinions. This results in either no decisions being taken or compromise decisions being taken or the 'boss' having to take a decision to overrule the meeting, showing himself up to be a dictator disguised as a democrat. 'You just can't win!' he exclaims.

Consultative

This is the management style of the group partner who holds a 10-minute 'briefing' session with all his group staff every morning at 9 am. He discusses the post, checks diary commitments and agrees priorities. He holds a regular weekly meeting of 20 minutes with all group staff to listen to information on clients and progress of major cases, and he gives out information about the firm. His monthly meetings take one hour and he goes through performance figures and clients' satisfaction reports and discusses problems and ways of improvement. All people in the group must be present because all must understand what each other does. On specific matters the group partner will mention a proposal and ask for comments. He will not say, 'Who's to blame for these complaints we are getting?' but rather, 'Let's go through these complaints and comments from clients received over the last few weeks. This sort of feedback tells us what some clients feel about our service. It's variable, most of our clients are delighted with what we do for them, but one or two are not. We need to keep up our standards. The firm has approved a client management plan which involves everyone on the firm. It also includes the use of client questionnaires. This is a sample. If you were a client, what would you think of this questionnaire? I propose that we try it out on a few clients and check their responses. Can you let me have a list of say 20 clients by lunchtime?'

Here the group partner remains in control and by asking his staff their views and by explaining why it's important and how they are all involved in doing this important task, he will achieve a greater degree of success than merely by imposing it from on high.

Job descriptions

All members of staff must know what the aims and objectives of the firm are and what their part is in it and what they can do to promote and reinforce those objectives. Noone in the firm should have the question 'Why am I here?' left unanswered. All staff should have a job description and this should contain some statement and reference that shows how that person or job holder is involved in the process of client satisfaction. Everyone's job description must show a link between the job holder and the client by showing how that person's job is designed to increase not only the efficiency and productivity of the firm, but also how that person's work is designed to increase client satisfaction, directly or indirectly.

The following job descriptions, for example, might include the following.

JOB DESCRIPTION – Word Processing Operator

To produce accurate, legible and attractive letters, reports, documents and other written material in response to client demand and their case managers and so help to project and reinforce the image of the firm as one which cares about its clients and which produces high quality written material and documents, etc ...

JOB DESCRIPTION – Office Junior

To assist case managers in carrying out the various administrative and support tasks in serving the interests of the firm's clients and which will ensure that the clients are satisfied with the work of the firm. You will be responsible to ( ) and do this by ...

JOB DESCRIPTION – Assistant Solicitor

To assist the partners in providing their clients with a quality legal service which complies with agreed specifications and which meets or exceeds the client's identified expectations and at a cost which the client will perceive as representing value for money. You will be responsible to ( ) as your group partner and you will do this by ...

Every member of staff must be involved in helping to satisfy the needs, requirements and expectations of the firm's clients, each must know what his part in this process is and by information, communication and annual appraisals each person must know how well the firm as a whole and the member of staff in particular has performed in achieving these objectives.

This culture can only emanate from what is actually done and by example. Statements of commitment to staff and client culture are not enough. The firm can demonstrate this by encouraging and rewarding the people in the firm who put effort and commitment into achieving measured levels of client satisfaction. You can involve the people in the firm in thinking about clients by asking them:

1 who are our clients?
2 where do our clients come from?
3 why do our clients come to us and not another firm?
4 what do our clients want and expect from us?
5 when do they need and expect it?
6 how can we ensure that we satisfy our clients in all this?

You and your staff can discuss how you can build these things into the daily work routine of the group and into the case and file management activities of the group.

Staff – overheads or assets?

Sir Robin Ibbs, Chairman of Lloyd's Bank, said at the Conference of the British Chambers of Commerce in Aberdeen in May 1995 that the competitiveness of a business depends on three things:

1 the talent and ability of its people;
2 their self-belief; and
3 their willingness to train, improve and be flexible.

In these days of costs cutting and overhead watching, more often than not the first costs to be cut are staff costs. Much valuable experience can thereby be lost to the firm. It has been calculated that in most businesses staff work at a productivity rate of only 40%. It is true that this rate rises a little where staff numbers are cut because the same amount of work has to be done by less people but it rises far more significantly where staff members are encouraged to be more involved in the work of the firm and are treated as valuable members of the team.

Competition makes it necessary for a business to be inventive, committed and industrious. The old ways will lead only to decline and ultimate failure. 'You ain't seen nothin' yet!' said Sir Robin. 'Change, innovation and training are gradually becoming embedded into management thinking. Pay increases must be earned by performance and jobs for life are gone. The keynotes now are: better products, better service and better value.' The people in the firm are the key to business performance with payment of best rates and performance related pay, training in customer services and product knowledge, responsibility and flexible working. 'We give more attention to our people than ever before and it's paying off', said Sir Robin.

The people in the firm are the key players in increasing service performance and therefore, staff management should become a key strategic objective of the firm.

The management of group staff

Tom Peters (*The New Masters of Excellence*) tells the story about the manager who thinks that his staff are great, that he could not find a better bunch of people to work with and that there is nothing he would not trust them with. He tells us also about the manager in the same company who thinks that his staff are no good, lazy and intent only on robbing him. Tom Peters says that both managers are right! How good or bad your staff are depends on how you treat them. If you distrust or dislike them, don't expect them to give you their best efforts. They will do enough by 'sufficing' in the workplace, doing nothing exceptional but also doing nothing overtly wrong. They will provide only average productivity. On the other hand, if you treat them well, if you value and respect their actual or potential contribution, if you consult them for their views before committing to a new course of action, giving credit where deserved, using mistakes as a learning experience, encouraging them to take some responsibility and recognising their individual contribution to the overall satisfaction of the client and the success of the firm, they will respond even more and the overall productivity of the group will rise substantially. Good staff management is good production management which leads also to good client management.

It's up to the group partner at a local level and how he wants to make it. He will set the tone and the work culture. He gets what he sets, no more and no less. If the firm's staff are under productive, it's because the firm, its managers, culture, systems and organisational structure makes it difficult for them to be otherwise. It's rarely due to a lack of individual ability of the staff. If your staff see that you are prepared to recognise and reward hard work, initiative, innovation and enthusiasm, then you will get hard work, initiative, innovation and enthusiasm. If they see that you stifle or discourage these things, if you jump on initiative, criticise new ideas, blame staff and pour scorn on innovation, then your staff will close up and 'switch off' at work. It's up to both central management and the group partner to create the atmosphere to get everyone at work to 'switch on'. Client management is one way of harnessing that innate ability and enthusiasm and converting hitherto untapped potential into increased client satisfaction and productivity.

People – the first resource

Anne Minto, Deputy Director General of the Engineering Employers Federation, at the BCC Conference in Aberdeen in May 1995, said that dealing with 'people' issues is now a key business strategy. The old, paternalistic ways of management doing all the thinking and then telling staff what to do and then measuring and controlling them to ensure compliance is no good any more – it's inefficient, ineffective and expensive to treat people like that. Control must give way to empowerment, enablement direction and coaching.

Empowerment means the encouragement of all staff to contribute, to become more involved with client satisfaction, to be better trained in product quality and service quality and client satisfaction, with better delegation and coaching and by working in teams being empowered to make decisions. Product innovation, staff empowerment and client service innovation should become the leading strategies in increasing the competitive strength of the firm. In order to achieve this, Anne Minto said that we need to recognise the following:

1 managers need to be trained in a whole range of new skills;
2 we need to change more quickly;
3 best practice yields profit performance; and that
4 leading businesses are those which adopt leading practices.

Applied to law firms this means:

1 group partners need to be trained to manage the financial performance of the group;
2 group partners need to be able to respond quickly and directly to client and market conditions;
3 group partners should manage the quality of case management within their groups; and
4 group partners get what they set.

In addition to technical skills, initiative, creativity, adaptability, responsibility and customer service skills are the key attributes that people in the business should be encouraged to develop. Staff alignment is vital for business success so that all of your staff should know and understand the firm's objectives and mission statement and how what they do as an individual or as a team member fits into the overall strategic development of the firm. Everyone in the firm must be able to state clearly and with confidence the answers to these questions:

1 'Why are you here?'
2 'What is it that you do and could do to help improve client satisfaction and the profitability of the firm?'

Training of staff is the single most important factor in improving the competitiveness of your business. Retraining, up-skilling, cross and multi-skilling are vital, not only in legal matters but also in client management and inter-personal skills.

John Monks, the General Secretary of the TUC, also a speaker at the BCC Conference, said that although many businesses are now saying, 'Staff are our greatest asset' and, 'People come first', many may be challenged to say what they are actually doing about it. 'People are not the company's best asset – they *are* the company' he said. The 'feel-bad' factor resides principally in the feelings of job insecurity and poor communications which staff perceive existing within their companies.

Leading edge firms have good communications and good staff relations. You will improve your competitiveness by recognising and rewarding each person's contribution to the success of the business. Businesses must replace the 'us and them' culture with a 'stakeholder' culture where the business recognises that its staff, who derive their means of support and job satisfaction in their working life from the company, do have a valid interest in the success of the company. We must replace the old control-based staff management styles with mutual value, trust and respect. The company is a community of interests and not just the preserve of the directors, shareholders or partners to do with it as they will. Staff, suppliers and customers also have legitimate stakeholder interests in the company or firm.

Ed Gillespie, General Manager of ARJO Wiggins Fine Paper, also a BCC Conference speaker, said that technology will only give a business a short-term advantage and that the real and lasting competitive advantage of a business will come from the quality of its people. In a client-driven age, technology only distances a business from its clients. We need to be driven by 'customisation' where the specific requirements of the individual customer are catered for. Customisation requires listening and response. The 1,001 moments of truth occur at every point of contact between a client and the members of the firm, because to your customer, you and your staff *are* the firm.

By 2001, demographic changes will force major changes in the workplace with more managers, fewer semi-skilled workers and fewer people in the 18–34 age band. Innovation is the key but where is innovation being taught and encouraged? Does the traditionally-run law firm encourage creativity? Where there is staff empowerment, however, orders become directions, control is replaced by leadership and teaching is replaced by coaching. The real competitive differentiation of the law firm will come from its people. People are different. It is people who add value by getting involved and by getting close to clients. 'If your workforce are not with you 100%, you will not achieve your targets, let alone exceed them', said Anne Minto. In order to keep good people, you must create the environment to make the right people want to stay.

Staff performance

Just coming into the office and doing the same old work routine from 9–5 without measurement, tasking or achievement may suit some people but for many others this style of work does not excite or energise. If you give someone a special task or responsibility then the pulse rate will quicken and performance and job satisfaction will increase. In order to achieve optimum productivity, each member of a law firm needs to be directed towards performance and results rather than just carrying out a process.

If noone seems bothered one way or the other what a person does, good or bad, if noone notices what you do, if there is no publicity or openness about the results of your work, then why bother? It has been estimated that only one person in 100 achieves his full potential without some form of measurement being applied.

One of the roles of the group partner and the managing partner is to develop a culture of empowerment, responsibility and reward that will enable a person to do his job to the best result, rather than just doing his job. Measurement linked to result and reward is fundamental to any successful business. This must be accompanied with open communication so that people can know what is expected of them and how well they and the firm are doing.

Measures of client service performance applied to an individual or a group might include:

1 the number of new clients per month, actual and target;
2 the number of lost clients per month with a brief report of the 'exit interview';
3 numbers of complaints per month with details;
4 the amount of written-off chargeable work in progress might indicate low perceived service benefits and consequent defensive underbilling;
5 quotation and tenders success rates;
6 aged debtors and poor recovery times may indicate service problems;
7 repeat work and introductions measures from existing clients may give some indication of service and client satisfaction ratings and performance;
8 client satisfaction reports and ratings;
9 late completions (deliveries), missed key dates and case plan overruns may indicate low staff morale; and
10 the number of recommendations and referrals per month.

Knowing what to measure and how to measure it, preparing the report and then getting the members of the firm to respond to it is part of the art of client and staff management which go together in this context. For example, rather than just coping with complaints, try looking for root causes and try to spot problem areas and trends and then discuss with the people concerned the appropriate remedial and avoidance measures and then implement and check for success over a period of time.

By agreeing, setting and then measuring and reporting on specific areas of performance, the firm gives an important signal to all members of the firm about the things it considers to be important and what should be done about it. As in the case of complaints, if they are measured and analysed, discussed and dealt with and then remedial measures are put in place, the people in the firm will realise that complaints are taken seriously, that client satisfaction really is important to the firm and that the firm does really care about its clients and their perceptions. If a firm only or primarily measures performance in terms of billing and time recording, without any measures of client satisfaction, then the implied message to staff is that client satisfaction is unimportant or less important or peripheral to the real work of time recording and billing. Job satisfaction will never rise substantially without some qualitative targets and measures of performance. If we don't measure it and only talk about it, the signals we give out are that it isn't really that important at all and that we couldn't care whether a client is satisfied or not. By measuring and reporting we signal priorities and values, which is reinforced further when linked to salary and compensation. These measures underline the cultural priorities of the business.

In the ultimate analysis, it comes down to how we see ourselves. If we see our work as lying in the file of papers and nowhere else, then we will have customers rather than clients and charge at time rates only. If we see our work in terms of client satisfaction, welfare of clients and the identification and provision of benefits, then that is our work and our productivity may be measured in value rather than in time. The general move away from the billable hour to fixed price or value billing that is already happening is evidence of this.

Motivation, morale and reward

Maslow's classic definition of motivators shows that people are not motivated primarily by money. The basic motivators of human life are food, clothing and shelter. If we are hungry, then food tends to dominate our thoughts and actions until such time as the pangs of hunger are assuaged. We can't do anything else until we have tended to this basic human need. Once we have eaten, we need to ensure that we are warmly and decently clothed. Fashion doesn't come into it if you are in an extreme of climate – in the Arctic you just don't care what you look like as long as you are warm and dry. You also need a place to live, where you can rest and enjoy some privacy.

Having secured these three basic human motivators of food, warmth and shelter, you then look for something worthwhile, interesting, fulfilling or challenging to do. You seek fulfilment and reward. This is partly why people come to work, not only for the income it produces to provide for our basic needs but also with the expectation that the work might also be interesting and possibly that it will help them to express something of themselves and find some fulfilment. As long as the salary is set at the market rate for the job, a person at work will seek to express himself and find fulfilment, as well as the wish to work with others in developing some bond of mutual achievement in team work.

Leadership, direction, communication, involvement and reward will do more to motivate the members of the firm and increase their overall morale, efficiency, effectiveness and productivity than any written office manual. Measurement promotes improvement by:

1 setting the culture;
2 focusing on key activities;
3 setting values;
4 focusing on results rather than processes;
5 setting goals and monitoring trends;
6 increasing job satisfaction;
7 increasing morale; and
8 indicating acceptable levels of performance.

The adage that 'what gets measured gets done' is exceeded only by 'what gets measured, recognised and rewarded gets done better'.

Departments, groups and teamwork

The traditional departmental structure in law firms was designed for the production of the work that lawyers undertook. Client managers design the structure of their firms around the clients and the benefits to be provided for clients. For example, a firm might decide to evolve from the old functional departments into just two client-based departments: business client and private client, each containing lawyers with the range of specialist skills, including contentious and non-contentious skills, required by that particular client type. Multi-skilled and multi-tasked client-based groups are the way of client management. In some firms with key clients of sufficient magnitude, groups could form around particular key clients, serving all their legal needs, with the client partner in overall control of both contentious and non-contentious work.

What is necessary is that we should organise ourselves in ways driven by the client instead of only our own internal and functional needs. The old way was designed around technical, functional skills which inhibited cross-selling because each group or department had its own type of work and style of service. The regular client of one partner often experienced a a different style or level of service when exposed to another department or group. This was the antithesis of putting the client first – it was putting the client last, or even worse, not even thinking of putting the client anywhere at all! It might happen that the people and even partners in one department did not really know what the other departments did. People gave their loyalties to their functional work group rather than to the firm as a whole or to the clients of the firm generally.

These traditional ways can now be perceived to impose restrictions on developing an active client management programme and culture that concentrates on putting the client, and not just their function or the firm, first. The firms that recognise that the emphasis has moved towards clients have begun to structure themselves into groups or teams which can supply the full range of legal services that their clients require. For example, the company and commercial department may call itself the 'business client department' and it will include people working with one, two or more lead partners supervising the litigation, property, company and commercial services for the business client. Litigators, conveyancers and commercial lawyers join together to work in a team for the benefit of the client type. Whatever the client's needs, they will be met by that group. Even where a one-off service that is outside the business client department's normal range can be dealt with in that group by temporary secondment or improved and effective delegation practices. What is cardinal is that the business client must maintain throughout the contact with the client partner he is accustomed to and he must not be exposed solely to the different, though no doubt equally competent legal work of a different partner, group or department. The client partner will retain overall responsibility to the key client for all legal products and services, even to the extent of the lead partner himself instructing the other department and becoming the client himself, perhaps with internal billing.

It means replacing the old 'function-based' approach with a new 'client-', 'group-' and 'people-' based approach. This will ensure that a client is presented with a consistent quality of service and a consistent quality of product for all his legal requirements. It does not mean doing work that you are not skilled in doing. It means using the person with the best functional skill for the legal product that the particular client wants with the difference that he is managed by the lead or client partner and is presented to the client by the person with the best client skills for that particular client.

This approach rejoices under the name of 'the trampoline' where a number of people with different skills all metaphorically bounce up and down together and are projected ever higher by the efforts of their co-trampoliners. This is what is meant by client and staff focus, where the grouping of people and skills is made to increase the overall group value as perceived by the client. It is also a supporting structure for those on it and thus is more natural than the old skill-based groupings. Whereas the old skill-based departments were helpless when faced with a problem outside their normal scope of work necessitating them seeking help 'from elsewhere', the new people based multi-disciplinary groups are stronger and more self sufficient.

These client-based groups will become formal and permanent groups and will be separately monitored as their own profit and cost centres. They will have a permanent 'core' of staff and partners. They will produce their own business plans and budgets. The members of the group will all share in group bonuses for exceeding agreed targets.

Lip service is the main enemy of client orientation because people tend inexorably to carry on as before, no matter how enlightened their avowed thinking becomes. People may leave the partners' annual conference enthused by the new client management philosophy saying, 'Yes, there really is a lot to be said for all this new client management stuff, but I must rush back to my office to prepare for court tomorrow.' People will tend to revert to the familiar functional activities rather than start upon the new client-focused activities. This is why a structural change with the client in mind will enable a firm to start to realign itself as a client-focused organisation. The implementation of a client-focused structure requires the simultaneous dismantling of the old skill-based groupings within the firm. It is often only by moving people around that you will get anything to move at all.

Staff involvement

It is vitally important for business and the bottom line that a firm should develop a culture and ethos that encourages people to come forward with ideas and suggestions in the confidence that they will be listened to. Lawyers have been prone to be dismissive about things and ideas that have not been done before. This is an inherent weakness for a business in a changing market economy. New ideas can first be tried out on a limited basis. If it's a disaster, no great harm will have been done. If it works, then there will be scope for more extensive use. For example, a suggestion might be made by the members of staff as follows:

We have made a comparison between the client care methods employed by the firm and those of two other firms and the following possibilities arose from our research which would be practical and relatively inexpensive to implement:

1 fresh flowers in reception areas;
2 improve the firm's brochure with colour and legible print;
3 place pencils, pens and firm's notepads in the boardroom for use of clients;
4 place daily newspapers and current magazines in the reception area;
5 hold social evenings with clients in the boardroom;
6 improve decor of areas that are open to clients;
7 place attractive display units for brochures and leaflets in the reception area;
8 place attractive and clear signs directing clients and visitors to the reception area from the lifts;
9 provide coffee, tea and biscuits in the reception area for waiting clients; and
10 escort clients to and from meeting rooms.

These are all simple and obvious things in client care but may be easily overlooked by those who see the firm only from the inside or who have stopped 'seeing' it at all anymore. The point in doing these things is to show that the firm thinks about and pays attention to the little things as well as the big things. No matter how wonderfully you are able to conduct the first interview and get the relationship off to a flying start, no matter how brilliant your legal advice, drafting or forensic skills, if your client has been kept waiting in a grubby reception area that has made no concession to human comfort, then you will be starting off with a disadvantage. If after conducting a brilliant first meeting, your client visits your unlit toilets (who is responsible for replacing light fittings?), or gets lost trying to find the lift, or has not been offered a coffee all morning, his impression of the firm will be affected, if not tarnished, by these impressions, impressions of which you may remain blissfully unaware.

This is why client care from members of the firm is important – the 1,001 little things done a little better all add up to the big message of whether or not the firm pays attention to the views of its clients. Client care opportunities suggested by members of the firm can provide many easy and inexpensive ways of reinforcing the vital message that you are trying to project to your clients – that you care and that you understand and that you are doing something about it.

Who manages your intangibles?

One of the main difficulties of coming to terms with client management is that it may all seem so vague and imprecise at first. When a busy solicitor looks up from his files for a couple of minutes, if you mention client perception, the client experience or the service intangibles, you may see his eyes glaze over, a worried look may appear on his face and he will dive back into his files as quickly as possible, noting with some concern your weakening grip on the real world. To the lawyer in action, the real world of law is about law files, contracts, meetings, court attendances and completions, not all this airy fairy nonsense about 'intangibles'. However, unbeknown to him his client may be waiting and wondering what is happening, why hasn't he heard anything? Is nothing happening? The intangible of client perception is busily at work all the time whether we know about it or not.

Whilst you're beavering away on the files, your secretary may be explaining to your client on the telephone why you can't see him before next Thursday, the receptionist may be keeping her waiting because she didn't make an appointment, or your office junior may be chatting to her in the lift. Maybe your key client is in another department with another solicitor who is busy, but unintentionally, wrecking the client relationship you have worked so long and hard to build up with your key client. So whilst you are busy doing your legal work, others may be busy (or not) creating other impressions in the mind of your client. In order to ensure that these intangibles are managed positively, it is essential that all who work in the firm are imbued with the same client focus. This means a high degree of communication and awareness of the importance of the client and client perception.

The word 'intangible' does not mean unimportant. What is not real to one person may be very real to the client. Being aware of and recognising the importance of and then trying to manage the service intangibles is part of the task of client management.

Client action teams

If you're really serious about putting clients first, why not invite some clients into your offices to meet you and your staff and discuss their service expectations and the client satisfaction measures that you are doing or proposing to do? A short client/staff session could be structured as follows:

1   invite five to 10 clients;
2   open with a short address about feedback from client question-naires and surveys and outline the client care and client manage-ment measures and initiatives being taken in response by the firm;
3   invite clients to complete a simple client service questionnaire;
4   open up for discussion and comment;
5   keep it general and don't get involved in individual cases;
6   note what clients say they like or dislike; and
7   follow with a buffet lunch and mix with staff.

A regular monthly session like this with a sample of clients would soon put the firm or the group in touch with real rather than assumed client perception. It would also involve your staff and so give the initiative some new energy and meaning. After each session you should hold a feedback discussion to identify problems and solutions. For example, it may go like this:

'Mr A said he often had difficulty getting through on the telephone – all the lines seemed to be engaged.'

'Yes, Mrs B said that as well. She also said that she is often kept waiting for a call to be switched through and doesn't know whether she's been forgotten or abandoned!'

After some investigation, the firm might decide to increase the number of lines, or perhaps offer direct dialling to case managers, avoiding the use of the switchboard altogether. This saves time for clients and reduces congestion at the switchboard. Other remarks might include:

'When I first came to your office, it took me 20 minutes to find a car parking space.' (Consider the cost/benefit of providing client car parking spaces.)

'I had to wait a week for my appointment.' (Consider staff ratios, delegation and time management. Consider adopting a Client Charter Statement such as, 'Appointments within two working days guaranteed'.)

'I was surprised that you weren't open on Saturdays – everyone else is!' (Consider Saturday opening, clinics, staff rotas, and supplying home telephone numbers to clients.)

'I don't know who to contact if Mr A is not there.' (Consider whether you are fully complying with Rule 15 and telling the client who to contact in your absence. Try using the case plan and client agreement.)

The client action team could make a report on client feedback together with proposals for new service initiatives and, once approved, could monitor whether or not the new systems are successful.

The use of a client action team will not only impress your clients by your willingness to listen and to do something about it, but it will also encourage your staff that you mean business with your clients by involving more people in the firm. You will be amazed to see potential being unlocked that you never suspected was there.

It was reported in the first issue of *News from Lloyd's Bank*, the bank's own newsletter to clients, that the bank had introduced customer panels to obtain feedback directly from clients. They wanted to know what customers wanted and liked or disliked. The initial results were encouraging with the view, 'Who better than our customers to tell us how we can improve our service?' A law firm could well consider instituting similar ways of regularly obtaining client feedback to improve its service systems.

Quality circles

Most people work in small groups of two to four people. It is quite possible that a client visiting your office could meet and speak to the office junior, someone from the word processing or accounts department, possibly asking for directions from the lift. It is important that all staff are informed and enthusiastic about client service as well as being trained to use every moment of contact or exposure to the clients in a positive and proactive way to project and underline the firm's overall care and understanding of the client.

How, for example, can the new office junior 'project and underline' the firm's client care philosophy to a client in a random encounter? The junior could go a long way to destroying it by careless gossip in the lift if he is overheard by the client. He as well as the receptionist should be included in a client management circle.

The 'quality circle' is a regular meeting of all people in the group which will discuss targets, performance and complaints, looks for ways of doing thinks better and agrees its own group implementation plan, all within the overall objectives of the firm. It is one of the main engine houses of change and improvement at client level because it involves the group who work directly with clients. Here people can see and experience directly the results and affect of their work with clients, whether it satisfies the client or not.

Human relations skills

When a firm actually starts to hold regular meetings with its clients to discuss and receive comments on service, then that firm is demonstrably one which is trying to get closer to its clients, which listens to its clients and which attaches great importance to client perception. If a firm also discusses proposed actions, remedial work, new services and proposed service improvements with its clients and then actually does something about it, then that firm will be increasingly able to match what it does with client requirements, to meet or exceed client expectation and so to achieve the overall objective of total client satisfaction.

The very process itself of inviting a few clients to give their opinions will in itself be hugely beneficial both for the clients' perception of the firm, which the client will perceive as a firm which cares about client's views, takes them seriously and does something about it, and also for you in your businesses where partners and staff will in various ways be involved in this new, exciting and valuable new way of talking to clients.

Clients will be seen by you and your staff no longer as people who just sit in reception and then in your offices, to whom we write letters, send bills and chase for payment. They will also be seen increasingly as people who are integral to your business, as people who are part of and not external to your business, as people who have an impact on how your business is shaped and how and what services you provide.

Lee Iaccoca, formerly President of Chrysler, was trained as an engineer but admits that the most valuable and useful training course he ever attended was an optional part of his degree course dealing with human relations skills. He said that most of the engineering students skipped this course, thinking that it was too vague and had no relevance to a career in engineering. His subsequent meteoric rise to become President of Chrysler is evidence of the importance of human relations skills. Training in people skills is fundamental to whatever career is taken because we can only reach our full potential by working with and through others.

Staff and associates

Given that staff play a crucial role in the delivery of client satisfaction and that as far as the clients are concerned, the staff are the firm, then we should give tangible recognition to this by looking at our staff as members of the firm or associates rather than just as employees. Certainly, all frontline staff would be worthy of this appellation and as we have seen that support staff also have job descriptions linked to client satisfaction, then they too should receive similar treatment. All associates should be named at each office, supplied with a business card describing them as such, for example:

```
┌─────────────────────────────────┐
│     JARNDYCE & JARNDYCE         │
│          Solicitors              │
│                                  │
│        Antonia Jobling           │
│        Word Processing           │
│     and Client Documentation     │
└─────────────────────────────────┘
```

Staff empowerment

Staff empowerment is not some anarchistic or revolutionary call to overthrow management. Rather it is about ensuring through active staff management that everyone in the firm has the ability and resources to work and perform and achieve results more efficiently and more effectively. It ensures that the investment in staff salaries and training costs becomes more beneficial to the firm. It does mean a move away from the traditional hierarchical control management styles to a more directive, coaching, consultative and team-based style of management. The maximisation of the client abilities and productivity of every member of staff is a challenge that will have a dramatic affect on the bottom line.

The key to staff empowerment lies first in the underlying culture of the firm and in staff training. Unless the ambient culture in the firm is one which recognises and encourages staff development and client orientation, then any proposals to develop staff in client management and staff empowerment will not be as fully effective as they could be.

Staff and client management

The days when clients were reserved for partners only have become too costly too maintain. Staff costs have risen but so have staff skills. The days when a productive solicitor could boast, 'I am able to keep two-and-a-half typists busy!' are gone, forced out by the cost of employment and the development of information and technology support. As all group members including partners and solicitors develop keyboard and information and technology skills, the traditional role of the secretary will be replaced by that of the paralegal. The need for word processor and typing support is being supplemented by the need for assistance in group work to satisfy the needs of clients. Instead of 'Word Processor Operator Required' we will be asking for 'Assistance required by the Business Client Group in servicing the legal requirements of a wide range of business clients. Must have keyboard skills and be adaptable and have or be prepared to acquire personal presentation and client support service skills which will be provided by the group. Legal experience is preferred, but training will be given.' Instead of 'Assistant Solicitor Required' we will see, 'Client and Case Manager required to service and develop the existing and prospective clients of the firm. High client satisfaction ratings required. Marketing and client management skills preferred. Must also be a qualified solicitor'.

Staff costs being high relative to available profit margins, the accent will be for added-value support staff. People work better in teams and client satisfaction, productivity and learning rates rise dramatically when teams work together with regular and open communications.

Client management is driven by the people in the firm, including client partners, case managers and support staff. A firm should invest time and resource in staff management as a strategic policy, because without it, client management will not be able to be fully developed to its potential.

Action checklist

1 Conduct an internal staff survey to assess the current state of staff morale.
2 Review the firm's staff management policy as appropriate.
3 Consider the implementation of 'investors in people'.
4 Consider introducing a compensation system linked partly to performance and achievement.
5 Consider the introduction of work groups and quality circles.
6 Consider the appointment of a marketing and client services manager.
7 Review for possible improvement the internal communications systems in the firm.

9 Marketing and client management

What is marketing?

The marketing orientation of a business has been described by Yallop Marketing as follows:

We make our profits by creating opportunities to more effectively satisfy our clients' needs within the constraints of our resources.

A market-oriented business should start by researching its markets and competitors and then design its products and services in accordance with the information gathered from that research. The business will then deliver its products and services more effectively to its customers and so achieve growth in turnover.

The Institute of Marketing defines marketing as:

... the management function which organises and directs all those business activities involved in assessing and converting customer purchasing power into effective demand for a specific product or service and moving the product or service to the final consumer so as to achieve the profit target or other objectives of the company.

This is a particularly interesting definition because it breaks down marketing activity into several parts as follows:

1 it requires market research to assess the potential demand for the product or service;
2 it requires actions to persuade potential customers to demand a product or service;
3 it deals with the delivery of the product or service to the customer; and
4 it defines these marketing activities as being linked to and motivated towards achieving the profit targets or other objectives of the company.

The definition does not deal specifically with the production of the product or service or with the nature or quality of the product or service itself. Such a definition of marketing is very wide and spans the whole business of the firm, except for the product or service itself. Perhaps in this definition can be found the reason for the problems that marketing has brought to some firms and individual lawyers. When law firms were first permitted limited advertising rights in the mid-1980s, law firms which started 'to do marketing' concentrated their efforts on brochures, advertisements, leaflets and so on, working on persuading clients to use their existing services. The approach was, 'This is what we do – who wants to buy?' Not unnaturally, many lawyers and law firms found this approach to marketing distasteful and contrary to their concept of professionalism. It was not very commercial or businesslike either because it completely ignored the other three elements of marketing – market research, delivery service and the integration of marketing with the profit and other objectives of the firm.

The leading law firms are now actively scanning directories and names and addresses of all businesses and potential clients in their own and within other law firms' areas of operation. All of your major clients have certainly been approached by other predatory law firms and many of your private clients will have been courted by local if not regional firms. The market, therefore, includes a firm's existing clients and so market research means more than just hunting 'out there' for new clients. Market research activities should be devoted also to researching the views, perceptions and opinions of a firm's existing clients. This is where most of a firm's work comes from and this is the client group that a firm needs to satisfy and retain. If a firm is unable to satisfy its existing clients or if the firm doesn't know whether it does or doesn't satisfy them or to what degree it satisfies them, there is little point spending the time and effort and money required to recruit yet more new clients. It must be a principle of the first order that a client once obtained is a client never to be lost. It is a principle also of the first magnitude that a client once obtained is a client who should be developed into using the firm for repeat and other work.

Another area of work contained in the definition of marketing which may easily be overlooked is the delivery of the product or service to the client. This is the area where we lawyers spend a great deal of our time and this is the area where the client actually experiences the value of our service to him. The delivery of the legal product or service to the client is one of the main areas in which client management operates. Client management operates in all the areas in which the client is involved or which form part of his experience and perception of the firm, including the presentation of the products and services to the client. Client management includes all of marketing rather than the other way around.

If client management is understood to include the whole range of activities which affects the client and which form part of his perception of the firm then it will be seen that marketing, in the sense of the presentation of the firm and its services to prospective clients, is only a part of client management. The client management spectrum, therefore, may be seen to include:

- market research;
- marketing activities;
- selling;
- presentation of the firm;
- presentation of its people;
- presentation of the benefits of its services;
- design of its products and services;
- delivery of its products and services to the client;
- review of client satisfaction levels;
- client feedback;
- service value assessment;
- pricing structure; and
- value, profit and satisfaction performance assessment.

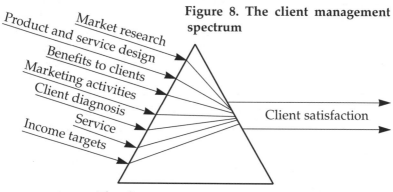

Figure 8. The client management spectrum

The client management spectrum

Seen in this way, marketing can be understood as being of fundamental importance to the business and all pervasive in its effect on the business. It will also be seen that client management, which encompasses marketing within its overall spectrum, is, and should be seen to be, the driving force of the whole firm because it affects all of the whole firm and all its activities.

Perhaps a better definition of marketing, particularly of a business which provides intangible services as opposed to concrete products, is that devised by Peter Drucker (*Management by Objectives*):

Marketing is the whole business seen from the point of view of its final result, that is, from the customer's point of view.

Marketing is here seen as not being confined just to front end-selling, but it is seen to encompass the whole business. Marketing is not, therefore, just about 'getting more work in' or about selling or about promotion – marketing is about the whole firm as seen by the client. Marketing activity without market research and client feedback is like shooting in the dark: noisy, exciting, flashy, expensive and almost a total waste of time and money.

The marketing brief

Client managers believe that for a firm to be successful it has to be seen as being different from its competitors in offering something which other firms do not. This difference could be pricing structure, client service levels, legal expertise, location or the quality of people in the firm and so on. Client managers try to identify what it is they do or could do that is different from their competitors. Based on client feed-back and market research, the firm will be able to identify what services it provides and to which clients and what the perception of the firm is that clients have. Then the firm will put the two together and identify those services which the firm can provide which are liked by the client and that other firms do not provide.

The problem with a law firm may then become clear: the firm may not do anything different from its competitors and appears to compete only on price. It provides the traditional range of legal services only, it is pretty much the same as the other firms, it is being underpriced by the smaller high street firms and is being out-skilled and out-managed by the larger city firms. The familiar picture emerges, the firm is too big and too expensive for the smaller client and too small and has not enough specialist skills for the larger clients. All is not lost, however, if the firm is able to respond to the following strategy:

1   based on market research, the firm decides what services it retains and what services it can develop to meet the ascertained client demand;

2 identify which existing and potential clients the firm wishes to retain and recruit for those services;
3 identify why those services are different from or better than those on offer elsewhere by its competitors;
4 identify what benefits it can offer to clients that its competitors do not;
5 conduct a client survey to find out what its existing clients like and don't like about its services;
6 develop and deliver those ascertained legal products and services; and
7 check for effect with questionnaires and a periodic survey.

Sales and production are inter-connected. You can only sell what you can produce, and you must only produce what is in demand. Good marketing work will be devalued if the production team, those who actually do the work and deliver it to the client on a day-by-day basis, perform badly in the opinion of the client. An efficient production team will never even get started unless the sales team can bring in the clients requiring that type of work. In law firms, the sales and production team are often the same people.

Three times as many clients are lost due to poor service rather than due to poor legal work or advice. An effective marketing solicitor will probably have the following attributes:

1 he is courteous;
2 he likes people;
3 he is aware of and enthuses over the different characteristics and needs of each client;
4 he understands his clients;
5 he is interested in his clients, keeps in touch and goes to see them;
6 he knows his product (the legal work) and his people;
7 he makes himself available to his clients;
8 he is reliable in that his clients know they can depend on him to provide the services and legal products in a consistent way; and
9 he is empowered to be able to get on with the job.

The turnover days (see Chapter 1) measured our performance in terms of bills delivered. That is a limited, though important, way of score-keeping but it does not tell us everything we need to know about performance. A more comprehensive and useful reporting system will contain details of:

1 the percentage of time spent with existing clients in a non-fee-earning role or capacity (client care time);

2 the percentage of time spent with potential clients (marketing time);
3 the client satisfaction ratings achieved with existing clients;
4 client development rating (the number of cases being developed from one key client into repeat instructions);
5 client introductions (the number of cases referred from each group in the firm to other groups in the firm);
6 the number and names of lost clients, with details;
7 the numbers, types and sources of complaints; and
8 inception statistics split between cases for new and existing clients.

Unlike many other product-based businesses, where sales and production are dealt with by different people in different places or departments, solicitors do their own marketing, their own production and their own delivery and presentations to the client. This is because, in the case of a service, it is the person selling, doing and delivering the work who is an integral part of the service itself. Therefore, it can be seen that in doing our legal work we are also already doing marketing as well. Client management is about doing what we already are doing but doing it more effectively with a different motivation and understanding. This concentration of marketing, production and delivery in the client manager can open up new opportunities and vistas when the principles and practices of client management are applied.

New ways for old

Perhaps we should start by reviewing the differences in the old and the new ways of doing things. A comparison of the old fee earner role model and the new client manager role model might illustrate this principle as follows:

The fee earner ...	The client manager also ...
... does the work within his own legal expertise.	... ensures that his client has the benefit of the firm's overall expertise.
... describes himself by his function.	... describes himself as the clients describe him – according to whether or not he meets their needs.
... works for himself or his own group.	... works for the firm as a whole.

... assumes quality in his work.	... measures the quality of his work according to two standards: 1 does it accord to objective standards and specifications? 2 does it satisfy the client?
... is a member of a learned profession.	... is a member of a learning profession which is constantly finding new and better ways of satisfying clients.
... his performance is measured according to bills delivered.	... performs according to the levels of client satisfaction.
... sells legal services.	... makes profits by providing solutions, benefits and welfare to clients.
... 'does marketing'.	... is motivated to keep and develop his best clients.
... has a turnover motivation.	... has a motivation driven by the desire to provide quality legal work, client satisfaction, value for money and profit.

The change in emphasis from what a solicitor does to what a solicitor does for his clients has been brought about by changes in the market as a result of competition. Formerly, a good solicitor was thought to be one who was a good lawyer and a hard worker, whereas now a good solicitor is one who is thought to be good by his clients, who understands their needs and who satisfies their expectations. We are now defined not by what we do but for whom we do it for. This repositioning and understanding of ourselves from the perspective of the client is the fundamental reason for the evolution from a fee earner to a client manager.

Selling services

Much has already been said about the differences and consequences of seeing ourselves as ones who sell service as opposed to selling legal products alone. Instead of the traditional law firm approach to selling by saying, 'We do conveyancing – who wants to buy?', where the accent is on the legal product and its price, there is with client management a 180-degree shift. The marketing attitude of the client manager is one which says, 'You are a unique client and we understand you and want to know more. We believe we can help you achieve your objectives and we can provide you with the benefits that you will find of value. Let's identify what it is that you want and then see how we can deliver it at a price acceptable to us both.'

The market for commercial property may have gone into a decline over the last five years but the market for satisfying clients' needs is almost unlimited where the need is defined by the client and not by us. For example, where a firm does residential conveyancing, instead of calling ourselves 'conveyancers' which is a functional definition of what we do, we could look at ourselves from the house-mover's point of view. They see us as people who help them in the process of a house move, advising on the financial and legal aspects, doing the completion and getting them into occupation and legal ownership. The benefit to them is that we help them with the legal and financial aspects of moving house. So instead of 'conveyancers' we are in the client's terms 'house move advisers'. This role opens up much wider opportunities for benefits and services than does the former functionally based word of 'conveyancer'.

In addition to 'doing conveyancing', we should also be identifying and providing benefits. For example, fixed fees, case plans, progress reports, pre-exchange reports, no cost additions without the client's approval, chasing for quick exchange or completion and so on. If we take only a functional approach to conveyancing, without stressing service and value benefits, we may limit ourselves to being able to complete only on price.

How do clients think in the process of deciding to use a solicitor? Perhaps a client thinks like this:

1 I am a person with occasional needs for legal advice and services.
2 I have just met or know a solicitor but I don't need one right now.
3 I have a legal problem – maybe I need a solicitor to help me?
4 How much longer can I put off seeing a solicitor?
5 I need to see a solicitor urgently!
6 Which solicitor shall I go to?
7 I know A and I've heard of B. It's one or the other.
8 I've chosen A because I met him once at a business lunch. I hope he doesn't let me down.
9 I've been to see A. I think I've made the right decision, he seems very understanding and interested in me.
10 A has looked after me well. I'm happy to use him again and to recommend him to others.

It is the client's perception of the service we provide for him that makes the service good, bad or unsatisfactory rather than how we as lawyers rate ourselves. This does not mean that being a good lawyer is not important or that our legal expertise is ancillary. In the new, client-driven marketplace our legal expertise and qualities as lawyers are important but they must, in addition, be linked to client management skills.

Tips from a salesman

In marketing legal services you are to a large degree selling yourself, because as we have seen in Chapter 6 ('Service is our business'), you are a major constituent part of the service. We have seen in Chapter 6 that a service comprises three elements which together provide a benefit or welfare to the perception of the client. The legal service itself, the service provider and the client form the service triangle. So in marketing yourself and the firm it is necessary to emphasise your own personal approach to service and benefits. You need to impress on the client that you will be available and easily accessible, that you won't disappear or let him down. Be careful and attentive when listening, ask questions and try to find out what the client really wants and needs. There are some techniques we can learn from the salesman in countering client resistance as follows:

Price resistance

Client: 'Thanks for the quotation but it's too much!'

This response is perceived to be a challenge to a lawyer's legal services and products which he knows are good but somehow the client just does not see it that way. It can make the lawyer feel undervalued as well as overpriced. What can he do? The first rule is never to reduce the quote and do the same work for a lower price. Not only is this bad for your business, it also undermines your overall pricing policy. Your response should qualify the product and increase the service specification as follows:

Client manager: 'You are right to be concerned about price. But it's true that you get what you pay for these days. We always try to meet a client's budget and match what we do to suit your needs wherever possible. Let's look at what's involved here in the standard case plan. Hmmm, look, if we cut out contingencies we can reduce the charges at this stage, if things change we'll have to look again at this. We could reduce travel time if you could come to us for meetings. This should produce a reduction in charges of £XXX. Will that be acceptable? We can also send you a weekly/monthly progress report for all your cases with monthly bills. In this way you can stay in control of costs and avoid any surprises! Let's set a maximum charge at £YYY and we won't exceed this without your prior approval'

Differentiation

Client: 'We use Kenge & Carboys for all our legal work.'

Client Manager: 'Well, they are a good firm, but our service also includes [weekly][monthly] printed progress reports for clients at no extra cost. This helps you keep fully up-to-date and keeps you in control of charges. It's very popular with our clients. We can also offer you, without charge, a legal healthcheck to look at your business overall and to make recommendations for action or review with charges agreed to suit your budget. This includes a review of your terms and conditions of employment for you and your staff. Do you think these benefits might be useful to you?'

Uninterested

Client: 'I don't need any legal work doing at the moment.'

Client manager: 'You are fortunate to have such a well-managed business. It's obvious that you understand that it's far better to avoid legal problems than to have things ending up in potentially costly and time-consuming court action. You might find that our free legal healthcheck would be useful. One of the points covered is a review of your terms and conditions of sale to ensure that your business is protected and risks are reduced. Oh, you haven't got any? You usually use your customers' conditions? You'd like me to suggest something simple? I'll let you have a draft tomorrow.'

Client complaint

Client: 'Last time I used your firm you lost my deeds and I was not pleased.'

Client manager: 'Did you make a complaint about that? Good. How was it dealt with? We found them after a thorough search? Good, I'm glad to hear you kicked up a stink, it's clients like you who keep us on our toes. Of course, that problem won't happen again because we have now appointed Harry Archive, an early-retired civil servant, to manage a computerised deeds database with our new, secure, fireproof deeds storage system. It's proving very popular with our clients and the deeds storage, document retrieval and copying charges are very competitive. Can we quote you for this new service? Plus you get access to your deeds and documents within 24 hours and should you need any information we provide the first 10 A4 photocopies without any extra charge. OK, good, send me your deeds and I'll get Harry to put them in store.'

Client criticism

Client: 'I think your firm is incompetent!'

Client manager: 'I can see that you were upset about that incident. There was obviously some lack of communication. Did you know that you can now call us any time day or night on our 24 hour helpline, so there may never be any more misunderstandings? I can personally assure you of a better level of service with this new facility. Here's my home telephone number, should you need it.'

Client scepticism

Client: 'I don't think your firm can really help me.'

Client Manager: 'We are in business because our clients think we do help them. I understand that 60% of your business is done in Europe? We can provide you with contacts throughout a network of law firms all over Europe. All offices speak English and provide local document translation and interpretation services as well as advice on national laws. Do you think that will help? Very well, I'll send you details.'

The close

In desperation to get an instruction or to 'win' a quotation or tender, we think, often mistakenly, that a reduction in price is the only thing to do. Instead, try to close a sale by emphasising a benefit such as:

'... and we will not exceed the agreed charges without your prior approval.'

'... and we can let you have a copy of our monthly printouts and monthly bills so you can keep track of costs.'

'We can let you have copies of all letters so you are kept fully up-to-date.'

'You won't need to worry about who's doing your work because I'll retain overall control and responsibility for all the services you get.'

Service as well as price is one of the key determining factors along with product quality and price. We must develop our services to be seen as user-friendly, different and flexible to meet the varying needs of different clients. Negotiating on service and product specification will be more satisfactory to both solicitor and client than merely haggling over price.

Marketing attitude

Marketing is more of an attitude of mind than a list of activities. It is a way of thinking that puts the identification and satisfaction of client needs as the first priority. It requires you to keep thinking of ways to provide services and legal products that will satisfy the client. It is based on client benefits as well as product excellence. This is why each case manager must be actively involved in marketing and this is why this attitude towards marketing must be embedded in the firm's culture. Vicarious marketing through a marketing partner or external consultant, no matter how well done, will only be of limited value, and opportunities thrown up by the marketing activities will be missed or underplayed. As we have seen, as each person in the firm *is* the firm and each person who delivers the service *is* part of the service, then everyone is and must be actively involved in marketing.

The often-encountered reserve in some lawyers about marketing and selling may be replaced by a different understanding of marketing in that in identifying and satisfying client needs and requirements we are doing what is the very essence and pinnacle of professional practice – the provision of benefits to clients by more accurately identifying and meeting the client's needs and expectations.

Classical marketing

Marketing experts tell us that marketing is comprised of the four main topics of product, price, place and promotion, as follows.

Product

In law this is the generic legal advice or legal process such as the transfer, the contract, the decree *nisi*, the writ, the forms, the law and legal expertise. We have seen in Chapter 5 that the legal product forms only about 20% of the perceived total legal service from the client's point of view. We have seen that legal competence is assumed. Apart from niche legal expertise, and even with niche legal expertise, marketing and competing on legal competence is only of limited value.

Price

The 1994 Solicitor's Remuneration Order is based on the premise that lawyers can fairly and reasonably charge a fee which is based on the cost of production plus a reasonable percentage mark-up to take into account a number of factors, including the value, importance and complexity of the matter. Whilst this may satisfy the Taxing Master, this approach to business and private clients will no longer be sufficient because it does not bring the client into the calculation. It is based on an objective assessment of cost rather than on the perception of value by the particular paying client. Clients don't want to pay for products and process as much as for benefit and value. 'Is it worth it?' they ask themselves rather than 'what does it cost?' Cost and process-based pricing structures yield to value-based charges in a competitive environment. Client managers understand that the amount a client is prepared to pay increases in direct proportion to the level of client satisfaction (see Chapter 14, 'Client Satisfaction – The Science of Clients').

Place

Solicitors have this tremendous advantage over many other businesses in that the case manager who is part of the service does much of the work for his client whilst he is face-to-face with the client. The service is direct, personal and is generated there and then before the client's eyes. The case manager is not remote from the client and the production of the legal work is not remote. He is perfectly situated to receive direct feedback from the client about perception and satisfaction if he is prepared to read the signals and ask the right questions. If you buy a car, you do not generally deal with the person who made the car. If you buy vegetables in the supermarket, you do not talk to the farmer who grew them. If you buy a house, you do not usually deal with the people who actually built it. Generally, personal service is only encountered in professional services where production and service converge, in the client and case manager.

Promotion

This is the action you take to ensure that your existing and potential clients are made fully aware and are kept up-to-date with the full range of services that can be of benefit to them. Brochures, advertising, entertainment and seminars are relevant here. The best promotion of all is spending time with clients and in providing benefits to clients by using client management skills.

It is necessary in client management to add to the classic four-part formula of marketing the function which is at the heart of legal work, a fifth 'p' for the presentation and delivery of the legal product to the client.

Presentation

The presentation and delivery mechanism of the legal product is where the added value and differentiation opportunities lie in abundance, by understanding and improving the client's experience and benefit of the legal product, by enhancing the welfare and benefit aspect of the product and by identifying and exceeding the client's expectations.

Brilliant legal advice can be blighted by the inaccessibility of the lawyer; state-of-the-art documents are diminished if they are sent out two or three days after the date promised to the client and the most well-controlled and conducted litigation case is appreciated less by the client who is not informed about what is happening. At both the apparent and subliminal levels, client satisfaction and the choice of solicitor is influenced more strongly by these presentation elements than by functional capability.

The marketing objective

Marketing is not really about selling at all. If the 'target' client is not in the buying vein, no amount of marketing will achieve a sale. All our marketing efforts cannot persuade a client that he should get a divorce or that he should buy a house. It's unethical as well as ineffective. Marketing attempts to create and maintain awareness of the firm's service benefits for potential clients, whereas traditional marketing focuses on selling the legal product, which forms only a third part of the client's perception of the overall legal service, the client manager's 'relationship' marketing objectives focus also on the service receiver (the client) and on the service providers (the client managers). This is where the new marketing objective is to be found.

Image of the firm or a person in it

Your target client may not be instructing solicitors right now, but he may be in six months' time. The image you create now of you and the firm may stay with him. The image being received by clients and target clients needs constant attention. Reputation is only a partial definition of image which needs constant reinforcing. Any bad experience suffered by the client or target client can ruin any positive image that has been built up over many months.

Competition

If a client or 'target' client is about to instruct a solicitor, he may be exercising some choice between two or more firms. He will know how well or badly you compare with your competitors. We should, therefore, include in our marketing activities some research about our competitors from the market's point of view. You may *know* that Kenge & Carboys lack your firm's expertise in certain types of legal work, but if they are more attentive and responsive to your client than you are, if they are spending more time with the client and getting to understand his needs better than you, you can be sure that Kenge & Carboys is where the client will go and stay.

Branding

A brand image which focuses on the firm's unique selling point or differentiation should be identified and constantly be reinforced by the firm's marketing activities. For example, 'Jarndyce and Jarndyce – Lawyers who put their clients first'.

Marketing in action

Assuming that the attitude and motivation towards attraction, retention and growth of the client base has commitment from all people in the firm, then there are four phases of marketing in action:

1 identify the needs of clients by listening, client questionnaires, surveys and market research;
2 design the product and service to match or exceed the identified needs and expectations of the client;
3 present and deliver the 'designer' product and service to the client; and
4 check and record client satisfaction levels at regular intervals.

The old ways of just doing the legal work left unexplored and unsatisfied many client requirements, needs and opportunities. A lack of understanding of client needs had the effect of encouraging a concentration on legal function rather than on the purpose and results of what we do for our clients – the benefits.

Market research

Research into client opinion, perception and requirements is where all business development or turnaround must start. Any other base for growth will be built on the shifting sands of assumptions about clients. Market research is driven by the attitude that understands that survival and growth in business are directly linked to the firm's ability to identify and satisfy client needs more effectively, more consistently and more economically than its competitors. Market research should start by asking a cross-section of existing clients:

1 'How satisfied are you with our existing services?'
2 'How do you think we can improve our services?'
3 'What kind of pricing structure would you find more acceptable?'

The use of client surveys and client questionnaires to achieve systematic and regular feedback is the essential first step towards building a responsive client management culture in the firm.

What do we do with all the information we gather and record about clients? Addresses, mobile telephone numbers, business types, etc are all very important, but does all this information just sitting there on the client database, or in our heads, actually satisfy the client? Do we satisfy the client? How well? How badly? Indifferently? Why? What can we do to maintain and improve client satisfaction?

A firm with a growing market share is evidently satisfying its clients. A firm with a static client base is evidently not doing anything new or additional in its service to clients. It's clients may just be waiting for a reason to make the final break. We can't go on any longer not knowing whether or not we are satisfying our clients and whether we are getting better or worse. We can't just assume client satisfaction. Assumptions like these find no place in client management because only regular and systematic feedback can be fully effective in putting and keeping a firm in the eyes of its clients.

What kind of market information is needed? The following are useful.

Client trends and perception

Client questionnaires and contact calls or visits at the end of each case, regular client surveys, client lunches, complaints feedback, lost client questionnaires, new client questionnaires and competence and performance reports will give the firm day to day information about clients direct from the coalface.

Legal and professional

What is happening in the law, the new rules, the new laws, the repeal of the old laws – these all offer new opportunities with clients. The ever growing and changing body of law provides an immense pool of opportunities for those who can see it and who take the time to familiarise themselves with new legislation and who then apply them to the known needs and requirements of their key clients. Your research team will be asking themselves, 'How will this new Act affect our top 100 key clients and their businesses? What advice and services can we design, introduce, adapt, change, modify or discontinue for these key clients? Which of our clients will benefit from these new services? Let's work up some ideas, go and see a few key clients and ask them and see what happens?' This is a firm at the leading edge of marketing and client management.

Strategic plan

When a firm combines this information with the activities above, it will say to itself, for example, 'If clients are seeing us more as service providers, should we not make it our prime strategy to train all our partners and staff in client management and client satisfaction service skills?'

The firms which care for their clients will leave nothing undone in trying to resolve a client's problem or need. The leading edge firm will already have known about and addressed the client's problems the day before yesterday. If all your client antennae are switched on and turning, probing the ether between you and your client, you will pick up the danger signals or opportunity signals well in time to do something about it. Often we do so only when it is too late.

The effective marketing and production matrix, therefore, comprises:

1 Listening to clients, spending time with them, getting to know them and understanding their needs and collecting, recording and measuring data about them.
2 Designing and developing your current products or introducing new products after discussion with key (and a selection of) clients, listening to feedback, adapting and then producing to the new client the case plan and care plan.
3 The new or amended product is carried out and reports and feedback gathered to measure its effectiveness. Does it work and does it satisfy the client and does it make a profit?

213

4 With feedback based on experience, you can work out what went wrong, what went right and what can be done better. Then do it and introduce the service on a wider basis.

The firm's marketing staff

Anyone in a firm who has direct contact with and influence on clients is a marketing person. Even a person whose work only indirectly affects the clients is a marketing person. The marketing partner who leads a successful presentation to a new client is the champion of the day but the credit control clerk chasing an overdue account from one of the partner's established key clients whilst he is out doing the presentation also has an important effect on the relationship between the firm and the client. Handled insensitively, it could alienate the client and lead to a drying-up of any further work, and all the good work and service you have supplied to the client will be put under unnecessary and avoidable pressure. Handled well, it will further confirm the client's view that he has chosen to deal with an organisation that is well run throughout at all levels and which is responsive to individual client needs. So virtually everybody in the firm needs to have some marketing and client management training in order to understand that:

1 the client comes first;
2 it is the client who pays our drawings and salaries; and
3 it is the client who we must satisfy in all that we do.

How can marketing be more relevant and effective to the needs of the 1990s where value rather than price is one of the main client concerns? Value to clients, improved client satisfaction and, therefore, improved billing performance will be assisted as follows:
1 Rather than trying to sell 'litigation', for example, we could instead say that legal services can help avoid or reduce potentially expensive court work. Where court work is necessary, the firm will discuss and agree with the client his needs and budget.
2 Recruiting fee earners and partners from people who enjoy being with people and show a caring, understanding and interested approach to clients. Then train them to be technically competent. Get the people with the attitudes and train them to be lawyers as well as the other way around.
3 Keep asking your clients and prospects for suggestions and feedback and then do something about it.

4 Handle complaints quickly and without being defensive, begrudging, reluctant or offended. Turn complaints into opportunities, not problems.

5 Look for the tell-tale signs of client distress (see Chapter 7) and then go to see the client to head off any problems.

6 Ensure that all your staff at all levels receive regular information and feedback about your clients and the firm's marketing activities. All staff should be able to meet clients at sometime annually.

7 Encourage staff to introduce new clients to the firm, with incentives.

The marketing spectrum

A law firm may be good at telling clients what it does, but it may not be so good in pointing out what it can do for its clients or how it is different from its competitors. This is very well explained in the booklet entitled *On The Art of Being Perceived as Better* issued by Hodgart, Temporal & Company. This makes a detailed analysis of lawyers' marketing efforts. Their view is that 'marketing flows from strategy' and may be illustrated as follows.

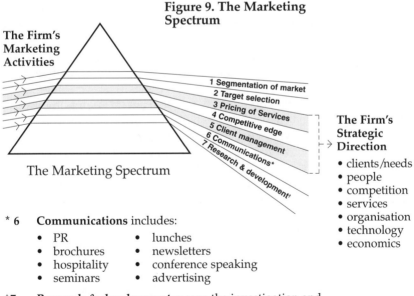

Figure 9. The Marketing Spectrum

* 6 **Communications** includes:

- PR
- brochures
- hospitality
- seminars
- lunches
- newsletters
- conference speaking
- advertising

†7 **Research & development** means the investigation and identification of clients' needs, and then the design and delivery of the legal service accordingly.

215

What a law firm may have been doing in its marketing efforts is to pay insufficient attention to sections 1–5 and to have concentrated almost exclusively on the communications aspect of brochures, seminars and hospitality. It concentrated on saying what they did rather than how they could provide benefits for the client. A more segmented and client specific form of marketing, produced by the firm's strategy and marketing information is now required. I can do no better than quote the statement of Hodgart, Temporal & Co about the importance of client management:

As competition for clients heats up, we see client management being of crucial importance in the whole marketing process. Managing the delivery of services to a client; ensuring the right resources are in the right place at the right time; ensuring the fees are appropriate to the value perceived by the client, managing the expectation of a client about value and fees, ensuring that all the client's legal needs that the firm wishes to meet are being met from within the firm and, above all else, ensuring that everyone who deals with the client does so in a way that achieves and maintains the firm's competitive edge over rivals – these are all part of the role of the effective client manager.

The second phase of marketing awareness and activity, expanding work with existing clients, both with repeat work of the same type as well as introducing new services, is very much the task of a service-oriented business. This is particularly true of the commercial solicitor who tends to do most of his work for a relatively small number of clients. He is very much dependent on the quality of service he provides to ensure that his major clients keep sending him repeat work.

Client management and marketing seen from this point of view are really only different aspects of the same overall focus on the client. Marketing is in effect saying to prospective clients, 'We can provide you with the benefits you need.' Client management says to clients, 'Aren't you glad you chose us to provide you with the legal services you need because now you can see that we do really understand you and that we are interested in you and we are delivering what we said we would and more.' The marketing activity of the client manager, therefore, can be seen in two parts:

1 to show potential clients that he is ready, willing and able to provide the benefits that clients need; and
2 to secure and improve client satisfaction and client retention by providing a quality service that satisfies or delights the client by meeting or exceeding his identified needs.

Don't try to be better – be different!

Can you tell margarine from butter? Can you tell one high street bank from another? Can you tell what brand of petrol is in the car tank by the way the car drives? Do you know the first names of your firm's accountants? Do you know why you use them and not the firm down the road? Do you know why your clients use your firm and not the firm down the road? Have you asked your clients?

A client will remember you if you have provided him with poor products or service. He will remember not to come back and he will tell others. No matter how long ago it happened, an unhappy client will remember you and tell his friends and colleagues, 'Kenge & Carboys? They're the firm who lost my deeds! I wouldn't use them if I were you. I can recommend Jarndyce & Jarndyce who looked after my last house move very well. They weren't the cheapest but they did a really good job for me.' The client's memory of one firm's poor service will for him be an eternal blight on the firm's name.

Your client will remember you for years when you have provided him with exceptional value. 'They're the really good firm who found my deeds that my former solicitors lost! They obtained a new set of deeds from the Land Registry and charged me less than my former solicitors who lost them! I've been telling everyone how good they are.' Good service is remembered and retold.

Your client will not remember you at all if you provided an indifferent service. 'No, I don't have a regular solicitor. There was a firm who did my house conveyancing three years ago but I've forgotten their name, so I came here after reading the *Yellow Pages*. Can you help me?' Just by doing the job, by meeting the client's needs but not his desires or expectations, the firm that did the conveyancing has lost a client and may not be even aware of it. It is that kind of firm which deals in customers rather than clients and which needs to know how to identify and meet and exceed client expectations. Client management will assist a firm in the transition from a customer focus to a client focus.

Have you ever lost a quotation or a tender after a detailed and time-consuming presentation or come second to another firm who you *know* are no better than your firm? You feel a sense of injustice and undervalue? Yet from the point of view of the target client, they feel that they made the right decision. Why is this? The client may have difficulty in accurately assessing legal competence and in many cases where routine work is involved, legal competence is assumed. The target client will look for something different or extra which Firm A offers and which Firm B does not, being benefits which *the client* thinks are important.

In the old days, law firms tended to be much the same as everyone else and this was reinforced by the monopoly and fee scales in conveyancing. But now in this deregulated and competing profession, it is the difference in products and service which need to be emphasised. If you do not think that you are different, you need to find ways based on client feedback to ensure that you do offer something which your competitors do not. Service differentiators are infinite and are limited only by the imagination of the lawyer. Some service differentiations might include:

1 offering a service which no other local firms provide – eg environmental law, intellectual property, employment law or legal aid;
2 you may provide clients with a work specification of standard work types which helps the client to understand and agree the stages of the work. This may be useful to a wide range of clients, both business and private;
3 you offer pre-exchange reports to clients giving them in one document a full technical report on the proposed transaction, rather than sending them long, technical and, let's face it, boring letters. Such reports are also useful for clients who will need to send a report (with your firm's name on it) to their board for approval;
4 fixed fee initial interview (gets the clients in and it shows you are interested in them);
5 free financial consultation (nearly all types of legal work involve finance in one way or another);
6 free emergency telephone helpline (for peace of mind);
7 retainer fee to cover standard preliminary legal work in a certain type of work (peace of mind, easy no extra cost access to legal advice);
8 free car parking for clients at your city centre offices (easy access);
9 all client telephone calls to you are free of time recording charges (encourages clients to keep in touch);
10 full computer narrative and breakdown of bills given to clients (aids client awareness);
11 agreed maximum charges not to be exceeded without clients' consent (puts clients in control but without limiting fees for reasonable and necessary additional or varied work);

12 free legal update or client newsletter (shows you understand clients' potential needs); and

13 [   ] (here insert your own idea for a valuable, low cost service differentiator).

This is the key – knowing and emphasising in all your service and sales efforts how a client using your firm and your services will receive benefits and extras that he would not get elsewhere. The benefits do not have to cost a lot, indeed they already exist in most firms but perhaps are not being marketed sufficiently well. Added-value items do not need to add to cost. The client will want to stay with your firm because he sees that you understand his needs and can work with him and that with the differentiators and added-value items you offer he thinks he's on to a good thing with your firm.

Service differentiation

Under the rules of compulsory competitive tendering (CCT), a points system is used to assess and compare tenders, typically as follows:

1 legal cost   30%
2 technical expertise   40%
3 relevant experience   10%
4 approach to the management of the assignment   20%

The service 'intangible' of 'approach' in 4, being given 20% is rated twice as much as relevant experience and half as much as technical expertise and two-thirds as much as legal costs. The approach, or the presentation and delivery of the legal product, which is client management, is officially rated as 66% as important as legal cost. So let's do something about client management.

Your concerns in quotations and tenders must match the client's concerns. If he is concerned about cost overruns, offer to provide him with monthly costs statements, interim bills and/or a maximum fee beyond which you will not go without his prior consent. You could also offer a cost review meeting and copies of your computer time recording print-outs.

If he is concerned about response times, offer to hold meetings at his premises, offer daily, weekly or monthly progress reports and a trouble-shooting 'hotline' to the named client partner.

If he is concerned about 'who will be in charge overall' then identify the client partner and the case managers and support staff who will be working on the matter. Remember, the people providing the service are a part of the service. It is not always essential to have a partner on call as long as the client knows who he is and is happy with the person taking overall responsibility.

A firm's differentiation strategies can be based on product, price or service. It is important to identify which. Product differentiation requires it to show that it offers legal products that its competitors do not, such as specialist planning, tax or environmental law skills and expertise, or that it offers a greater depth of product knowledge by showing a more specialised team with special expertise in a particular area.

Price differentiation is perhaps more familiar to most firms who are under pressure to build up or regain turnover or to expand their client base, produce fee packages and cost reductions calculated to beat the competition and so increase the flow of work. This strategy is fraught with dangers, because there is often no escape from the downward spiral of cost cutting. New customers who shop on price alone tend to move on when the discounts are exhausted and repeat work is being charged on higher scales. The reduced profit margins of the work so gained put even more pressure on cash flow and can strain profitability to breaking point. Price differentiation alone is a losing strategy.

Service differentiation is the more attractive and viable marketing strategy and is the principle strategy of the client manager. Having won the new client, your main strategic marketing objective is to apply your unique client management techniques and methods to the new client to show that you understand and are interested in the client's business or affairs, to ensure that value-added factors are applied and that your service differentials reinforce the new client's decision to reinstruct you in additional work.

Cut prices or added value?

We work in a competitive market and price is crucial, but not always critical, in the client's decision to use a particular law firm. A lot depends on the service and legal work required, the type of client and the level of expertise required for the work. Cutting prices to the bone and holding yourself out as being 'a friendly law practice' may not always be the most effective strategy. If a fixed price is agreed which is linked to an agreed work specification or case plan, then in addition to such extras as telephone helplines, client partners, monthly progress reports, etc the client will be able to form his perception on value rather than on price alone. Of course, with commodity work such as conveyancing, debt collection, insurance litigation work and so on, fixed prices for a fixed commodity are the norm and no amount of added-value items will affect the decision on that particular service. It may, however, generate interest in the firm's other services of which the client may not have been aware.

The internal survey

The marketing attitude of the people in the firm can be given a jolt by a visit from the bank manager, by the loss of a major client, by the defection of a partner or department to a rival firm, or by the gradual decline in the number of large clients, repeat work and new inceptions. Waiting until there is not enough work to go around is leaving the marketing effort until it's too late. It is, therefore, necessary to start with doing an internal audit of the attitudes of partners and staff, preferably on a group or departmental basis. It is also necessary to find out:

1 What percentage of fee income comes from repeat work?
2 What percentage of fee income comes from new work?
3 What are the income percentages from different client types?
4 What are the income percentages from different work types?
5 What are the income percentages from key clients (eg 80% of income comes from 20% of clients with 10 or more cases per year in the firm)?
6 What are the different levels of profit of the different services and client and client types?
7 What is the cost of resources tied up in the above services and the relative return of profit for each one?
8 Does group A produce more profit than group B?
9 Do the people in group A produce more profit per person than the people in group B?
10 What are the relative client satisfaction rating levels for each service and for each group?

A firm may get more income from client A than from client B, but the firm may make more profit from client B. This presents some strategic, management and client management issues with which the firm needs to deal. A firm may do an internal questionnaire:

1 Why do clients choose us in preference to our competitors?
2 In what ways are we different from our competitors?

3 Would clients pay more for (i) better legal work; or (ii) better service? or (iii) both?
4 Do clients choose mainly on (i) price; (ii) service; or (iii) value?
5 What is the image in the marketplace of (i) the firm; (ii) your group/department; (iii) you yourself?
6 Does your knowledge of your competitors include details of (i) their prices; (ii) their client satisfaction levels?

Try to quantify what the members inside the firm think that the firm's image is in the marketplace. Try the following questions, collate and count the results (1 = poor, 2 = fair and 3 = good). A score of over 24 might indicate a good firm image or it might mark an over confident self appraisal. Only when compared with the external survey of what clients and referrers themselves think will the results be of any real value.

Question			
	Poor	Fair	Good
1 How good is the firm's image in the marketplace?			
2 How good is the quality of your legal work?			
3 How good is the quality of your service?			
4 How do we compare with our competitors?			
5 How good is our best local competitor?			
6 How do we compare with the best local competitor?			
7 How good is our understanding of clients?			
8 How good is our interest in clients?			
9 How good is our accessibility to clients?			
10 How good is the value of our products and services?			
11 How well do we look after our clients?			
12 How well do we make clients aware of what we can do for them?			
Total			

The external survey

Ask your clients to reply to the questions contained in the internal survey above, adapted only slightly for the client. Clients should mark these 1 to 3 as appropriate for 1 = poor, 2 = fair and 3 = good. A high rating of 24 or more may be encouraging but what is really important is the comparison between the results of the internal and the external survey. Where a clear mismatch is shown, this is where work needs to be focused.

In addition, the external survey should ask clients and referrers to answer the following questions:

1 What do you find satisfying about our existing services?
2 What do you think we could do to improve our services?
3 What kind of pricing structure changes do you think would make paying legal costs more acceptable?

A sensitive and discreet use of these questionnaires with analysis, recommendations and implementation of appropriate measures will produce client value service improvements and differentiation.

Marketing made easy

If the marketing attitudes in the firm as revealed by the internal survey are not highly developed, then the marketing plan will need to be kept simple as follows:

1 all staff to be encouraged to introduce clients with an introductory commission. Details of introductions to be published internally, with appropriate measures to maintain client confidentiality;
2 all fee earners to be tasked to introduce one new client each week;
3 all fee earners to be tasked to refer one existing client per week to another group or department for an 'introduced' service;
4 all associates and partners to introduce one new major clients a month;
5 all associates and partners to introduce one potential 'key client' every two months;
6 all associates and partners to lunch at least once a week with a client;
7 all associates and partners to lunch at least once a month with one key client;

8 all associates and partners to visit one key client at his workplace at least once a month;

9 all associates and partners to telephone at least five 'dormant' clients per month; and

10 all partners to submit a monthly marketing report to the marketing partner and to attend a marketing and client co-ordination meeting.

Marketing need not be expensive, difficult or unpalatable to lawyers. By adopting these or similar procedures, you can proclaim, 'we use the most sophisticated marketing methods available – we talk to our clients!'

Client diagnostic report

If you don't advise your client fully on a wide range of pertinent and necessary matters, he'll either get no advice and so incur problems now or in the future, or else someone else will provide him with those services. 'Oh, I didn't know your firm did that type of work!' is a cry too often heard. It is unforgivable. So often we tend to concentrate on our own particular type of work and forget the overall needs of the client and the range of work the firm could provide. 'How do I market divorce work?' cries a partner in the matrimonial department rather than 'I explain to all my matrimonial clients the benefits and services that my firm can provide in conveyancing and probate and financial advice, as well as other services which may appear particularly relevant to that particular client.'

Test your own diagnostic skills on the city financier client who consults you about making a will and who presents you with this preliminary layman's draft:

> To my wife I leave her lover and the knowledge that I wasn't the fool she thought I was.

> To my son I leave the pleasure of earning a living. For 35 years he thought the pleasure was all mine. He was mistaken.

> To my daughter I leave £150,000. She will need it. The only good business her husband did was to marry her.

> To my valet I leave all the clothes that he has been quietly stealing from my wardrobe over the past 10 years.

To my chauffeur I leave my cars. He ruined almost all of them and I want him to have the satisfaction of finishing the job.

To my partner I leave the suggestion that he takes some other man in with him if he expects to do any business.

And lastly to my cousin Louis who always wanted me to remember him in my will – 'Hello, Louis!'

After flattering your client about his youthful looks and undoubted longevity, you focus the discussion, with your new clients' obvious pleasure, on the problems in his business and personal life and what could be done to improve or protect his position as far as legally possible. Your client is receptive to your advice which is proactive and wide-ranging. What range of legal advice and services could you offer to him? A sample of what might be discussed might include:

- Making a will (and subsequent codicils);
- tax planning;
- family law (divorce, separation);
- trusts;
- financial services;
- employment advice;
- criminal law;
- partnership deed;
- limited liability company formation;
- Mental Health Act.

The competitive edge

The way to deal with competition is to provide a differentiated legal service which satisfies clients more in terms of product quality, service and value for money. It is not necessary to be 'better lawyers' in the legal sense alone. Look at the banks, they don't attempt to differentiate on the thickness of the walls of their strongrooms or the accuracy of their bank statements. When they do attempt differentiation, it is in service and customer care. So when Jarndyce & Jarndyce wants to say that they are better than Kenge & Carboys, what do they really mean? Are they better lawyers or nicer people or in that terrible phrase, 'friendly' solicitors?

More and more firms are realising that this 'betterness' is to be found not in our contrasted legal abilities, but it is rather a 'different-ness' in our ways of presenting and delivering our legal products to our clients in ways which the clients perceive as being of value.

225

The banks all used to be seen as the same but now they all say they are different because they have developed relationships with their customers. Is this true? What are the main features you associate with the big four banks and how are they different? Difference and service are not achieved by statements of intention in marketing brochures and mailshots but only in what clients perceive. Bank managers are now all saying that the 'relationship' between the customer and the bank is what it's all about. On being introduced to a bank manager, I was informed by him that he 'managed 54 relationships'. Each client is assigned to a manager who takes overall responsibility for the business of that client throughout the whole banking empire. This is similar to the concept and practice of the client partner or lead partner in law firms. He has to develop an understanding of that client and keep in touch. He advises the client not only on the usual services that the client uses, but also advises the client on new products, on better and more appropriate services becoming available to him. He does not just respond to needs but also takes new products and services to his clients. Competing on service and relationship features can give a firm the competitive edge.

Spending time with clients

Time spent with clients is an important and effective use of the client manager's time, both during the working day and at social or business entertainment events. The types of entertainment are varied and include the following:

1 formal dinners (Law Society, Chambers of Commerce, IOD);
2 sportsman's dinners with guest speakers from the sporting world;
3 sporting events – rugby, cricket, a box at a football match, etc;
4 wine tastings;
5 golf days;
6 musical and theatrical events;
7 clay pigeon shooting;
8 a pie and a pint, etc.

As we have seen, the legal service is such that the person delivering the legal product and the person receiving the product are both part of the legal service. Therefore, whether you are actually in chargeable time mode or not, when you are spending time with your clients the service itself is being experienced, except without charge.

Any time spent with your client, whether chargeable or not, is therefore a 'live' performance. As the provider of the service you are part of the service whether you are actually giving legal advice or not at any particular point in time. Therefore, spending time with clients whilst the clock is not running is one of the most effective ways of increasing client satisfaction on terms which you can control and manage. This is an important part of client management. You don't have to suddenly swing around on your client at the end of a dinner or sporting event and say, 'Well, you know what all this has been leading to, don't you? We want some work from you!' Of course, this approach might actually work with some clients, but generally you don't have to do it because in client entertainment you are not trying to get work but rather to reinforce the relationship. The event is not wasted just because you don't return to the office the next day laden with promises of work and new instructions. You should have made the impression that you are good to do business with, keen and able to deliver the product and the service to meet the client's expectations. This is what entertaining is about: it's not about selling, it's about the continuation of the service relationship beyond the context of a specific case.

Service to sales

One of the fundamental principles of client management is that by providing your client with a level of service which meets or exceeds his expectations you will retain the client and receive more repeat work as well as more recommendations. The relationship will develop because it is based on good service and personal relations and this will inevitably lead to new work. Maintaining client relationships, developing new work from existing clients and attracting new clients by your reputation for looking after your clients is marketing activity which also derives from successful and effective client management.

It has been estimated that there are three times as many clients lost due to poor service than due to poor legal work or advice. This is consistent with the client perception survey which shows that the generic legal work itself comprises only some 20% at most in the perception of clients of the overall total legal service. It is the total client experience of your firm that goes into this perceptual matrix in the mind of the client. It may go as follows:

1 a recommendation to the potential client to use your firm;
2 the potential client's pre-existing perception of your firm;

3 the potential client notices your firm's advertisements in the local press;
4 the potential client meets someone who works in your office;
5 the potential client makes the first telephone enquiry;
6 he notices the voice and manner of the receptionists;
7 he notices the voice and manner of the case manager who may give a quote;
8 he makes a comparison with other law firms;
9 he makes the first appointment, he travels to your office, he may have some trouble with car parking, bus queues, finding your office, asking someone for directions, getting lost, waiting for the lift, a crowded reception area with everyone noticing his arrival, waiting in reception, reading yesterday's newspapers, accepting a coffee but noticing that they forgot the sugar, experiencing a few minutes delay, and then being told, 'Mr Kenge will see you now.' As he shakes the hand of Mr Kenge who takes a minute or two to find his file, preparing for the interview, the client has already had a number of experiences of the firm and many of his pre-existing expectations and perceptions of image may already have been formed or changed. So even before the brilliant Mr Kenge gets to work, the client is already a long way along the path of the client experience of the firm.

You can't manage the traffic and the bus queues although you could perhaps make appointments quicker and car parking easier. You may even sometimes make a point of visiting clients at their offices. This is the start of client management, being aware of how the client experiences dealing with your firm.

Client managers accept that to succeed by providing excellence in what you do is not enough. It is necessary that you should provide excellence in what you do for your client. Facts must give way to perception because perception is all important to the client. He may be influenced by facts but this is only part of his overall perception of the firm.

In the transition of the profession from a function to a service culture, where it was once comprised of a number of independent law firms all doing much the same work in much the same way for much the same fees and where client satisfaction was ancillary to the work being done, we need to evolve into meeting client requirements, dealing with complaints and successfully meeting clients' needs most of the time. This will become a profession peopled with firms which meet or exceed clients' needs and expectations all of the time and who can occasionally delight the client with new services or old services delivered in new and more useful ways. This is being truly responsive, and a responsive firm will never be short of clients because by providing good service, more work will be obtained and retained.

Introductions and cross-selling

A client of one partner is a client of the firm as a whole. If that one partner does only commercial property work, for example, then the client may never come to explore the possibilities with him of further and different work being done for that client by you or others in the firm. Time and again, when asked, clients say, 'I didn't know you did that sort of work as well!' The lack of a diagnostic approach to the overall needs of the client can and does produce many missed opportunities, both for the firm and for the client.

The Client Inception Form (see Chapter 10 and Appendix 5) provides some basic information and opportunities for discussing other services. Of course, you don't read a list out to the client and just tick boxes in columns but rather from your initial discussion with the client you can ascertain fairly easily whether the client needs other services and advice and it is your duty as a professional adviser to take an overview of the client's legal affairs and exposures and to offer to provide these services.

The effect on most clients I have dealt with like this is either to say, 'I didn't know you did all that!' or a positive response to your care and concern. Not all such discussions will lead immediately to further work, but this is not necessarily a sign of failure or lack of client management or selling skills or a lack of interest from the client. Even where the client goes away without taking up your offer of other services, he has taken with him the knowledge that the firm is interested in providing a wide range of services that may be useful in the future. Also, he will take away an impression that you are interested in him and his business and that you are thinking about him and trying to help on a wider front. Such discussions will bear fruit sooner or later, in one form or another.

Client packages

Client management requires us to take a wider approach to the client and his needs than just the immediate legal function under current instructions. We can with some types of client take a 'packaged' approach and prepare a 'bundle of services' that might typically be offered to a client with identified needs as follows.

Client setting up a new business

- company formation or partnership agreement
- independent financial advice
- employment contracts for staff
- director's service agreements
- lease or purchase of business premises
- terms and conditions of sale
- advice on copyright or trademarks, etc

The new business client will need access to advice for the first 12 months and may be interested in paying a retainer for advice and basic 'hand-holding' legal services.

Overseas client setting up business locally

- company formation
- location and acquisition of business premises
- staff contracts
- supplier contracts
- director's service contracts
- terms and conditions of business
- joint ventures
- EU law
- grants and relations with local and public authorities

Doctors in general practice

- building contract for new surgery
- building contract for surgery refurbishment
- partnership agreement for retirement and admission of partners
- fundholding and independent financial advice
- employment contracts for surgery staff

Your experience of dealing with different client types will be a start from which to work out a range of typical packages. You could discuss your ideas with an existing client and get to understand his views and needs. Having produced a few packages this way will enable the firm to offer a fuller range of services rather then just 'doing a lease' or amending a set of memorandum and articles of association. A firm doing this will become client-driven rather than function-driven. This is the overall aim of client management.

Client database mailshots

Have you discovered the gold mine in your office yet? This does not mean the cabinet full of unbilled work which you're keeping back for a rainy day. It means the computer database of client information, or the inception book, or even the Christmas card list. Whatever it is that you have that has been used to record the names and addresses of clients is of immense potential value in looking after existing clients and of developing more work, if you know what you're looking for and if you know how to use it.

The client database when used incorrectly can be dangerous and destructive. For example, a partner may decide to mailshot all property clients on the database about his expertise in environmental law. So he lifts a huge slab out of the client database and sends out 100 standard form letters saying what he does and encouraging clients to contact him for further details and advice about environmental matters. He has the expertise and is available to advise. Sounds perfectly reasonable so far, doesn't it? But within a few days he will start getting telephone calls which may go like these:

Caller: 'It's about your letter. Well, Mr Smith doesn't live here any more, he moved to Hull about a year ago when I bought the house from him. Didn't your firm do his conveyancing?' *Ooops!*

or

Caller: 'This is Mrs Smith. I was very upset to receive your letter, my husband died three months ago, your Mr Heap is dealing with his estate. I'm surprised you didn't know this. Don't you people talk to each other?' *Groan!*

or he may receive a letter along these lines:

KENGE & CARBOYS
Solicitors
Chancery Lane, London

Dear Sir,

We have received a copy of your letter dated 29th ult. addressed to our client Mr Smith. We are instructed by our client to inform you that he objects to receiving unsolicited correspondence from your firm and that in the event of any recurrence we are instructed to apply forthwith and without further notice to the court for an injunction to restrain the same, with costs.

Yours faithfully,
Kenge & Carboys

He may even get a telephone call from a professional friend:

Caller: 'Hello, Simon, this is Mark [a rising young associate solicitor with your 'friendly' competitor law firm down the High Street]. Look here, I've had a call from Mr Smith. You know, Tom Smith. Well, it's about the letter your firm sent him about environmental work. It was from your firm, wasn't it? Well, uhm, I thought you knew that he transferred all his legal work to us last year? Didn't you know? Oh, dear, I thought you did! Well, our partner Mr Forsyte, who specialises in environmental law, does his work and I do his court work. I thought you knew. Ah, well, never mind, that's business! By the way, are you still OK for squash tomorrow lunchtime?' *Embarrassed silence.*

He reflects worriedly, as he stares out of the office window at the grey drizzle of a summer's day, 'This database mailshot and marketing game isn't as easy as I thought! I must (a) try harder (b) stop fooling around with all this marketing nonsense, or (c) get back to some real work.' As he turns back to his desk, he is comforted somewhat by the familiar but rather uninspiring pile of files on his desk awaiting his time and attention. Just as he reaches for the nearest file, the telephone rings once more:

Caller: 'Hello, Simon, this is Fred Smith calling. It's about your letter. Well, it's funny it should arrive just now because I've been thinking of extending the factory, remember, you did the purchase for me six years ago? Well, now seems as good a time as any to do something about it. We've got plenty of new orders coming in. We need the extra space. There's a problem though – the land next door has got planning permission for industrial use but I'm told there used to be an old chemical factory on it. Can I come to see you tomorrow? What, you can come to see me and take a look at the site? That's just fine! By the way, we're moving house to Newtownsville and I wonder if you would handle the conveyancing for us? Good! I'll expect you tomorrow about 12 o'clock. How about some lunch afterwards?'

Bingo! One out of three responses is an excellent rate of strike for a database mailshot. The worried partner reflects that maybe there is something in all this marketing nonsense after all, and only half-suppressing a smile he asks his assistant to leave a message for Mark, with apologies, to rearrange squash for next week instead of tomorrow on account of an urgent client meeting! Mailshots can be good for business and good for the client. They can be potentially disastrous if used incorrectly.

The database must be kept up-to-date, the entries must be regularly reviewed, someone must build up personal knowledge of the clients of the firm, not just the clients of one partner. As an environmental law specialist he was not to know that a Mr Smith died three months ago, but his probate department knew. Did they know that Mr Smith was a client of his? Did they know he was going to do a mailshot? Has he got the time to communicate on all these points? Does he really have to check first with his probate department before using the client database for environmental law mailshots?

Well, they were both right according to the old rules which concentrated on function and departments but not on clients. They are both wrong in relation to the new rules which put the client first. Here is a valuable object lesson – if you start doing new things that have not been done before, then unless you think it all through first very carefully and very thoroughly, unless you consult with all concerned, unless everyone else knows what you're doing, and unless you know what everyone else is doing and unless you try and test on a small sample first, then disaster may follow. These are the ground rules of client management. This does not mean that you should give up or not try at all. It means that you should recognise that client management and marketing are skills that can and must be acquired. It's not a natural talent and skill, perhaps, for every lawyer, but it is a people skill that can be learned by all.

The design of the client database is important. To do this, you have to know what you want from it and how you intend to use it. Because this is new to many lawyers and because many of us have not used a database like this before, we don't know how to get started or if we do start, we may get it wrong. If you are serious about clients, if you are serious about client management, if you are serious about prospecting for gold in your client database, then you should get serious about training, about getting the right people in to design and operate the system and about getting a dedicated person to run it in support of the partners and client managers in the firm. It will pay for itself many times over, not only in new fee income generated, but also by the reputation you will develop for staying in touch with clients, for helping them on a wide range of issues, for being interested and for being proactive and available. The field is wide open: few, if any, other law firms do it or do it well, yet. The whole culture of the firm will gradually swing around to prospecting for new work with existing clients by using the client database in new and more effective ways.

The marketing manager

Making client management happen throughout the firm in a consistent, comprehensive and controlled way needs management by a trained person who will act in support of the client and marketing objectives of the firm. If the firm's objective is, 'To exceed the levels of clients' expectations' then a detailed action plan needs to be prepared, first to identify exactly what are the expectations of clients and second to devise ways of implementation and report. Partners will need to have the full time support of a trained marketing manager to assist them in carrying out the client management and marketing initiatives of the firm. The role of the marketing manager in developing a client management programme typically might include:

1 implementation of a system for gathering feedback on client perception and client satisfaction using surveys and questionnaires;
2 analysis and discussion of results with management with recommendations for a client management and services plan;
3 preparation of a client management plan for approval;
4 preparation and circulation of a client newsletter;
5 design and provision of leaflets and brochures and other ways of keeping clients fully informed of the services provided by the firm;
6 carrying out regular stakeholder surveys of clients, staff, partners, referrers and suppliers;
7 assisting with handling complaints;
8 production of monthly client reports for management;
9 training for members of the firm in client management; and
10 assisting with marketing and client entertainment.

Whilst partners and client managers are the best people to deal with marketing and client service, many of the ideas generated and activities to follow through are left undone without consistent attention and work. When partners dash back to their offices and clients, it is the marketing manager who will be responsible for follow through action and report.

A detailed description of the work of a marketing manager is contained in Chapter 16 at p 359.

Marketing and client management

Marketing strategy is moving away from placing the accent on the generation of the one-off sale to the pursuit of client satisfaction and the development of longer term relationships with clients. If 80% of the average law firm's work comes from existing clients, we should spend more time ensuring that this increases to 100% (a 25% increase in turnover) by ensuring that every existing client is satisfied and in turn gives us more work. What high budget marketing plan can claim to do that?

Marketing is often thought to be about the getting of new clients. It is also very relevant to the getting of new business from existing clients and its success here depends directly on the quality of client management. You are much more likely to get new and repeat business from an existing client who is satisfied and who knows you and the service you deliver than from prospective clients who initially can assess you on the sole criterion of cost.

A firm with a good marketing and client focus will be getting some feedback from clients about new services and products and perhaps even designing some new services and products to meet a specific need of a specific client. Suggestions from clients for improvements will be a regular feature of the firm's daily business life.

The more advanced client management firms will be regularly getting market research data about what clients think and need now and in the future and of new and future opportunities to anticipate market requirements and plan in advance to be ready to satisfy them.

Sales and service go hand in hand. If your best salesman brings home the bacon, you won't keep it long if you fail to deliver a quality legal product, with a satisfying service delivery system. If you deliver well and satisfy clients, you need to be able to tell your potential markets about it. It can be seen that marketing is only part of the overall client management activities of a law firm. Marketing without client management is largely a waste of time. Client management includes the whole spectrum of client-related activities from the presentation of products and services to the client and through to the delivery of those products and services to the review of the effect and result. Seen in the wider context of client management, marketing is but one aspect of the client activities of a firm.

If marketing is about selling, then client management is about buying. The former sees service and products from the firm's point of view ('We pride ourselves on the quality of our legal work and service to our clients') whereas the latter sees the service and legal work from the point of view of he who must be a payor – the paying client. Effective marketing should address both buying and selling, and the service that links them together.

Action checklist

1 Reconsider your approach to marketing as being not about selling but being about the strategic direction of the firm in managing its resources to most effectively providing benefits to clients.
2 Recognise that the effect of deregulation and competition has put the client first and that this has had a profound affect on the way a law firm goes about its business. The whole firm, its people, structure and resources have only one validating factor – does it or they increase client satisfaction?
3 Determine that your service strategy is part of your marketing strategy.
4 Start by getting market research and regular feedback from existing and potential clients and then design your legal products and service to meet identified client needs.
5 Build into your marketing and service strategy the two key ingredients – be different and provide a better service than your competitors.
6 Employ a marketing manager to assist in design and implementation of a marketing and client management programme.
7 Invest time with clients and reap the rewards.

10 The client manager's toolkit

This chapter contains a number of client management tools which a client management firm could put into practice, perhaps individually or incrementally. It is not suggested that all be implemented at once and the reader is directed to Chapter 16, 'Responding to the Challenge' for a suggestion of various client management implementation programmes. These will depend on the current culture and client orientation of the firm comprising its staff and partners.

You are a client-oriented solicitor or firm to whom client management has been second nature for years. What happens when you're away ill or on holiday or unavailable? What resources can the client expect to fall back into? Most of us are 'good with clients' when our client is sitting across from us at the other side of the desk, listening to every word of our legal advice. What happens when you are not available? What happens if, having carefully and skillfully nurtured a 'new' client and converted him into an 'established' client, you start to pay more attention to the getting of other new clients to the detriment of your established client? The system of client management must be able to cope and carry on. This is where the real profit from client management is to be found, rather than in isolated pockets of client service skills in the firm. Once set up, the client management culture will develop its own momentum.

This chapter contains some basic techniques and tools of a client management programme. Some of them are practices no doubt already current in many firms, and others are ideas to experiment with on a limited sample basis with a few selected clients in an appropriate group or department. Some are more radical in appearance.

A client management programme needs to be adapted to fit each firm. It is not possible or advisable to import a client management programme wholesale. It must reflect and be appropriate to the current culture of the firm, its size, location and client base to be effective. There is no one perfect system.

'The profit's in the system'

Client management, like marketing, is more an attitude of mind rather than a list of things to do with clients. To say that someone is 'good with his clients' tends to suggest that a person either has or has not got 'it' and that nothing can be done about it. This approach is not only defeatist but is unacceptable in client management which holds that everyone can learn and improve their service skills to clients because, as we have seen, a person who delivers a service to a client is actually part of the service himself. Whilst it is accepted that it will not be possible to turn everyone into a dynamic and effective client manager overnight, it is in taking the first steps towards the establishment of a systematic and firm-wide client management culture and practice that will mark out your firm as one which is serious about client satisfaction and one that is doing something about it.

Client inception form

One of the first steps in client management is to get to know your client and to put the basic details on your client database. The use of a well-designed and informative client inception form is a first requirement. The accent here has been changed from the traditional matter inception form in order to place a new accent on the client rather than just on the case.

A sample client inception form is contained in Appendix 5. It can be adapted to suit each firm's own particular requirements, being more or less detailed to suit the firm's client management and computer systems. The form will need to be completed by the client manager or group secretary as appropriate and be signed by the group partner or client partner. The form, or part of it, could be completed by the group secretary with the client before the client comes into your room, depending on the type of client and the work involved. The secretary takes down the client's name, address, telephone numbers and occupation and other information on the form in accordance with group practice.

Is the client a new client to the firm? If so, where did he come from? Was he recommended by a satisfied client? Which client? Was the client recommended by a member of the firm? Who? Was the client referred by a professional adviser? Who and why? Did the client contact the firm due to an advertisement? Which one and where? Is the client an existing client of the firm? Who dealt with him previously?

Who is the client partner? We need to know and enter this information on our client database because we need to understand where clients come from and why. This way we can better direct our client management and marketing efforts in the future. If, for example, we discover from this information that 20% of our inceptions for last month are with new clients, this represents a sizeable part of our current business. Did we have 20% this month last year? What is the trend and what does this tell us about the way our business is growing? More importantly, perhaps, it reminds us that 80% of our new work comes from existing clients. Why does so much work come from existing clients of the firm? Are they really satisfied? Why do they keep coming back? Can we provide an even better service to our existing clients, and, if we do, will it improve turnover and reduce fee resistance? If our service levels slip, will this source of work decline?

Again, if of the 20% of inceptions which come from new clients, 10% for those come through *Yellow Pages*, then again, we know that *Yellow Pages* is an effective way of attracting certain types of new client but that it accounts for only 2% of the firm's total inceptions. If last year, new clients accounted for 22% of our inceptions, then it may be disturbing to find that this has reduced by 2% this year. Why was this? Did we forget to renew our *Yellow Pages* advert? It could be as simple as that. What is not so simple is to ask the right questions and to get the answers and to do the things which are pertinent and necessary to the running of our client-oriented businesses.

We need to know what our clients do for a living. Is it of importance to the company and commercial partners in head office to know about branch office residential conveyancing inceptions? Do they need to know about a Mr Jones instructing a branch office to deal with his house purchase in moving into the area? Is it really that important? Perhaps, perhaps not. However, client managers do not leave clients to chance and all new client inceptions will be studied with interest. A client-focused firm does not take the risk of missing an opportunity. Suppose that Mr Jones is the Chief Executive of ICI? Does that make a difference? To a client-oriented, commercial law firm it makes all the difference! That sort of information would be viewed at head office with great interest and attention. Arrangements would be made for a follow-up contact. Yes, of course ICI has its own regular lawyers but, if Mr Jones is buying a house in your area, there may be a relocation or expansion or diversification of the company being planned. Mr Jones may decide he wants to use some local legal services. Mr Jones may not even have thought about it, but if he finds that the legal work on his house purchase is done efficiently by someone in the firm and with service beyond his expectations, if he finds that he is given information about how what the firm does can benefit him and his business, if he gets to meet one or two partners in the process, who knows what can happen? Client managers try to make these things happen and don't just leave it to chance and wait behind their brass plates any longer. So, as can be seen, we can't leave it to chance any longer to find out who each and every Mr Jones really is!

By using the client inception form as part of the client antennae of the firm, what used to be a chore can become a marketing and client management tool involving both the group secretary and the client manager. When these forms are reviewed by the marketing manager, the appropriate partner(s) in the firm will be alerted and the client management machinery will swing into action. Every inception form and every new and existing client will be carefully logged and checked for the information it may yield, now or in the future.

We may have ascertained that the new client, Mr Jones, from the branch office is not, in fact, the Chairman of ICI, although the name did cause a momentary flutter at head office (they are now so alert to the possibilities of the new client inception form!), but we do know why he came to us, where he lives and what he does. That information used to be enough, didn't it? But the days are gone when clients just tumbled in abundance through our doors.

In competing on service excellence, which only clients can judge, we need to know more about each client, we need to know the quality and potential of the client and of the instructions. What is the actual and potential quality of the present instruction in terms of fee income? How much is the case worth and when and how will we be paid? So the case manager is also required to state on the client and matter inception form, for analysis at head office, his estimate of how long the case will take, how much it will be billed, when the bill will be sent and when and how the bill is to be paid. This will also help to cure the ulcer of your worried finance director who would regularly be reduced to a gibbering wreck just three days before each month end with as much as 45% of budgeted bills still remaining unbilled. He is beginning to breathe more easily and to actually sleep at nights because the financial information in the client inception forms helps to give him a financial picture of where the firm is going and what is in the pipeline in terms of agreed bills to be delivered.

Estimates of bills and payment dates have been notoriously inaccurate in the past. But, with the use of case plans and costs plans and the agreed charges section of the client agreement (see Chapter 11), it will be increasingly easy to plan each case and to more accurately plan and agree the charges for each case. Your finance director will no longer be content to know whether you are 'busy' and whether you think 'things may be picking up' or in your opinion that 'there's not much work about' and other such partneresque *obiter*. He will need to have more precise details and this information can and should be gleaned at the outset and be included in the client and matter inception form. This information can then be built into the monthly finance and management reports of the firm.

The client inception form should also contain details for introductions, or, as it is incorrectly often called, cross-selling. Client managers do not cross-examine their new clients at the first interview and they certainly do not try to 'sell' client services he doesn't want or need. In their initial discussion with the client and in their preparation of the case plan, they may come across instances where the client may need other legal services, now or in the near future. For example, Mr Jones, the branch office client buying a house in the area, may be a director of his own small company and he may be also looking to take a lease of an industrial unit nearby. He is proposing to employ some new staff and may need some advice on contracts of employment. A number of his existing staff are moving into the area and will also need conveyancing services. A client manager may suggest to Mr Jones that he may be interested in speaking to the partner who deals with employment contracts and who may be able to help him in this. Mr Jones may not immediately take you up on this offer, but provided you have identified a need, provided you have told him that you can help, provided that you diarise to mention it at a future date and provided you complete the client and matter inception form, then these opportunities to assist Mr Jones further and to provide a more comprehensive service to him will leave an impression of you and your firm with him. He will see you as being someone who understands his business needs, who is interested in him and who is willing and able to assist him further. The process of obtaining this information will indicate to Mr Jones that you care and are interested in him as a client rather than as just as another case or matter. You never get a second chance to make a first impression.

The firm's marketing and service personnel will be interested in seeing every client inception form for the information to be gathered about both individual clients and trends and to ensure that the appropriate action is taken to follow through leads and to take supportive action with the client partner. Firms that employ marketing and service professionals will be particularly well placed to make use of this information.

Client information pack

Establishing a good relationship with the client at the outset is vital to the 'client for life' concept of client management. All too often we lawyers tend to get so involved in the detailed legal work and priorities and pressures of the case that we sometimes forget or overlook the importance of keeping the client fully informed about what other things the firm can do for the client. Does each fee earner always remember to tell the client about other services of the firm which may be of benefit? Do we always remember to hand out the appropriate leaflets and information about the firm and how it can help the client? Are these brochures and leaflets up-to-date? The client information pack is one way to ensure that this is done in every case and with every client without fail.

The front end of the case presents a good opportunity to send out to clients information about how the firm can help them, both in the conduct of the present case and also for other potential needs and requirements of the client. This publicity must be user friendly and of a quality that the client is less likely to bin it than to put it on one side or in a drawer for future reference. The pack could be sent by the partner or his secretary, or in larger firms by the marketing manager, working on information from the client and matter inception forms and liaising perhaps with the introducing or client partner.

Typically, the client information pack would include:

1 'welcome letter' from the firm;
2 Rule 15 letter or client agreement;
3 client's guide to the firm;
4 terms and conditions of business;
5 personnel directory;
6 appointment card;
7 relevant services brochures, eg buying your house with us, making a will, advice to company directors, etc;
8 details of any special offers, eg 'make a will week';
9 the firm's brochure; and
10 partner and staff profile of the relevant work group.

The client manager will ensure that he keeps an up-to-date stock of client information packs for clients to take with them when they leave after the first meeting. Yes, we all hate being inundated with bumph which we promptly consign to the waste bin. Most people will retain the paperwork if it is clearly and quickly seen to be useful and relevant to the recipient. This is the challenge – making the client information pack interesting, relevant and useful to the client by stressing the present and potential benefits to him in particular.

It is necessary to design the pack to be interesting and relevant from the client's point of view rather than just from the firm's point of view. It is necessary to do some client research and client questionnaires to get some feedback from clients. Then try sending out some samples in order to ascertain feedback about client opinion and perception. Sending Mr Jones the leaflet on 'Liabilities of company directors' could be very useful but also sending him a leaflet on 'Problems at home?' might be inept, or maybe not. Moreover, the long and closely typed screed on 'The commercial property department' may be found by Mr Jones to be too detailed and boring.

The client is really not interested in 'The commercial property department' or what the firm does. As a commercial property partner, the department may absorb all your time and interest, but you are not the client and the client will not see it as you do. Mr Jones at this point is only interested in what you can do for him and the benefits of using you as his solicitor. So, rather than sending information about what you do, stress the benefits to him there are in what you can do for him, eg 'local', 'available', 'responsive', 'flexible', 'value', 'client satisfaction'. The distinction between information about what you do and what you can do for the client is vital, from the client's point of view.

Client profiles

Over a period of time the client partner will get to know a number of key clients particularly well. He will know their businesses, he will have visited their factory or office, he will know the managing director, the finance director and the chairman. He should also have got to know the middle managers and the up-and-coming managers who are or will be the future of that business. He will know their secretaries' first names and the firm will probably have done their conveyancing work. He will know the company, its subsidiaries, its holding company, its bankers and accountants. He will know what the directors do out of the office, he may play golf with them, he may have entertained them at home for dinner. All this information is important towards making and cementing a good relationship with the client.

In addition, other people in the firm may also deal with this client from time to time. Other partners with specialist skills may do work for the client and other support case managers may have done some work for this client. Do they know the managing director's mobile telephone number, should they know, does the managing director want or permit them to know? Do they know information that the client partner does not know? The sensitivities of clients can be easily trampled on if this sort of information is used inappropriately.

By producing a client profile for each key client and by putting it on the client database (subject of course to security codes for named partners) which you will keep regularly updated, the main current details and information regarding each key client of the firm are recorded for all partners and authorised staff to see and use. This is useful where more than one client or group deals with the key client.

If each partner names the top 10 clients for whom he acts and if each client partner prepares a client profile for each of his named top 10 clients, then in a 10-partner firm this would produce client profiles of 100 key clients. This information when viewed by 10 partners and, perhaps, the client and marketing manager (subject to confidentiality, security passcodes and the terms of the client agreement with each client) could produce all sorts of cross-fertilisation of ideas and information. Each partner with screens on their desks would be able to spend just a few minutes a day learning a little more about the 100 clients on whom he depends for his living.

In case of absences of the client partner, or where work is transferred from the client partner to another specialist group, the people concerned can quickly come up to speed in their knowledge and information about the key client from using the client profile. In addition, any useful or relevant information about the client picked up by the other group personnel could usefully expand the firm's knowledge about the client and its ability to provide services and benefits.

Partner and staff profiles

Leading directly on from client profiles is the use, where appropriate, of partner and staff profiles. As we have seen in Chapter 8, the people in the firm who provide the service form one part of the service and the client himself forms another part. It is important to the client to know who is doing his case work and who is the partner in charge and who the assistants are and who he can contact in case of absence or emergency. Both Rule 15 and the client agreement recognise the importance of the named personnel and this is the reason it is important, because they are part of the service.

The firm could produce a number of short personal profiles of the partners and other members of the firm, perhaps on a group-by-group basis. This will be more immediately relevant to the client's needs, and will be linked to the personnel named in the Rule 15 letter or in the client agreement. The use of these profiles could be tried experimentally at first with a sample group in order to gauge client opinion and reaction. It needs sensitive treatment as well as the consent of the persons involved. Rows of pictures of grinning lawyers may be hard to take for some clients. External professional advice should be considered before going too far in this direction.

Progress reports

Having completed the case plan and client agreement with Mr Jones, the first meeting comes to a close. Mr Jones has paid you something on account, he has agreed what you're going to do and how long it's going to take and when he's going to pay you again. He knows when the next meeting or point of contact is going to be and the stages of the work you will be doing initially. You already know a bit about him, his business and family, where he comes from and what else you or the firm can do for him now or in the future. (Check that client contact diary and complete that client inception form!)

So, you have made a start on Mr Jones's case as agreed. You've already done much of the initial work in planning the case with him present. In so many cases, it is this thinking and planning time at the outset that is so important in determining how the case runs overall. As Mr Jones knows what you're going to be doing in the next four weeks and as he will need to have some input, you will probably have agreed to see him again in three weeks time to go through the contracts, searches, pleadings or reports. Nevertheless, it would be appreciated by Mr Jones if you, or perhaps your secretary, should telephone him briefly after a week to say that things are going well, that you have sent off all the searches (or issued the writ, etc) as agreed (and paid for in advance by Mr Jones) and that you have received the draft lease (or specialist report, etc) and that you look forward to seeing her again shortly as agreed.

The progress telephone call might run like this, 'Oh, by the way, we are pleased to say that the draft lease has been received. It probably won't need much amendment or negotiation and we will be ready to go through everything with you next week, so we can see you in a week earlier if you like, or pop in to see you, if you prefer.'

A progress report to the client generally goes down well even when, as here, it was not strictly necessary from the file's or the case's point of view. It is beneficial, however, from the client's point of view and this is an important point taken by the client manager. He will give regular progress reports to the client on progress, or the lack of it. 'Progress' includes not only what's been done but also what's happening or being done now. It need only be a telephone call or it can be a file note copied to the client for the price of a stamp or fax. Avoid writing letters wherever possible – they are expensive, slow and often not user friendly.

It is human nature for clients to think that if they hear nothing, then nothing is happening, whereas many lawyers, who are also human, often take the view that the client assumes that everything is okay unless they hear to the contrary. In client management, no news is bad news to the client. There is a mismatch in these assumptions made by client and solicitor. It is important to tell the client what's going on and even if nothing is happening, to telephone him to tell him that nothing is happening. So often the client will then tell you that the deal has changed anyway! The fact and act of communication in client management often is more important than the message that is communicated. By making a progress report like this, you are in effect saying to your client, 'I have done all that we agreed, I'm in control and on schedule, you're in good hands with us and I understand that you want to be kept in touch.' As both the client and the solicitor are part of the service, then communication by keeping in touch is part of the service and not ancillary to it. The case may have faltered, but the service must continue.

The ultimate test of communication is that you should never get a 'chasing' or surprise telephone call from your clients, that you have anticipated their requirements and that you have acted in advance. Can you pass this communication test? All the time, or most of the time, or just sometimes?

In the case of key clients, it is often useful to produce regular, perhaps monthly, progress reports (see Appendices 3 and 4). This can be produced on a word processor and updated monthly. It sets out each case, a description to identify it, who is dealing with it in the firm, who is instructing on the part of the client, the current position as to progress and maybe also the position as to fees, with amounts billed together with a figure for recorded work in progress. Once the basic information is put onto a standard shell report, then the client partner can update it monthly. He will have received progress reports from all other case managers working for that key client. If not, he or his secretary will chase them. Partners and staff soon get used to being chased and soon fall into line with the progress reports. The client partner can then update the progress report, follow up queries on quality or fees internally, check the credit control report for that key client and then send off the progress report to the key client. In many cases, where there is a close working relationship, the client partner will meet with the key client, sometimes without charge, at the key client's premises, to go through the progress report to amplify where necessary and to take further instructions. He will take notes of client queries and follow up action. 'This case is now urgent, that one is being re-negotiated, you can send me a bill on that one' says the key client.

With some clients, the monthly progress report will be presented to their own monthly board meeting, to which you may be invited. What an opportunity for showing that you have delivered a differentiated service! Even if you are not invited to attend the board meeting, it is likely that your progress report with your firm's name on it will be circulated to board members. Even if it does not get circulated at board level, the director reporting will be using or relying on your report which makes his job a little easier. At least he will be mindful and grateful for your service assistance. The progress report can also be linked to the agreed monthly bills.

Keeping in touch

Some time ago I came across an assistant solicitor shaking the hand of a client outside the doors of the office, saying, 'Goodbye!' I asked him later what was going on. 'Oh, that was Mr Smith. We've just had a farewell lunch and we won't be seeing each other again.' I asked if Mr Smith was emigrating or going out of business or if he has a terminal illness or if the assistant was leaving the firm. He replied, 'We've just won him very substantial damages after a long and hard case and he was so pleased he took me out for lunch as a 'thank you'. It's a pity really – the case was very interesting and we got on well with the client. I'll miss him!'

I took the assistant quietly aside and whispered a few words in his ear. Gone are the turnover days, when clients just presented themselves at our offices, when we did the work and then the client disappeared into the ether. These are the days of the client and the client is for life. 'When are you seeing him again? What other help does he need from us? What business is he in? How is he going to spend or invest his damages? Has he seen our financial services adviser? When do you follow up?' and so on.

I explained that there was a golden opportunity to help the client further and also to develop the firm's services to that client. It is so easy to let these opportunities pass through being 'busy' doing other things or simply by not even appreciating how important that opportunity is.

It may be appropriate for a contact interview to be done here. The marketing manager could follow up with a service questionnaire or a client satisfaction rating telephone call. Even better, the group partner could get in touch, congratulate the client on his win and offer to provide another relevant service.

The client database should diarise to follow up after three months and then at six months. Contact should be maintained and the key client should be put on the mailing list and on the client partner's telephone list. It is vital that in one way or another a way should be found to maintain contact with that client.

Be careful of using the client database to keep in touch or for use in mailshots. Out-of-date or incorrect information can play havoc with client relations. Upset clients may respond by asking for their records to be deleted from the computer. It is a sensitive task which needs constant attention and diligence.

Monthly client telephone list

The name and contact number of 'former' and 'dormant' clients should be kept on a list and once a month at or near to the first day of the month there should be a telephone contact call. Over a period of one year I will have spoken to at least 120 inactive clients. After some initial small talk to re-establish the relationship and retune to the client's wavelength, the contact call may typically go like this:

Solicitor: 'Is everything okay with that lease/contract/service agreement/court order/settlement, etc that we did for you?'

Client: 'Yes, no problems. In fact, I'm glad you've telephoned, you've saved me a call, I've been meaning to telephone you. Can you help us with ...?'

Solicitor: 'Of course, we would be glad to help – I'll call in to see you tomorrow.'

I have estimated that out of every 10 calls made like this, about five result in an immediate instruction of some sort or another. As for the other five, it is difficult to be precise but it is certain that some of those clients do come back at such time as they need legal advice or services. Even if they don't make contact for several months, an impression will have been made or reinforced that the firm is one which cares about its clients, takes a long-term view of them and keeps in touch. It's this keeping in touch that is important because it may be perceived to be a continuation of the service. As not many solicitors find time to do it, the field is wide open for client managers to make a positive and proactive impression on their clients and 'former' clients. It costs very little and does not take much time. You can ask your secretary to help you with this. Apart from being good client care and good business, it is also a pleasant way to spend a few minutes, as a break from the incessant demands of legal work. Talking to clients outside of the ambit of a particular case is a 'free' service.

The DDR form

As a group partner you are responsible for all the clients and all the cases being handled by the case managers in your group. But if you have one, two, three or more assistants within your group, there may be several hundred current files and current clients and it will not be possible for you to meet or speak to every client that passes through your group. Nevertheless, you have overall responsibility for them and it is your task to ensure that every client receives the level of service for which you wish your firm to be known. How can you do this? You can't know every case and you can't know every client but you can make it your business (and as a partner it is your business) to make contact with as many of your group clients as is possible.

The DDR form may help. Every day your secretary, perhaps assisted by the marketing manager, places on your desk a yellow sticker and written on it is the name and telephone number of a client of the group, together with the name of the case manager in your group dealing with the matter and a brief description of the matter. You may also be given a copy of the client profile or even better, you may be able to call it up on the screen on your desk from the client database. All you have to do is pick up the telephone and dial the number. The following conversation typically might ensue:

Group partner: 'Good morning, I'm [name] the partner having overall responsibility for the clients within my group. I see from [name of case manager] that you are a new client to my firm and that [name of case manager] is dealing with your [purchase/sale/lease/court case, etc]. I have not been able to say 'hello' yet but I thought I'd just telephone briefly to introduce myself. I hope that [name of case manager] is looking after you satisfactorily?'

Client (somewhat amazed to be graced with a partner's attention and maybe a little suspicious at first): 'Yes, [case manager's name] is dealing with my case. Things are going alright, I think.'

Group partner (he only 'thinks' it's all going alright – doesn't he know, hasn't he been told what's happening? Some bridge-building may be required here!): 'Of course, [case manager's name] is very experienced in these matters and I have a daily meeting with him. Has he contacted you recently?' (The big question!)

Client: 'Well, he did say he would contact me if there were any problems so I assume that everything's okay.'

Group partner (relieved to hear that there is no actual problem other than only a lack of progress reports and communication (only!)): 'I'll have a word with him and get him to telephone you. I'd like you to know that I'll keep an eye on your case and that you can telephone me direct if you have any concerns or if you need any other advice'.

The client hangs up, thinking, 'Well, that's the first time a partner has contacted me. What's he up to? Is there a problem? Well, I don't think so but I'll see if [case manager's name] gets in touch. Maybe the firm really does care about its clients. I know who to contact if necessary. He's keeping a special eye out for me and my case!'

The group partner hangs up thinking, ' Well, that seemed OK. I'll have a word with [case manager's name]. I must do this sort of thing more often, tomorrow in fact!'

And so it goes on. Contact and communication with clients is never a waste of time. It maintains the service link and often leads to new business.

Why are they called DDR forms? Well, by speaking to a client of the firm on a daily basis, you will have been in touch with the front line, with the real world of real clients, with clients you would otherwise not have spoken to. Over the course of a year you will have spoken to 200 clients with whom you would not otherwise have had any direct contact at all. You have made service your business. This is your 'daily dose of reality' repeated every day for a year. I wish it was my phrase but it is not – it comes from Tom Peters, *The New Masters of Excellence*, who expounds the power and importance of this message far more forcefully than me.

Appointment cards

This is an idea taken from dentists. They always give you an appointment card during treatment and when treatment is completed an appointment is always booked for a check-up six months later.

An appointment card could be issued to the client at the beginning of the case with details of the next meeting. The group secretary will complete the appointment card with the client before he leaves the office and diarise it in the group office diary. The appointment card will be updated as the case progresses. The reverse side of the appointment card contains useful information about the firm so that the client will keep it with him at all times, such as telephone number, an emergency contact number and so on

After the case has been finished, the appointment card can be used or reissued where appropriate for a 'legal checkup' in three, six or 12 months time. This helps to maintain contact with the client and keeps the service going even though on hold.

The firm may adopt different practices for private, business and legal aid clients depending on its own client management style. The overall impression given to clients by use of the appointment card is one of planning, organisation and client focus. It may also help to ensure that not only will the client remember to come back but also it will impress upon all members of the group the importance of keeping in touch and provide one way of doing it.

Case reviews

It is a fundamental principle of client management that one of the purposes and objectives of doing legal work and providing a service to a client is to ensure that the client's expectations are equalled or exceeded and that the client is at least satisfied and preferably delighted with the service he has received. Just doing the legal work and collecting payment of the bill is not enough because it falls short of the last and vital stage. Client managers do not assume that just doing the legal work is enough to satisfy the client, they both need and want to know that the client is satisfied. In addition, client managers in their constant quest for service improvements need to receive client feedback to know what clients like and what clients don't like and then feed this information back into the service and product design process.

The case review looks at the case both from a quality assessment angle and also to assess the client satisfaction rating. It should be a rule to follow with all clients and in all cases. At the end of each case, there should at least be an internal review to check how the case was handled, how the case plan worked out in practice, and what was the overall profit or loss on the case. This deals with product quality. A client satisfaction questionnaire (Appendix 6) will assess the client satisfaction rating achieved in the case.

Initially, there could be a review with every tenth client. Was the client satisfied, did he get value, were there any problems and what comments, if any, does the client have? This is all vital information that needs to be gathered and to be fed back into the system to ensure that client concerns are properly catered for in our systems. It is this review and feedback process that is at the heart the work of a client-oriented firm.

Annual service client reviews ('ASK')

Where you act as a client partner, you will keep a regular overview of the affairs and cases of your key clients on a monthly basis. You will also arrange on an annual basis, if not more often, to visit your key clients at their factory or office to meet with the managing director and finance director in order to conduct a review of the year's work. This will include costs billed, cases done, credit control periods, rates of charge, feedback about the performance and service provided by your case managers and an adjustment and agreement of new terms where appropriate.

At a recent annual service client review I carried out, the client voiced his concerns about who did the work of a certain solicitor when he was away. He thought that noone seemed to see or action the client's work in that person's absence. It was not made as a complaint, but a little 'niggle' that could be, and was, nipped in the bud before it grew into an issue or a complaint. The client concluded by saying, 'Yes, we get a good service and a pound spent with you seems to go a long way!' Well, we still act for that client and perhaps it's due not only to the work we do, but also to the service we provide and the systems we have in place to ensure that we listen to the client and then do something about it.

Group partner's monthly client management report

We are familiar with monthly management accounts and we are familiar with targets and performance measures either of individual case managers, or departments, or perhaps more appropriately of groups centred around one partner and his clients. These reports are currently based mostly on financial performance such as billing, work in progress, credit control, disbursement control, write offs and so on, comparing this month with last month and last year.

But with the advent of changes in firm management style and client management practices, and with the expanding roles of group partners as discussed above, the group partner should also prepare and submit a monthly report on client management. Appendix 11 contains a sample of a group partner's monthly report on the management of clients within his group. It sets out a report on the main activities that comprise a partner's work with both existing and potential clients.

We have already established that whilst a partner must be a fee earner for at least 60% of his time, he is wrong to keep his head down doing legal work that in many cases could and should be delegated to support staff within his group. He should be spending up to 20% or 25% of his time doing the things set out in the report. This is how he manages the perceptions of the clients in his group and this is how he ensures that one of the main objectives of his work is achieved and maintained, namely client satisfaction.

The firm's monthly client management report

With the monthly management accounts there should also be a report to partners on the clients of the firms – inceptions, details of new clients, where they came from, what they do, why they choose this firm, categories of clients, lost clients and so on – all vital information to keep us informed of trends in the marketplace. A sample of the report is contained in Appendix 12.

It is a truism that that which is targeted, recorded, measured and reported is that which tends to get done. The whole point of the reports, systems and forms used in support of client management activities is to set targets for effective client action, to measure it, to report upon it and to review it. This ensures that things are done. Thinking and talking about client management is not enough.

All partners are accustomed to receiving the thick brown envelope once a month containing management accounts of the previous month and to setting an evening aside to plough through the monthly accounts before the next partners' meeting. However, in order to assess the performance of the firm in ways additional to the way of the accountant, a firm can also measure and report upon its performance in client management. A firm that actively manages its clients as well as its finances, will also need to see reports on clients in a regular and systematic way.

The 'welcome' letter

When a new client joins the firm, it would be a nice and inexpensive gesture to send a 'welcome' letter to the new client. Apart from being an indication that the firm is aware of and appreciates having the new client, such a letter could also fulfil other uses such as enclosing the firm's literature, the client information pack, details of special offers and of client discounts on certain services.

The letter needs to be handled sensitively. It may not be appropriate, for instance, to issue a 'welcome!' letter to a new client instructing you on a family or personal matter, or where there has been a recent bereavement in a probate case. It may be ideal to send to a young couple who are newly married and buying their first house through the firm, or to a new client taking advice from the firm about setting up in business for the first time and so on. The 'welcome!' letter will be of value when used in the right circumstance but it could do harm otherwise. Ideally, at this level of client management, the firm may need to have a trained marketing manager who will be able to assess what is appropriate to the client by looking at the client inception form and by having a brief word with the case manager, group partner or client partner concerned.

The 'thank you' letter

Rather like the 'welcome!' letter, this is very effective when used appropriately. It may be ideal to send it to the address of a newly-moved conveyancing client, but could be clumsy and insensitive if sent to a newly divorced or bereaved client. The message here is clear: both the 'welcome!' and the 'thank you' letters give out useful and effective client orientation signals on the part of the firm but if these letters are not used correctly then not only will they fail to be effective but they may also give the very opposite impression that the firm is trying to create. There is no second chance to make a first impression, so such letters need to be handled with care.

After sales service

The culture and practice of the turnover days (see Chapter 1) was to measure the firm's performance in terms of the number of current cases and the amount of bills delivered rather than in the quality of service as perceived and assessed by the client. The end of the case and what happened afterwards were not treated with any great attention as we moved on to the mountain of new cases awaiting our attention. In client management, however, the qualitative 'client for life' culture is encroaching upon and superseding the former file management quantitative culture.

When we have brought in a new client, when we have provided a service to him, when we have completed his 'case' and when he has paid our bill, then stage one only of the client relationship has been achieved. This may be the time to 'drop' the file but not to say 'goodbye!' to the client. Instead, it is the time to look at diagnostic advice for other services and to diarise the subsequent contact intervals, mailshots, newsletter circulation and follow-up telephone calls.

This all needs to be handled with sensitivity and care in order to avoid overwhelming or pestering the client with unwanted or untimely communications. Depending on the type of client and the work you have done, each case on completion should contain an 'after-sales' service plan that should be put on the client database and allocated to the client partner.

Fixed fee interview

One of the barriers between solicitors and their clients is the perceived barrier of cost and uncertainty. By not discussing costs at the initial interview, particularly with a new client, and then by sending out a bill later without agreement or discussion with the client, ('billing by ambush') we not only risk not being paid, but we also perpetuate the myth of being expensive and uncaring. We also risk losing the client. An alternative would be to proceed as follows:

1 offer a fixed fee diagnostic interview of half an hour;
2 ensure that the interview starts on time;
3 when you start the interview, explain to the client that the charge for the first half hour is fixed. If the interview continues beyond the half hour, you explain that the client will be charged at your hourly rate;
4 the client can pay his bill by cheque, cash or credit card at the end of the interview and be issued a receipted standard bill 'For professional charges for advice given in respect of ...'.

This approach will have achieved a number of things:

1 the client will know and agree the charge at the outset;
2 both the case manager and the client will be in control of the time taken;
3 both the case manager and the client will be able to control the cost;
4 your diary will not be disrupted;
5 the client will get what he expects; and
6 you will get paid immediately, as well as getting a new client.

Legal health check

Client managers will have produced a profile of legal advice and services which they consider to be necessary for the well-advised client, based on their own range of services and the information received from clients. For example, they will have built up a profile of the business client who will have the benefit of advice from the firm in the following areas:
1 business premises;
2 terms and conditions of sale;
3 employment contracts;
4 company formation or partnership agreement;
5 copyright and trademarks;
6 debt recovery procedures;
7 company secretarial services; and so on.

The private client will also have a profile of services which may include:

1 house conveyancing;
2 making a will;
3 financial services including mortgage, insurance, pensions and savings;
4 tax planning;

5 trusts;
6 family law advice;
7 employee advice; and so on.

The firm will be concerned to ensure that all its clients are well advised in the basic range of services that the firm can provide. By using the legal audit, the firm can suggest that the client should consider being fully advised and protected as far as legally possible.

Telephone helpline

Information and advice need not always be communicated by personal 'attendance'. The perceived benefits of emergency and 24-hour helpline calls can be great but can be provided at relatively low cost. There is a comfort factor to some clients in knowing that legal advice is available throughout the day, night and at weekends. The helpline also helps you to stay in touch with your clients.

The helpline could be one which is manned by an internal rota of partners and solicitors. There could be a 'duty' solicitor on call throughout the day to deal with emergency calls and enquiries. He would take preliminary details and refer the client to the most appropriate person in the firm. He may be able to give some initial advice himself. At evenings and at weekends the rota could work so as to divert calls to the duty solicitor's home number without revealing what that number is.

Alternatively, during office hours the marketing manager could be detailed to deal with new clients and general enquiries, making preliminary notes and then transferring the enquiry to the appropriate legal expert.

The CSR board

Whilst sitting in the waiting room of the local hospital, I was intrigued to see a large information board displaying various performance measures under the heading of 'Patient/customer performance targets'. Using symbols of beds, people and large injection needles, the chart illustrated the targets that the hospital had set itself and the performance actually achieved. Some figures related to waiting times for an operation, to see a consultant and waiting times generally and punctuality on being seen for fixed appointments. I noted that the target time for seeing 'patient/customers' in this waiting room was within 30 minutes of the time fixed for the appointment. A red sign above the information board kept flashing up messages such as, 'There is only one doctor on duty this morning (it was Sunday at 9.15 am). You should be seen within 30 minutes.' The waiting room was quiet and there was a relaxed and friendly but professional atmosphere.

Whilst glancing through an up-to-date magazine from the waiting-room table, I set my wristwatch, checked the people who were waiting and settled down to unobtrusively observe the proceedings. Every few minutes a nurse with a clipboard came into the waiting area and called a name, and another patient/customer was taken to see the one and only doctor on duty. Within 15 minutes the waiting room was clear. I didn't see anyone wait for more than 10 minutes. I was seen within 16 minutes and 23 seconds of my appointed time and went away feeling quite impressed. The actual treatment from the doctor was no different from any other hospital – it was about what I expected. The big difference was that I was happy not to have been kept waiting without knowing what was going on. Everyone there seemed happy to wait for a few minutes because it was in a managed and informed situation. The hospital had set itself realistic and comfortable targets, which they out-performed. I was prepared to wait for 30 minutes. Had the hospital promised to see their patient/customers within 5 minutes, which noone expected when they arrived, there might have been grumblings if they had been kept waiting for 15 minutes. The lesson for the client manager is that client dissatisfaction often arises from a lack of information and communication about what is going on rather than from the actual case itself. It is important to set realistic targets based on past measured performance, allowing some time for margins and to communicate these to clients. Everyone knows where they stand and what to expect. Clients don't always want speed, they just want to know a definite time or date and to be kept informed about progress.

The firm could even publish the performance figures, good and bad. Why not put up a large board in the reception area, attractively designed and easy to read with the following performance statistics:

1 the average waiting time for clients for an appointment in the last 12 months was same day/next day/two days/three days;
2 the average time clients were kept waiting in reception for their fixed appointment was five/10/15 minutes;
3 the number of appointments starting on time or within five minutes of the appointed time was [87%];
4 the other 13% were kept waiting no more than 10 minutes on average;

5 the number of complaints from clients over the last 12 months numbered 87, of which:
   23 were about delays
   43 were about costs
   21 were varied;
6 the complaints received were dealt with as follows:
   26 within two days
   45 within three days
   16 within seven days;
7 the overall client satisfaction rating for the firm during the last 12 months was 73%, the highest was 97% and the lowest was 23%.

Clients who arrive early in reception might be asked to complete a short client questionnaire and to put it in the client feedback or ' suggestions' box on the wall or hand it to the receptionist.

The client manager's toolkit

The techniques featured here are only a few suggestions of what could be done to improve the service to clients. Each firm will be able to make its own client management tools depending on the client base and the feedback it actually gets from its clients. There are few fixed rules other than to try something new and if it works and if clients like it and if it increases clients satisfaction and profitability then to keep on doing it. Client management is pragmatic and practical.

Action checklist

1 Consider whether a firm can benefit from using the client manager's toolkit.
2 Introduce each 'toolkit' practice one at a time, perhaps department-ally, and assess results. If it works, adopt it on a wider basis and go on to the next item in the toolkit.
3 Be pragmatic and practical – if it satisfies clients and is cost effective, do it and keep on doing it.

11 The client agreement

'What does the contract say?'

How many times after listening patiently to a client's tale of woe have you asked, 'Did you get it in writing?' How many times have you seen the shrug and heard the sad but almost inevitable reply, 'Well, it seemed all right at the time.' How many times have you advised the client, 'It all depends on what the contract says'? How many times have you explained to your client that a contract does not necessarily have to be in writing but that it's better to have something in writing to avoid problems of evidence? How many times have you then allowed the client to leave your office and then permitted yourself to commit large amounts of time and responsibility doing work on his case without a written agreement about the contractual terms? What does your contract say about the work to be done? What does it say about the charges? What does it say about the timescale? Why didn't you get it in writing? Why don't we do what we advise our own client's to do? It's an indefensible position from both a legal and a client management point of view and needs remedying for the benefit of both the solicitor and his client.

Appendix 1 contains a sample form of client agreement. It contains a printed version of a firm's terms and conditions of business including details of the firm's complaints procedure. This will ensure compliance with Rule 15. But it also contains client details, and as such is a useful file management and inception tool. It also has an agreed charges section (optional under Rule 15 but recommended by the Rules of Professional Practice) for discussion and agreement with the client.

The benefits of getting a signature to the client agreement at the beginning of a case should not be under-estimated, for both the client and the solicitor. The solicitor will have complied with Rule 15 and beyond, he will have secured a clear agreement with his client as to charges and he will have to a large degree planned the case, or the first part of it, with his client. The client in turn will, therefore, have a contract in his hand, feeling surer and, therefore, happier about costs and knowing who in the firm is going to do what and when.

Rule 15 and beyond

There are two parts to Rule 15 as follows:

(1) Every principal in private practise shall operate a complaints handling procedure which shall *inter alia* ensure that clients are informed who to approach in the event of any problem with the service provided.

(2) Every solicitor in private practise shall unless it is inappropriate in the circumstances:
   (a) ensure that the client knows the name and status of the person responsible for the day to day conduct of the matter and the principal responsible for its overall supervision;
   (b) ensure that clients know whom to approach in the event of any problem with the service provided; and
   (c) ensure that clients are at all relevant times given any appropriate information as to issues raised and the progress of the matter.

It is not necessary to provide the client with a written complaints procedure and it is not necessary to give a fixed quotation for fees. Whilst these are not legal requirements, it must be obvious to any business person in competition with other similar businesses for the same clients and doing the same sort of work in the same sort of way that simply abiding by the letter of the rule will not in itself guarantee that the client will instruct you or that you will always have a satisfied client. Compliance with regulations does not necessarily assure client satisfaction.

Apart from the Code of Professional Conduct, the introduction of Rule 15 was perhaps the first serious attempt by the Law Society to introduce into professional rules some basic standard of 'client care'. It was, however, received with mixed feelings by many practitioners. It can feel awkward to have to alert a new client at the outset, or to tell a long-established client, about the firm's complaints procedure. It can be both insensitive and uncommercial if handled unskillfully. If client management is taken seriously, there is much more that we need to agree with the client at the outset for mutual benefit.

The bare necessities

How many times have you got half-way through a case and realised that you haven't actually seen the client yet, or that you don't have his fax number or that you haven't realised that the timescale was urgent? How often have you got to the billing stage and wondered how on earth you're going to recover all that work in progress and justify them to the client? How many times have you written off your profit margin with a sigh exclaiming, 'The client/case just won't stand the cost!' How often have you blamed the overheads for making you unprofitable?

Many good things can stem from completing of a client agreement and agreeing a case plan with the client at the outset. A few minutes at the front end of a case, though hard to find, will repay ample dividends during the middle and at the end of the matter, if you can manage your time for preparing the case plan at the beginning of the case. As the case plans are intended to be prepared in the presence of and by agreement with the client, the time spent on case planning is not non-chargeable time, but an integral part of the case and file management process and the vital first stage in the service to the client. Also, by using the case plan format, it can act as a useful checklist and can also make it easier for the solicitor to cover the bare necessities, including the financial aspects of the retainer.

First, using the client agreement, take down the basic client details. Then discuss who will be responsible for conducting the case and who will be assisting in it. Name your assistant, even better, introduce your assistant to the client there and then. Name your secretary and any other person who might cover for you in case of absence. This is important from the client's perception of the service, who depends so much upon the personal aspect of the case, rather than upon the innards of the file which clients rarely, if ever, see.

You should try to cover a number of things with the client by the end of the first interview including the following.

Client details

The name, address and telephone number of the client are the usual details taken but, additionally, client managers are interested in finding out, if a new client, where he came from, why he came to us, who referred him or made a recommendation and what if any differentiation he expects. Details of his occupation or business, together with status and other contact names, can be useful. Client managers are seeking to understand their clients better so that they can provide them with a better service. The client is the intended recipient of the proposed legal service, and as he himself forms a unique and important part of that service, the more we know about the client the better the service will be.

The case manager

As we have seen, the person providing the service actually puts his or her own personal stamp on the service and actually comprises part of the service. This is why it is important to understand Rule 15's requirement to state the name of the person doing the work. We are, in effect, defining and specifying the service by naming the case manager. This is why the case manager or fee earner doing the day-to-day work on the matter needs to be identified, because he or she is part of the matter and the service.

The group partner

Where a partner has the overall responsibility for the management of the production of the service, as a group partner, who does not do all the work in the group but who may direct or advise the case manager or his group on their work, he also forms part of the service and so again must be identified to the client as part of the service specification. The legal product and services do not just hang in the air; they are a product of the people providing them. It is also important for quality systems to specify the control mechanism to ensure consistency of work and service.

The client partner/senior partner

The client will need to know the name of the partner or person to whom complaints or problems can be referred as a last resort. This may be a named partner or the senior partner or a client manager. A client-oriented firm will operate a clear and simple complaints procedure because it recognises that complaints are one of the best and cheapest sources of client feedback and market research. Complaints are best not to be seen as negative criticism but as pointers towards client management improvements.

The objectives of the work

A service has value only to the extent to which it achieves a result or a benefit to the client. Clients do not want to pay for the process of law but only for the result to be achieved, for example, to defend an action and counterclaim with costs, to recover damages, to obtain possession and damages, to get a divorce and to claim a rightful share of the matrimonial home and so on. It is logical, therefore, to ask the client what his objective is and to agree it in writing.

The case plan

Rule 15 requires that clients be given appropriate information regarding the case and its progress. If the whole case cannot be accurately planned at the beginning, the client should know how the work can be taken in stages and what work will be done up to a certain point in time when the case plan can be reconsidered. The demystification of legal work is an essential step towards client management. It seems obvious business sense to ensure that your client should be involved in the case planning process because, as we have seen, the receiver of the service is part of the service and also because it will reduce the chance of misunderstanding and future fee resistance. Case plans can be standardised, bespoke or broken into stages but it is best to keep them simple.

The agreed charges for the work

Now more than ever before the accent of legal work is on cost. Clients will nearly always go for the lowest cost option, no matter how good the product or service you outline in your presentation or quotation. Therefore, it is necessary to give the client what he wants. This will require the agreement of a fixed charge for a fixed amount of work and time. If you can't plan the work too far ahead because of possible variables, plan it in stages according to the 'salami principle':

If you challenge an expert to eat a whole salami, he simply smiles, sits down at table, produces with a flourish a napkin, plate, and knife and cuts up the salami into bite-size pieces and proceeds to eat it in slices until he comes to the last piece when the whole salami has been eaten. A gourmet would also have produced some fresh bread and half a bottle of chianti to help things along.

Adapting the salami principle for a client who wishes to claim damages from his employer for an accident at work, the first stage is to obtain evidence, statements and a medical report in order to assess liability and quantum. In addition, you may recommend that counsel be instructed to advise. You cannot say at this stage how strong the case is and whether it is worth pursuing, though it may look hopeful from your preliminary discussion with the client. So you would say to the client:

I think there is the basis for a successful claim here but, if it is defended by your employer and if the case goes all the way through court, it could be expensive. I suggest that we should get the report from your doctor and the specialist, and that we should get a statement from the foreman at work where your accident occurred. Depending on what they say, we may need to get counsel's opinion on the amount that you could claim and the chances of success. We can then decide whether to proceed further. To get to that stage will take about four weeks. Counsel's fee will be about £XXX and our charges will be £YYY, both plus VAT. If you're happy with that, I propose that you pay me £ZZZ now and the balance in four weeks' time.

Client management requires us to plan the case with the client at the outset by completing a case plan. Having planned the case or the first part of it, it is necessary to agree charges with the client. It is quite easy to work out and agree a fixed fee for a fixed amount of work. If the work is uncertain in time and content, it's best to say so as soon as possible. If it is commodity work, the costs are probably standard anyway. Client managers must be able to plan their work and cost it out and agree the charge with the client and manage the work to stay within the agreed case plan and cost plan.

The names of legal assistants and secretary

Over the course of a matter your client will speak many times to your secretary or assistant albeit only briefly perhaps. But, while your client is speaking to your secretary and not to you, your secretary becomes your stand-in and also becomes the firm and part of the service. This is why it is important to name her because she will form part of the service in the perception of your client.

The name of your assistant(s)

Solicitors do not work in isolation. Even if we have no permanent or regular assistant, when we are out of the office or away ill or on holiday, the person who looks at your mail or takes your calls is perceived by your clients to be your assistant and part of the firm and also forms part of the service. This is why you should name the person who the client can speak to if you're not available when he telephones, because he is part of the service that the client is paying for. It is so important to clients to know that someone else knows what's going on or can find out.

The next meeting or contact date

After the first meeting, your client leaves the office with some idea of what was said but very soon he may have forgotten the advice and what was agreed to be done and when and by whom. Research has shown that clients retain an impression of the firm and the service of which only 7% relates to what was said. With client management, a client who leaves your office after the first meeting will have a case plan and a client agreement. In addition, the appointment card can be very useful for some types of client as a reminder of the next meeting.

Introductions to other services

We have seen that calling ourselves 'conveyancers' or 'litigators' is using old functional terminology. Clients are attracted to you because of you and what you can do for the client, not because you are a conveyancer or litigator. It is you that is part of the service and it is you that the client wants. It is not just your expertise. Therefore, you need to explore with the client his overall needs for legal advice and identify what benefits or solutions can be achieved by the various services that you and the firm can offer to him. You are not just cross-selling but rather you are providing the complete legal service. To a matrimonial client, for example, you will not only ensure that she gets her divorce, but also that her property requirements are serviced, that she updates her will and reviews her financial position.

Your home telephone or other contact number

You are part of the service and so is your client, and the service is provided when you are on 'live' with the client. When you are not in contact with the client, then the client may perceive that the service is interrupted is suspended. You may be beavering away at the paperwork or file in the office but, unless the client knows that, there is not a great deal of perceived value to it. If you're out of contact with your client you may be perceived as not providing the service at that point in time. It's often more perception than reality that counts. 'I don't need to contact the client just yet' is heard time and again from the function-oriented lawyer. This is never heard from the client manager who understands that direct client contact, even when nothing important in the case is happening, is still important to the service as perceived by the client. Where you do give an emergency or contact number to a client, it is rare indeed that a client will use it, but he does feel that he can get in touch if he needs to and, therefore, is satisfied that the service is continuing in some way.

The client agreement

The first stage is one of the most important stages of the client relationship, where it is agreed with the client what the client wants, what the solicitor is to do, when he is to do it and when and how he is to be paid. It is perhaps surprising that we as lawyers, who never let our clients do anything unless it is recorded precisely in writing, have been content to accept instructions from the client without more precision. He gets on with 'the file' and 'the case' and only contacts the client when necessary for the case or the file. Long narrative bills dictated after the event are sometimes done to explain or justify what they have done so they can charge for it. This is case planning in reverse. This can lead to client dissatisfaction which can easily be avoided by advance case planning by agreement.

The client agreement should be dealt with as follows:

1 it should be agreed and completed at the first interview;
2 it should be in writing;
3 it should be signed by the group partner, although in routine work it may be acceptable where the policy is first agreed by the group partner for the assistant solicitor or legal executive or case manager to sign on behalf of the group partner;
4 it must be signed by the client and he must be given a copy of it;
5 it must be written in plain English.

The client agreement acts as a checklist for the work, it creates the basis for the relationship to develop, it is clear and unambiguous, it complies with Rule 15 and it is produced *with* the client rather than being imposed *upon* him. It records the fact that the client has had some input into the legal service process.

The client agreement also contains the firm's terms and conditions of business and so reduces the overall paperwork. Where a case plan is agreed, it can be attached to the client agreement. There is room for supplemental and reviewed charges by agreement. It can also contain details of other services which the client may need from the firm.

A copy of the client agreement goes on the file for your checklist and worksheet, a copy goes to the finance department for billing support/centralised billing purposes, and a copy is given to the client. The quality and client management firms may require a copy to go to the quality manager who will check that all cases have properly completed case plans and client agreements.

The client agreement avoids the use of jargon and uses modern English such as, 'We promise ...', 'You ...' and 'Us' rather than 'Jarndyce & Jarndyce may require security for costs ...' A full form of a typical client agreement is shown in Appendix 1.

Case plans

At the beginning of most cases, the vast majority of clients express the view that their case will be simple and straightforward. They think that the documentation need not be lengthy or complex, that the charges need not be excessive and that it will all be over within a few weeks. The vast majority of practising lawyers know from experience that things are not always that simple, that paperwork can become long and sometimes complex, that things can change as the case progresses, and that time and cost estimates can change. This imbalance of understanding between lawyer and client can be reduced by use of the case plan which is an important part of the client agreement. Rather than doing a long narrative bill after the case is over, the use of the standard case plan at the outset to agree with the client what work is to be done, by when and by whom and at what charge is part of client management. Rather than recite these each time in a 'client care' letter, it is possible to use the standard case plan, amended where necessary, and agreed with the client. Then attach the agreed case plan to the client agreement.

As a requirement of Rule 15 as well as of a quality system, it has become necessary for lawyers to be more proactive with clients and the management of their work and to agree as far as possible at the outset what work is to be done, how long it will take, what the charges for the work will be and who is to do the work. The lawyer also needs to identify the work involved in advance so that not only can he explain it to his clients, but also so that he can agree charges for the work based initially on a pre-prepared standard work plan. The lawyer needs to know that the work will be effective and sufficient to achieve what is required, ie that there will be no errors, omissions or mistakes.

The case plan is designed to stand alone or to be attached to the client agreement. Its design parameters are:

1 it sets out the basic standard stages for the case;
2 it can be tailored to suit the client by agreement by adding or even deleting certain items;
3 it must not exceed one or two sides of A4 paper; and
4 it can be varied by agreement as the case progresses.

The case plan is agreed with the client at the first meeting. It explains to the client (if he wants to know) what work will be done. Professional clients like them. The lay client may be interested to know what he is paying for. The case plan will become the work sheet for the file and can be ticked off as each part is done, giving a progress chart and performance sheet at the same time. Not only is this a good way of controlling the case, but it also gives instant information to anyone else who needs to look at the file (should you be off sick) and it ensures that no vital step is missed. It is also a good way to teach and train your assistants and paralegals. The case plan is not, however, a detailed checklist for doing the legal work where the case managers will need access to precedent checklists and case management systems.

The benefits of case plans include the following.

Quality control

Standard case plans will ensure consistent standards and work practices throughout the firm. Case plans are reviewed and updated at regular intervals by the professional and quality group of the firm. Case plans are suitable for internal quality audits.

Quality assurance

The client is assured that the work will be carried out in accordance with accepted professional and agreed standards.

Communications

By discussing and agreeing the work stages at the beginning of the case, the client will understand better what is involved and the amount of work to be done as well as being able to follow the case as it progresses.

Less fee resistance from clients

When clients understand better the work involved, they are more content to let you get on with it because they know what 'it' is. Having agreed the case plan, they have also agreed the costs and, provided any subsequent variations to the case plan and charges have been agreed, there will be little, if any, fee resistance when the interim and final bills are delivered. Bills also tend to be paid quicker.

File checklist

One copy of the case plan is put onto the file with a copy of the client agreement and it acts as a checklist for things to do and to be ticked off as the case progresses. The case plan is designed for client information, it is not designed to be a detailed legal checklist for the case manager.

Teaching and training aid

When explaining to other members of the group what needs to be done in a certain matter or in a certain type of matter, particularly where there is a client transfer (see Chapter 12), the case plan gives a clear and easy picture of the work involved. It gives the trainee or delegatee an overview of the whole case rather than a snapshot of the work immediately to hand.

Consistency of work

Case plans used throughout the firm will provide more standardisation and consistency of work practices and quality. Even the largest firms depend on the skills of the individuals within it and individual practices can vary widely even within the same firm. If all groups and departments use authorised case plans, then the quality of the legal work is made to be consistent throughout the firm.

Computerisation

As more types of work are computerised, such as residential conveyancing, probate, wills, personal injury and so on, the use of case plans will build into these systems the stages of work and precedents that need to be included. More work will be able to be processed by fewer people more quickly, to a higher standard, and with better profit margins.

The legal process, the case plan and the client agreement

Having completed and signed the client agreement, you will have a new client, you know where he's come from and you know quite a lot about him. You've even agreed a service level and agreed charges. Well done! This for many of us represents a considerable advance. We are becoming interested and knowledgeable about the clients. We are not just talking high client ideals, we are actually now doing something about it and making a new and proactive impression on the client.

The result is a happy client who thinks that you are responsive, which you are; and not stuffy, which we aren't any more. You then complete a written case plan based on the form contained in Appendix 2. This is capable of many variations, but what is important is that first, you are working to stated standards of practice laid down by your firm for quality control purposes. By agreeing or amending the specification with the client, you are adding into it the client's input and quality assurance aspects.

The client agreement and the case plan are kept on the file and are used as an instant reminder and quick guide to critical information about the client and the case and the costs, for you or for someone else in your absence who will be able to pick up the file and carry on. The case plan could be produced on coloured paper or card to be easily identifiable on the file. In most cases, a copy of the case plan will be given to the client.

The client now knows what the work involved will be over the next four weeks, he knows that the work may vary after that depending on the acknowledgement and he knows how much it will cost to that point and how and when he should pay. You have even told him that if it is not defended, the overall costs will be around £Z, but that you will be able to give a more definite figure in four weeks' time.

Case plans and client agreements provide a framework for and a record of what is necessary to be dealt with at the beginning of each case and with each client. There is no special magic in the forms, except only that without them, much of the important initial work for the case and the client relationship may be omitted.

Contingency fee agreements

Following the limited introduction of contingency fees in personal injury and debt recovery cases, it has become apparent just how

important it is to ensure that the precise terms of the agreement between the solicitor and the client are agreed at the outset. The risks of the solicitor of incurring substantial abortive costs in the event of losing the case and the liability of the client to pay fees at a higher rate to reflect this risk, have made written agreements necessary in these situations.

A form of contingency fee agreement has been recommended by the Law Society. It is not dissimilar to the client agreement used by client managers. There is no reason, therefore, why client agreements should not become more widely accepted and used in the profession, whether or not a contingency fee is proposed, as the risks to both solicitor and client can be substantial in both.

'No deal, no fee' agreements are becoming increasingly common in non-contentious work where the lawyer has to consider the risk of losing a fee against that of taking a share of the 'profit' of a done-deal.

The first interview

Legal cases can last for a few days, a few weeks, a few months or even a few years. It is, therefore, vital that the work done at the first interview is adequate to start off the case on the right footing and also to start off the client relationship as well as can be done at that important first stage.

Usually, the first interview is taken up with listening to the client, asking a few questions to clarify one or two points, giving some initial general advice and then taking down some details about the client and his case. We may talk generally about costs but it is often difficult to be precise about charges in advance of the case and the service to be given. The case plan and client agreement go a long way towards defining the case and the service in advance, and makes it less difficult to agree charges with the client at the outset.

The legal costs are often uppermost in the mind of the client at the first interview. He expects it to be dealt with. He may be disappointed or confused if you don't deal with it there and then. The charges as well as the case must be dealt with in a way that gives the client a choice and some input. Initially, the client manager may find it difficult to agree a precise case plan and the agreed specification may be drawn in fairly wide terms such as:

Sale of 123 Blackacre with discharge of first mortgage to Abbeyshires Building Society; or

Issue of divorce proceedings for decree absolute, no children, undefended.

The first expansion of this is to agree some anticipated timescale, in order to give the client an estimate and also to deal with possible cost overruns due to unexpected delays or complications. Here you give a best estimate based on the information available at the time and agree a timescale with a review of the case plan and charges at that time if the matter is not completed. In the case of standard and routine work, it is possible to produce standard case plans setting out the stages of work involved.

Where a comprehensive case plan is not possible, then the case plan will deal with the first stage, for example, 'Advice in connection with building dispute, writing to builder's solicitors, obtaining copy contract and invoice statements and advising on recovery of sums paid and damages, taking approximately four weeks and charges not exceeding £X plus VAT.'

Where there are urgent instructions, there may not be time to agree and sign a detailed case plan and have a confirmatory case plan could be sent to the client within a day or so for signature. Where the urgent work will absorb substantial time in the first day or two, it would be better to get a case plan agreed and signed with perhaps a payment on account.

For form's sake!

You may by now be exclaiming that all these forms are not necessary. Perhaps not in an ideal world, but the point is that a form can be a useful checklist. There is no magic in the form itself, it's done to ensure that you do what needs to be done, it contains what needs to be communicated to those who need to know. The completion of the right form at the right time makes the service to clients easier and more consistent.

The benefits of these forms include:

1 improved communication with clients;
2 consistency of work practices;
3 quality standards assured; and
4 capable of revision.

The care plan

What level of service does the client want or need? Do we provide the same level of service for the client with a house purchase or debt recovery case as we do for the long-established and treasured plc client who provides 10% of the firm's annual fee income? But didn't that plc client start with us 20 years ago because we handled the managing director's house purchase? From little acorns ...

So, the first dilemma. Some would say that we should treat all clients with the same level of service. Some would say that's impossible to perform. Well, there's no one answer and each firm must decide its own policy in this. But don't forget the client – what does he want and expect? Does he want to be copied into all correspondence, does he want a full written report on everything, does he want copies sent also to his managing director, finance director and so on, does he want us to use first class post, does he prefer us to fax everything to him, should we telephone him or does he telephone us? By offering various service levels and letting the client make a choice at the outset, then parameters can be properly set and consistency be managed and maintained.

There are clearly different levels of service that are needed as dictated by the case as well as by the client. Take debt recovery. You are acting for a new client suing for £250 – a simple and straightforward case for the computer – a fixed service for a fixed fee. It's commodity pricing. But, if you are suing for £250 for the key plc client, do you give it the same treatment? If the client is one of your major debt recovery clients for whom you have hundreds or even thousands of debt cases on the go at any one time, he may have agreed with you that you will send him a monthly or weekly report, that there will be a monthly account meeting, that enforcement action will be taken automatically rather than waiting for a decision by him. He may even have endowed you with discretion to take whatever action, within certain cost and risk parameters, as you think best. So, different service levels are appropriate and necessary to suit different clients. The point here is that it's not really for us to decide what level of service we will give to our clients, but rather one of offering to the client a range of service level options *for the client to choose!* The client will decide the type and level of service he requires.

Having discussed the options with the client at the outset, or discussing it on the regular client review from time to time, it is necessary to record what the client wants and expects and write this into the care plan. It could also be entered on the client profile so that all concerned with that client can see that the client, for example, wants all letters copied to him by fax. A sample client case plan is contained in Schedule XIV.

Variations and additions

The client agreement and case plan are not intended to restrict the basis of the relationship between a solicitor and client but rather to form the basis on which the relationship can be developed.

There may be some objection that agreeing a fixed fee at the outset creates a problem where the case becomes more complex than originally thought or where delays are incurred through no fault of the solicitor or the client. These fears are easily countered because the client agreement clearly states that the agreed charge is based on the agreed case plan. Any changes to this are to be dealt with by subsequent agreement with the client. Just because it is not always possible to accurately plan the whole case from day one and to calculate the charges precisely does not mean that an attempt should not be made to plan the case at all. Where solicitors try their best to give an estimate of charges to cover a variable situation, it often sounds to be suspect and evasive from the client's point of view. It also might suggest that the lawyer is not able to plan and control the case, which is not an impression that you wish to create.

The client agreement and case plan creates a framework for the relationship, covering the basic legal issues and a path forward as the case progresses. Clients are generally willing to accept that the course a case will take cannot always be precisely predicted, but they do want to know the likely stages and the likely costs. Clients will no longer agree to an open-cheque-book costs-based approach to case management. Agreement and planning are here to stay.

Action checklist

1 Review your Rule 15 procedures to check, first, whether full compliance is being made with the Rule and secondly, the response and perception of clients to your letter of engagement. Is there room for improvement?
2 Prepare a draft client agreement containing also your terms and conditions of business.

3 Try using the client agreement with a small sample of clients, perhaps initially in only one group or department and check with both client managers and clients for responses and comments.
4 Determine to ensure that clients are better informed and more involved than before about the case work and the services and benefits the firm can offer to them.

12 Client transfers

One of the things that clients seem to dislike most is being swopped around between fee earners in the firm for the same or different work to be done without being consulted and often without even being notified who is doing their work. For example, a regular client with partner A who does all that client's commercial property work may be involved in some litigation. The client consults partner A who advises that the specialist litigation skills of partner B's group are necessary. Partner A makes a quick telephone call to partner B and sends him the file and perhaps a scribbled note. Some time later partner A is surprised to hear that his client is not satisfied and that all is not well. On investigation, he finds that partner B's new file is perfectly in order, the litigation advice was sound and that the procedural aspects of the case appear to be under control and in hand. So what is the problem?

You, your service and your client

It has been seen in Chapter 6 that the person supplying the legal product is actually himself an important and inseparable part of the service from the client's point of view. This is what personal service means, it involves input from the people involved, both supplier and receiver. Therefore, the simple fact that there is a change in the person supplying the legal product means by definition that the service will be different. If one part of the service relationship is changed, then the client will experience a different service. The legal product element of the service may be perfectly in order but the client will have experienced a difference in the person and, therefore, a difference in the service and that is where client perception is mostly influenced. The legal product of partner B may be every bit as good as that which partner A dispenses but it is nevertheless still different because partner B and partner A are different and the client's experience of the service will change. If managed well by the client manager, the transfer can be seamless and even positive, in providing added value and specialist expertise but, if left unmanaged, the situation often causes unrest amongst clients.

The management of the client transfer has to deal with three key elements:

1 to ensure that the client is informed about the proposed transfer and that he agrees to it;
2 to ensure that partner A, the client transferor, keeps in touch with the client, not so much to check that partner B, the client transferee, supplies a quality product, but rather to ensure that partner B provides a service which is satisfactory to the client; and
3 to ensure that the client partner, if other than partner A or B, keeps in touch with the client with a service overview which assures the transferred client that he has not been 'dumped' or abandoned by his established and trusted legal adviser.

The client management technique of the client transfer ensures that the person in the firm with the best and most appropriate legal expertise for the case is used whilst the person with the best relationship with the client maintains the service continuity. This technique will also help to avoid or reduce the problem of 'client hogging' where the client partner will attempt to do all types of legal work for his key clients rather than transfer them elsewhere in the firm. Client hogging preserves continuity of service but at the risk of product quality, whereas the client transfer preserves service continuity as well as promoting product quality, both of which improve client satisfaction and overall client profitability.

The client partner

All clients should be allocated a client partner who will take the responsibility of ensuring that all of a particular client's legal affairs which the firm is handling, and not only those cases being carried out in his own department or group, are handled with the quality of service that the firm sets out to deliver to all its clients.

The allocation of a client partner to a client should observe the following principles:

1 he should be the partner who is closest to the client;
2 he should be the partner who has known the client the longest;
3 he should be the partner who gets on best with the client;
4 he should be the partner who does most of that client's work in the firm, usually of one particular worktype;

5 he should be the one who can be relied upon to accept personal responsibility for that client's overall experience of and satisfaction with the firm; and

6 he should be the one with whom the client feels satisfied and comfortable, having explained the role to the client.

The role of the client partner has been examined in detail in Chapter 7.

The appropriate legal expert

The general practitioner may be seen by some as a thing of the past as far as legal expertise levels are concerned, but the great strength and advantage that the general practitioner had over our modern skilled specialist was that he took an overall view of the client, his family, his business and financial affairs. This depth of knowledge of the client was an invaluable factor in enabling him to give best advice to his client. He was the lawyer through whose hands all the client's legal affairs were conducted. He advised as much on the basis of client knowledge as of his legal knowledge. This understanding of the client is what clients like and it is only when the levels of the product expertise required made it impossible to continue giving advice on all legal subjects that the service levels between different lawyers in the same firm were noticed to be different from the client's point of view.

It is best if the person doing the job has the day-to-day control and management of the case and also has immediate and direct access to the client so that he can work efficiently and measure feedback from the client direct. But with service levels being so important, it is necessary that the client partner keeps a watching brief, not so much on the legal details, but on progress, client access, billing and client satisfaction. Client managers use a new form of delegation in order to meet the expectations of the transferred client.

Response service criteria

When a client transfer is done, the transferred client may need time to acclimatise to partner B. This is where reference to the client profile as well as to the client partner and staff profiles will be of particular benefit. A glance at the care plan for the client will quickly inform partner B that the client likes to receive copies of all correspondence but that it should be sent to him at his office marked 'private and confidential'. The care plan might also note that the client likes to receive a telephone progress report at least weekly, and to receive a copy of the monthly work in progress figures for his particular case(s). These 'little' items of client care may seem insignificant to the firm but they may be very important to the client.

Billing arrangements

The client will have become accustomed to certain types of billing arrangements with partner A, arrangements that may have been developed over the years but may not have been recorded. Some clients expect to receive time recording printouts with their bills, some prefer percentage fees, some like to haggle and others like fixed fees. I have heard of lawyers who have worked for key clients for years, who enjoy their client's complete trust and confidence, who socialise and go on holiday together but who fight and rail like cat and dog every time it comes to the bill. Some clients like to discuss, consider, make a counter offer and then agree a figure. Whatever the arrangement, it is sure to have its own peculiarities and needs expert and sensitive handling. You can imagine the client reaction when partner B who is unaware of the client's billing arrangements with partner A comes to deliver his first bill to the key client of partner A without first consulting with partner A!

Even worse, partner B could show himself to be less or more expensive than partner A and this will unsettle the client and annoy partner A. If partner B is more expensive than partner A, the client will complain quietly, at first, to partner A and then partner A may have a word with partner B about his bill. If partner B is less expensive than partner A, partner A may feel embarrassed and enforced to adjust his own established billing rates.

The client may not like having to start again with partner B in fee level negotiation. There are two ways of avoiding or reducing this problem:

1 by using an internal client transfer agreement, partner B can 'bill' partner A who will then be able to sort it out with the client; and
2 by using the client profile (see Appendix 7), partner B can quickly and easily read the billing arrangements between the client and partner A and, by discussing the billing arrangement with partner A, he will be able to deal with this sensitive area of internal client transfer more accurately, more quickly and with less client dissatisfaction.

Progress reports

Partner A will be concerned to know that partner B and his group are progressing the case for his key client. He will not simply be able to assume that all is well. Client managers do not make that assumption. Therefore, on completing the client transfer agreement, he will specify that he wants to receive a progress report from partner B at specified intervals, say, weekly or monthly, depending on the client and the case in question. He will not just leave it until he hears a complaint from his dissatisfied key client.

File audits

Quality firms conduct regular file audits and each partner has responsibility for doing audits for named partners. In the case of internal client transfers, partner A could do the file audits on the files of his key client that are being worked upon by other partners or groups in the firm. This would give extra impetus both to client management and to quality management, with both being focused on the specific client and not just on the file. Linking file audits to key clients may make it more pertinent and possibly open up new ideas and approaches to that particular client.

Client satisfaction

At the end of the case being dealt with by partner B, there will be the usual client satisfaction questionnaire sent out to the client and the reply will be considered by both partner B for his own group assessment and also by partner A for his assessment of the work done for his key client. Any major discrepancies will be discussed at the monthly client review meetings.

There will be a file review and client satisfaction rating at the end of each transferred case. Partner A will be able to say what he thought of the service and legal product provided by partner B in a frank and constructive way. This will be a very positive way of building up internal communications, quality product and client care systems. It will highlight the practices and problems of the client satisfiers, the client dissatisfiers and the client sufferers and point to remedial measures. It is, of course, a sensitive issue between partners and fee earners, but constructive criticism must be an essential part of the overall quality client management systems of the firm.

As firms grow bigger and more complex, with more people assuming a wider range of roles, it is more important than ever before to ensure that quality and client satisfaction are maintained at consistent and reliable levels. This will be achieved by setting the internal client transfer policy and then by identifying and measuring performance. If you receive instructions internally from another case manager to do something for his client, does it go on the top or bottom of your in-tray? Do you give priority to your 'own' clients? Do you satisfy the transferred client and, if so, by how much?

Hand-overs, backup and holiday cover

Who looks after your cases and your clients whilst you are away on two weeks' holiday? What happens to them if you're away on sick leave? Who 'picks up' the file when a case manager leaves the firm?

In situations of temporary short-term absence, an assistant or partner will look at the post and deal with matters that require immediate attention. It can be difficult for another already fully occupied case manager to take over all the absent case manager's files. What is important is that the clients of the absent case manager should know that their cases are being supervised and who they can contact.

Where the case manager knows he will be away from the office for more than a few days, he should leave detailed notes on each 'active' file and notify his clients the name of the person who will be dealing with their cases. He should, of course, also notify the other case manager, discuss priorities and, where possible, introduce him to the client.

The client transfer agreement

Where a client is transferred internally from one group to another, one way of doing it is that partner A will instruct partner B on behalf of the client, a file will be incepted by partner B and the 'bill' will be made internally by partner B to partner A. Partner A will act as the internal client whilst partner B does the specific legal work. Partner A will deal with the day-to-day instructions to partner B and partner B will report to partner A. In this way, the key client will remain with partner A whilst obtaining the benefit of the specialist skills of partner B.

It may be more efficient, of course, for partner B to deal with the client direct and to take instructions direct from the client, depending on the type of legal work involved and the type of client relationship. Progress and billing would remain an internal matter between partner A and partner B.

The key point in dealing with client transfers is that the firm should have a policy and a system, that clients should be kept fully informed and that the case management and client service stream should be continuous.

Action checklist

1 Examine your own internal system for transferring clients between the specialists within the firm. Does it always work effectively and to the client's entire satisfaction? Ask a few clients and case managers for their views.
2 Discuss what should and can be done to improve the system.
3 Design an internal client transfer system.
4 Introduce the new transfer system for a trial period and check for effectiveness and measure the levels of client satisfaction over a period of time.
5 Check your back-up systems for temporary absences of case managers.
6 Provide training on delegation skills.

13 Costs and the client

Competitive pricing

It is a truth universally acknowledged, that a solicitor, in possession of the most competitive quotation, must not be in want of a client. In the post-recession, de-regulated and competitive market conditions of the mid-1990s, clients are demanding the keenest charges from the law firms which do their legal work. Where a firm tenders to a prospective client for a general retainer to do its legal work or only for one specific matter, then the legal expertise, size, quality accreditation and reputation of the firm seem to count for little to the client unless the charges quoted are the most competitive of all. Unless the price is right, a firm may not be given the chance to show what it can do for the client.

This predominance of price over the other features, which clients consider in choosing to instruct a solicitor, seems to be at odds with the findings of the survey of law firm clients referred to in Chapter 5, which puts the understanding of and interest in the client shown by a firm and the quality of its professional staff as the most important concerns of a client in choosing which solicitors to instruct. Most clients stipulate that they want good service, and many put service as their first concern, but experience teaches us that unless the price quoted is the most competitive, few clients in a quotation situation seem prepared to prefer service over price.

This apparent inconsistency can be puzzling. Clients demand both the keenest of prices and the best of service from responsive and competent professionals. The firm's experts, quality and service systems are in risk of becoming an expensive and under used resource unless the firm, through its competitive pricing policy, can attract and retain clients and legal work in sufficient volume that will enable it to keep its production costs and its profit margins adequate in order to continue supporting the competitive fee levels it is quoting.

It is a prerequisite of attracting legal work that a firm must be able to respond satisfactorily to a client's question of 'How much do you charge?' The right price is determined by the first law of economics – the amount that a client is prepared to pay.

Superior value

The maintenance of low prices and high service levels presents a firm with a conundrum – how can it deliver the highest service to its clients whilst also quoting the most competitive charges? An answer may be found if we consider the analysis of the complete legal service in Chapter 6. The legal product, defined as the generic legal work in the case, may be seen as forming only one of the three constituent parts of the overall legal service. The product delivery service provided by the firm and the achievement of benefits or welfare for the service receiver are the other two elements of the overall legal service. Whilst the generic legal 'product' is common to all competent law firms, the two other elements are two service variables which a law firm should address as part of its competitive strategy. A competitive pricing policy should be the bedrock on which product quality and service differentials are constructed and displayed to clients.

In a quotation situation, therefore, whilst the legal product can be quite accurately specified in an agreed and written case plan, it is the service potential of the firm which is still an unknown at that stage, as far as the client is concerned. Although the service features can be specified, they cannot be experienced by the client until the firm is doing or has done the work and until the client has received the service. It is an intangible which only the service receiver can assess as and when the product is being or has been delivered to him.

Where the client is established and has been regularly receiving legal products and service from a firm, then where the service is perceived by the client to be superior to that which can be obtained from other firms, then clients do not always insist on re-tendering where the firm's charges are also perceived to be competitive. Where the client has built up an established and beneficial relationship with members of the firm, then the service element appears to form a greater part of the client's consideration in choosing to stay with the firm. Where the service element is perceived by the client to be inferior, where service levels have slipped, or where there is the perceived indifference factor referred to in Chapter 15, then the client may feel that he may just as well go out to the market for a tender or re-quote, even though the firm's prices are fairly competitive.

Drawing these apparently disparate features of the legal service together, it appears that a firm needs to be able to quote the most competitive charges in order to attract work from a new client, and to remain keenly price competitive in order to retain work from existing clients. What can be seen to be equally important but which works in a different way is the no-charge 'extra' of superior service which helps to attract and more particularly to retain a client. Superior perceived service in delivering quality legal work will convert a firm's competitive pricing policy into superior perceived value. Whilst the lowest price may attract a client, it is superior value that will retain the client in the medium to long-term. Where service levels are perceived to be high but the firm's charges are uncompetitive, then, likewise, the client will not perceive value and may consider a re-tendering exercise.

As far as costs and the client are concerned, therefore, it is not simply a matter of dealing with the question of 'How much?' – there is a requirement for superior product quality, superior service delivery, superior quality of people and superior value in a firm's pricing policy. Whilst clients must be satisfied that they have been given the most competitive prices, the best value that they demand is a product also of product quality and service.

Client managers endeavour to match the selling experience of the firm and the buying experience of the client. In the ultimate analysis, a client management firm competes on value, not only by its superior competitive pricing policy but also by finding out what it is that clients value and ensuring that its products and services are seen by its clients as being worth the price agreed.

Managing price and service

Low service levels cost as much to provide, if not more, than high service levels. The attitudes, systems and practices of client management do not have a high 'cost' to install, maintain and develop because they are predominantly people skills which can fit in with a firm's existing infrastructure. Client management techniques do not require additional investment in premises, hardware or software. There is a training cost in developing a client management programme but, as much of this can be done internally with coaching rather than teaching as a training method, the training costs are not high relative to 'black letter' law and other training costs. The actual cost to a firm of low service in terms of unattracted, unretained and underdeveloped work for existing clients, if precisely calculated, would be much higher in relative terms.

The competitive power of a client management firm is found in its ability to quote the lowest competitive charges in order to attract new work from new clients and then by the superior perceived quality of its legal work, its people and the quality of its service delivery system, to work effectively to retain the client and develop repeat and newly introduced work from a client who perceives value, benefits and satisfaction. A client management firm recognises that its charging policies are an integral part of its management policies, and that the prices it can afford to charge to its clients must be a function of the cost at which the firm manages to do the work. The charges it is able to quote and sustain at profitable levels are determined by its ability to manage the costs of the firm's overall resources.

A firm's pricing policy must be competitive on the one hand and it must be sustainable on the other. It is not just a turnover issue of getting more work in at the lowest competitive cost, but it is also a management issue of improving its product quality, its staff management and its client management in order to maintain and develop its profitability. If a firm attracts work only on price, without managing its resources, its margins and it's clients' perceptions of its service, its medium-term future may not be as secure as it may think. If a firm manages to consistently provide its existing and potential clients with superior legal products, superior perceived service, superior quality people and superior competitive charges, then superior perceived value will be the result.

The Solicitors' Remuneration Order 1972 (repealed)

The question of costs was not always as thoroughly discussed with the client at the beginning of the case as is generally the practice today. The Solicitors Remuneration Order 1972 required that legal costs for non-contentious work should be 'fair and reasonable having regard to all the circumstances of the case'. The method of assessment was based on a number of objective criteria contained in s 2 of the Order which included the complexity of the matter, the skill involved, the time taken, and the amount of money involved. Only the eighth criterion, 'the importance of the matter to the client', involved the subjective view of the client himself.

Such an assessment was more of an art than a science and it was possible to arrive at different charges for different firms, both of which could be justified as being 'fair and reasonable'. It was not easy to explain the workings of the Order to a client and, generally, costs were not dealt with until after the case was completed. If the client was not happy with the charge, his remedy lay in making an application for a remuneration certificate at which the charges were reviewed in the light of the eight criteria of assessment.

The 1972 Order was not designed to provide an accurate costs plan for clients upfront but, rather, it provided a basis for assessment of costs once all relevant factors were ascertained, generally after the case had been completed. Sometimes, the client had no detailed idea of the work being done and no real idea of how much the charges would be until the bill was rendered after the case had been completed. It was difficult for a client to budget and manage the legal costs he was incurring and which could lead to problems when the bill was finally delivered. This pricing policy, sometimes called 'billing by ambush', was not entirely satisfactory to the law firm either because it could lead to the firm carrying high amounts of unbilled work in progress as well as credit control problems.

The Solicitors' (Non-Contentious Business) Remuneration Order 1994

The 1994 Order has moved some way towards recognising the changed market conditions of the 1990s. Section 3 recognises more of a balance between the concerns of the solicitor and his client by requiring that a solicitor's costs should be 'fair and reasonable *to both solicitor and the entitled person* having regard to all the circumstances of the case' (italics added). The fundamental requirement has moved from an almost entirely objective test of reasonableness towards a more subjective test involving both the solicitor and his client.

Whilst the 1994 Order goes on to repeat all the 'old' eight criteria of cost assessment contained in the 1972 Order, it introduces a new criterion requiring regard to be had to:

(i) the approval (express or implied) of the entitled person or the express approval of the testator to:
(i) the solicitor undertaking all or any part of the work giving rise to the costs; or
(ii) the amount of the costs.

Both the Written Professional Standards and the introduction of Rule 15 had earlier laid greater emphasis on the importance of agreeing the charge or the basis of charge with the client at the outset of the case, and the revision of the Order has established the importance of obtaining the client's agreement (express or implied) to the work and the legal costs.

Increasingly, clients have been demanding a clear and simple way of understanding and dealing with legal costs, and the 1994 Order enables and encourages the practice of solicitors reaching an agreement with their clients about the work to be done and the charges to be made. In client management terms, this refers to the client agreement and agreed charges. Before considering these in detail, however, it may be useful first to look at a few other ways of dealing with costs and the client that have been used variously and more or less successfully in recent years.

The fixed price quote

Many cases, particularly standard and commodity legal work, appear to be simple, straightforward and predictable at the outset. A firm could calculate the likely time and other internal costs necessary to bring the case to completion and, having considered the market rate for the job, it could then propose a fixed price quotation to a client. As the case proceeds, it often happens, however, that more work is involved, that things change, that the matter takes longer through no fault of the firm's and that the client starts making urgent demands. The recorded work in progress quickly overtakes the now rather sick looking 'fixed price' quotation and the solicitor finds himself financially challenged by both his client and his own Finance Director, whilst the legal work in the case continues to pile up. He hardly dares mutter 'swings and roundabouts' any more as it seems it's always the roundabouts he seems to be getting to deal with these days.

The many imponderables, that may appear as the fixed fee case unfolds, present the solicitor and client with a 'win-lose' billing policy because it is based not on the cost of the work to be done but on price only. A fixed price for an unspecified amount of time and work is not a particularly sensible policy if something preferable can be agreed with the client. Some firms may indulge in it and, on a swings and roundabouts view, may regard it as sustainable.

The list price quote

When you are busy and your services are in demand and there is plenty of work about, you may be able to afford to quote the firm's list price rates and may be surprised and gladdened to have them accepted. More likely, you will see your prospective clients as well as some of your established clients shopping around for a lower figure. You may pride yourself on the work you do and the service you provide and so you may refuse, even at the cost of losing some clients, of doing quality work at cut-price rates. 'I refuse to do cut-price work! There are standards to be maintained after all!' You may be galled to see your old clients frequenting new and cut-price firms who are 'just buying work in' whilst you find previously unknown time for polishing up your checklists and reviewing your precedents.

The realistic quote

My favourite way of quoting for work which worked successfully on the whole but, more recently, I have found to be unreliable used to go something like this: a prospective client/tenant telephones to ask: 'How much do you charge for doing a lease?' I dutifully asked a few questions about the amount of rent, term of lease, rent reviews, service charges, timescale and so on. From the answers received, I could usually develop a feel for the likely work involved and, from experience, could estimate that the case would cost about £XXX. Such quotes were usually accepted with little apparent resistance.

More recently, some prospective clients, on receiving such a quotation from a firm, may stagger as though smitten with a mighty blow. 'I ought to tell you that I have received a much lower quote from another firm' the prospective client might warn. If the firm decides to slug it out toe-to-toe and talk about its expertise in dealing with rent reviews and service charge clauses and, if it tells the prospective client that the firm is 100 years old and that through its departmental structure it can provide a full range of legal services, the now less than prospective client appears unmoved and rings off to 'think it over'. He does not call back. The firm later hears that the other firm which got the job eventually charged as much as its own first quote. Quotations can be a daily lottery to the practising solicitor.

Hourly rates

The 'billable hour', as enshrined in the book and the film, *The Firm*, became one of the major factors in billing practices over the last 10 years. The billable hour, usually calculated in accordance with the Law Society's 'Expense of Time' formula, is based on the cost of production rather than on the value to the client. As long as the work kept coming in, then the billable hour was a sustainable pricing policy. Problems started to arise during the recession, where the volume of work started to decline and firms were left with high overheads which demanded high charge-out rates. In some cases, these rates began to look excessive to clients, who had also become highly cost conscious in their own businesses and who began to look around for better rates. Hourly rates began to drift away from the cost of production towards market-driven rates of charge, and the charge-out rate wars began.

Many clients are no longer prepared to accept the billable hour without reliable pre-estimates of time and the work involved, further details of the time spent as the case progresses and controls on the maximum agreed to be spent. A pressure point has arisen – the client does not want to pay hourly costs without knowing what he is getting for his money, and a firm may be reluctant to take on work for which it may not be properly remunerated.

Estimates

The estimate is a valiant attempt to achieve a compromise between giving a client a fixed price quote on the one hand and quoting hourly charge-out rates on the other hand. 'Based on the instructions I have received and assuming that the case is straightforward with no unforeseen problems, difficulties or delays, then I would estimate that our costs should probably be in the region of about £XXX, but I must stress that this is an estimate only and things can change. If the deal has to be substantially re-negotiated, or if additional documentation is required, then it is difficult to accurately estimate how many more hours work will be involved. My time charges are £YYY an hour and are recorded on our computer.' Whilst this sort of estimate may fairly reflect the legal position, it is confusing to the client and uncommercial.

Value billing

This has the attraction of being simple to calculate and easy to understand. The problem is that high value transactions produce billing levels that are no longer acceptable to the client and low value transactions produce an uneconomic return to the firm. In some cases, the generic legal work involved is similar for both low and high value work, though the responsibility and ultimate risk is higher for the higher value work. Whereas 0.5% to 1% and other graded or 'sliced' decimal point percentages of value were often the basis of charge for property and other non-contentious transactions, they seem to be the norm now for only the lower value work and are unacceptable to clients for work containing a higher value element.

How much does the file weigh?

This billing policy is a relic of the 1970s where, at the end of a case, the solicitor would thumb through the file, sift the enclosures, count the letters sent and received, check the documents, feel the weight of the papers, consider the client's perception of the case and then pronounce the amount of costs to be charged. It is a declining art form, but it was wonderful to behold and it will be sadly missed by both solicitors and clients because it had the advantage that, although imprecise, it did take into account the client's level of satisfaction.

Contingency fee agreements

This relatively new billing arrangement has only become permissible in restricted types of litigation cases and time will be needed to assess its impact and success. In that it requires discussion about costs upfront with the client and the completion of a written Contingency Fee Agreement, it is to be welcomed by the client manager as an advance in client relations.

Abortive and contingency fee agreements for non-contentious work are becoming more common as the profession aligns itself closer with its clients and their markets and assumes an element of risk in return for sharing an element of profit. 'I'd be quite happy to pay your bill if I had some money coming in!' a client might remark. When money does 'come in', a client may display little fee resistance except for the stipulation that the fee quoted should be final and absolute for the client's budgeting purposes.

Price versus value

Competing on price alone, without competing on value and service, can be a self defeating policy in the medium to long-term because clients demand not only the keenest of prices but also superior service and value. The cost-cutting and price wars that some firms indulge in are dangerous strategies for a number of reasons:

1 profit margins are squeezed producing low re-investment;
2 legal product quality is endangered;
3 the expectations of clients are difficult to convert into higher value billing once cut price legal work has become the norm; and
4 some clients migrate between law firms, feasting on introductory discounts, and then moving on with little or no client retention being achieved.

Cut-price legal work is a short-term policy that has a negative long-term affect on the firm. Provided a firm's charges are competitive, which means that they are within 5% of the average market rate, then charges should not be the only relevant factor when an existing client decides whether or not to re-instruct Firm A or to seek a quotation from Firm B. Cut-prices may win a new customer but service and value at competitive rates of charge will convert him into a client.

Clients are not so much concerned with whether you charge on fixed fees, percentages, or time, as long as they can clearly see that the charges are competitive and that it produces value and benefits to them. A value based billing policy starts by establishing what the client wants and is prepared to pay for by discussing the work and cost options at the outset of the case.

Agreed charges

Section 57 of The Solicitors Act 1974 contains provisions for solicitors to enter into non-contentious business agreements with their clients. The 1994 Remuneration Order allows the competing service professional to adopt the client management way of agreeing charges with a client at the outset of a case, based on a written work specification and identified client expectations.

The first stage of any case is the most important by far. The meeting with the client, the case planning and the agreement of charges will determine not only how the case will proceed, but also how the relationship between the solicitor and his client will develop as well as how profitable the case will be. Agreeing charges with the client at the outset does not necessarily mean agreeing fixed charges. Clients do not always insist on a fixed price, whereas they do require a clear agreement as to how charges are to be made and they will want to have some input and control in the process. If a firm has some form of charging innovation and flexibility, then the client will have a wide range of options for agreeing his charging arrangement. For example, a firm might consider offering the following cost options:

1 written case plan;
2 introductory discount;
3 fixed fee interview;
4 fixed fees for commodity work;
5 value fees based on an agreed percentage of the value of the transaction loyalty discounts;
6 interim billing;
7 case and cost plan reviews;
8 contingency fees;
9 various methods of payment – standing orders, instalments, credit cards, etc; and
10 discounts for prompt bill payment.

The lottery of perpetuating a pricing and quotations policy based on production cost, estimates, or swings and roundabouts can be avoided with the use of client management techniques. By adopting the profitable case management techniques below, a firm can regularly and systematically ensure that each and every case and client will produce an acceptable and predictable level of profit as well as satisfaction to the client.

Costs versus agreed charges

An article in the *Times* on 9 November 1993 proclaimed:

City firm spells out details of charges.

This may have seemed radical at the time and it did mark a significant step forward in client relations. It failed, however, to comply with the basic tenet of client management that charges are not only to be spelt out, which is the old way of telling clients how much things cost, but that charges are to be agreed in advance with the client to fit his particular needs and budget. Client management replaces the old 'win-lose' relationship with a new 'win-win' relationship where a firm instead agrees with its clients what is to be done, by whom and at what charge. A headline article about a client management firm might now read as follows.

Lawyers agree fees to suit clients

Mr John Jarndyce, senior partner of leading law firm Jarndyce & Jarndyce, has announced that in response to client requirements his firm is setting a new trend in its pricing policy. The firm has developed a new client management system containing a pricing structure which sets charges by agreement between the lawyer and his client. The firm's new approach to pricing, which has been developed on a trial basis with a number of existing clients, is based on having a written client agreement between the firm and the client at the beginning of every case, specifying the work to be done, the name of the partner taking overall responsibility for the case, the names of the lawyers who will be assisting him with the case, the timescale and the charges, all discussed and agreed with the client to meet the individual client's requirements. 'We are putting our clients first and we are experiencing unprecedented growth' said Mr Jarndyce. The firm of Jarndyce & Jarndyce has gained a reputation in the marketplace over the last five years as being a firm which has developed an unrivalled commitment to innovation, quality and client satisfaction. Other law firms will be watching closely for the next move from Jarndyce & Jarndyce.

The vast majority of commercial enterprises do business on the basis of agreed or published prices. Standard products are sold at prices which are discounted, reduced or increased in accordance with market demand. Where a manufacturer is asked to produce something new or unique for a particular customer, a detailed specification is agreed and linked to a delivery date and a price. Law firms advise their business clients how best to document these transactions to protect and promote their legitimate business interests. Client managers follow their own advice and do the same with their clients.

The 'A' to 'Z' service

This is a quotation technique that more accurately enables you to cost, quote, explain and charge for the work you actually do and is popular with clients. It typically runs along these lines.

Client: 'Can you do this lease for me, and how much will it cost?'

Solicitor: 'Yes, I'd be glad to help you. Our charges for doing the lease in accordance with our standard case plan will be £YYY plus VAT. There are additional expenses for stamp duty and land registry and search fees of £XXX. Now let's see, yes, that's a total of £A.' (This is the 'A' quote.)

Client: 'I see. Hmmmm. To be frank, that's more than I was expecting. Can't you do it for less than that?'

Solicitor: 'Yes, I could, but it will mean doing less work and spending less time on the case. What legal costs did you expect? Do you have a budget figure in mind? What's your timescale? Hmmm, I see. Well, let's have a look now. Well, we may not need a second meeting if all goes to plan and we may not need an agreement for lease if you can get your fitting out plans approved quickly. We may not need to make many amendments to the lease if you're happy with it as drawn. It looks fairly standard, but I will need to read it all to be sure. I think we could get the charges down to £ZZZ plus VAT and expenses if we do complete by the day you require and if there are no complications. That meets your budget figure, doesn't it?' (This is the 'B' quote.)

Client: (relieved and a bit surprised at this new commercial approach) ' That sounds more like what I was expecting. Do you think the lease will be okay, though?'

Solicitor: 'Well, I have dealt with that industrial estate before and the leases are all standard. The landlord doesn't like to amend the lease. Of course, we're in a tenant's market at the moment and I may be able to negotiate a break clause for you. It may take a bit more time and cost a bit more though!'

Client: 'Well, a break clause could be useful. Does that mean the landlord can bring the lease to an end early as well? I see. Well, I think I would like it if you think you can get it. The agent never mentioned it. How much do you think it will cost? £250 more? Ok, try it but if you can't get it, I'll still go ahead. Please proceed on this basis.'

Solicitor: 'OK, I'll try for a break clause, and won't exceed that figure without your approval. Are you happy with that? Right, I'll give the landlord's solicitors a ring today.' (this is the 'C' quote.)

In many cases, the cheaper 'B' or 'C' quote ends up costing as much or sometimes more than the 'A' quote but with no fee resistance from the client. This is because the dialogue has helped to identify and explain the benefits the client wants as well as agreeing a base for charges. The

'A' quote is often found to have been underpitched for you to cover the actual cost of doing the work, and overpitched for the client at the outset who was not aware of all the work involved. It leaves no way to renegotiate without pain. In many cases, the lower 'B' quote often results in a better profit margin, because the work to be done is specified in advance and not exceeded, thereby leaving your profit margin protected. It is also generally more acceptable to the client, who gets exactly what he agrees to pay for by accepting the 'B' or 'C' quote.

The traditional quotation system which says, 'It will cost £XXX' is in need of review because it is unilateral and excludes client input and agreement. It is inappropriate to case planning and client management. Rather than saying, 'It will cost £XXX', the new approach is to achieve by discussion and specification at the outset an agreed charges plan (see Chapter 13) where the client has had an input and an agreement has been reached. You are adjusting your product and service to your client's budget. This does not mean that you are cutting your prices and profit margin. It means that you are being responsive to your client, that you are planning the case and that you are managing the case, the client and your margins better.

The types of quotation are, therefore, infinite or at least from A to Z. The 'A' quote is based on the standard case plan and the 'B' quote is the agreed charge for the amended case plan after discussion with the client. It is far better to start with a standard tariff and case plan and then to discuss and agree amendments with the client than to have no standard or discussion at all. The imposition of rigid pricing structures and work plans is anathema to client management. Quality law firms will have a range of standard case plans already prepared and reviewed at least annually which set out the standard stages of work to be done in the range of standard transactions which the firm undertakes. See Appendix 2 for a sample case plan. By linking your costs plan to the case plan you not only show the client what should and can be done, but you amend it to suit him and what will be done and thereby customise it to suit the particular client. You thereby are highly likely to consistently win the instruction from the client, whilst leaving it open for the client to instruct you to do variations and extras at the client's request and with an amended agreed charge.

The rule is to quote a fixed price for a fixed work specification agreed with the client. You must never quote a lower figure than the first figure without adjusting the specification – not only will you be reducing your profit margin unnecessarily, but you will also appear to the client to have attempted to overcharge him in the first place. Client management is about winning the work, satisfying the client and making a profit.

Profitable case management

Five rules of case management can be applied to all cases to ensure that every case is a profitable case. It is an effective low-cost, high return pricing and practice financial strategy. It comprises five rules or stages as follows.

1 Agreed charges

The first and fundamental rule is that you should agree with your client in the first interview or during the first telephone call, the charges to be made for the case. Note here, the first point, that we are not talking any more about how much it 'costs' to do the case but about how much the agreed charge will be. Your charges may take into account the cost, the time, the value or the other bases of charge contained in the 1994 Remuneration Order. The approach taken is not so much: 'This is how much it will cost' but more along the lines of: 'We can do the work specified in the case plan for £XXX' or 'We can do this much work for the figure you had in mind'.

The agreed charges should state what charges will be made for a specified amount of work within a specified period of time. If you have a series of standard work specifications for standard work types, these can be used as a basis for quotation, as well as for the Client Agreement and, subsequently, as a checklist to which to refer whilst carrying out the case. You should also agree the dates or periods when interim bills and the final bill are to be delivered, the method of payment and the credit period, if any.

2 Time recording

Whether or not the agreed charges plan is based on time charges or otherwise, it is important that you and your group case managers, or anyone else in another department or group who works on the case, should fully and accurately record the amount of chargeable time spent in the matter. The words 'chargeable time' means time that is actually spent on the case and which is *potentially* chargeable, without any deductions or discounts being made. It is the group partner who will decide the amount to be billed when reviewing the file diary containing information on all the time recorded. If case managers make discounts and reductions or adjustments as they go along thinking, 'The case or the client will never stand this charge so I won't record it', it will not be possible to get an accurate time management record which gives one measure of how much it costs the firm to do the job.

3 Variations and additions

One of the main problems with estimates and quotations is that in many cases it is not possible at the outset to give the client an accurate figure because the work itself could be subject to many variables. The cost is not linked to the amount of work actually done and can often lead to cost overruns where the work is extended. It is another example of a 'win-lose' situation which can be an unnecessary drain on a firm's income.

By using a standard work specification for charges, by using the 'salami principle' of dividing a potentially big case into smaller stages, by estimating the work in each stage in weeks rather than months, by agreeing and planning what work will be done in the first few stages, a firm can present its work to the client in a clear and simple way. A case manager will advise the client at the outset of the case about possible variables in the work and charges which depend on future events. The case manager will review the work at each stage as the case progresses and, if the timescale or work does materially change, he will discuss this with the client and get his prior agreement to any additional work or charges.

By dealing with the agreed charges, by highlighting at the outset the possibility of additional work or charges, you put the client in the picture and in control, right where he, as a satisfied consumer of your legal products and services, should be. At the same time, you ensure that you always produce a low, realistic, and competitive quotation. If, at a later stage, the case does change, your client is prepared for a review to be made.

4 Regular and prompt billing

If the agreed charges plan states that bills will be presented monthly, then a firm needs to make sure that it does deliver its bills monthly as agreed. If a firm has agreed that charges will be paid on completion, it must make sure that it does bill and collect on completion. Billing is part of the perceived service and so, like other case plan 'promises', it is important to stick with what has been agreed. Bad billing practices are bad for the firm and its financial controller and they are also bad for the client. Centralised billing support from the finance department to the busy case manager, as discussed below, may be useful to ensure that good billing practices are maintained.

5 Collecting payment

Remember the three 'Cs' in Chapter 1? The second (or first) 'C' stands for costs, and the rule that it's no good a firm doing all the legal work if it doesn't get paid. So all that has gone before in profitable case management, agreeing the charges, time recording, dealing with variations and billing promptly as agreed, needs the final requirement that the case manager should be responsible for bill collection. Some firms separate the functions of legal work and credit control. This may be efficient internally, but it is not particularly good for the client relationship, where the work, the service and the bill are all part of the perceived service and the value for money mix. Case managers and the group partner should be responsible and accountable for collecting payment promptly, or within one month of the bill date. The measurement of bills paid is as important as the measurement of bills delivered. Client managers regard bill payment as a 'completion' of the relevant service period, where the five stages have been successfully managed.

These five rules of profitable case management, if fully and effectively applied to a case, will ensure that the case is done in a measured way, with financial control and in agreement with the client. When applied to non-contentious work, a firm's case management will become more controlled, with a steady rise in client satisfaction and profitability.

How to agree legal charges

Clients are more discriminating than ever before, they want keen prices and they also want good service. There is no point in trying to sell the client a Rolls Royce service if he only wants to pay for a Metro or a Vectra. Client management firms, therefore, first find out what it is the client wants and then try to agree a cost with the client commensurate with that. The client has an input to make in both the case plan and the agreed charges. In this way, a client management firm can sell both a Rolls Royce and a Metro and a Vectra service side by side, and with equal profit and equal client satisfaction, by providing different services and different work to different clients which each respectively has specified and agreed to pay for. The stages of the agreed charges quotation may go as follows:

1 ask the client to identify his objectives;
2 establish what the work is likely to be and how long it will take;
3 identify who will do the work;
4 outline the standard product specification or case plan;
5 discuss the client's particular requirements;
6 break the case down into stages where it is likely to take more than four weeks;
7 try to ascertain the client's budget or if he has received any other quotations;
8 calculate a fee based on time charges, value etc and then quote a fixed fee to the client for the fixed and agreed amount of work;
9 if the client does not feel comfortable with the figure, the case manager may identify where it is possible to make one or two reductions in the case plan and consequent savings. Perhaps the number of meetings could be reduced, perhaps only one or two stages of the case plan will be carried out initially? The case manager should never reduce the charges without altering the case plan;
10 advise the client that, if the work or timescale change, there may need to be a revision in the agreed charges with the client's approval. Point out the possible changes that could result in work and price variations; remember that the client is always right and is entitled to get what he agrees to pay for. The charge should match the work all the way down the line through the case plan;
11 discuss and agree optional times of payment such as on account, instalments, interim monthly, disbursements in advance and so on.
12 discuss and agree optional methods of payment such as cheque, cash, credit card, on completion, from proceeds of sale, trust fund monies, re-imbursement by third parties, etc;
13 complete the client agreement and attach the agreed case plan to it;
14 confirm in writing what was agreed and get the client to sign the case plan and the client agreement or acknowledge receipt.

The essence of the agreed charges method of case and cost planning is that there should be discussion, planning and agreement between the case manager and the client at the beginning of the case. This can set the relationship off to a good start and reduce misunderstandings and confusion. In this way, it can be seen that it is not necessary to provide a Rolls Royce service for a Metro price and that both can provide acceptable levels of profit.

The financial spectrum

The best way to improve credit control is to improve the process of agreeing charges with the client at the start of the matter. The better a firm manages to cover the financial aspects of the case with the client at the beginning of the case, the more likely it is to be paid properly and on time. Agreeing costs with the client at the outset of the case has strong and beneficial ramifications throughout the whole case management process. It may be helpful to think of the whole process covering the financial aspects of a case as a spectrum as follows:

- discussion with client of financial parameters;
- agreement of specification of product and service;
- quotation of standard rates;
- agreement of charges;
- time recording;
- agreement of variations and additions;
- interim billing;
- final bill;
- collecting payment.

Where agreed charges are developed across the whole firm, the firm's overall financial performance will become better managed. Financial management at both macro and micro levels is necessary – case managers proactively managing their cases and reporting to their group partner, and the firm's management team being able to budget and plan more reliably.

Centralised billing

Some larger firms may find it more efficient and effective for bills to be generated, collected and processed through a central billing department rather than each fee earner and secretary doing their own accounting, bill production, delivery and credit control with greater and often lesser effect and regularity.

The case manager and group partner should retain responsibility for agreeing the charges and any variations, and they should also remain accountable for the collection of the bills from their clients but, with the advent of client management, it will be seen that this aspect of accountancy, once agreed between the fee earner and the client, can be effectively supported by the cashiers and accounts departments. Most other businesses operate in this way.

As a halfway house between individual billing practices and centralised billing, a regular monthly account management meeting between the group case managers and the financial controller may be held to identify billing opportunities, deal with accounts transactions, credit control and discuss performance to targets. Such meetings may be designated as 'billing days' although, as these meetings become a part of the regular working practices, less time will be required as efficiency increases.

The ultimate test of client satisfaction

When a firm delivers a bill to its client, how would it be perceived by its client if it included in the bill a question about client satisfaction and value? It might, for example, include a scale marked '1–10–20–30–40–50–60–70–80–90–100' with the following question addressed to the client: 'Please say how satisfied you are with the value of the legal work and service you have received by marking the scale from 1 (totally dissatisfied) to 100 (totally delighted). Please be fair and reasonable.'

Whilst the initial stage of agreeing charges with a client is one of the service high points of the case and client management process, the point of bill delivery is also a service high point. In dealing with agreed charges at the beginning of the case, the case manager is in effect saying to his client: 'I have agreed to do this amount of work during this period of time and at this charge which I have agreed with you.' At the point of receiving the bill and deciding whether it is fair and reasonable, the client is in effect saying: 'My perception of how you have dealt with the case, the legal work you have done, the time you have taken, the way you have kept me informed about progress and the benefits you have achieved for me is excellent/good/fair/poor/unsatisfactory.'

Many complaints about costs are found on investigation to be about the client's perception of value for what he has received from the firm. The client is not always saying that the costs are too much but rather, that he does not think it was worth the cost, or even that he did not know what the costs would be until he received the bill after the event. The causes of this sort of complaint can be substantially reduced by dealing with costs and the client as a professional client manager.

Pricing policies and billing practices are highly sensitive subjects in which there is no one right way. Every firm and client manager will have its or his own particular of dealing with these matters and it is not possible to be prescriptive. What is important is that there should be some system and policy which involves the client in a way that both the firm and the client consider to be satisfactory and to be of value.

Action checklist

1 Consider whether your current quotation and billing practices are always successful and profitable.
2 Do you think that a satisfied client would offer less fee resistance than a client who is dissatisfied?
3 If 'Yes', write down the things that you do to satisfy your clients. Have your clients told you that these are what satisfies them?
4 Can you state one good reason for not agreeing costs with the client at the outset?
5 Introduce, train, manage and measure the performance of financial case management in one control group or department over a period of 12 months and then compare this with other groups. If it has been successful, it can then be developed throughout the firm.

14 Client satisfaction

A satisfied client is one who feels that he has had good service from his solicitor, who believes that his case has gone well and who on paying his bill thinks that the benefits and service he has derived are fairly reflected in the amount of the bill. In short, he is satisfied that the case and the service are worth it. Service, as we have seen, is something which is experienced by the service receiver and only he can assess whether the service is good, bad or unsatisfactory. The service provider cannot truly claim to give good service unless this is supported by responses to client feedback, client questionnaires and client satisfaction ratings.

Complaints from clients about the legal costs charged for a matter as being 'too high' are often cases where the client is in effect saying, 'Your bill seems to me to be more than the case and the service are worth. I don't see that the service I have received is worth what you are charging.' This attitude is perhaps not surprising if the case is not planned or agreed in any detail at the outset and the client's expectations are left unidentified. In this scenario, where the solicitor starts off doing what he does on the assumption that the client will accept this as being self-evidently of value, it is perhaps not surprising that the levels of client satisfaction remains unacceptably low where fee resistance levels remain high. It is a fundamental principle of client management that, by first identifying what it is the client expects and is prepared to pay for, client satisfaction will increase and fee resistance will diminish.

The meaning of the word 'satisfaction' is to be found in the word itself. It is comprised of two Latin words – 'satis' being the word for 'enough' and 'facere' being the verb 'to make' – and literally means 'to make enough'. Translated into the 20th century legal profession, the client revolution means that now the paramount task of the solicitor is to do enough for the client rather than just to do the case well. The pre-client revolution days of working hard to do the job well and leaving the case to speak for itself are long gone. A job well done which, for whatever reason, does not satisfy the client is no longer a job well done because the nature of the work that we do for our clients has changed. The clients have changed it for us. Legal competence is assumed but client satisfaction has to be achieved and measured. Our legal training prepared us to do the legal work and now client management training will help us to ensure that in the process we also ensure that client satisfaction is achieved, measured and improved. Client management is a quality system with client satisfaction as its objective and improved profitability as a result.

The science of clients

How precise can we be about service and client satisfaction? Is satisfying the client a knack that some of us have and others haven't? Are the intangibles of service incapable of definition or measurement? Is it all a matter of chance? If there are no practical answers to these questions, then client management is just smile technology, where pleasing the client is just a matter of good manners.

Client managers do propound certain principles based on their observations and experience of providing legal services to clients. Some of them can be reduced to mathematical formulae as follows.

Formula one

The level of fee resistance in a client varies in inverse proportion to the level of client satisfaction:

$$FR \propto \tfrac{1}{2} CS$$

Formula two

The amount of the bill which is acceptable to the client increases in direct proportion to the level of client satisfaction:

$$AB \propto CS$$

Formula three

Product quality plus the client's perception of service plus the client's assessment of value together equals the level of client satisfaction:

$$PQ + CPS + CAV = CS$$

In the above formula, the following abbreviations apply: FR = fee resistance; CS = client satisfaction; AB = amount of bill acceptable to client; PQ = product quality (legal work, knowledge); CPS = client perceived service; and CAV = client assessed value.

A client who is satisfied with the case and the service he has received will be more amenable to paying his bill, even to the extent that the amount of the bill may be a little more than the market rate. Good service will justify some amount of premium pricing up to 10–15% above market levels. In the reverse, low levels of service perception may lead to 'discounting' on bills before delivery and to further discounting or credit bills after delivery and complaint from a dissatisfied client.

Client management stipulates that service is an integral part of the overall legal service along with the quality of the legal product and the price, which all taken together form the basis on which the client assesses value.

The quality of the legal product is discussed elsewhere in this book and the pricing structures also. It is the third vital ingredient of service in the overall legal service that is in need of attention and development. Service improvements will produce the immediate and substantial results to be expected of a business which produces a quality product in response to its clients requirements and at a price that clients consider to represent value.

Each part of the above formulae requires client input to what the solicitor does but the result, value, is one that lies in the perception of the client only.

The management of clients on a firm-wide basis, particularly where the firm is large or has several locations, needs to be systemised. You can't rely on the bush-telegraph or chance encounter in the corridor or at lunch with another member of the firm to pick up valuable and strategic client information.

Here, such information and classification of clients needs to be kept up-to-date on the database to which all branches and departments need to have regular access. The importance of this will become apparent when it is put into execution, but the time required to collate and update such information should not be underestimated.

Client satisfaction and bill delivered

Long bill narratives may signify case planning in reverse. It is often only then, after the work has been done and the client reads through the long bill narrative, that the client begins to understand what work has actually been done, what the case was all about and the stages it went through. It can come as a shock to the client who often thinks that his case is straightforward and who protests, justifiably on the facts, that, 'I never asked you to do all that so why should I pay for it?'

Client study – 'How much and when?'

In the case study on page 124, all the client wanted to be assured of was:

1 that the new factory would definitely be open and in production by 9.30 am Monday 12 March in order to meet an order from an important new customer;
2 what sums would need to be paid in building costs, rent and fees?; and
3 when would the said sums need to be paid, please?

It did turn out that the lease was completed on time and production started on schedule, with the client's company operating 24-hour shifts for several weeks in order to meet the delivery dates stipulated in the important new order. A couple of months later on having lunch with the company's manager I asked, 'Oh, by the way, how did that important new order go? Was the customer satisfied with the product?' He looked slightly perplexed and answered, 'Actually, we don't know yet. I went to see the customer last week and all the deliveries we made were still standing in their warehouse with the packing cases unopened. When I remarked on this I was told, "Oh, we will use them when we're ready. We insisted on those early delivery dates to test how good you were at meeting deadlines."' Delivery dates, a service rather than a product or price feature, was the critical factor. My bill was delivered and paid promptly.

Needs, expectations and aspirations

As we have seen in Chapter 5, 'needs and expectations' are words which are often used interchangeably or generically to describe client objectives but the terms do actually mean different things. The 'needs' of a client describe the basic requirement for the legal work to be done properly and competently. This is a basic necessity. Client ' expectations' encompass the service attributes that the client expects to accompany the production and delivery of the legal product, such as meetings, letters, and telephone calls.

The third category of client objectives may be called 'aspirations'. A client aspiration is what the client hopes to achieve as a result of the legal work being done, namely the benefits, welfare and solutions which a client hopes will result when the case and service have been completed. 'Why should I pay you when you haven't done anything for me?', was the distraught complaint I once heard from a client as I presented a bill. We had worked hard but ultimately unsuccessfully in defending a divorce petition on his behalf but the result was that the petition was granted to his former wife with maintenance and costs against him. The legal work had met his needs because it had been done competently, his expectations of service had been met because there had been meetings, letters and so on. But his aspiration – to stop the petition and to avoid maintenance payments – had been unsuccessful. This kind of client dissatisfaction can be reduced by advising the client at an early stage about the realistic chances of success. By definition, only 50% of litigants can 'win' in a two-sided case and to that extent there will always be some element of client dissatisfaction, but a dissatisfaction which need not adversely rebound on the client manager who will have agreed and identified client expectations and advised realistically on client aspirations at an earlier stage in the case.

Client study

One day, as a young assistant solicitor, I was passing by outside the boardroom and noticed several agitated people hovering around the door leading into the unknown inner sanctum. As I walked past, the senior partner's secretary called out, 'John, where are you going? Come on, they're all waiting for you in the boardroom!' I looked around thinking there was some mistake, or some other John, but no, it was me she was calling! Like a lost sheep, I was shepherded quickly inside, to the smell of cigars and the sound of popping champagne corks. I was led across deep-piled carpets, into the wood-panelled, chandeliered room towards the buzz of satisfied and expectant voices. I was left in the middle of the room, surrounded variously by the senior partner, other partners and several very important clients who I vaguely recognised. Hands were thrust towards me to shake, smiles beamed around me and 'Well done, John!'

rang in my ears half a dozen times. A chilled glass of champagne was slipped into my hand and I was offered salted peanuts in a bowl. Was this a mistake? Was I dreaming? Had they all gone mad? It slowly dawned on me that I was being personally thanked for settling at the doors of the court a multi-million-pound and 'difficult' case that had been rumbling along for several years and about which few, if any, people, including me, understood all the intricate legal issues. The boundless goodwill towards me was matched by their evident relief at the satisfactory settlement, in which otherwise heads other than mine might have rolled had it gone to court and if judgment had gone 'the other way'. I had in fact played only a relatively small part in the case which had been dealt with on joint instructions with another firm, but the other firm weren't anywhere to be seen that day. I had just about enough sense, even at that tender age, to say nothing but mused long and hard afterwards on the nature and causes of client satisfaction and delight. I concluded that one should never ignore or under-estimate the importance of client aspiration and perception. In this case, which everyone had tired of and felt worried about, it was the client's wish that it be settled in a satisfactory way. My legal input was not particularly brilliant. The settlement having been achieved with no rolling heads, everyone was happy. The conclusion is: if the client is happy and believes he has been well served, then so be it, he has been well served. The client is always right!

The ingredients of client satisfaction

In the above case, the level of client satisfaction was high, but why? H James Harrington, *Total Improvement Management,* says 'The level of client satisfaction is directly proportional to the difference between your perceived performance (not your actual performance) and the client's expectations' (here meaning aspirations and not needs). In order to understand what it is that actually satisfies the client, there are two things needed; first, the identification and specification of what it is that the client hopes to achieve, and secondly, how your performance as perceived by the client measures against it.

What creates client satisfaction? Are we talking about the client's need of a competent legal product? Are we talking about his service expectations? Or are we talking about the even higher level of client aspirations, which may be different from his needs and his expectations. Client satisfaction can comprise a mixture of these three things in his mind. For example, the client might have the following needs, expectations and aspirations:

The client needs ...

... you to get the facts right about his case;

... you to give the correct legal advice;

... you to use the correct forms and procedures;

... you to bring the matter to a conclusion.

The client expects ...

... that you will have one or more meetings with him;

... that you will write one or more letters;

... that you will make some telephone calls;

... that you will send a bill.

The client has an aspiration ...

... that he will find in you an adviser who understands him and his business;

... that on winning or completing the case he will have achieved some benefit or welfare;

... that you may be able to help him increase or improve the benefits or welfare to which he aspires;

... that ... [add here something from your own experience].

Different clients will have different needs, expectations and aspirations. Often, the needs are more basic and obvious than the expectations and both are based on his previous experience with you or other service professionals. Whatever the client's needs and expectations are, he will assess your overall performance by whether or not and by how much you have exceeded or fallen short of those needs and expectations. If you can met those needs and expectations, then client satisfaction will usually follow.

Client delight, as opposed to satisfaction, lies in the aspirational zone, where what you have done has helped the client achieve or exceed the benefit, solution and welfare to which he aspires. The client didn't need or expect it but you have done something for him which has delighted him. The client's needs generally relate to legal and product features whereas client expectations relate more often to service features. The client expects you to be available and accessible and he needs you not to make a mistake. The aspirational zone is where the client manager seeks 'to boldly go'.

The measurement of client satisfaction

In order to measure client satisfaction in a regular and systematic way, it is necessary to agree at the outset what the client needs, expects and aspires to by completion of a case plan as well as a care plan. If at the end of the case you have ticked off all of the points on the plan, then the client will probably be satisfied. If you have fallen short, he may be dissatisfied. If you have done more and have exceeded the clients' expectations, if you have approached or even achieved some of his aspirations, you will have a delighted rather than just a satisfied client.

The rating of client satisfaction will be low where you just do the job he needs. It lacks perceptible differentiation and added value. By delivering a legal product which works, you will have done what the client needs, which is fitness for purpose. Clients will not get excited about this *per se*. The conveyance conveys – no more, no less. Meeting client expectations with service extras and differentials will help to satisfy your clients. Doing more than this, by doing what the client desires but doesn't expect, is the way to achieve client delight. The objectives of client management are to promote client satisfaction, client retention, market growth and increased profitability.

In the legal profession, we have perhaps not placed enough value or importance in developing our client satisfaction skills. So often we do our legal work well, doing what the client 'needs', but sometimes we fail to satisfy the clients and under-recover in our bills because we fail to identify and meet client expectations or aspirations in the service features of what we do. The message here is that if clients pay for satisfaction, benefits and service, if client satisfaction is about perception rather than just hard fact, then if we design our systems and services to ensure that the client's expectations and aspirations are identified and achieved, that client satisfaction is a measured objective and that client service is a way to increase our margins, then we can under our own management and direction improve our profitability on a case-by-case and client-by-client basis.

The management of client satisfaction

A client management programme should embrace all aspects of the client relationship. If we only mechanically do what any other trained lawyer can do, then we will not differentiate ourselves to attract and retain clients and nor will we maximise the profitability potential that each case and each client presents. It is a principle of client management that these service and client 'intangibles' are important to clients and that they should and could be managed in a systematic way as much if not more than we manage the production and administrative aspects of our business.

Most firms employ a cashier or accountant to manage their finances, the bigger firms might employ a personnel manager to manage their staff and perhaps even a quality manager to ensure compliance with and development of quality systems and practices throughout the firm in a comprehensive and consistent way. The management of clients can and must be done at the point of service delivery by the case manager and, in addition, there are roles for the group partner (client supervision), the client partner (overall client responsibility) and the senior partner (individual and firm-wide complaint responsibility).

Client satisfaction ratings

It is often said that what gets measured is what gets done. It's easy to measure bills delivered and credit control performance and these are important indicators to past performance. Bills measure performance from the firm's point of view and only indirectly, by virtue of gaining payment of the bill, from the clients point of view. We can measure the bill we have delivered but it does not necessarily measure the satisfaction generated in the eye of the client. Even if the bill is paid promptly, it does not necessarily tell us whether or not the client perceives that he has received value. We simply assume so because the bill is paid.

It is said that IBM do not assess the performance of their sales managers in terms of sales volume but instead they assess them in terms of customer satisfaction ratings (CSR). For example, executive A has a CSR of 70% and executive B has a CSR of 50% and so on. These are the figures used in assessing the success of the sales manager as well of assessing, in aggregate, the overall success of the company.

We need to find whether and to what extent and why the client is satisfied or dissatisfied with the work, the service and the value perceived. This needs to be defined and measured in order to be of any use in monitoring performance and in making service improvements. The CSR may be assessed by asking clients as follows.

317

JARNDYCE & JARNDYCE
Client Satisfaction Rating

'How satisfied are you with the legal service that you have received from us?' (Please tick the box and number which most closely expresses your view.)

Delighted		Very satisfied		Satisfied		Disappointed		Dissatisfied	
100	90	80	70	60	50	40	30	20	10

Please write any comments you wish to make about our service and about how it could be improved for you:

Thank you for your response. Your views will be noted and acted upon.

The client is asked to tick the box nearest to his own feelings about the case and to provide further comments if he wishes. This latter point is important because otherwise we would end up with accurate figures telling us that our clients are satisfied or otherwise, but with no information as to the reasons for their satisfaction or otherwise. If we know what clients like and dislike, we can plan to increase the former and remedy the latter by building the causes of satisfaction into our training plans and systems. Likewise, when we know what it is that causes dissatisfaction, we can alert partners and staff to these things and adjust our procedures and systems to reduce or eradicate these problems altogether.

Client feedback pool

Listening to the client is one of the most important ways of measuring success. We don't do our work for clients in order to dissatisfy them. We don't do it to leave a neutral or indifferent experience. We do it because we have the skills and know that we can achieve the clients' objectives. All client contact details should be feed back into a client feedback pool. The chance words, the gratuitous comments, the throw-away line, the letter of thanks or of complaint – everything should be recorded and sent in to the client feedback pool.

The marketing manager will analyse these reports, assess whether there is a strength, weakness, an opportunity or a threat (SWOT). He may question the reporter further, he may go to see the client. In a large firm, it is the gathering and treatment of this information which will put the firm beyond the reach of all others. For example, clients could be asked:

1 was the bill correct?
2 did it contain any surprises?
3 were any increases in costs unexpected?
4 how well did we respond to your needs and requirements?
5 did we help you to achieve your objectives?
6 how would you rate our service overall from 0 to 100?
7 would you use us again?
8 would you recommend others to use us?

It is as important to identify and understand the causes of client dissatisfaction as it is for the causes of client satisfaction because the reduction of the former leads to an increase of the latter.

Client satisfaction reports

The information gained about clients should be collated, analysed and be put into a monthly management report to the firm as the monthly client report. In time, this will become the report that all will look to and respond to more than any other.

The survey report should provide partners with an accurate and updated report on the four key attributes of the firm's client satisfaction achievement by supplying reliable data on the following:

1 the clients' perception of the service received;
2 their rating of the firm generally;
3 their comparison between this firm and others; and
4 what the firm can do to improve the client's perception of the firm's legal work, service and value for money

See Appendix 12 for a specimen of the monthly client management report.

How well do you satisfy your clients?

How many of a firm's clients are dissatisfied in one way or another and are contemplating changing their solicitors? This could be higher in low client-service-rated firms and lower in high client-service-rated firms. Not knowing which we are is dangerous and a firm should do a regular client satisfaction survey to 'save' its 'at risk' clients and retain its satisfied clients. The survey results will show the other services and legal products which clients are looking for, but which they may not be able to source in the firm at the moment.

I recently visited a company boardroom where the walls were festooned with performance charts. The first chart was headed, 'Objective One – to measure and improve our customer satisfaction ratings to agreed target figures over 12 months.' The chart showed a number of groups, departments, branches and company-wide customer satisfaction targets and alongside each one the actual measured performance figures. Most targets had been achieved and all were going in the right direction. It was simple, open, brave and effective. The chart addressed, measured and communicated to all staff and others one of the key issues for the success of the company. A firm which measures its client satisfaction ratings might consider a similar reporting system.

Solicitor–client inter-dependency

We depend on our clients for our living – they do not depend on us for theirs. A client management programme must start with a healthy respect for clients from everyone in the firm. 'We have no future if we don't have satisfied clients', we should all be saying all of the time; 'The clients are why we are here' and 'Client satisfaction means job security.'

So start by asking your staff, every single member of the firm, what they think client satisfaction is and what they think clients think it is. Then ask them to say how their job at the moment actually does contribute towards client satisfaction and what they think they could do to improve client satisfaction.

The firm culture can be gauged by its own language. If we talk about clients as 'them out there' or think of them as the necessary payers of bills, and if we rarely talk about clients at internal meetings and if we treat complaints defensively, we are probably in a culture which is distant from clients and which does not understand them as well as could be. 'Be careful with clients – they'll criticise you for being slow, they'll blame you for mistakes, they won't pay your bills, and they'll sue you if things go wrong!' some may say. Client orientation here is very strong, but pointed in the opposite direction from a client manager's point of view.

When clients are often in the office, when you're on first name terms with them, when your staff get to know them as well, when you could list from memory the names and annual turnover of the firm's top 10 clients, when the names of new clients are notified to other partners, then the firm is showing some of the characteristics of a truly client-oriented firm. All this leads to the classification of a law firm, being the sum of its members including both partners and staff, as achieving a high, medium or low level of client satisfaction. Most firms currently classify their performance in terms of turnover, profitability, bills delivered and numbers of fee earners, etc. This may imply that there are high levels of client satisfaction. Firms which are growing must be satisfying some clients, but are they satisfying them all and how much? As a rule of thumb, how much time do you and your partners spend at partners' meetings in discussing clients? High client satisfiers spend 50% plus of all management time in discussing 'what we can do for our clients' whereas low client satisfiers spend most of their time talking about turnover, financial results, expenditure, domestic matters, premises and computers, with only some 25% of this crucially important management time being devoted to the core business, that of satisfying clients.

Planning for client satisfaction

Most people will agree that client satisfaction is important but they may not all agree about how to achieve and increase it in a systematic way. Many firms proclaim in their brochures and publicity that they are 'committed to the highest standards of client service'. Does your current business plan put client satisfaction as the first, key strategic issue? Does it contain a detailed plan for gathering client feedback and for the implementation and review of specific measures to achieve and increase client satisfaction? Is the achievement of a measured level or increase in client satisfaction your number one priority or is your business plan stuffed full with medium and long-term strategies, marketing, budgets and financial projections? These are all, of course, very important and essential to law firm management but with nothing more than this they will not in themselves produce any substantive improvements in performance. In order to achieve improvement, new methods and ways of working need to be specifically planned, implemented and measured.

Seven out of the 10 companies with the highest customer satisfaction ratings in Japan are not manufacturing businesses but service businesses. They assess the three keys to high performance in customer satisfaction as being:

1 superior products and services (it works better and is more reliable than those of its competitors);
2 superior sales and delivery staff (people to people means better service than its competitors); and
3 superior after-sales service than its competitors.

Note the word 'superior' is used as opposed to 'excellent'. You have to be not only good but also better than and different from your competitors. If all law firms were as good as you, you would lose the differential that good service is designed to give to you. Law firms no longer are deemed equally able and competent – those days have gone. The key strategic development in law firms is to compete on differentiated service and client satisfaction levels. If your competitors get better, you must get better more quickly. Therefore, rather than proclaim, 'We provide high levels of service', a firm should be planning to deliver levels of client satisfaction which will justify the mission statement that, 'Our mission is to ensure that our clients choose our service above all others.'

Action checklist

1 Ask your clients what it is that satisfies them and what they value.
2 Set up an effective client management system.
3 Measure and report on the client satisfaction ratings.
4 Plan to increase the bottom line by increasing client satisfaction.
5 Recognise that client management is also hard-nosed, bottom-line financial management.

15 Complaints

Complaints and opportunities

Every firm will get some complaints, even if it does not have an effective complaint handling system in place. These complaints may be regarded in client management terms as a free, ready-made and valuable client feedback system. Every complaint provides you with an opportunity to listen to a client who cares enough about your service to make a complaint. Every complainant provides the firm with an opportunity to improve and an opportunity to save a potential lost client.

If you don't get many complaints, you might reasonably assume that your clients are generally happy and that you are good at looking after them. But according to the USA White House Office of Consumer Affairs:

- 96% of dissatisfied customers never complain and of those customers who are dissatisfied, 90% never come back in the future;
- one dissatisfied customer will tell at least nine other people about how he is dissatisfied with your firm; and
- it takes five times as much time and money to win a new customer than it does to keep an existing customer.

These startling figures are a stark lesson and provide a principle of client management – time and money spent reducing and avoiding the causes of dissatisfaction to existing clients and in dealing with complaints is five times as effective as the same amount of time and money spent in chasing new clients. Seeking client feedback, even at the risk of hearing some unpleasant things about ourselves that we would otherwise not have heard, and dealing constructively with complaints are both strategic activities with a high potential yield. Client managers no longer regard complaint handling as a secret process dealing with personal, service or product failure, but instead see it as an integral, essential and constructive part of client management.

Research by IBM has shown that customers who had their complaint dealt with satisfactorily were *more* likely to buy from IBM again and *more* likely to recommend IBM to others than those customers who had not had any problems at all! Thus, dealing with complaints responsively and satisfactorily is good market research and good marketing and so is good for business. Complaint handling should not be seen as a negative and unproductive activity because when dealt with by the client manager it can be very useful and positive.

Unless you respond quickly and satisfactorily to a client's complaint, the client is likely to find another solicitor and tell nine or 10 others about his dissatisfaction with you and your firm. The benefits of dealing with complaints effectively and constructively far outweighs the perceived problems and inherent distaste usually associated with such activities.

You need to make it easy for clients to complain and make comments and they need to believe that something will be done about it. Complaint handling methods should include:

- a client questionnaire sent out during a case may enable something to be done for a dissatisfied client before it's too late, nipping the compliant in the bud whilst being perceived as being responsive to the client;
- a client questionnaire sent out routinely at the end of each case may provide valuable information about 'niggles' which fall short of complaints.

When you do get a complaint from a client, or rather, when you are told by a slightly embarrassed senior or managing partner that so-and-so has been in touch with him about you, do you seethe with feelings of rage, do you turn on the client and blame him or do you just feel hurt and undervalued? Do you try to keep it quiet and sweep it under the carpet, do you regard it as an unavoidable part of the job, or do you deal with it dutifully in accordance with your firm's complaints procedure?

At first sight, client management may (incorrectly) be thought to be only about dealing with complaints. It is seen as a negative and unproductive thing, made mandatory by Rule 15 and the Office for the Supervision of Solicitors. But dealing with complaints effectively is one of the first and most important things a firm can and must do in developing a client management programme.

Apparently, the Chinese do not have one word for 'problem' and another word for 'opportunity'. They have one word for both which translates as 'interesting situation which is capable of going in one of several different ways depending on how it is handled'. This Chinese word would be very apt to describe complaints: they are interesting situations which can be resolved positively or negatively or not at all, depending on how they are handled and by whom. Complaints put service on trial. So, treat a complaint, save a client and win an ally and advocate for the firm.

Rather than setting up or handling complaints with faint or reluctant hearts, it is, therefore, necessary and beneficial to grasp this nettle in order to make the whole operation a positive, constructive, learning situation where no one is blamed but where lessons are learnt and systems are changed to ensure that the cause for complaint is reduced or eradicated altogether.

By making a complaint a client has given the firm a golden opportunity to turn a perceived failure into a demonstrated success. The ability to solve a legal problem is a mark of a good lawyer but the ability to keep clients happy and to be able to resolve problems satisfactorily is the mark of a good client manager.

The origin of complaints

If you are a manufacturer of a concrete and tangible product such as a television, a car or a widget and if your product fails in the hands of a customer, it is generally fairly easy to identify the cause of failure and to replace the faulty part. If you do it quickly and positively, with no fuss or cost to the customer, then it is likely that customer satisfaction may be maintained. If you do it really quickly and better than your customer expected, you will improve the relationship and secure repeat orders and recommendations. The customer's awareness of the product has been raised, he had experienced a disappointment in the product's failure but, on receipt of exceptional service, his perception of the product and its service support system and of the firms has been heightened. Complaint handling is a continuing and integral part of the legal service because it involves both participants. A complaint may be regarded as a key point in the client's experience of the firm which when handled professionally and skillfully could enhance the client's service perception of the firm.

As a service provider, dealing with a complaint from a client is not so straightforward as dealing with a product failure. It is difficult to identify what exactly went wrong and why exactly the client is complaining. Time and again I have dealt with complaints where, on examination of the file, I find that the advice recorded and the work being undertaken was perfectly correct and without fault. Nevertheless, it was apparent even in these legally correct matters that the client was seething with discontent for some reason that was not immediately apparent. In virtually every case it was found that the problem lay not in the legal work or advice itself, but in how that advice was given, delivered or communicated to the client. The complaints were predominantly about service, about the case manager's presentation and delivery of the legal product.

Delays and overcharging seem to form the basis of the majority of complaints. These are often found on further investigation to be complaints about poor communications. The basis for these complaints are capable of being reduced or avoided entirely by the practical implementation of the principles of client management.

A complaints handling system

Everyone makes mistakes from time to time and every business can have lapses in its service systems and will receive complaints. The mark of a client-focused business is not that it never makes mistakes or that it never gets complaints, but that it deals swiftly and effectively with the complaints that are received and in remedying its mistakes. A client management firm will have great pride and confidence in its complaint handling system. In order to ensure that the firm has an effective complaint handling system, there are a number of prerequisites as follows.

Commitment of management

The management team in a firm must acknowledge that complaints are inevitable regardless of how good a firm's service system is. They should recognise that complaints are a form of client feedback and market research as well as being a part of practice development. We have seen that a complainant client can be converted into a long-established client and advocate of the firm's service abilities if his complaint is dealt with promptly, fairly and constructively. As long as complaints are seen as a sign of failure, fault and blame which are to be hushed up and handled in secret, then the firm's culture will not be able to advance and the opportunities presented by complaint handling will not be realised.

Other members of the firm should also be made aware of the partners' resolve to deal with complaints constructively and positively. It is often the staff, including fee earners, case managers and other support members of the group who receive the complaint and it is important that they see the firm dealing with complaints positively and in accordance with established procedures. Serious complaints which may lead to an insurance claim must of course be dealt with confidentially but the vast majority of complaints do not involve such serious consequences.

Publicity

The complaints system must be made known to clients, both in order to comply with Rule 15 and also in order to make it fully effective. Details can be contained in the initial letter of engagement with the client, the terms and conditions of business or the client agreement. The explanatory wording should not be that of reluctant compliance with an imposed rule but rather words which reflect the firm's enthusiasm to deal with complaints, should any arise, positively, fairly and constructively. This approach in itself often takes much of the sting or rancour out of a client's complaint.

All members of the firm should also be made aware of the complaints handling system in a positive and constructive way. Details of its operation should be contained in the firms' office manual and even in specially prepared literature on the subject for clients to use. Staff should be encouraged to report all complaints, even informal comments and compliments as well, in order that a full and accurate picture can be assembled and maintained of client perception.

Problems or people

Where a complaint may involve a specific partner or member of staff there may of course be some understandable reluctance in that person about reporting it. Whatever assurance the firm may give that the complaints system is to concentrate on problems and their remedy rather than to punish individual members of the firm, these assurances will go unheeded unless the firm openly demonstrates consistently and regularly that this is indeed what is actually done. A blame-free emphasis on the problem, rather than on the person, and the accent on remedial measures and client satisfaction is what is required.

Of course, if complaints over a period of time do indicate some weakness in a particular person or group, then this must be addressed with discussion and perhaps counselling and training. The emphasis in client management, including complaints management, is upon learning from experience and continuous improvement rather than blame and fault. In this sense, the profession can become a learning profession as well as a learned profession.

Objectives of complaint handling

A client-focused firm which holds an open and positive attitude towards dealing with complaints from clients and which sees them as a potentially positive form of communication with clients, may decide to issue a leaflet to clients about how to complain. Rule 15 does require a firm to operate a complaints system and to tell clients the name of the person to whom complaints should be addressed. In order to extend this part of the service, the client leaflet may be seen as a positive and open way of introducing the subject to clients.

The main objectives of operating a complaints system include:

- to turn a dissatisfied client into a satisfied client;
- to create or restore the bond of trust and confidence that is essential to the solicitor/client relationship;
- to turn a complaint into an instruction for further work;
- to retain a client 'at risk';
- to strengthen the relationship; and
- the restoration of client satisfaction.

The complaint report

A form of complaint report (see Appendix 13) should be used for recording all complaints. A pad of copies should be issued to all group partners. When a complaint is received from a client, either in writing or verbally, the matter should be referred immediately to the group partner and a complaint report will be completed stating briefly the name of the complainant, the case reference, the group and client partner, the case manager and brief details of the complaint. A copy should be kept in the group complaint file and copies should be forwarded to the senior partner, the client partner and the marketing manager. Whilst the partner closest to the point of complaint is the best person to deal with the matter, it will be necessary for him to consult others about the most appropriate way of dealing with the complaint.

This form of consultation and guidance, when combined with his own knowledge of the client, should enable him to deal with the complaint in a positive and constructive way. When the group partner from whom the complaint emanates is not the client partner, he should also consult the client partner concerned who may take it on himself to deal with the complaint with the client.

Internal investigation

As soon as the complaint is received, it should be acknowledged and the client should be informed that the complaint is being investigated and that a response will be made within seven days. This acknowledgement may be made by telephone but it should always be followed with a letter. This is not only a courtesy but also may help to temporarily pacify an irate client.

The person who takes the responsibility for dealing with the complaint will consult the fee earner or case manager and other persons around whom the complaint is centred. He will also call for and examine the file and check for compliance with the service and case and client management procedures that the firm may have adopted. He will then make his report on the complaint form.

The firm should aim to be able to respond fully to the client within seven days of receiving the complaint or within such other reasonable period as may be appropriate. It cannot afford to be lax about this aspect of service where the client may be armed and dangerous. The response must be made personally either by telephone or preferably by a meeting in person. The client may be invited into the firm's office specially or be seen on his visit to the office if it coincides with the same timing. It is probably not a good policy to go the client's office or workplace for the response. A lot depends on the circumstance and the client in each situation but it is generally better to see the client on your own territory.

The complaint meeting

The inquiry and response to the client's complaint where a meeting is held should contain a number of parts.

Listen with patience

It is important to start by listening to the client. He feels upset and perhaps angry and so must be given the chance to say what he feels. The client should be allowed to have his say without interruption – it may be the first chance of making a service input he has had, albeit rather late.

Empathise

Most clients do not complain and so when one does, you can feel sympathy for his distress. It is not necessary to agree with his interpretation of the facts of the problem, but it is essential to acknowledge his feelings. If you tell the client that he has misunderstood the situation and should not be dissatisfied, you will only make the situation worse.

A good complaints handling policy is to try to find ways of acknowledging the problem from his point of view. 'Yes, I can see that you must have been upset/been surprised/felt that nothing was happening, etc.' Try to use 'and' rather than 'but', because 'and' is constructive, whereas 'but' tends to erase what has gone before. Also use 'I' more than 'you', since it comes across as being less threatening.

Don't explain

Listen to the client's version of what happened and try to establish the facts. You may be tempted to explain your version of what happened and to justify events, but this is your perception and not the client's and it will only serve to make matters worse. The techniques of dealing with complaints show that it is generally not good policy to explain what went wrong and why, or to try to justify what was done. This serves only to inflame the client and to confirm his doubts about the firm not really understanding him. If the complaint was that a deadline was missed, it's no good saying, 'It would not have happened if our computer operator had not been away with flu at the time and the key date on our computer database was missed.' It's much better to concentrate on the remedial action which the firm proposes to take.

Agree the facts

The responder should have found out and mastered all the facts from the file before the meeting. In this he will have an advantage because not many clients keep a contemporaneous file as does the case manager. The responder should have the file with him and it should be visible to the client but not open. The responder should not open it unless a fact is questioned or contested.

Speak to the people

The responder should also have spoken to all relevant people involved including the case manager, the group partner and the client partner. They may be defensive and blame the client, saying, 'The client doesn't understand!' or worse. All views should be checked before responding to the client.

Identify the problem

The problem and the facts should be identified and separated from personalities as soon as possible. For example, 'Well, it appears there was some delay. I have spoken to our Mr Guppy and it appears that he was doing his best to get a response from the other side, as these three attendance notes and two letters on the file to their solicitors shows. Perhaps he should have contacted you to say that he was having a problem here, so at least you would have known what was going on. Don't you agree?'

Reaching agreement

It is vital in complaint handling to secure the client's agreement to each stage of the complaint response. He must be invited to agree the facts, he must acknowledge the people involved and he must come to accept the root cause of the problem. This process is not easy because the complainant client may be emotional or even angry. He will want to vent his fury on someone. He needs someone to do some active listening. He may want sympathy or for the first time in his experience of the firm, someone to really listen to him and try to understand him. It will be recalled that understanding and interest are the two most important things to a client. If he feels he has been taken for granted or treated as a case and not as an individual, this part of the complaint-handling process is a vital and integral part of the solution, by simply listening and showing interest in the client, perhaps for the first time since the case started.

It is important here not to confuse sympathy and understanding with agreement. The client may be abrupt with the responder or rude about the person involved. 'He showed no interest in my case at all and did absolutely nothing for me!' The responder does not have to say, 'Yes, I agree, he really is useless!' but rather, 'Yes, I can see that you were upset' or, 'Yes, I can see how you must have felt.' Acknowledge the client's perceptions without necessarily agreeing with his version

331

of the facts. The worst thing to do is to dispute how the client should have felt or to suggest that he over-reacted. Client perception is the pith and essence of service for, as we have seen in Chapter 3, the client is always right. By agreeing and accepting the client's response and perception and by empathising with this experience is all part of the complaint handling process. Telling the client he is wrong to be upset is not the way of the client manager.

Identify a solution

After some time the client will have calmed down and this will be a cue for the responder to move the discussion forward towards identifying possible solutions and to get the client's agreement to a solution. 'Well, Mrs Jones, I think I understand why you were upset. The case was being done as well as possible in the circumstances but you would have appreciated to have been kept better informed. Are we agreed on that? Well, I have spoken to our Mr Guppy and we thought you might find it helpful if he sent you a copy of each letter on the file as it comes in and a copy of the letters he writes. Would that be helpful, do you think?' The client may accept this as a step forward. She may want more. 'Well, perhaps, Mrs Jones, we could send you a brief monthly report or simply telephone to let you know what's happening, even if not very much is actually happening?' If the client is not satisfied, it may be necessary to ask the client what she thinks would be useful and acceptable. It is vital to keep looking forward to solutions and not backwards at problems or explanations.

Agree a way forward

It is important to agree what action will be taken, when and by whom. Not only is this important in dealing with the actual problem, but it will also show the client that his complaint has been successful, and that he has got 'something done about it'. The firm will also be showing that it does understand the client, that it is responsive and that it is in control of things. If you say to the client, 'Yes, I'll check into it and get back to you within seven days' then on the seventh day the client will be expecting your response.

Summarise the discussion

When a solution has been agreed, and often these are simple and obvious, it is necessary for the responder to sum up the facts, the problem and the agreed solution and so point the way forward. By this time, a new and better degree of client empathy may well have been formed and a satisfied and mollified client will leave your offices. He will believe that he has had it out, that his views have been established and accepted and that the firm has responded positively to his just complaint.

Resolution

The client interview must be followed up promptly with a letter to the client referring to the meeting, confirming the agreed facts and problem and then confirming the solution that was agreed with the client. There might be an apology for the upset caused to the client, and a statement that the firm will do its best to ensure that the problem does not recur. The very process of dealing with the complaint itself is often more than 50% of the solution from the point of view of the client. This is why the complaints-handling procedure should be seen as an integral part of the service rather than as a appendage which becomes necessary as a result of failure.

Apology

If the firm finds that a complaint is justified, it can be good practice to actually apologise to the client. You might say, 'Well, we're sorry about what happened and I suggest that we now do ... .' It is generally poor policy to dwell on what went wrong and over-explain because it can sound defensive and an attempt to justify what happened. It's better to admit the problem and then move on directly to deal with remedial action that will be taken with the client's agreement.

Whilst apologising to the client may be appropriate, the responder must be careful to avoid making expressly or by implication any admission of negligence or legal liability. Such an admission may avoid the firm's professional indemnity insurance as well as being grounds for disciplinary action. The responder should have formed a view and taken advice before the client meeting about this possibility. Where negligence or legal liability is an issue, a different approach may need to be taken (see below).

Communication

Where a particular solution has been agreed, it is important to tell the people concerned about the agreed solution immediately. If you have agreed to copy all letters on file to Mrs Jones, then Mr Guppy, the case manager, must be told and he must also acknowledge that he has been told and confirm that he will comply. A variation has occurred in the care plan and he must acknowledge this. Both the client partner and the group partner must be informed. The simplest way is to send a copy of the completed complaint report to the relevant people and to get them to acknowledge receipt.

Check for action

Having gone to all this time and trouble to deal with the client, it is incumbent on the firm not only to do what was agreed but also to check that it has been done. There really can be little hope for a firm that neglects this final but vital step in the compliant handling procedure.

Effective complaint handling

The factors which will ensure an effective complaint handling system include:

- all people concerned should know the rules and the services and the products of the firm;
- listen to the client and encourage him to be frank;
- keep it simple and positive;
- outline the benefits of the remedial action;
- don't get personally involved; and
- treat your client as you would like to be treated if you were a client.

Closing ranks and stonewalling is not the client manager's way of dealing with complaints. Having identified the problem, the responder needs to move the complaint forward with the objective of reaching agreement with the client about the problem and the agreed solution. Blaming the client and being defensive is an approach which, though understandable, will not yield either client satisfaction in the complaint or produce any valuable lessons for the firm.

Complaint management reports

Performance to financial targets and variances are reported regularly to the firm's management team. These reports assess the success of the firm's activities, but in only one aspect, the financial aspect. The firm is there to make a profit. The firm is also there to satisfy the client and, whilst billings may give some indication of the success of the firm with its clients, bills delivered do not necessarily indicate the levels of client satisfaction achieved by the firm. In order to do this, regular reports are required which will include information about complaints, numbers, causes, remedial action taken and subsequent client satisfaction levels.

The marketing manager should produce a monthly report to the firm for the previous month, with variances over the previous month, three months, year-to-date and this month last year. In this way the firm will be proactively managing and controlling the complaints process, raising the overall awareness in the firm of clients and be reducing the causes of complaints for the future.

Linked to these reports will also be reports about client suggestions, client satisfaction ratios and client compliments in order that the firm can be made accurately and consistently aware of what pleases its clients and what does not and so learn to develop client-oriented service and product features.

All complaints, comments and compliments should be logged at group or departmental level and collated firm-wide on a monthly basis for analysis not only for dealing with specific complaints but also for assessing client perception.

Learning from complaints

The complaint report will also include recommendations for remedial measures for the service system generally with costings. This is a vital and often overlooked part of the complaints system. If a firm is to develop a client-focused and learning culture, it must see complaints as one way of learning and of improving its services. If a number of complaints are made about 'delays' and where these are found upon enquiry to be more about communication, the firm may decide that service improvements are required. These may include regular methods of communicating to clients about the progress, or even lack of progress, in their cases. In the above instance, sending copy letters to clients may be a partial answer. Specially prepared, monthly client reports may be necessary for other clients. Whatever the response and the solution, the firm should consider building these features into its standard service system or at least offering them to clients as an option in its care plan. In order to convert the negative aspects of complaints into long-term positive aspects, it is necessary to ensure that complaints are reviewed and that trends and lessons are noted and service system improvements are made. It is obvious that in order to take advantage of the opportunities that complaints can offer, the firm does need to have made the commitment and allocated the resources and personnel which are necessary.

Complaints, comments and compliments

A complaint is only one type of feedback from clients, and not all feedback is negative or critical. It is a fact of everyday practice that individuals in firms also receive comments and compliments. We all treasure the occasional letter received from a client thanking us personally for doing a good job for them.

A client suggestion scheme or a client feedback scheme may perhaps sound more positive than simply 'complaints'. Ask your clients for suggestions of how they think your service could be improved rather than just telling them how to complain. Seeing a complaining client as just another problem is a losing strategy in a competitive world where added value and client satisfaction are the key winning strategies.

The firm may decide to be as open as possible about complaints and feedback, both positive and negative. We all get letters of compliments from clients from time to time and these are a form of client feedback which provides valuable information to the client manager. Instead of concentrating just on complaints, the firm may wish to refer to client feedback or suggestions in a broader sense. The firm may implement a client suggestion scheme, by post, by survey and by suggestion box and this may be useful in obtaining confidential and spontaneous client feedback.

Responding to complaints

Complaint handling has a vocabulary of its own and the careful selection of words and attitudes can be vital to the response process. Some responses can be classified into 'weak' or 'strong' as follows.

Responding to complaints	
Weak response	*Strong response*
Being defensive	Being open
Denying the complaint	Accepting the fact of the complaint
Disputing the facts	Agreeing the facts
Blaming the client	Focusing on the problem
Retreating from the problem	Being up-front
Feeling hurt	Welcoming feedback
Feeling misunderstood	Trying to reach an understanding
Being aggressive	Apologising for client inconvenience
Looking to blame someone	Identifying the problem
Explaining too much	Agreeing remedial action

It is of course necessary that in dealing with complaints that you stay within the guidelines laid down by professional indemnity insurers and within the constraints that may be laid down in the individual's contract of employment with the firm or in the partnership agreement. It is generally the case that no admission of negligence may be made. It is important that the complaints procedure is clearly understood and complied with by all concerned.

Quality and complaints

A number of quality control and assurance systems contain requirements for the handling of complaints, including BS 5750. In this context, a complaint is seen as an item of 'non-conformance' which may be presented as follows:

Control of non-conforming services and corrective action

Objectives	1 To ensure that any service or product problems are identified, analysed and resolved to the client's satisfaction 2 To prevent recurrence
Scope	All complaints received from clients and others
Responsibilities	1 For handling clients' complaints 2 For identifying problems with the quality of work and services to clients 3 To rectify sub-standard work 4 To prevent recurrence
Personnel	Quality partner/senior partner/client services manager
Documentation	1 Central complaints book 2 Complaints reports 3 Non-conformance report
Procedure	1 Receipt, logging and processing of all complaints 2 Identification and correction of sub-standard work and services 3 Production of non-conformance reports to identify problems with products and services 4 Making recommendations for remedial and product and service improvements 5 Carrying out corrective action

Everyone knows that Marks & Spencer always replace faulty goods with a refund. This 'no-quibble' approach to customer returns has itself given them an enviable service reputation in addition to its product quality reputation. If the clients and the market knows that your firm takes a positive and systematic approach to dealing with client complaints, this is usually seen as a positive and valuable differentiator rather than as an admission of fallibility and failure.

Perceived indifference

One of the biggest problems, as shown in Chapter 5, is that many clients think that their solicitors don't really understand or care about them. Perceived indifference is given as the main reason for clients leaving one firm for another. This perception is often in the client's mind when making a complaint. He may in effect be giving the firm a last chance to redeem its reputation in this respect. By dealing with complaints actively, openly, constructively, promptly and fairly, the firm can do a lot to make a complainant/client realise that the firm does care and does do something about it. Conversely, if the firm deals with the complaint in a slow, cumbersome, reluctant and defensive manner, the client may feel, rightly, that the firm does not really care and is operating the complaints system out of duty rather than out of a genuine interest in client satisfaction.

Complaints are not a sign of failure but a sign of life. Sometimes a person or firm needs to make a few mistakes to show that an effort is being made to satisfy its clients. 'How many mistakes have you made recently? None? Well you're not trying hard enough!'

Dealing with difficult clients

It is the few difficult clients that demand the most attention and can cause the most stress and absorb the most time. The experienced client manager will not find dealing with them easy but he will have a number of techniques to help him deal with the more usual 'difficult' client situations:

- stay calm at all times, even if you are seething inside with indignation at the client's complaints. Your voice, body language and attitude are a key part of managing the client's reactions;
- offer a range of options for action. This will make an angry client calm down so that he can consider the matter rationally;
- never be rude or aggressive in response. By staying calm and by repeating the options and listening, you will be able to keep it constructive;
- never try to justify the matter that the client is complaining about, it will only make the situation more difficult;
- you should consider, 'Am I the best person to be dealing with this? If not, who is?' You may need to hand the matter to the group partner without letting the client feel that he is being given the run around;
- never touch the complainant, particularly if the person is emotional or angry. Such actions may be misread and escalate into violence;
- noone is expected to tolerate verbal abuse from a client and, if this happens, immediate help should be summoned or the meeting be terminated immediately. Noone should go alone to see an angry

client, particularly any female member of the firm. If in doubt, ensure that the responder is accompanied; and

● try to find points of agreement and common values.

The ability to deal successfully with difficult clients is perhaps one of the greatest tests of the client manager's skill. Some clients, it has to be acknowledged, can be so demanding and unreasonable that no skill or technique will be of avail and that a termination of the relationship is the only sensible resort. Whilst a change in the client partner or case handler may often work wonders with a difficult client, on some occasions the firm itself may need to terminate the relationship. It is useful for the firm to reserve such rights in its standard terms and conditions of business.

All clients great and small

The Video Arts booklet 'Coping with customers' contains some valuable insights into customer types, which can be applied to dealing with difficult client 'types' in a law firm. Clients appear in all shapes and sizes and all are different in their expectations and perceptions of the firm. There are, however, some general observations that can be made about certain characteristics of clients and being familiar with them and having some understanding and knowledge of how to deal with set-piece situations can form a useful part of the client manager's toolkit.

The rabbit

She talks and talks so much that it's difficult to get a word in. Don't interrupt her or cut her short and don't bully her or be rude. As she pauses for breath, try to get in a pertinent question, such as – 'So he gave you a black eye, did he? Can you remember the date and did anyone else see him do it? Were you examined by your doctor?' In this way, Mrs Rabbit is able to express herself and the solicitor is able to put together some viable instructions.

The warthog

He is rude to you, and everyone else, so don't take it personally. Don't let him rile you or make you angry and make you say something you would rather not. He complains a lot and may even be offensive. Don't admit anything, try to identify the problem and agree to investigate a specific point and get back to him within an agreed timescale.

The tiger

He is a very powerful and intimidating client and has a reputation for aggression with his professional advisers, sometimes 'fatal'. The best tactic in dealing with this sort of client is to stay within your own area of competence and not to allow yourself to be drawn into unfamiliar territory where your knowledge and experience may be inadequate. If drawn on out of your depth, tell Mr Tiger that this is not your principal area of expertise and that partner A in the firm will be able to help him.

The camel

She is awkward and thankless to deal with no matter how hard you try. With such a client, deliver the legal service in a straightforward way without trying harder to satisfy her, because you will always fail.

The lion

He thinks he is the only client you've got and always demands full and instant attention, which you always give for fear of annoying him. Instead of allowing him to interrupt you when you are dealing with another client, send a message to him that you will return his call by a stated time. Before you telephone him back, ensure that you fully brief yourself on Mr Lion's case and call him back sooner than you said. Mr Lion will be surprised and taken off guard by the early response. He may falter and even be impressed with your grasp of the facts and progress of the case. You are telephoning on your terms and at your time and this will give you the necessary advantage in dealing successfully with this powerful and intimidating client. By inviting him to your office, you will have the additional advantage of dealing with him on your own territory and not his.

The bear

She is strong and wild and will tear you to pieces if she gets you cornered. She can also be very kind and friendly when the mood takes her. The problem is that you never know which mood she will be in when she telephones or when a meeting is held. Bears like honey so make sure, in dealing with this type of client, that you have some interesting news or information to give her.

Hissing Sid

This type of client says one thing and then later denies it or interprets it or the advice you have given in an inaccurate way. In dealing with this sort of client, it is important to be direct and unequivocal in the advice you give and to ensure that the advice is recorded not only in an attendance note on the file but also in a letter, perhaps marked 'private and confidential', or in a report sent to the client for acknowledgment and signature before contractual relations are entered into. Sometimes, it is as important to protect yourself against some clients as against 'the other side'.

Professional negligence

Noone likes to talk about professional negligence. A client-oriented firm, however, will endeavour to have an open learning culture which is not only prepared but is also willing to look at its mistakes and to learn from them and to do something about them. Many firms will have a cabinet with the files containing the professional negligence actions, generally kept under lock and key by the senior or managing partner and marked 'private'. The claims cabinet is looked on as a shameful thing, a wound in the side of the firm, an admission and evidence of human frailty. It is handled with hushed and discreet attention by authorised partners only.

It is, of course, necessary in the interests of confidentiality to keep such matters private and confidential. However, each case should be examined and the essence of it, without client names or details, be put into a report for perhaps selected client managers to see. For example: claim A is a claim made due to the writ not being issued within the limitation period. It could easily have been avoided in several ways:

- the key dates diary was not completed or checked;
- the lawyer concerned did not make adequate diary notes;
- the firm did know that time was critical but it did not prepare the case sufficiently for the writ to be issued in time;
- the writ was defective, etc; and
- liability was wrongfully admitted by the lawyer in question.

In the above circumstances where liability has been improperly admitted by the lawyer concerned, the firm may resolve to take the following corrective actions:

- the office manual prohibits any person even a partner from admitting liability to a client. The insurance cover may be invalidated in this respect. The lawyer concerned is due for disciplinary action;
- the senior partner will write to the client to apologise and to tell the client that the claim is being dealt with by the firm's insurers and that action has been taken within the firm to ensure that such a thing does not happen again;
- disciplinary action on the lawyer concerned takes place;
- review of procedures for making entries into the key dates diary. Who is responsible for making the entry, who keeps the diary, what happens if it is lost, should it be kept in one place, should it be put on computer;
- review of the office manual;
- training or publicity to staff on procedures for the key dates diary; and
- review group supervision and case management procedures.

The follow-up measures are vital to raise the firm's awareness about procedures and key dates. The firm will accept that complaints are inevitable and perhaps even necessary as a part of client feedback but that claims are really a result of system or individual failure. The firm will have embarked on a new and open culture in learning from error and constantly up-dating its procedures.

A vindictive attitude towards 'transgressors' will not help this culture develop. A *laissez-faire* or fatalistic approach towards complaints will also not improve matters. The culture is a balance that needs to be carefully maintained. Research in the United States has shown that the incidence of actions for professional negligence is greater against highly technically able professionals who have low client management skills than against professionals who have good client skills but who may be only of moderate though adequate technical ability. Whilst a client is unlikely to have grounds to sue for service failures alone, such as poor communications, where these are linked to professional incompetence or negligence he is more likely to sue than where service levels are good.

The National Consumer Council

The National Consumer Council (NCC) has been quoted as saying, 'Solicitors have a far rosier picture of their practices than their clients and are not as good at communicating information as they think they are. Only one in 10 firms actually seeks feedback from their clients.'

In 1994, the NCC published a report called *Solicitors and Client Care* which contained a number of recommendations based on the research behind the report. The contentious part of the report was whether these recommendations should be made mandatory and prescriptive. Whether they are made mandatory or not, it must be obvious to any business manager that if firms do not provide good service, they will decline and perhaps even go out of business. In this the clients and the market will be the final arbiters. Clients can legislate for client care here in their own way, with their feet.

The NCC was associated with the production of a booklet called, *How to Get the Best From Your Solicitor* which encourages more openness between the solicitor and the client at the outset of the case.

Failure to do what is outlined in Rule 15 is bad for business, not just because it would be a breach of professional standards but because Rule 15 points the way towards a greater openness with clients. It is far better for a firm to deal internally with complaints by using an effective complaints handling system than to allow complaints to be referred by frustrated clients to external organisations for resolution. This new openness is essential for growth and survival in this new competitive era where clients demand service and where clients exercise choice. The demystification and client orientation of the profession are the new business rules which have been made mandatory by the clients.

The way forward is that complaints will become fewer and less serious as client management systems kick into action and provide the framework where misunderstanding is minimised. With the advance client management work in place, there will be clear agreement as to terms of business, an agreed work specification, agreed charges, named personnel and even a care plan may be formulated. With all this in place before the work is begun, the risk of under-recovery is also minimised. So, client management and complaints handling go hand-in-hand with profitable practise management.

How to reduce complaints

Some typical client complaints include:

'The quoted costs were exceeded without my knowledge or agreement';

'The case took far too long';

'There were too many delays';

'I didn't know what was going on';

'I didn't ask for that to be done'; and

'You haven't achieved anything for me'.

All these are complaints about the delivery of the work rather than about the work itself or the costs. In this there is a powerful message in that by providing a service that equals or exceeds client expectations we can have satisfied clients, less fee resistance and more profitable case work. The powerful message is that after all, we were not being criticised by our clients for the quality of our legal advice, in which most of us take professional pride. Clients are criticising us largely not for the quality of our legal knowledge or advice, but for the service element, which has only in the past few years become to be seen as an important, if not the most important, part of the legal service process. We were not trained to provide a service to the client but we can be (re-)trained and we can learn and we can do it. This is one of the big messages of client management for solicitors.

The vast majority of complaints result from poor communication, failed expectations and misunderstandings. Communication, understanding and expectations can and should be dealt with at the beginning of the case through the use of the client agreement, the case plan, agreed charges and possibly the care plan. These all help to establish clearly the basis of the relationship and the contract between the solicitor and client and thereby to reduce the possibility of complaints in the future. If these steps are not taken, the recipe is set for future problems. The incidence of complaints is largely a matter of client management rather than of professional or legal incompetence.

It can be seen that dealing with complaints is a way of writing the client agreement in retrospect and case planning in reverse. In the vast majority of cases and clients, the complaints would never have arisen at all if a few minutes had been taken at the outset to agree with the client and to specify the basic issues of case plan, agreed charges and care plan.

If the case handler identifies and agrees up front what will be done, how long it will take, what it will cost, who will do it and on what terms and conditions, he will be dealing proactively with client expectation in a new, dynamic and profitable way, in the way of the client manager.

Action checklist

1 Accept that complaints will arise even though the firm may never hear of them.
2 Use complaints as an instant and readily available source of free client feedback.
3 Learn the techniques of dealing with difficult clients.
4 Avoid and reduce complaints by implementing a client management system.

16 Responding to clients

You get what you set

Not many solicitors would disagree that the quality of the client relationship is one of the key factors in determining the success of a law firm. Many solicitors would say that client care and client management *are* the main factors for success of a law firm. *All* clients would expect that their views and feelings should be the guiding force in running and developing a client-focused law firm.

The performance of a firm is a direct and inexorable result of the attitudes, actions and motivation of the people in the firm. Whatever the performance of the firm actually is, it is a result of what has been thought, said and done by the firm, and by noone else. Many firms suffered during the recession from lower demand for their services, lower charges and lower profitability. Firms had to learn how to respond to lower turnover and profitability. Firms that responded slower suffered more than those that read what was happening and adapted accordingly. By continuing working and managing during and after a recession in broadly the same way as in the pre-recession boom, save only with less staff and reduced overheads, is a survival policy that will not produce growth in the changed post-recession profession and economy.

Noone is expecting a boom to return anymore and few actually want one. Most businesses both inside and outside of the profession seem to have accepted that a flattish economy lies ahead and that any growth will have to be earned by new and better products and services rather than hoping to see profits buoyed up again by a property fuelled boom. The 'feel flat' factor is perhaps a more appropriate expression for the post-recession late 1990s than the so far elusive 'feel good' factor.

If nothing more is done than to continue as before but with fewer staff and reduced overheads, then perhaps it will still be possible to squeeze flat profits from existing legal products and services. If, on the other hand, a firm determines to improve its range of legal products and services, with the introduction of product quality systems, staff management development, financial management and client management systems, then increased profitability can be attained from static or even slightly reduced turnover. However, with such new systems on board, it is likely that the firm will have a greatly increased expectation of seeing itself develop pre-eminence amongst its competitors and see its market share, turnover and profitability grow.

This is the challenge to a law firm as to any other business – whether and to what extent it can adapt and respond to the permanently changed business realities of the late 1990s. No longer can we blame the recession for our performance because we have had sufficient time to recognise the market changes for what they are and to determine what we are going to do about it. Whatever happens, what we get will be what we have set, by decision, act or omission.

The first step

The past casts a shadow over the present, and some of the attitudes and principles which were effective in the pre-recession days can now be a substantial inhibition in responding to the opportunities of client management in the post-recession world. Which of the following statements, if any, do you think most closely resembles your own opinions?

1 'We are here to do legal work for clients and can only react to their requirements.'
2 'The most important thing is to control expenditure.'
3 'It is obvious that we satisfy our clients because we don't get many complaints.'
4 'I've been in a successful practice for years – you can't tell me anything about clients!'
5 'Work hard, get the bills out and keep expenditure down – that's the way we've always done it and I see no reason to change!'

Each of the above statements may often be followed by an admission which goes like this: 'Well, yes, I admit that our profits are not what they were five years ago, but ... .' It is true, however, that some firms have been able to increase their profits notwithstanding the recession. According to figures published from time to time in the *Law Society Gazette*, these appear to be the larger firms where management practices are perhaps more developed than in smaller firms. The gap in turnover, market share and profitability seems to be widening between the better-managed firms and the rest. Whatever the size or location of the firm, however, it is still those firms that provide satisfaction to clients that are on the growth path.

When a firm has been through times of falling profitability, when it has had sobering advice and reduced facilities from the bank manager, when it has talked itself out and suffered all the anguish of indecision and the challenge of change, its management may come to the point when they say, 'OK, let's give this client management a try, but let's take it steady, we don't want to upset the clients, er, I mean, we don't want to spend too much non-chargeable time with all this client management, er, well, I know it will be productive but ...' or words to that effect. These first faltering steps mark a huge quantum leap in the cultural direction of the firm.

Once a firm has reached this stage, then things will start to move more easily and with more speed. Like any new system, it may well be felt initially that things are getting worse and there are two reasons for this. First, the new heightened awareness that client management brings may depress the firm with the realisation of how much work needs to be done. Second, having let go of strict adherence to the former mainly functional ways of working but not yet having derived the benefits of client management, it may feel that it is adrift in the middle of unchartered seas. This is the real test of the firm's determination to continue and if it can get through this low patch and maintain its commitment to client management, then gradually things will be seen and be felt to improve.

Taking clients seriously

Yet saying that it is important does not necessarily mean anyone is actually doing anything about it. Whilst a professional firm might accept the need for improved attention to client requirements and client perceptions, it may not have developed the policies and systems for ensuring that client orientation and client management are integrated into its everyday working lives.

Even where attitudes gradually change towards client management, it still requires new work practices to be designed and carried out in order to do something effective about it. In most businesses, however, nothing much is done until there occurs what John Trowers, former chief executive of Rover, calls a 'compelling reason' such as mass migration of clients away from the firm, bank pressure, high levels of negligence claims or increasingly fierce local competition. Such a reason will make the firm do something, but until such time it may prefer to continue as before. It is rare that a firm will spontaneously start doing things differently because 'it's a good idea'.

Propounding the need to change may, therefore, not be taken seriously by many until such time perhaps as a 'compelling reason' forces change or acts as a catalyst to change. The need to adapt and respond to changed market conditions is serious and the price for not doing so can also be serious.

Getting serious

In the absence of a 'compelling reason', the first stage towards change is usually a growing awareness of the need to improve communications with and understanding of clients. Becoming aware of the need to improve client awareness and client systems in the firm can bring about immediate dissatisfaction. A firm may realise how much needs to be done, how most, if not all, of its systems and work practices will need to be reviewed and changed in whole or in part. Change brings stress and stress brings resistance.

So, in order to actually do something about it, a firm needs to be able to convince staff that client management is a serious matter. If client management is not taken seriously, and if it is regarded as peripheral to legal work, then a firm will not be able to enjoy its fruits.

So here lies the critical point which must be overcome before any serious or effective work can be done in developing client management techniques throughout the firm. It is absolutely essential to obtain the commitment of all the management team to the client management project because without it the project will fail to be fully effective. The way to obtain commitment is to get people to realise themselves the benefits that can be achieved by client management practices. (See Chapter 17.)

Planning and implementing a client management system

Once the principles of client management have been accepted to be a matter requiring serious attention, then it is necessary to move towards implementing its practices. The key to dealing with client management is to find new ways of working for client satisfaction and to invent new ways of measuring that performance. The approach to implementation must be planned and phased and perhaps only a few of its principal practices may be put in place initially. The stages of implementing a client management system may be as follows:

1 Evolve the emphasis on performance from just 'fee earning' to include 'client satisfying' by introducing regular measures and reports for client satisfaction to be produced alongside the usual financial management reports.
2 Develop the firm's complaints-handling system into one which is positive, open, responsive and uncritical of individuals. The system should concentrate on the problem, the possible opportunities of client satisfaction, and improvement to existing practices, rather than being one which is perceived to be about fault and failure.
3 Issue a service questionnaire to clients at the end of every case and record and analyse the results with a monthly management report.
4 Appoint a marketing manager to produce, *inter alia*, a monthly report to partners on the results of the questionnaires and to make recommendations for product and service improvements.
5 Involve all staff in client management and client care measures.
6 Hold a regular series of client management and client care training workshops with compulsory attendance for all, including partners. Even if the partners and other case workers are brilliant with their clients and perhaps don't need any training, they must be seen by others in the firm to be supporting the client management and client care initiative and sharing their expertise.
7 Publish performance figures of client satisfaction and complaints internally to all staff.
8 Include client care and client satisfaction measures in your staff appraisal and compensation assessment criteria.
9 Review the standard Rule 15 for use by all the firm and check with clients for altered perception.
10 Prepare monthly reports on all inceptions, new clients and complaints.
11 Carry out an active and varied client entertainment programme.
12 Produce a report on 'People in the Community' – what do partners and associates do outside the office in official, semi-official or voluntary capacities and assess how these are or how these could be beneficial to the firm and its clients.
13 Report on the activities and initiatives taken by people in the firm with clients over the last month.
14 Prepare a continuous client management and client-care training programme spanning a period of at least 12 months.

15 Take an overview of firm's typestyles and letter-writing formats to clients and assess the 'client friendly' factor with feedback from a cross-section of staff and clients. Are too many letters being written? Are they too long? Are they too technical? Would an enclosed report would be better?

16 Open an 'hospitality received' book to record all gifts to partners and staff from clients, including reasons and comments.

17 Ensure that monthly progress reports are offered to major and key clients.

18 Require that a client agreement be completed at the beginning of each case.

19 Introduce a 24-hour telephone legal advice service for clients.

20 Keep and regularly examine a listing of all incoming telephone calls and review how general enquiries are being dealt with.

21 Introduce a visitors book for reception and then examine and report upon its statistics about the number and frequency of client visits, waiting times and client feedback from reception.

22 Conduct a client survey every 12 months with a cross-section of the firm's clients and link the analysed results to the autumn conference, business plan and budgets.

23 Use a variety of client questionnaires to obtain regular client feedback.

24 Appoint a client partner to take an overview of the firm's client management programme and to make reports on complaints, inceptions, entertainment and marketing.

25 Conduct a series of client satisfaction surveys in different branches, departments and groups to identify where service improvements are most required.

26 Carry out an annual internal audit with staff to ascertain staff perception and morale and suggestions for client service improvements.

27 Carry out an annual external audit with stakeholders (referrers, suppliers, etc) to assess the firm's image in the marketplace compared to its competitors.

28 Review and redesign where necessary the firm's client database to include client profiles, key clients, major clients and business and occupation details. Ensure that client managers are linked by screens to the database.

29 Design and send out to all new clients a client information pack containing all relevant information about the firm which may be useful to the client including details of the firm's personnel and services.

30 Produce a practice guide to be given to all clients containing essential information about the firm, including telephone numbers,

opening times, emergency contacts, parking places, complaints procedure and so on.

31 Request staff to form a client action team or teams to meet monthly to consider client feedback and to make recommendations to partners for service improvements.

It is not recommended to try to implement all of these measures at once but rather to concentrate initially on two or three main projects and to get these up and running and embedded in the firm's practices before moving on to further stages.

Involving the members of the firm

If we agree that clients are important, if we accept that in a service business it is the people in the firm who are the firm and who are part of the service, from the client's point of view, if we agree that we must do something about it, then a firm should involve its staff in the client management initiative.

For example, a firm may decide that, in order to save cost on reception and switchboard, and in order to speed up linking clients with the fee earners, the switchboard will switch calls through to the relevant group secretary, who would then take on the responsibility for connecting the client with the partner or group fee earner concerned. No longer will the client be kept waiting on the switchboard whilst reception tried to locate the partner or fee earner when noone answered or noone knew where he was. Instead, the group secretary would take on the role. She would know and make it her duty to know where the fee earners are and to link them with the client or take the message.

If the new system is introduced but the group secretary is not told or has it explained to her why it was important, very soon the group may have an irate and confused secretary. She may exclaim in exasperation, 'I'm spending so much time dealing with clients that I haven't got time to get on with my work!' When she is reminded that dealing with clients was in fact what her job was really about, her confusion may still not subside. Without training and a planned phasing of the client management programme, the benefits of client management will not be fully realised. Her attitude is understandable, and highlights the difficulty of bringing about change without informing and consulting with those concerned.

It has been said, 'Treat your staff in the same way as you would like them to treat your major clients when you are out of the office.' How can a firm look after clients if it doesn't look after its staff who provide the service? Both are part of the client service process.

If a firm decides to start a client management programme, it should first get the commitment of the management team for the training and resources required as well as new working practices to put this into effect. The firm must accept that a client management programme will fundamentally change many of the ways in which it has traditionally gone about its business.

The need and importance of (re)training

Once the firm has committed itself to both the ideas and practice of client management, a training programme will need to be produced for all partners and staff in order to develop the culture and attitudes needed for client management as well as to learn the associated techniques, practices and systems. The programme may differ in detail between partners, case managers and support staff but overall the training programme should be held in common, concentrating on work groups and client types rather than upon the old classifications of work types, legal skill types and rank.

An initial word is necessary, however. Before you can realistically embark on a client management programme, you must consider whether you also have an effective staff management programme. You can't expect your staff to share your newly found zeal and enthusiasm for client management if you have for years treated them like serfs. Chapter 8 deals with the important aspect of staff and client management.

The traditional training for law firm work involved black letter law and the updating of legal knowledge called 'maintenance' training. These are of continuing importance but increasingly they will be supplemented by management, marketing and client management training. The changes and re-engineering of organisations and the people who together make up the firm is a training project of major strategic importance.

Client management skills can be learned by all in the firm. There will inevitably be some hostility or resentment to be encountered with some people in the firm. The partner who has successfully built up and maintained his practice in the firm may resent it even being suggested that some training or retraining in client management skills may be helpful. In introducing client management training, it is not being even remotely suggested that what people have been doing or are doing is wrong or inadequate – rather it seeks to hone client skills and develop them on a firm-wide basis. Client management training is not critical of people and is non-judgmental. It is pragmatic and looks at problems as opportunities for learning and development.

Where some resistance is encountered, it might be appropriate (as well as politic) to invite a partner who is sceptical about the theory of client management and who is an accomplished client manager nevertheless, to introduce the training session himself and so pass on some of his client skills to others in the firm. The enthusiastic but untrained marketing partner or the highly skilled technician may feel threatened by any hint of a suggestion that some training is required. For these reasons, it is probably better that everyone in the firm, without exception, should be asked to attend the client management training courses, in groups or departments rather than as individuals. The groups should reflect the people who actually work together, including the group partners as well as assistants and support staff. Even your most exalted client partner and rain-maker should be encouraged to share her experiences and skills and to encourage others to acquire them. It's in hers and the firm's interest overall to do so.

Client management is ideally suited to internal workshop-style training and skill sharing. Only the firm and those in it and its own client are the experts and, with only some little direction and emphasis being provided by an outside trainer or consultant, the partners and staff within the firm can share and transfer existing skills and knowledge about the management of client relations.

Stimulating a client management culture

Firms rarely are able to generate culture change solely from within. There is a need to bring in new ideas and new people to enthuse and convert the doubters and to drive through the necessary changes by the force of their vision, drive and enthusiasm. Ways of encouraging this process include:

1 invite a key speaker to address partners and senior staff on the nature and need for client management;
2 hold internal meetings to decide whether anything needs to be done;
3 do a client survey to obtain a broad view of the firm as perceived by a cross-section of clients;
4 do a sample case survey on service satisfaction from 10% of your cases over the next month;

5 get one branch or department to use the client agreement 'to get it in writing' with clients and gauge client reaction to it after a trial period of three months;

6 start using case plans in routine work types for quoting and as quality checklists;

7 try using the care plans with a small sample of clients in order to establish what's expected by the client and review this practice after three months;

8 use the agreed charges section of the client agreement. This will involve some preliminary costing work and use of standard case plans. You can only quote a fixed charge for work that is specified in advance. This helps the client and protects you from cost over-runs; and

9 design your case management techniques so as to reduce the possible causes for complaints by the following steps:

    1 all telephone calls to be returned on the same day;

    2 regular monthly progress reports to all clients;

    3 use of client agreements, case plans and care plans and agreed charges;

    4 designate the client or account partner to take overall responsibility for the work of your key clients;

    5 aim to deal with complaints within seven days (see complaints schedule);

    6 start the move overall to total quality management by defining and measuring performance in client management, staff management, financial management and quality management; and

    7 form a client group comprising the client partner, marketing manager and two others to meet each month to review all new inceptions of clients, to check allocations of client partner roles and look for introduction opportunities.

The successful and thorough implementation of these measures will gradually out-perform all the firm's cost-cutting attempts to improve the bottom line. The accent will then be on client satisfaction, staff involvement, open communications and quality work.

The effective strategies in developing a client management culture include the following:

1 be responsive (as distinct from reactive) to client needs;

2 be easily accessible to clients at all times;

3 be reliable and always do what you say you will do;

4 be convenient and proactive in identifying and achieving client objectives;

5 be user friendly;
6 be adaptable with your products (legal work), your services (how you deliver your products), and your charges to match the client's needs and expectations; and
7 understand your clients and be interested in them and not just in their cases.

This new emphasis on client management could have a substantial affect on your profitability within one to two years if comprehensively and consistently implemented throughout the whole firm.

The role of the marketing manager

By now, many readers' eyes will have glazed over and they will have exclaimed, 'Well, that's all very well, but I've got a firm to run and work to do. I haven't got time for all this client management stuff. We can get our secretaries to do it, can't we?' Here lies one of the main stumbling blocks to the whole client management issue. You know it all makes sense but you're not equipped with the ways and means of doing it. If we're going to take client management seriously, we will have to be prepared to take on a whole new system of training and to change many of our traditional work practices.

This is the real test and the substance of Tom Peters' epic challenge, 'While you're busy doing the business, who's going to manage the intangibles?' Many of these client management practices deal with the intangible aspect of service rather than the core product itself, the legal work. But whilst we are busy doing the legal work, which we have seen may comprise only as much as 20% of the total legal service as viewed by the client, who is managing the other 80%? Receptionists, telephonists and secretaries are all in daily contact with your clients, yet many of them have had no specific training in client care or communications skills.

There is so much here to do that we need assistance from a properly trained person who has good marketing, client service and communications skills in order to support partners and staff in 'managing the intangibles'. Managing the intangibles is new and hard work. The work of the marketing manager will vary depending on the size, location and culture of the firm. The activities of the marketing manager may include the following.

Client information

Preparing, communicating and reviewing information clients.

Training

Organising and conducting training sessions and workshops with partners and staff on client care skills and client management methods.

Issuing the client information packs

Groups and individuals may not always have to hand the relevant and current literature about the firm when they issue Rule 15 letters to clients. By copying the client inception form to the marketing manager, she will be able to send appropriate literature to the client with the client information pack.

Complaints

Assisting the senior partner in dealing with the firm's complaints handling system.

Client database

Reviewing and updating the client database to ensure that client information is up-to-date, accurate and relevant to support the marketing and client management activities of the firm.

Group partner's monthly client report

Assisting group partners in preparing their monthly group client reports.

Marketing and strategic development

The marketing manager should attend these meetings to advise on and produce statistics about clients, trends and perception.

Budget

The marketing manager should produce a budget for marketing and client management activities for approval by management.

Client entertainment

The marketing manager should be responsible for organising the relevant partners and clients for 'at home' lunches and entertainment activities.

Service manual, tariff and directory of expertise

Most of us think these are a 'good idea' but who has ever had time before to produce one or keep it up-to-date? Once set up, the updating process will be managed by the marketing manager.

Staff outfits

They may be worth trying for receptionists and front line support staff. The marketing manager would advise on what is appropriate, having consulted with staff and obtained some feedback from a few clients.

Christmas card list

What was once the only client database needs to be developed into an effective client management and marketing tool.

Client mailshots

Mailshots can cause problems where client information is out-of-date. Targeting at specific clients is preferable to the 'blunderbuss', 'all things to all clients' approach.

Client newsletter

Producing a good and pertinent newsletter for clients is time consuming and requires a number of skills, not just legal knowledge.

Client referrers

Keeping a database of people and organisations who do or could refer work and clients to the firm is an important part of marketing and client management.

Partner and staff profiles

The people in the firm *are* the firm and they are the people who attract, satisfy and retain clients. Some form of information about the people in the firm may be useful to clients. A short biographical note, details of skills, experience and specialisms and perhaps a photograph might make the firm's brochure more interesting and helpful. Clients don't really want to read about departments.

Key client profiles

Understanding and knowing about the client is an important part of client management. Building up a profile of key clients, over and above the basic client database details, could give the firm new insights in to the needs and attributes of its most important clients.

'Welcome!' and 'thank you' letters

In the pace of legal work, it can be easy to overlook the civilities of welcoming new clients, perhaps linked with a client information pack about the firm's people and services. It can be easy to forget to thank clients for using the firm when their cases are completed and perhaps enclosing a check-up appointment card for three or six months hence, a helpline card or a firm diary or calendar, to be of use to the client and to keep the firm's name in his mind.

Appointment cards

As a reminder of the next appointment, with details of telephone numbers, opening hours, access and parking, etc, these may be appropriate, particularly with private clients.

Client surveys and client questionnaires

The regular dissemination of questionnaires and surveys, and the gathering and analysis of client opinions, perceptions and satisfaction ratings is one of the fundamental tasks of the client management firm. It takes time, effort, organisation and planning to do this effectively.

Client satisfaction ratings management reports

The client manager's two principal objectives are to increase client satisfaction and to improve profitability. The former needs to be regularly measured on a case-by-case, sample and firm-wide basis, and from the basis of a monthly management report.

DDR forms

The practice discussed in Chapter 10 of the Daily Dose of Reality form, where partners and other client managers are required to contact one existing but not personally known client per day, can be organised by the marketing manager, if necessary.

Client annual reviews

Busy fee earners can forget to arrange and carry out the annual client reviews or to follow through the agreed amendments or recommendations. Support from the marketing manager can be useful here.

General enquiries

Is your legally untrained receptionist also the firm's director of operations and legal resources? Is she the person who deals with new clients and potentially important new enquiries? She may do it extremely well, but could someone do it better and more professionally? The marketing manager may herself undertake this task or else she will advise how this front line outpost of client management could be improved.

Introductions and cross-selling

Many professional people have an intense dislike for the word 'selling', and the phrase 'cross-selling' conjures up the image of a door-to-door salesmen with his foot in the door saying, '... and can I interest madam in our completely new range of shrink-wrapped legal products specially designed by our resident technicians to be suitable for every possible household legal problem?' Opening his briefcase to reveal an array of glossy brochures, he continues, 'Based on extensive research, each has its own unique colour and cost coding ...' Client managers approach their clients as professional consultants who diagnose their clients' real needs and only propose other services when he has ascertained the client's need. The marketing manager can support and promote these activities by ensuring that brochures, the directory of expertise and client packages are kept relevant and up-to-date.

Directory of experts and expertise

The people in the firm *are* the firm as far as clients are concerned. Their skills and expertise should be documented in order to ensure that the 'appropriate expert' concept is put into and kept in practice.

These are just a sample of the range of client management activities that do not fall easily within the skills, expertise or proclivities of the busy fee earner but yet are important to be done by someone. Client management firms recognise the importance of these activities and ensure that they are done in a managed and effective way.

Every partner, fee earner and front line support person is already a client manager whenever he does something for a client or which has an impact or influence on a client. The best marketer and client manager is always the person doing the legal work for the client. The marketing manager does not replace or encroach upon this role but rather works in support and promotion of it. The marketing manager does not need to have a high profile with clients but works to assist partners and client managers in being more effective in client management and client satisfaction. The marketing manager does not replace or even overlap in the role which only the service deliverers can play; he or she acts in a support role to partners and staff to help ensure that all client initiatives and efforts are for the benefit of the firm as a whole.

In one way, this role could be seen by a firm as 'our resident in-house client' because the marketing service manager to a large degree is there to see the firm as the client sees it, to keep the firm on its toes and to raise the whole awareness of the firm about its clients. In employing and using effectively the marketing manager, the firm will indicate its commitment to client management systems. It will be employing someone to help the partners to 'manage the intangibles'.

What gets measured is what gets done

Client management is not something just to talk about or theorise over – it is a practical, day-to-day system of attitudes, practices and systems for dealing with client needs, expectations and aspirations, which is designed to achieve and increase client satisfaction and the profitability of each and every case. In order for such a system to be effective, it is necessary that client management practices should be designed, implemented and operated in such a way that performance can be both targeted and measured. No matter how good an idea, if it can't be measured, it can't be managed.

Throughout this introduction to client management, the accent has been very much on systems, targets and measurement of performance because only by doing this can the benefits of client management be fully realised. The Appendices contain various forms of questionnaires, surveys and reports which are designed to do just this – to set standards, to aim at targets and to measure performance as part of the essential growth path of client management which is continuous improvement.

The file management approach to legal work needs to be superseded by a client satisfaction approach. This will need to be capable of measurement. The firms who are measuring performance only in financial terms are the score keepers. They need to see the direct correlation between better service and improved profit.

Responding to clients

The leading 85% of United Kingdom companies agree that customer service is important to retain existing business. It has been estimated that United Kingdom business is forfeiting £100 billion per annum in the cost of lost business and marketing costs to replace that business which has been lost due to poor customer service.

Apart from the 15% of leading companies that do not acknowledge the customer as king, in the case of those 85% who do, there is not much evidence that these enlightened companies are actually doing much to convert theory into practice.

Price Waterhouse have done a survey which shows that, despite the huge costs of replacing lost clients and lost opportunities to develop new and repeat work from existing clients, fewer than 10% of businesses actually measure the number of clients they lose each year. Only 50% of the companies questioned in the survey admitted to taking any steps to find out the needs and concerns of their clients, and more than 60% said they never compared their own customer management policies with those of their rivals. Forty-five per cent admitted that their sales personnel were ill-suited to the present needs of their customers.

Some firms seem to be obsessed with using head count reductions in staff to improve performance rather than in improving client retention, where only a couple of percentage points improvement will improve profitability substantially. If you don't get the product right, if you don't get the service right, and if you don't provide value to clients, fewer clients will buy and your marketing costs will have been wasted. In order to be effective, you have to get the whole firm thinking, talking and doing something about client service. It is not a secret for partners around the partners' table, it is not a burning bush, it must not be consigned to the obscurity of a firm's mission statement or business plan. The lead must come from partners and be enthused throughout the firm. Senior management at Marks and Spencer and Virgin are frequently to be seen on the sales floor or in the aircraft checking what customers think and then they go away and do something about it.

A firm should compare its client service with that of its competitors. The barriers that we have erected and unconsciously perpetuate between us and our clients must be identified, reviewed and wherever possible be dismantled. Our methods of doing business with the client, from top-to-bottom and from side-to-side, need to be thoroughly reviewed and redesigned without exception with the client in view.

Action checklist

1 Decide to do something about client management before your clients and competitors decide for you.
2 Hold your next partners' and staff meeting jointly to outline a new client management programme which will involve everyone in the firm.
3 Encourage a culture change towards clients by inviting client and staff feedback and ideas for service improvements.
4 Recruit a marketing manager to make the drive more effective.
5 Design and implement a series of measures, targets and reports to promote client management practices throughout the firm.

17 The benefits of client management

Do you want to get more work, have more clients, improve your profitability, be less stressed at work, be more in control, have a happier and more productive staff, produce quality legal work more consistently and reliably, and do you want to have clients who are so satisfied with your services that they not only remain loyal but also introduce more varied work and recommend you to others?

The benefits of client management are many and various and can be classified under seven main headings as follows:

- financial benefits;
- product quality benefits;
- staff benefits;
- client benefits;
- strategic development;
- a sharpening of the competitive edge; and
- business growth.

Because clients and the satisfaction thereof are fundamental to the firm's success, then all things in the firm are affected by the quality of client satisfaction achieved. Each heading will be looked at in turn.

The financial benefits of client management

Client management is designed to increase client satisfaction and, therefore, to increase profitability in each and every case. Client management is about the bottom line like no other aspect of law firm management because it focuses not only on the process or on the files or on the law but also on the person who is expected to pay the bill and contribute towards a firm's profits. Client management concentrates on both process and result, the result of creating a satisfied client. Client management is result-oriented because it is about doing the things that are most likely to ensure success in the case, satisfaction of the client and in getting paid.

The effect of successful client management on a firm's financial performance and its profit and loss account are many and profound and include the following:

Turnover

A satisfied client will during the course of his case be prepared to discuss other aspects of his personal or business circumstances with the case manager or client partner which in turn may lead to introductions to new and additional services. The client manager's diagnostic skills will enable the client to have the full benefit of the firm's range of legal products and services. If he's buying a house, you will also be able to help him with his will, with independent financial advice, possibly employment advice where he is moving house for a new job and so on. Company clients may be willing to instruct the firm in their property affairs and patent clients may also bring in other work where they are pleased with the service received. No longer will clients be heard to say, 'I usually use Kenge & Carboys – I didn't know you did that sort of work in your firm!' The many previously missed opportunities will be picked up increasingly and unerringly by the client manager, thereby bringing in more work to the firm and increasing its turnover of cases and billing performance.

Profitability

Getting in more work is not necessarily a good thing in itself unless you can do the work and all other work in the firm profitably on a case-by-case basis. Through the practice of profitable case management (see Chapter 13), the profitability of each case can be more effectively managed and improved. By observing the five rules of profitable case management, the client agreement, time recording, dealing with variations and additions, prompt and regular bill delivery and collecting bills delivered, there need no longer be the low profit work, nor the loss leader. Even *pro-bono* cases can be made less unprofitable by keeping them within defined limits and ensuring that they do, in practice, lead to more profitable work rather than just leading to more losses. If a firm can ensure through the practice of client management that each and every case systematically yields a profit, then the overall profitability of the firm will see a substantial and solid increase.

Cash-flow

Your satisfied client whose expectations have been identified and met by the client manager will already have agreed the charges or the basis of charge, the payment intervals and the method of payment and so there will be less delay in account payment. Much avoidable delay in bill payment is caused where fees have not been discussed and agreed in advance. Client management ensures that there will be few if any billing 'surprises' for the client. Moreover, the client manager will have discussed and agreed the bill with his client before sending it out to him. He will probably also have collected bill payment on or before the 'billable event' and in many cases will have received payment in advance or an account. The cost benefit of improved cash-flow to the firm's bank balance will be substantial.

Work in progress

The total value of billable but unbilled work in progress at any one time should comprise no more than one-quarter to one-third of the firm's annual income budget. These figures will vary upwards in a legal aid practice where payment is slower but less risky and will be lower in a conveyancing practice where costs from high turnover clients are collected on completion. Where the client agreement has been used to agree billing intervals and billing events, then control and management of billable work in progress should improve. The firm will set itself a target for its billable work in progress at any one time not to exceed, say 33% of its annual budget turnover. Individual groups will have work in progress targets varied as appropriate to its client base and work type, with legal aid work in progress being as much as 50–60% of annual budget target, and conveyancing being about 20–25% where case completions are quicker. These figures will vary for each firm, the point is to have a target and to monitor progress against that target. If the work in progress target is greatly exceeded, this may indicate poor interim billing; too low a level of work in progress may indicate not enough work being recorded, done or incepted. Client management promotes regular interim billing and 'housekeeping' write-offs of billed work in progress. A healthily man-aged, well recorded, regularly billed and written off work in progress indicates good client and financial management and is a joy to show to your bank manager, if asked.

Credit control

In general, the profession is fortunate in not having had a serious bad debt problem but there are many unfortunate cases where slow payment of bills delivered is a problem, with many firms still working with 60–90 days aged debtors. Many of the credit control problems are found upon enquiry to be a direct result of poor client management, particularly where there has been a failure to agree charges with the client at the outset of the case or where 'billing by ambush' has occurred. Where the basis of billing and billing intervals are agreed between the client manager and the client, then clients by and large conform and credit control problems are reduced or avoided entirely. The aged-debtor performance of the firm should reduce to a healthy 30–40 days with active and systematic client management. Good client management is also good credit control management.

Cash in your lock-up

Where the aggregate total of unpaid bills delivered on average at any one time equals 20% of a firm's annual turnover and the aggregate total of billable but unbilled work in progress at any one time equals 30% of a firm's annual turnover, then the total amount of costs 'locked-up' with clients may equal as much as one-half of the firm's annual income budget. The cost of providing an unpaid and unsecured loan to clients totalling one-half of the firm's annual turnover, particularly where the firm is working with bank overdraft or fixed term finance, is immense. For example, a firm having an annual turnover of £1 million may have £500,000 at any one time in 'lock-up' and the cost of this at, say, 10% is £50,000 per annum. If the firm is working on a profit to turnover percentage of say 20%, generating profits of £200,000 per annum, it can readily be seen that its 'lock-up' costs are as much as 25% of its annual profits. For less efficiently-run firms the figures are far worse. Even on a static turnover, client management can be seen to be able to increase profits by up to 25% by reducing the unbilled work in progress and aged debtor figures, without incurring any marketing or development costs.

The cost of bills delivered and unbilled work in progress is one of a firm's biggest overheads. The billing practices that we have inherited from our former regulated and uncompetitive years, when profit margins were sufficient to sustain bank charges and costs as 'hidden' overheads, need to be replaced by client-focused billing practices. The markets and the clients have changed and so should our billing and client management practices.

Interim billing

Most firms are now familiar with regularly sending out interim bills, although as recently as five years ago some solicitors thought that there was something underhand and dishonourable in billing before the case was done and dusted. It was reported at a practise management conference I attended only a couple of years ago that one commercial partner in a leading law firm complained to his financial director, 'I've got this big new client but I'm really worried – he has asked to pay our accounts monthly as we go along.' The realities of modern economic life have disabused us of the expensive and unnecessary practice of billing only at the end of a case. I have heard few, if any, complaints from clients who have gone on to interim billing provided it was properly explained and agreed with them first. So, by extending the service element to include up-front communication and regular contact with clients over fee levels, we will effectively reduce our unbilled work in progress to targeted managed and realistic levels. This will make us popular with our clients, with our partners and with our bank manager.

Price premiums

Good service, quality legal work and value for money are the hallmarks of good client management. Where the quality of service and of the legal product are different and better than the competition, then price premiums of up to 10–15% above the market rate may be acceptable to clients because if the client is totally satisfied then fee resistance will decrease. Product quality is generally taken for granted, but service quality will be a significant differentiating factor.

Reduced fee resistance

Your satisfied client may know that you are 'not the cheapest' but he will be comfortable in paying your 'list price' fees for the service you have provided. Where you have agreed the charges or the basis of the charges at the outset, where you have kept him informed, where there were no surprises, where the client felt he was in control of costs, and even though they may have exceeded the original agreed charge but the client is still satisfied because he was consulted and agreed to the variation in advance, where you were nearly always available when he called, where you called back promptly and without fail, where you visited him at his office or work place, then here the client will more readily pay the account and with less drama than under the old 'billing by ambush' regime where bills were rendered with long bill narratives, explaining after the event what the client is expected to pay for. Lawyers wouldn't instruct third parties on behalf of a client without establishing in advance exactly what costs were involved and we should not expect our clients to expect otherwise of us. 'Billing by ambush' should be outlawed.

Client management has the double objective of increasing client satisfaction and profitability. The former begets the latter. Whilst other financial management measures are aimed primarily at cost control and reduction, client management provides a method and system for dealing with the challenge, 'If you want to charge more, you'll have to provide a better service!' The systematic, comprehensive and effective implementation of a client management system will improve the bottom line far more than any financial budgeting, control and recording system because, rather than just measuring performance, it improves performance across the whole firm.

The product quality benefits of client management

Client management, like product quality, is a matter of ensuring that you are putting the right ingredients into the top end of the client management mincer. When you put a quality legal product (legal knowledge, efficiency and expertise) plus a quality client service into the top of the mincer, then in the absence of mismanagement in the rest of the business, this will produce the conditions for financial success. The right results will follow if you do the right things – you get what you set.

We have seen in Chapter 4 that quality is comprised of two things: the degree of conformance to an agreed written specification and the degree to which identified client expectations are met. Quality in product excellence needs to ensure that the product is agreed first with the client. There needs to be a preliminary discussion and agreement of the product specification in terms of the client agreement and the case plan.

Product quality is, therefore, promoted and improved by client management because it requires the client manager to agree and produce a case plan at the outset of each case. For standard and routine work, there may be a series of standard case plans that will vary little from client to client. For other less standardised work, there may be an outline case plan containing the basic structure and stages of the case, leaving extras and variations to be agreed with the client as the case progresses.

Case planning requires the case manager to be proactive, to think ahead, to plan the case in advance and to manage its progress in a systematic way. Instead of just starting off with the first letter before action or sending out a contract and then sitting back to wait for a response, the case manager will have done most of the legal and strategic thinking about the case at the outset. The savings in time that this produces during the case can be substantial.

Product quality also depends on legal knowledge, efficiency and expertise. These are enhanced by client management rather than reduced because they are seen in their proper context as being a part of the overall legal service. Being understood as such, product quality is maintained with service improvements rather than being reduced by product feature cuts or production costs generally.

The staff benefits of client management

The politics and economics of employment are daily putting greater stress on the importance of increased staff productivity across the whole business spectrum. In the legal profession, where as a people business even greater emphasis is put on the value of personal attention and contact, it is even more important to ensure that every single member of the firm operates and is perceived by its clients to operate as an asset in the generation of client satisfaction throughout the firm, whether directly or indirectly. The cost of training and employing staff is such that the traditional 'doing' roles of typing, filing, accounts, etc are no longer capable in themselves of justifying a salary without also having some linkage with client satisfaction. Many, although not all, members of staff will want to be involved in the firm's client management programme and will find it both stimulating and satisfying.

Client management is perhaps one of the best strategies in raising productivity and performance throughout the firm because it involves everyone in a common drive, it is oriented towards people and results rather than process, and because it breaks down like never before the 'us and them' syndrome that limits the potential of people in many law firms. The traditional training method within the legal profession is that of learning from example, by watching what the experienced practitioner does and then by emulating what is seen. This is beneficial where the example is good but so often the trainee may be exposed to less-than-perfect experiences and examples which may inculcate inadequate or even bad habits. What we learn at this stage has, however, the tendency to stay with us throughout the remainder of our careers. Client management encourages the active transfer of client management skills from client masters to others.

Some specific benefits on staff of client management include.

Staff turnover and morale

The members of the firm, who are perceived by clients as being part of the firm and who after several years service should be regarded as stakeholders in the firm, must be recognised not only as assets but as people with a legitimate interest in the success of the firm. The cost of recruitment and training is high, and a firm stands to gain on its people 'investment' where valuable members of the firm are retained and developed. It is a major loss where someone leaves the firm for reasons other than retirement, removal or for other personal, non-work-related reasons.

Where members of the firm are involved with clients as part of the strategic development of the firm, then such persons will not only be perceived as being important in the firm's performance but they will also perceive themselves as playing an important and defined part in the success of the firm and see themselves as an integral part of the firm. This attitude will not only improve a person's morale at work and reduce the urge to leave for greener pastures but it will result in a more stable, able and reliable body of people who together comprise the firm.

Productivity

Many members of the firm do not see the figures for the firm's financial performance and have no way of assessing for themselves how well the firm or themselves in particular are doing. At the client management level, however, members of the firm can see whether clients are being treated well and whether clients are satisfied with the firm's services. By being more involved in client management, and receiving more client feedback, then people will identify more with what the firm is doing from a service point of view and, by being more involved, will naturally put more effort and more of themselves into the task. As we have seen in Chapter 8, many people at work only 'suffice', working at productivity levels of only 40%, doing what they do without praise, criticism or known result. An increase in the level of involvement and activity which raises a person's productivity by a further 10% to a moderate 50% will, if continued across the firm, mean a productivity increase of 25% firmwide. Such improvements are possible as a result of client management.

Job satisfaction

We have all had bad experiences with clients as well as from other members of the firm from time to time. The art of human relations is perhaps the most important of all skills, both in business, at home and with friends.

'Why am I here?' and 'Where does what I do fit into the firm and its activities and plans?' and 'Noone appreciates what I do!' are all familiar calls for help from staff that may or may not be answered. Where a member of staff does understand these things and has his questions answered and his work given credit and his position in a group or team is reinforced by the managers of the firm, then he will feel he is doing a worthwhile job, with reduced levels of stress and frustration.

Absenteeism

Stress is the leading cause of illness in the workplace and the cost of absenteeism due to illness is a heavy burden on all businesses. Absenteeism can be a sign of low staff morale and needs to be given active attention. Absence due to illness caused by stress is more severe and can indicate not only low morale but perceived pressures that can cost the business dear in terms of lost productivity and morale. Where client management is used effectively together with the other three essential management activities (finance, clients and product quality), then the well-regulated firm that results from this should be able to show improvements in performance in terms of lower recorded absences due to illness caused by stress.

Job security

One of the greatest of all human motivators is the need for security and this is particularly important in the context of employment. The recession, the advance in technology and the inexorable march of progress towards skill and discretion-based work away from routine and manual work, has put many, if not most, people in fear for their jobs. All this talk of change and re-engineering and teamwork and client focus can be perceived by some as threatening and dangerous. It is not always clear how jobs will be affected by change and in this scenario, the co-operation and enthusiasm required from people may be reduced accordingly.

It has been remarked in Chapter 8, that you cannot develop client management without also having an effective staff management system. Members of staff will view with suspicion and perhaps hostility any 'new' management changes in culture, direction or work practices without adequate and credible staff management improvements. Where client management is put successfully into place and where the underlying culture is supportive and encouraging in people issues, then people are more likely to feel secure and, therefore, to give of their best in the tasks required of them.

Client management skills

These are learned and transferred between practitioners more quickly and more effectively by focusing specifically on client relations and client management as skills in their own rights rather than being seen as merely ancillary to legal skills. If it is true that clients assess our overall legal service on the basis of 20% for the legal work and 80% for the product delivery and service skills (as seen in Chapter 5), then it will be abundantly clear that the involvement of all staff in client management is essential.

Training

Client management training provides a uniquely different approach to training than the traditional pure 'black letter law' approach which is knowledge as opposed to skill-based. Client management is complementary to existing legal skills and serves to enhance them with a new focus on client perception. Client management skills enable us to more effectively and more profitably present and deliver our legal product knowledge to the client.

The quality of people

After several years of deregulation and increasing competition, it has become clear that just being a good lawyer or a good law firm is not good enough in itself to guarantee survival, profitability and growth. We need the people who have the ability to satisfy clients, to make a profit and to be able to work effectively with others in addition to having legal skills. Staff management is a key strategic objective.

In a service industry where the legal product is delivered by the service provider to the service receiver, the management of both parties' needs and expectations is necessary in order to be fully effective. Client management will flourish more abundantly in a firm where enlightened staff management policies prevail in which all members of the firm are recognised, involved, respected, valued and rewarded as legitimate stakeholders in the success of the firm.

The client benefits of client management

A satisfied client will come back to you for more work, recommend you to others and use other services of the firm. The client himself will receive the benefits of increased satisfaction, product quality and value. The benefits to the client will include the following.

Client satisfaction

One of the dual aims of client management is client satisfaction. We do not do legal work in a vacuum or for its own sake, for the intellectual challenge or for the money. We do it in response to a client request which when the work is done will have satisfied his request. Our work must always be directed towards client satisfaction and we must measure it in each and every case and with each and every client.

Product quality

The client will benefit where the quality of the legal product is improved by client management. The legal advice and services will be geared to meeting client objectives more precisely, the legal process will be managed in planned and agreed stages thereby reducing delays and mistakes. The product will 'work' better and the conditions that give rise to mistakes and claims will be reduced.

Service quality

The second limb of quality, that of meeting client expectations, will by now have been seen to be the main area in which client management operates. By first identifying and then managing and finally by measuring the satisfaction of client expectations, client management can be seen to be of equal importance to the management of product quality.

Many firms have been successful in putting into place some sort of quality system, ranging from the legal aid franchise standard, to the Law Society's own 'Practice Management Standard'. Some firms have achieved BS 5750 or ISO 9002. These are all creditable and noteworthy achievements but in themselves only go part of the way in conforming with the definition of quality. The next big step, which comprises the second 'limb' of quality, is to ensure that client needs and expectations are identified and met systematically on a case-by-case basis. This will involve the implementation of a client management system in one form or another which involves dealing with abstract and intangible concepts. Client management involves another, the client, and ostensibly abstract and intangible things such as client expectation and client satisfaction. This is the real benefit, however, of a quality system and, for those who have complained volubly against the imposition from outside of apparently useless, form-filling systems, the real pay-off and benefit will not appear until the second stage has been successfully implemented. It is true that quality systems will achieve some improvements in operational efficiency, but the real benefit of a quality system will not be felt until an effective, quality, client management system has also been implemented to deal with the second part of the quality requirement.

Value

Overall, clients want value, and this is specifically the objective of client management. By managing the overall client experience of the firm, including both its product and service features, and by agreeing the charges or the basis of charges in advance with the client, value is virtually guaranteed. It is measured at the end of every case and any loss of perceived value is taken into account in redesigning the product and service delivery system.

Recommendations

The adage that 'a job done well speaks for itself' is perhaps more appropriate to the old pre-deregulation and uncompetitive days than to the present and foreseeable competitive market conditions in which we now seek to make a living. With client management, the job is specified at the outset and it is done well or badly to the extent to which it conforms to the agreed product and service specification, and to the extent to which measured levels of client satisfaction are achieved. An amended adage seems now more appropriate: 'a job is done well or badly to the degree of measured levels of client satisfaction'.

Where the client is satisfied and believes the job has been done well, he is more likely to recommend the lawyer or the firm to others.

Client retention

A client is a client for life in client management terms. If one job is done satisfactorily, it is expected that the client will return and introduce other work to the firm over a period of time. The client will have the security of knowing that he can rely on the firm for most, and perhaps all, of his legal service needs.

Client attraction

Whilst client retention is one of the main objectives of client management, it can also attract new clients at the tender or quotation stage. The client manager explains to the prospective client the benefits of the firm's client management system, with a brief description of the case plan, progress reports, product specification, agreed charges and client satisfaction measures. Many prospective clients will at this stage clearly see that the client manager is skilled in dealing with client expectations and may form the view that this person and this firm appear to be good to do business with.

Repeat work

A satisfied client will not only remember you for the legal service you have provided in one type of case by referring similar types of work to you, he will also consult you for his other legal needs, provided you have told him what else you and the firm can do. It's amazing how often clients will say, 'I didn't know you also did that sort of work!' ('You' meaning the firm overall.) By using the client information pack and the client manager's diagnostic skills, the client should know all about what you and the firm can do for him.

Client endorsements

The professional rule about not disclosing client information is not breached where the client agrees to his name being used in marketing and tendering material. The fact that you and your firm already represent a number of substantial and satisfied clients can be a potential marketing asset. 'We include amongst our satisfied clients ABC plc and ZYX Company Limited' may be a useful indicator to the prospective client of the nature of the legal products, service and value your firm can provide. If, in addition, ABC plc and ZYX Company Limited are also prepared to speak to a specified prospective client, then the endorsement will be further strengthened.

Perceived market pre-eminence

When the firm enjoys a reputation in the market of being one that satisfies its clients with product quality, service extras, differentials and perceived client value, then the firm really will be the market leader. An active and progressive client management programme will promote all these features across the broad front of its activities.

Client loyalty

A satisfied client is an asset to the business but the permanence of the client with the firm is one that can be notoriously unpredictable. Where client management is put into practice, far more is found out about the client including accurate indications of client satisfaction ratings. When measured client satisfaction ratings are being reported monthly as stable or rising, then the firm can take considerable comfort in that report.

Introductions

Introducing clients to the wider range of services of the firm is the duty of all client managers and the benefits of doing it accrue both to the firm and to the client. The client is generally better advised where all or most of his legal service requirements are handled by one firm, and the firm itself benefits from more work, greater use of its products and services and a higher turnover.

Market share

Market share can be increased by price wars, merger, practice acquisition or by managed growth. The first is interpreted to mean cost cutting and 'buying work'. The second and third are client annexation policies. A better way of growing clients is to keep and develop all those you already have and to acquire new clients by specific targeting, using client management practices to retain and attract new clients. This kind of growth is solid and reliable and need not rely on the cut-throat battles which can be observed taking place in various parts of the country.

Less complaints

Because client management focuses on client expectations and their experience of the legal service and because it deals with them in a pro-active way, it becomes less likely that complaints about delay, inattention or costs will arise. Each of these will be dealt with by the client agreement, agreed charges, progress reports and regular client feedback.

Less claims

Most complaints are based on service deficiencies rather than product failures, and most can be resolved with an effective complaints-handling system. Even those few complaints which do involve product defects, and which may lead to a claim being made can be reduced by client management where standard case plans are used. No system is perfect and noone is infallible but the chances of receiving a claim are likely to be far less where a client management system is in place than where there is none at all.

The true test of the effectiveness of a client management system in a firm is the degree to which each and every aspect of the management of the firm is geared towards maintaining and increasing client satisfaction by adding to the benefits received by clients from the firm. The result is measured in increased profitability.

Strategic development

Some firms spend large amounts of time and money in casting about looking for the strategies that will lead them into profitability and growth. Going commercial, developing new legal services such as environmental law, employment law and so on, are all thought to be part of the answer. Setting and measuring financial targets, imposing accountability and putting staff on performance-related pay are all ways of helping towards that end. But these strategies in themselves may not be yielding the results which many firms need and expect. The introduction of quality standards may help iron out inefficiencies, but none of these strategies deals specifically and fundamentally with an assurance of client satisfaction.

Perhaps the area for key strategic development lies right under our noses in the work we do and the way we present and deliver it to our clients. Certainly, it is necessary to develop new services to meet changing laws and identify existing or potential client legal needs, certainly, it is necessary to reduce or even abandon old and unprofitable services but, whatever we do, it is necessary that we do it in a way which is most likely to meet or exceed client expectations.

In this context, product quality is a key strategy because legal knowledge and expertise cannot be taken for granted by law firms and needs to be maintained and developed with active research and development. It is obvious that if a firm puts all its efforts into developing new products without first ensuring that its existing products are producing the maximum potential profit, development costs may be unnecessarily incurred. Legal training, continuing professional development, case planning, legal updating and product research and development are key aspects of a product quality strategy that a successful firm must adopt.

An equally important strategy is to ensure that with every client at least a minimum level of client satisfaction is achieved. It's all very well working away at product development, marketing, and cross-selling, but it's a short-sighted strategy unless the firm also takes active steps to ensure that client satisfaction, which after all is why we take on the work in the first place, is achieved consistently and systematically throughout the firm and at levels which are being actively improved also throughout the firm.

By actively implementing a client management programme across the firm, there will slowly, but surely, be achieved the strategic advantage of satisfying your clients better and differently from your competitors, whether it be in run-of-the-mill debt recovery, niche intellectual property or management buy-out work.

Sharpening the competitive edge

The result of successfully pursuing a strategy that seeks first to identify and then to satisfy client needs and expectations is that the firm and the people in it will become known in the marketplace for looking after their clients' interests and in providing extraordinary levels of service and satisfaction. If a firm, which already competes successfully with niche legal products, adds to its work and activities the client management strategy which ensures increased client satisfaction, consistently and reliably, then the scythe for gathering in the client harvest will be sharpened on both sides and be doubly effective.

A firm which manages its clients and increases its profits by one and the same system, namely client management, is one which does not fear competition from any quarter, except perhaps from another client management firm. Other law firms are sure to be courting your key clients, even as you read this book. If you're not listening to what your clients need, expect and value, and if you are not doing something about it, there are plenty of other firms out there who will and who do.

Business growth

We have seen that 'a business exists to create a client' (Peter Drucker) and we hear the management gurus telling us that the first objective of any business is to stay in business, and that to stay in business the first requirement is to make a profit. Survival and profit are not only the objectives of a business but they are also the requirements to remain in business. In order to work to create a profit and survive, the business has already to be making a profit so that it can survive to make a profit. This poses the enigma facing many law firms: that, in order to survive as they are and without change, they are compelled to accept lower than formerly acceptable profit margins. This also means that changes in culture and work practices are resisted because they are seen as being too expensive or too risky or just because they are different.

Client management offers the strategy that can lead a firm out of this predicament in to a new era of growth and profitability if the bold though measured step towards client management can be taken. If the firm has no other or better strategy for survival and growth, or if its current strategies are not yielding the hoped-for results, then what better strategy to adopt than one which focuses on its lifeblood, its own clients?

In short, the challenge facing a law firm is a management challenge. Managing its finances, the quality of its work, its staff and its clients is the essence of the challenge. The best managed firms are the ones that will survive and thrive.

It is not claimed that client management is the one and only strategy to win success but, along with the other key strategies of product quality, financial management and staff development, client management will give the firm the final and convincing result and accolade of success, its perceived pre-eminence in the eyes of its clients and in the marketplace in which it does business for its clients.

Action checklist

1 Consider the benefits to be gained from client management – is the firm so successful or are your own particular practices so good already that nothing further needs to be done? Check whether your clients agree with your answer. If not, client management can assist in achieving improvements in both.

2 Examine your quality systems for the ways and means of promoting client satisfaction and consider whether these are fully and effectively implemented in the firm. Do you think that client satisfaction is an equally important part of quality as conformance to specification? If so, client management may offer tangible benefits.

3 Adopt client management as your prime strategy for developing the firm and for competing more effectively in the marketplace by being known as providing different and better levels of client satisfaction than your competitors.

Appendix 1

Jarndyce & Jarndyce Solicitors
Client agreement

AN AGREEMENT made on the   day of   199[ ]
BETWEEN

1. You, the Client
Name (1)   ....

Name (2)   ....

Address   ....

Tel ....(home) ....(work) ....(mobile)

2. and the Guarantor(s) (if any)
Name(s)   ....

Address   ....

3. and Us, Jarndyce & Jarndyce,
Case manager   ....

Client partner   ....

Assistant(s)   ....

Secretary/Paralegal   ....

4. The Case
This agreement concerns the following case: (brief description)

....

A case plan has been agreed between Us and You

                                                    Yes/No/attached

Estimated timescale to

[completion /judgement / other: [   ] – [   ] weeks/months

Case number .... Client number ....

IT IS AGREED that You, the Client, have instructed Us, Jarndyce & Jarndyce and that We have agreed to provide You with the legal advice and services in connection with the Case in accordance with the terms and conditions of this agreement.

5. Agreed charges

You have agreed to pay Us the following Agreed charges for the Work:

Fixed charge £..............   Hourly rate £..............

Estimated charge £.............. to   199

Maximum charge £.............. to   199

Other:

Agreed charges to be reviewed on: 199

6. Expenses (disbursements)

You have agreed to pay Us in advance the following expenses which We will need to pay out on Your behalf in dealing with the Case:

Description	Amount
1	£..............
2	£..............
3	£..............
4	£..............

7. Payment of Agreed charges

You have agreed to pay the Agreed charges to Us as follows:

– costs on account £...........

– interim account – 4 weeks   on exchange

– interim account – 8 weeks   on completion

– interim account – 12 weeks   on ....199[ ]

– when work done >£250 Legal Aid Yes/No..............

– when work done >£500 payment/contribution by third party?.....

– Other ....   No/Yes – Amount....................

Credit terms agreed: payment on account delivery/within 30 days of account date.

8. Method of payment

You have agreed to pay the Agreed charges as follows:

Cash/cheque

Credit card

Direct debit after account delivery

Standing order (completed form attached)

Deduct from proceeds of the Case

Third Party re-imbursement

Other ....

9. Signatures

By signing this Agreement, You, the Client and We, Jarndyce & Jarndyce, agree to be legally bound by the terms and conditions contained in it and You acknowledge receipt of a copy of this Agreement.

Signed: Signed:

Client (1)...............................   ....
                                 for and on behalf of
                                 Jarndyce & Jarndyce
Client (2)...............................

Conditions

1. Definitions

In this agreement the words and phrases below have the following meanings:

'You, Your' means each person(s) named as the Client on page 1;

'We, Us, Our' means the partners of Jarndyce & Jarndyce Solicitors of Chancery Lane London;

'Guarantor' means the person or company (if any) specified on page 1;

'Case manager' means the person dealing with Your Case specified on page 1 or other person notified to you;

'Client partner' means the partner who has overall supervision of and responsibility for Your Case;

'Case' means the case described on page 1 and in the case plan and any work or variations or additions which are at any time agreed between You and Us;

'Work' means the work agreed to be done by Us in the Case as described in the case plan or as a agreed from time to time;

'Agreed charges' means the charges specified on page 4 and all expenses, interest and other payments by the Client due under this Agreement or as agreed from time to time;

'Expenses' means any expenditure (disbursement) to be incurred in the Case;

'Agreement' means this Agreement and any variations to it which are agreed in writing;

'Conditions' means these Conditions or Our Conditions from time to time in force or as may be varied between You and Us in writing.

385

2. Interpretation

2.1 In this Agreement, wherever appropriate, the singular means the plural and the masculine includes the feminine and neuter genders and vice versa;

2.2 Where the Client specified on page 1 includes two or more persons each of You will be fully liable to Us individually under this Agreement. Your individual liability will not be affected by the fact that there are two or more persons named as Client or whether or not someone else was supposed to sign or whether or not there is a Guarantor. This liability is known as joint and several liability.

3. We agree with You ...

3.1 to provide legal work and advice for the Case as agreed from time to time;

3.2 to carry out the Work in a professional manner.

4. Conduct of the Case

4.1 The Case manager and/or such other persons named in section 3 of page 1 will deal with Your Case;

4.2 The Client partner named on page 1 will have overall responsibility for the Case;

4.3 We will arrange for outside agencies or consultants where appropriate and agreed with You to assist in the Case. All such agencies are listed on a List of Approved Agents. We cannot be responsible for such part of the Work carried out by them;

4.4 Where an estimated timescale is agreed based on information available at that time, we will endeavour to complete Our Work within that period, but We cannot guarantee to complete the Work within such time, and We cannot be liable for delays due causes beyond our control.

5. Complaints

5.1 We will endeavour to satisfy You with our Work;

5.2 If You have any complaint, comment or concern about Our conduct of the Case, please contact the Client partner named on page 1. You may also or instead contact the Senior partner of Jarndyce & Jarndyce (who is the first named partner on Our letterhead) who has overall responsibility for Client satisfaction;

5.3 We encourage You to be frank and tell Us what You think of our Work. In this way We will be able to improve our service to You by understanding and dealing with any problems which might arise in the Case.

6. Quality

6.1 We are bound to comply with the professional rules of the Law Society and by the Rules of the Supreme Court;

6.2 We are regulated by the Law Society in the conduct of investment business;

6.3 We carry out Our Work in accordance with the [   ] Quality Standard;

6.4 You agree that your Case file may be subject to a quality audit by others from time to time. We agree that all efforts will be made to ensure that Your confidentiality is protected.

7. Data Protection Act

7.1 We are registered under the Data Protection Act 1984;

7.2 By signing this Agreement You consent to the storage and retrieval of information about You on our computers.

8. Agreed charges

8.1 You have agreed to pay the Agreed charges in the amount and in the manner and at the times as described in sections 5–8 inclusive;

8.2 We will keep You regularly informed of the progress of the Case and of any reason for a change in the Agreed charges;

8.3 If You ask Us to do any additional Work then the Agreed charges will be varied and agreed between You and Us;

8.4 The Agreed charges are based on the Solicitors' Remuneration Order 1994 and Our agreement with You;

8.5 Agreed charges are subject to periodic review by Us which will be notified to You in writing;

8.6 Where the Agreed charges or a part of them are to be paid by a third party We will endeavour to recover these on Your behalf and until such time You will remain liable for payment of the Agreed charges.

9. Expenses

9.1 It may be necessary in carrying out the Work for expenses to be paid out by Us on Your behalf — these have been discussed with You and these are listed as far as possible in section 6 and are payable in advance;

9.2 We shall notify You in advance of any other or additional Expenses and You will pay Us in advance or within seven days of a bill being sent to You;

9.3 We are not liable to pay any Expenses on your behalf unless You have paid us in advance or on request. Any Expenses of which We have given You advance notice and which We incur on Your behalf and which You do not pay to Us as above will bear interest at 2% per month.

10. Value Added Tax

Value added tax will be charged in addition to all agreed charges and expenses as appropriate at the rate prevailing at the tax point once a bill is delivered.

11. Late payment

11.1 All bills are due for payment on the date of delivery;

11.2 We shall be entitled to charge You interest on the balance outstanding of any bill unpaid 30 days after the date of the bill calculated from the date of the bill;

11.3 We shall be entitled to make a charge of £15 which will be added to the outstanding balance for each statement or overdue account reminder letter sent to You;

11.4 We are entitled to transfer monies held on Your behalf in Our client account in order to discharge any outstanding bill which has been sent to You;

11.5 Where You or some other person or company (for example, a bank or building society) are required to pay monies to Us in connection with the Work other than in respect of our bills (for example, the balance of purchase monies due on completion) such payments must be made to Us not less than three clear working days before the required date;

11.6 Where We have given adequate advance notice to You or such other person or company requiring payment to Us of monies and such monies are not received at least three clear working days before the due date We shall be entitled to charge interest on such uncleared funds calculated at a rate equal to 1.5% per month above the lending rate from time to time of [   ] Bank plc.

12. Interest on Client account

12.1 We will pay interest to You on Your monies held in Our general client account at the ordinary deposit account rate paid from time to time by the bank in which such monies are held;

12.2 If first agreed between You and Us in writing, monies liable to earn interest may be kept in a separate designated deposit account to be opened by Us for that purpose;

12.3 You will be liable to pay all bank charges for opening, operating and closing such account together with Our reasonable administrative charge for dealing with the account and supplying a statement of interest;

12.4 We shall be entitled to deduct the amount of any outstanding accounts from any payment of client account interest to You.

13. Legal aid

13.1 You should ask Us to advise whether or not You are entitled to legal aid in the Case;

13.2 Our charges for Work which is legally aided will be explained to You by Your Case manager.

14. Storage of deeds

14.1 We will store Your deeds and documents without charge except for non-standard items;

14.2 If You ask for any deeds to be withdrawn from storage or for any copies to be made, We will make a charge in accordance with current published rates of charge. A standard deed retrieval fee of £[   ] will be made in addition to photocopying charges at our standard rate.

15. Critical future dates

Once the Case is completed We cannot accept any further responsibility for reminding You of important future dates such as dates for service of notices or rent reviews. Any such reminders given are made without charge and without incurring any liability on Our part.

16. Copyright etc

16.1 We retain copyright and all other intellectual property rights in all materials produced or used by Us in connection with the Work;

16.2 You will pay and indemnify Us against all charges if You pass on or disclose any such material to others without our prior written consent.

17. Taxation of fees and Remuneration certificates

17.1 Any request for a taxation of costs and any request for a Remuneration certificate must be made to Us in writing within one month of the date of a bill;

17.2 Your rights to challenge Our invoices are restricted by this Agreement.

18. Waiver and Variations

18.1 Any failure by Us to enforce any part of this Agreement shall not be a waiver of the terms and conditions of this Agreement which shall remain in full force and effect;

18.2 Except where agreed in these Conditions, any variation or waiver of this Agreement must be agreed in writing;

18.3 We reserve the right to amend these Conditions at any time after giving You reasonable advance notice.

19. Governing law

19.1 This Agreement is governed by English law;

19.2 It is agreed that any legal action relating to this Agreement shall be dealt with only by the courts of England or Wales except where We take legal action in another country in which You may be resident.

20. Notices

20.1 You must notify Us immediately of any change of Your address;

20.2 Your address for all purposes including correspondence and the service of notices shall be the address specified in section 1 or such other address of which You shall have given Us written notice;

20.3 All notices shall be sent by pre-paid first class post and shall be deemed to have been received two days after posting.

21. Guarantor

21.1 The Guarantor (if any) specified in section 1 agrees to be bound by and carry out all the obligations and liabilities of the Client under this Agreement including payment of the Agreed charges;

21.2 If We release You or the Guarantor from any obligation under this Agreement this will not reduce the liability of the other;

21.3 Where there are two or more Guarantors their liability under this Agreement shall be joint and several as described in Clause 1.

22. Cancellation

22.1 You may cancel this Agreement at any time on giving Us written notice but such notice will not cancel existing rights under this Agreement;

22.2 If You give notice of cancellation this will be conditional on You immediately paying all outstanding invoices and subject to these Conditions You shall pay our final invoice for Work done up to the date of cancellation;

22.3 We may cancel this Agreement at any time on giving You written notice but such notice will not cancel existing rights under this Agreement.

23. Acceptance

23.1 By signing this Agreement or by continuing to instruct Us following any variation to this Agreement You are deemed to have agreed to these Conditions;

23.2 These Conditions replace any previous agreement between You and Us whether written or oral.

Appendix 2

JARNDYCE & JARNDYCE			
CASE PLAN			
Purchase of Freehold – Purchaser			

Client/Purchaser: ....

Property: ....

Date .... Estimated timescale: ....

Case reference: .... Agreed charges £ ....

PRE-EXCHANGE	Action		Action
Instructions from client		Title and requisitions	
Searches:		Preliminary Enquiries	
– local		Draft Agreement	
– mining		Draft Transfer	
– commons		Funding/mortgage	
– Land Registry		Planning	
– Land Charges		Other: environmental	
– Company		VAT	
– Other		Report to Client	
EXCHANGE TO COMPLETION	**Action**		**Action**
Sign and exchange contracts		Other:	
Insurance		– consents required?	
Engrossments			
Completion Statement		Completion:	
Bill to Client		– consents required?	
Pre-Completion searches		– transfer and title deeds	

POST COMPLETION	Action		Action
Report and account to Client		Diarise dates	
Stamping and Land Registry		Client Questionnaire	
Notices, options, etc		Case Plan Review	
Signed: .... (Client)	Date:	**Signed:** .... (Jarndyce & Jarndyce)	

Appendix 3

Jarndyce & Jarndyce Solicitors
Progress report (multiple)
Date: **199**

Client:
Case manager:
Client partner:

Dear [Client],
  We are dealing with a number of your cases and enclose a brief note
  of the progress made to date with them. Please let us know if you
  have any comments or if any facts or circumstances have changed
  by completing the section marked 'Client Comment' and returning
  the Progress Report to us in the pre-paid reply envelope.

Matter/Reference   **Progress to date**   **Client Comment**

☐ We attach a Statement of Account detailing outstanding accounts
  for your kind attention.

      Total due at   /   /   199   £.....................

☐ We enclose an interim account to date for the above case reference
  numbers:

Yours sincerely,

Case manager/Client partner

Appendix 4

Jarndyce & Jarndyce Solicitors
Progress report (case)
Date: **199**

Client:

Case description:

Case number:

Case manager:

Client partner:

Dear [Client],

We are dealing with your case and enclose a brief note of the progress made to date. Please let us know if you have any comments or if any facts or circumstances have changed by completing the section marked 'Client Comment' and returning the Progress Report to us in the pre-paid reply envelope.

Progress to date:

Agreed charges

☐ We attach a Statement of Account detailing any outstanding accounts in this Case for your kind attention.

☐ We enclose an interim account for Work done to date.

Client Comment:

Thank you for your instructions and we will contact you again shortly.

Yours sincerely,

Case Manager
Jarndyce & Jarndyce

Appendix 5

Jarndyce & Jarndyce Solicitors
Client inception form

Client details

Client reference:
Name:
Address:
Post code:
Telephone:
Home:
Office:
Mobile:
Fax:
e-mail:
Contact name/Position:
Occupation/Business:

Client Classification:
Business/Professional/Private/
Legal aid/Agency/Joint/Referral

Introduction

New client
Existing client
Advert
Referral
Recommendation
Other:

Group details

Client partner:
Group partner:
Case Manager:
Assistant(s):

Secretary/Paralegal:

Client care

Client agreement:
    Yes ☐ No ☐ Date [＿＿＿＿]
Case plan:
    Yes ☐ No ☐
Care plan:
    Yes ☐ No ☐
Rule 15 letter:
    Yes ☐ No ☐ Date [＿＿＿＿]
Client information pack:
    Yes ☐ No ☐
Client profile:
    Yes ☐ No ☐ Update ☐

File details

Case reference:
Branch/Office:
Work type code:
Inception date:

Agreed charges

Agreed charges £
(copy attached)
Estimated charges £
Disbursements £
First interim bill due: /   /
Credit period agreed: [   ] days

Case details

Description:
Work type code:
Estimated timescale:

Signed

Case manager:
Group partner:
Copy to: client partner
Date:

Notes

Appendix 6

Jarndyce & Jarndyce Solicitors
Client satisfaction questionnaire

Dear Client,

We are carrying out, or have recently completed, a case for you and we hope that you are satisfied with the legal service you have received.

The partners and staff of Jarndyce & Jarndyce believe that you, the client, are the best person to judge the quality of our legal services. We would like to know your opinions on the legal service you have received from us.

In order to help us help you better, we would be grateful if you would spare just a few minutes to respond to the questions on this form and then return it to us in the pre-paid envelope. Please be frank. Your views will be given careful consideration and will be treated in complete confidence.

Thank you for your help.

Yours sincerely,

John Jarndyce
Senior Partner

Please indicate your views by putting a number in the box against each question as follows:
5 = excellent; 4 = very good; 3 = fair; 2 = poor; 1 = unsatisfactory

Quality of legal work

1. How do you rate the quality of legal advice given to you in your case?

2. How do you rate the quality of the legal work done in your case?

3. How well was the legal position explained to you?

Quality of service

1. How well do you rate the way we discussed the case with you at the beginning and kept you informed of progress during the case?
2. How well do you think your case manager understood you and the case, your needs and expectations?
3. How well do you rate the quality of our service to you?

Value for money

1. How well do you rate the way we discussed the likely charges and agreed them with you at the beginning or during the case?
2. How well do you rate the way we kept you informed about any increase in charges during the case?
3. Overall, how well do you rate the value for money in your case?

General

1. How would you rate your overall satisfaction with the legal service you received from us?
2. How would you describe our firm to colleagues, relatives or friends?
3. If you were to consider using our legal services again, how would you rate the service you would expect to receive?

Comments

Please make any other comments on our work or our services:

Please complete the following (optional):

Client name: ....

Address: ....

....

Telephone: ....

I would like to receive a reply: Yes ☐ No ☐

Thank you for your response. Your views will be carefully considered.

Appendix 7

Jarndyce & Jarndyce Solicitors
Client profile
Private and confidential (restricted access)

Client information

Client reference number:
Client:
Address:

Telephone:
Fax:
e-mail:

Principal business activities:

Accountants:
Managing Director:
Finance Director:
Company secretary:
Other contact names:
Managers:

Holding and associated companies

Names:

Chairman:
Directors:
Group company secretary:
Other solicitors (if any):
Accountants:

Brief history of client relationship

Jarndyce & Jarndyce

Client partner:
Other partners:
Case managers:
Principal work types:

Financial status

Agreed charges:
Credit period:
Average age debtor performance:
Bills delivered in last financial year (to [   ] 199[   ]) £ [   ]
Projected bills for current financial year:
Special billing arrangements:

Annual client service review meeting

Due in [   ] each year.
Last meeting held [199] See notes.
Client satisfaction rating at last review: %

Client plan

See client care plan attached.
Monthly reports:
Introducing other services:

Confidential

Access restricted to: [   ]

Notes

Client financial year:
Last Annual Report on file?   Yes/No   for year [   ]

Appendix 8

Jarndyce & Jarndyce Solicitors
Annual client service review

Client:
Client partner:
Client number:
Review date: Place:
Present:

Review of preceding 12 months

Review of specific cases in last 12 months

Service review for last 12 months

Ability to meet deadlines:
Attention to detail:
Progress reports:
Case planning:
Value for money:

Case manager performance

Other:

Complaints

Client comments – general

Client satisfaction rating

Delighted □   Pleased □   Satisfied □   Not satisfied □   Displeased □

Preview of next 12 months

New instructions:
Client requirements:

Review of agreed charges

Projected fee income:
Hourly rates:
Percentage charges:
Fixed fee:
Case plan and Agreed charges:

Introducing other services

□ Commercial property
□ Company
□ Commercial
□ Litigation
□ Debt recovery
□ Employment

□ Conveyancing
□ Intellectual property
□ Probate, trust and tax
□ Financial services
□ Family law
□ Other:

How likely will the client require the above services in the next 12 months?

Action agreed

Next client service review date: [   ]

Copies to

Appendix 9

Jarndyce & Jarndyce Solicitors
Client plan

1. Client details

Name:
Address:
Telephone: home   business   mobile   fax
Occupation/Business: Type:
Client Number: Category: private/business/Legal Aid
Client Source: existing/new/referral/recommendation
              advert/*Yellow Pages*/other:
Client Profile Number:

2. Group details

Group Partner:
Client Partner:
Lead Partner:
Case Manager(s):
Assistants(s):
Group Secretary:
Paralegal(s):

3. Matter details

Case number:
Work type code:
Client agreement date:
Letter of engagement:
Costs plan agreed?
Client information pack sent:

4. Costs plan

The following charges have been agreed with the client:
Agreed Charge: £   Linked to Case Plan?   stage 1 to [   ]
Interim billing every one/two/three months
    OR work in progress of £250+/£500+/£1,000+
    OR on completion
    OR at stage [   ]
Method of Payment: cheque/cash/standing order/instalments
                   direct debit/credit card/proceeds of sale
                   other:
Third party contribution / costs undertaking? Yes / No
                              (client retains liability for payment)
Credit terms: on bill delivery / 30 days.

5. Client objectives

Case and Client Objectives:

6. Diagnostic report

The client has requested/may benefit from information/advice/
    services as follows:

☐ Buying/selling a house
☐ Making a will
☐ Property development
☐ Financial services
☐ Family law
☐ Company/commercial
☐ Tenancy agreement
☐ Housing
☐ Debt recovery

☐ Business tenancy
☐ Employment law
☐ Probate/trusts/tax
☐ Landlord & tenant
☐ Starting a business
☐ Charities
☐ Planning
☐ Personal injury
☐ EU law/other:

Notes

Appendix 10

Jarndyce & Jarndyce Solicitors
Client questionnaire

1. Jarndyce & Jarndyce

1. Why did you choose to instruct Jarndyce & Jarndyce?
   Recommendation   Personal contact   Reputation   Charges
   Existing client   Location   Advertising   Other
2. Have you used other firms of solicitors?   Yes/No
3. Were they different from this firm?   Yes/No
4. If yes, in what way?

2. Your case manager and your case

Do you think you received enough personal attention?	Yes/No
Would you have liked to have seen someone else?	Yes/No
Was your case manager nearly always available?	Yes/No
Were your telephone calls promptly returned?	Yes/No
Was your case fully explained to you?	Yes/No
Were you kept informed about progress of your case?	Yes/No
Did more than one person do your work?	Yes/No
Do you prefer to use the same person on all matters?	Yes/No
Do you think your case manager understood you and your case?	Yes/No
Was your matter dealt with promptly and courteously?	Yes/No
Do you think there were any mistakes?	Yes/No
Were you kept waiting?	Yes/No
Was your case handled professionally?	Yes/No
Were there any delays?	Yes/No

3. The office

Did you visit our office?	Yes/No
Was our office convenient to your home/office/ workplace?	Yes/No
Would another place have been more convenient?	Yes/No
Do you think the offices and facilities were satisfactory?	Yes/No
Would you prefer appointments at your workplace/ home/other?	Yes/No

4. The service

Were the members of Jarndyce & Jarndyce helpful and courteous?	Yes/No
Was the matter completed to your satisfaction?	Yes/No
Do you think there were any problems?	Yes/No
If 'Yes', was the problem solved to your satisfaction?	Yes/No

5. The charges

Were the costs satisfactorily discussed with you at the beginning of the case?	Yes/No
Were the agreed charges exceeded/maintained/reduced?	Yes/No
Do you think the charges were: too much/too little/ about right?	Yes/No
Do you think we are more expensive than other firms?	Yes/No
Did you get value for money?	Yes/No
Is price the most important factor to you?	Yes/No

6. General

If you have one main complaint, comment, compliment or criticism about our service, please let us know:

7. Complaints

Do you have any complaints or comments?	Yes/No

If 'Yes' please comment:

Would you recommend us to a friend/colleague/ another business?	Yes/No
Would you be likely to use this firm again?	Yes/No

8. About Jarndyce & Jarndyce

Do you know about all the legal services we can provide to both the private and business client?	Yes/No
Did you receive a copy of our Practice Guide?	Yes/No
Have you received our firm brochure and Client Information Pack?	Yes/No
Would you like to be put/kept on our mailing list?	Yes/No

9. Confidentiality

1. Do you have any objection to the following:
   - your name and/or product and/or service being mentioned to existing or potential clients? — Yes/No
   - your name and/or product and/or service being mentioned in our publicity? — Yes/No
   - your name or photograph of your product being displayed at our offices? — Yes/No
   - our clients to be introduced to you as possible customers? — Yes/No
2. Do you require strict confidentiality in all matters? — Yes/No

10. Other legal services

Have you now or in the near future any interest in the following services?
- Making a will for you or your relatives? — Yes/No
- Buying, selling or leasing property? — Yes/No
- Company formation or restructuring? — Yes/No
- Business start up? — Yes/No
- Redundancy, contracts of employment, dismissals? — Yes/No
- Commercial premises on lease, sale or purchase? — Yes/No
- Debt collection? — Yes/No

– EC or international law?	Yes/No
– Other	Yes/No
If so, may we discuss your requirements with you?	Yes/No

11. Your future requirements

Will you need legal advice and services:
 now/in three months/in six months/within one year?   Yes/No
Can you say what these may be?

Do you think you would consult us on these matters?	Yes/No
If 'No', can you tell us why not?	Yes/No

Do you wish us to contact you now?	Yes/No

Thank you for completing this questionnaire. Your comments and views will be given careful consideration.

We hope that you are satisfied with the work we did for you.

Appendix 11

Jarndyce & Jarndyce Solicitors
Client management report (group partner)

Group partner: Month ending:

1. New case inceptions

This month   *Previous month*   *This month last year*   *Monthly target*

2. Client origin

Current   *New*   *Dormant*   *Ex-client*   *Recommended*   *Other*

3. New clients

This month   *Previous month*   *This month last year*   *Monthly target*

Principal new clients this month
Name   *Business/Occupation*   *Comment*

4. Key clients

What contact and development has been made with your key clients
    this month?
Key client – name   *Contact/development*   *Comment*

5. Group clients

The Group Partner has responsibility for all clients dealt with by the
    case managers in his/her group.
Has the Group Partner spoken to/met all new group clients this
month?   Yes / No / Comment:

Has the Group Partner reviewed progress in all case/matter lists with the case managers in his/her group this month?
Yes / No / Comment:

If some clients have been transferred from another Client Partner or group, have you made progress reports at least monthly to him/her?
Yes / No / Comment:

6. Client diagnosis, introductions and transfers

What major or significant new services have you introduced to your current and key clients this month?

Client name   *Introductions*

What services from other groups or departments in the firm would be useful to your clients?

Which clients have you transferred to another group or department this month?

Client name   *Transferred to*

Do any of your clients use other firms of solicitors?
Yes / No / Comment:

If 'Yes', please state why, which other firm and what steps if appropriate you are taking to provide such services?

7. Prospective clients

What three prospective clients have you made contact with this month and with what results?

Prospective client contact   *Prospect rating*   *Comment*
                                      Good/Fair/Poor

1.
2.
3.

8. Marketing and other outside activities

Please state what marketing activities you and any group members
have been involved with this month:

1.
2.
3.

9. Entertainment

Spending time with existing and potential clients aids mutual
understanding and may lead to new business.
Please state what time you have spent with clients this month and how:

Client lunches   *Client dinners*   *Sporting events*   *Other*

10. Referrals

Some clients come from referrals. What referrer's have you contacted
this month?

1.
2.
3.

Please state what clients/cases have been referred to you this month:

11. Complaints

Please list all known complaints received by the group this month
with remedial action:

Complainant/Client   *Nature of complaint*   *Report number:*

Has any complaint been referred to the Finance Director?   Yes/No
Have all complaints been dealt with satisfactorily to the client? Yes/No
Please complete the following:
  'As far as I am aware there are no potential negligence
  claims in my group'   Yes/No
  'As far as I am aware, no member of my group has
  admitted any negligence'   Yes/No
  'There have been no referrals to our PI insurers this month' Yes/No
  If no, please give details:

12. Client questionnaires

Client Questionnaires sent out this month [   ] Returned [   ]
Client comments received:

13. Client satisfaction rating

Based on responses to questionnaires, what is the client satisfaction
 rating for your group this month?

Group Partner: ☐   *Case Manager*(s): ☐   *Group average:* ☐

Last month: ☐   ☐   ☐

Average YTD: ☐   ☐   ☐

[5 = delighted; 4 = pleased; 3 = satisfied; 2 = not satisfied; 1 = dissatisfied]

14. Lost clients

The following clients have left or been lost to the firm:
  Ex-client name   *Reason for loss/leaving*

Unless you have had some contact with a client within the last six
 months that client may be a 'lost' client. What key clients or other
 clients should now be contacted?

  Client name   Contact name   Telephone
1.
2.
3.
4.
5.

Do you use appointment cards?   Yes/No
Are diarised contact dates checked?   Yes/No

15. Quality of service

We are always looking for ways to improve service to our clients. What
 service improvements have you made or could suggest?

Do you need support from our Marketing Manager?   Yes / No

16. Group partner – comment:

17. Marketing manager – comment and recommendation

18. Managing partner – comment

19. Signed

....
    Group Partner   Marketing Manager   Managing Partner

Appendix 12

Jarndyce & Jarndyce Solicitors
Client management report (firm) for [month] 199

To: All partners
From: Marketing Manager/Managing Partner
Date: 199

1. Overall comments

2. New matter inceptions

Last month	Previous month	Last year	Target	Variance %	YTD	Target YTD

3. New client inceptions

Last month	Previous month	YTD	Last YTD
1.			
2.			
3.			

4. Existing client inceptions

Active clients	Non-active clients	Dormant clients

5. Client inceptions classification

	Last month	Previous month	Last YTD	This YTD
Business clients				
Private clients				
Legal aid clients				
Other				

6. Major new clients or introductions to existing clients

New Clients	Work	Group
1.		
2.		
3.		
4.		
5.		

Introductions Client	Work	Group
1.		
2.		
3.		
4.		
5.		

7. Sources of new clients

Recommendation	Referral	Marketing	Advertising	Other

8. Client questionnaires

	Last month	Previous month	YTD
Questionnaires returned			
Analysis of client comments			

9. Client surveys

A client postal survey was carried out during [   ] in the [   ] Department followed by a telephone call. Surveys were completed with [   ] clients with the following comments:

1.
2.
3.

10. Entertainment

The following activities and events with clients took place last month:
1. [   ] with [   ] from the firm and [   ] from clients
   Comments:

2. Seminar on [   ] was held at [   ] on [   ] with [   ]
   from the firm and [   ] from clients and an invited audience.
   Comments:

3. Other:

11. Client satisfaction rating

The client questionnaires and surveys revealed the following average
levels of reported client satisfaction:

Private client	☐	Business client	☐
Legal Aid clients	☐	Litigation	☐
Company/Commercial	☐	Probate	☐
Commercial property	☐	Other	☐

[5 = delighted; 4 = pleased; 3 = satisfied; 2 = unsatisfied; 1 = dissatisfied]

	Last month	*Previous month*	*Average YTD*
Average CSR for the firm overall			

12. Complaints

	Last month	*Previous month*	*YTD*
Complaints received			
Sources of complaint by group			
Complaints actioned			
Client satisfaction			
Main causes for complaints			
Client comments/ compliments			

419

13. Comments and recommendations for action

Signed: .... Date: ....

                    Marketing Manager

.... Date: ....

                    Managing Partner

Appendix 13

Jarndyce & Jarndyce Solicitors
Complaint report

Complainant/Client name:
Address:
Telephone:
Case manager: Client partner:
Group partner:
Case reference: Date of complaint:
Complaint responder: [Senior Partner]/[Client Partner]/ ....

Complaint description

Action taken (with dates)

Complaint acknowledged to complainant:
File located and checked:
Discussion with Case Manager:
Discussion with Client Partner:
Discussion with Group Partner:
Discussion with complainant:
    telephone call/meeting

Response to complainant

Comment by complainant

I think that the way Jarndyce & Jarndyce handled my complaint was:

Excellent ☐   Good ☐   Fair ☐   Poor ☐   Unsatisfactory ☐

Other comment (if any):

Signed: ....
                Complainant/Client   Responder for Jarndyce & Jarndyce

Jarndyce & Jarndyce

Internal action taken:
Remedial action:
Review due:
Other:

Appendix 14

Jarndyce & Jarndyce Solicitors
Client care plan

Client:
Address:
Case reference:
Case Manager:
Case description:
Date:

Client care specification

Case plan completed	Yes / No
Weekly telephone progress report	Yes / No
'As and when necessary' telephone progress report	Yes / No
Letters out — copy to client	Yes / No
Letters in — copy to client	Yes / No
Written report to client	Yes / No
Meetings at our offices	Yes / No
Meetings at client's business premises/home/other	Yes / No
Progress reports — multiple case/monthly	Yes / No
Progress reports — case/monthly	Yes / No
Client Partner supervises	Yes / No
Client Partner reports to client	Yes / No
24-hour telephone contact required	Yes / No
Extra copies of letters to:	Yes / No
Letters to client marked 'Private and Confidential'	Yes / No

Other client expectations/needs/requirements:

Appendix 15

Selection factors

Survey results

Has a real understanding of the client's needs	1
Quality of professional staff	2
Being a specialist in the relevant field (technical ability)	3
Reputation for obtaining results	4
Ability to come up with imaginative or innovative ideas	5
Experience in the client's sector	6
Speed of response to initial enquiry	7
Competitive fee levels	8
Previous experience with your firm	9
Size of the firm	10

The above selection factors have been ranked by clients in order of importance to them. Understanding the client's needs and quality of professional staff at 1 and 2 indicates the importance of the service 'intangibles' of the relationship between the solicitor and his client. Technical legal skills are rated highly by clients at 3, but still less highly than 'relationship' skills. The ability to come up with imaginative or innovative ideas is ranked perhaps surprisingly high at 5. Experience in the client's sector or business is ranked lower than would be expected at 6. Competitive fee levels ranked down at 8 is perhaps the biggest surprise of the survey whilst the lowest rankings of client loyalty and size of firm at 9 and respectively 10 presents opportunities for a competitive firm.

Appendix 16

Glossary of terms

Agreed charges – a written agreement between solicitor and client recording what has been agreed as the charge or basis of charge following a discussion of the case plan. In a competitive client driven profession, it is no longer acceptable to clients to be told by their lawyers how much the work costs. Cost of production is no longer relevant to clients but rather price and value is. It is, therefore, preferable to discuss charges at the outset and to agree them with the paying client.

Agreement (client agreement) – a written agreement signed by the solicitor and the client at the beginning of each case outlining details of the client, the supervising partner and support staff, the matter, client objectives, the case plan, agreed charges and standard terms and conditions.

Agreement (client transfer) – an internal form used where one client is passed by the client partner to another partner or group for other legal work.

Annual client service review – an annual meeting between the client partner and the key client to discuss service levels, case managers, cases and client perception/satisfaction over the last 12 months and to discuss charges and work projections over the next 12 months. Best done in the last quarter for budgeting and planning purposes.

Appointment card – useful for private clients to know when the next stage of the case or meeting is planned. Contains useful information about the firm for client's benefit. Also ensures that the client manager plans the next diagnostic or follow up meeting before the end of the case. Helps to maintain the service link.

Benefits – the essence of what clients want and are prepared to pay for; it is not what we do that clients pay for but what we do or achieve for them.

Billing support – active support from finance department in the production, issue and collection of bills; and the management of group financial performance and compliance.

Body language – the unspoken and unwritten communication signals that we all give out and receive and which need to be understood by the client manager.

C's – the three basic concerns of the client manager are doing the Case competently, collecting Costs and looking after the Client.

Care – clients respond to service as much if not more than to the detailed legal work. At the outset of each case, identify what the client wants and expects in the way of service and then base the agreed charges on that. Meetings, venues, copy correspondence, progress reports and so on can be part of the care levels agreed.

Case – the legal knowledge, rules and procedures that we learn at college and from books and which we apply in practice; one of the 'three C's'.

Case manager – the person who has the day to day control and management of the case; the person who does the routine legal work.

Case plan – there are two kinds of case plan:
1. a standard case plan is a detailed legal checklist to be attached to the file and used by the case manager as a guide to the conduct of the case. It is ticked off as the case progresses. It promotes quality, consistency and proactive case management as well as reducing errors. It is also suitable for file audits.
2. a client case plan is an outline plan of the case agreed after discussion with the client at the outset of the case. It can be amended to suit the client's expectations and requirements. It is divided into stages should be reviewed monthly. It may be attached to the client agreement.

Case review – at the end of each and every case, a short review of the case plan, costs and client satisfaction is necessary in order to check how effective the client management has been so that errors can be avoided in future and benefits be increased. Without this vital review stage, we are working blindfold. Were the client's expectations and needs met? Did the case plan work? Were there any complaints or compliments? What went well? What went wrong? Was the client satisfied? What was the client satisfaction rating? Did the lawyer learn anything? Is there a useful lesson or precedent? How much profit/loss on the case was there? Why? Lessons for the future? Contact client again when?

Charges – agreed charge is a more appropriate term than costs in the de-regulated and competitive 1990s. In client management, charges or the basis of charge should be agreed with the client at the outset of the case and be kept under review, particularly where the work changes or the time is extended.

Client – a person or company who contributes towards your income in return for the benefit, welfare or solution he perceives that you provide for him through your legal advice or service. A client is a regular user of a firm's legal products and services.

Client action team – an internal group which reviews the client management reports of the firm and from groups; it recommends action for improved service; it can also means a multi-skilled group which is dedicated primarily to service the needs of one client or for one specific project.

Client agreement – a written record produced after discussion with the client at the first meeting of what the case manager has agreed to do and what the client has agreed to pay; can incorporate terms and conditions; may have a case plan attached to it.

Client audit – a review of the status of a client's legal affairs or business with recommendations for legal advice and services as appropriate.

Client care – the 1,001 'little' things which can provide a low cost, high perceived benefit to clients.

Client charter – a published list of client focused promises or standards to which the firm commits its service performance.

Client database – the goldmine of information about clients which can be built up about clients from data in files, cabinets, address lists, computers and in personal knowledge and which is vital to developing the relationship between the client manager and his client.

Client focus – the suite of attitudes, culture, values and activities which puts the client, his needs, expectations and perceptions first.

Client information pack – a package of information about the range of benefits which the firm offers in response to the identified needs and aspirations of the client.

Client partner – the named partner who takes overall responsibility for all legal work done by the firm for a particular client. It can also refer to the partner in the firm who takes overall responsibility for client management in the firm.

Communications – the essential and delicate link in the service chain between the service provider (the client manager) and the service receiver (the client) which in itself is part of the service, as perceived by the client. Where communication stops, the service stops, where communications are interrupted or hindered, so is the service from the client's point of view. The better and more regular the communication links, the better the service as perceived by the client.

Complaint – a free source of feedback and market research that can be invaluable to the client manager in remedying and developing the particular client relationship as well as the general client culture of the firm.

Costs – charges based on the cost of production (internal) rather than upon the value and benefits to the client (external).

Culture – the essential characteristics, features and ethos that makes a firm what it is. This means its people, both partners and staff, and their attitudes and work practices towards clients, legal work, finance and each other.

Customer – a person or company who has used a firm's legal product or services once only and who has not given any repeat work to the firm. Technically a client but in reality only a customer until the client manager has converted the customer into a client by eliciting repeat work, introductions or recommendations and referrals by the quality of the service, legal work and value he provides.

Decision – a decision has seven parts parts: (1) recognition of the problem and the need for something to be done; (2) consideration of alternative courses of possible actions and their relative risks, costs and benefits; (3) the act of choosing a course of action; (4) communication to those concerned and accountable for implementation; (5) implementation; (6) review for effectiveness; and (7) adjustment or redesign and decision. A decision is incomplete until it has completed all seven stages.

Diagnosis – the procedure used by client managers to identify client needs for legal services now and in the forseeable future. It is preferable to 'cross-selling' which focuses more on what the firm does rather than what the client wants and needs.

Differentiation – the identification and promotion of those unique and special things about the firm's service which clients like.

Effective – usually means the opposite of 'busy'. It involves achieving the things that you know are important but that you hardly ever get the time to do.

Group partner – the named partner who manages the production of legal services in a group of people which may include associates, solicitors, legal executives, paralegals and support staff. He is responsible for the product quality, staff management, financial performance and client satisfaction of his group.

Indifference – the main reason for client seepage is where clients perceive that the firm or solicitor does not seem to care or be bothered about the client during the case. It can be countered by regular communication and the client contact call.

Intangibles – the things, other than the generic legal work, which together add up to the client's overall experience and perception of the service received.

Key client – a client who regularly instructs the firm and who has a number of current cases at any one time with the firm in one or more groups or departments and who ranks significantly in terms of billing and profitability.

Lead partner – the named partner who takes overall responsibility to the client for a particular case, project or series of transactions.

Management (case) – management of the legal process including analysis of facts, legal advice and case conduct.

Management (client) – management of the relationship between the service provider and the service receiver which produces profit for the former and value for the latter.

Management (file) – management of correspondence, documents and paperwork in the file of a client's matter.

Managing partner – the sixth most important person in the firm, ranking after the five top clients. He must be able to run the firm on a day-to-day basis whilst also driving it towards continuous improvement and innovation. He should be market and client-driven as well as financially able.

Marketing – the culture, attitudes and activities which focus on what a firm does and which (may) be of interest to a client. It looks at and approaches the market from a seller's viewpoint. Marketing legal services can be ineffective where the relational aspects of service are undervalued or ignored.

New – the attitudes, culture, vocabulary, values and work practices that have been made necessary by deregulation, the recession and increased competition. Generally market-driven.

Old – the attitudes, culture, vocabulary, values and work practices that pertained before the recession, deregulation and increased competition. Generally supplier-driven.

Paralegal – a new class of entrants to the profession are people trained with keyboard, client management and legal skills. The traditional role of the secretary will be transformed into and replaced by the paralegal offering value added client, documentation and legal skills.

Perception – the way in which clients experience and perceive the service offered by the firm or received by the them. Only clients can assess this.

Price – a unilateral supplier quotation that invites the client to say 'yes' or 'no'.

Proactive – planning the stages of a case in advance, dealing with as much work in a case as is possible at any one time, discussing the next date for review/action/follow up and driving the case forward to meet agreed timescales and achieve identified client objectives.

Process (legal) – what lawyers traditionally spend most of their time doing in gathering the facts, giving legal advice and conducting the case. Client managers also plan the work to be done, and review for effectiveness and client satisfaction.

Product – the legal work involved in handling the case, including legal knowledge, legal advice and conduct of the case. The 'product' needs to be distinguished from 'service' which is the client's assessment of how the legal product is presented and delivered to the client.

Profitability – the key financial measure of performance on a case-by-case, group-by-group, departmental and firm-wide basis. Whereas turnover measures activity, profitability measures results.

Quality – the degree to which something conforms to specification and client expectation. Quality requires inputs from both supplier and receiver. There can be no quality without active client inputs.

Reactive – activity stimulated by external events.

Responsive – activity stimulated after identifying client needs and expectations and which is unlimited in scope.

Satisfaction – the degree to which the client perceives and assesses that the result, benefit or welfare that he wanted from the case has been achieved. Clients come to law for satisfaction and so client managers must first identify client objectives and then measure how well they have been achieved.

Selling – the attitude and marketing activity that says: 'This is what we do, who wants to buy?' In promoting a service, a client manager looks at the buyer or service receiver and says: 'We can do things that will help you achieve your objectives. Let's talk!'

Senior partner – the partner holding this non-executive role should lead and direct the vision, culture, direction and style of the firm. With his eye on the horizon, he must be prepared to introduce new and perhaps controversial issues for debate. He must be client-driven.

Service – the way in which we deliver the legal product to the client as perceived by the client; service is what the client experiences as a buyer and as a receiver of the service.

Service (after sales) – by maintaining the relationship after the case that has been developed during the case, client managers can keep the vital service link alive and so promote a realistic expectation of further work.

Service (delivery) – clients experience service delivery more so than product quality. Service provider and service receiver have equal prominence in client management.

Service to sales – the strategic policy that:

1 understands that an estimated 80% of new instructions come from existing or former clients;

2 recognises the tendency of satisfied clients to stay with the firm and give repeat instructions, use other services within the firm and make recommendations to others;

3 puts resource and attention to ensuring that the presentation, quality and delivery of legal services to its clients is such that client expectations are identified and satisfied in each and every case; and

4 ensures that the solicitor-client service link is actively managed and maintained both during and between cases.

Small talk – the dialogue between a solicitor and his client that precedes a meeting and which is essential to enable them to 'tune in' to each other's wave length by establishing common views and values. Holidays, the weather, last night's television, the news and so on give an opportunity to the participants who are about to engage in serious and technical matters to establish a bonding or common value system to enable those forthcoming discussions to go smoother and better. Often follows a meeting to re-establish common direction and purpose.

Stakeholders – those people or groups of people who have an interest in the success of the firm, including partners, staff, clients, suppliers and referrers.

Transactional management – management of the day-to-day business of the firm in accordance with established practice.

Transformational management – management of the process of changing the culture, structure, objectives, policies and work practices in a firm whilst also maintaining the commercial and financial viability of the business. Particularly appropriate to a firm moving towards a client management culture from a case and file management culture; sometimes called 're-engineering'.

Turnover – the performance measure that tells us about activity and volume in terms of gross bills delivered; extremely pertinent when supplemented with a profitability analysis.

Value – value is the assessment made by clients based on their perception of service, product and price.

Vision – the idea(s) supported by a detailed plan and budget of what and where the firm hopes to be and to have achieved within a stated timescale.

INDEX